The New
New Zealand

The New New Zealand

The Māori and Pākehā Populations

WILLIAM EDWARD MONEYHUN

McFarland & Company, Inc., Publishers

Jefferson, North Carolina

LIBRARY OF CONGRESS CATALOGUING-IN-PUBLICATION DATA

Names: Moneyhun, William Edward, 1946– author.
Title: The new New Zealand : the Māori and Pākehā populations /
William Edward Moneyhun.
Description: Jefferson : McFarland & Company, Inc., Publishers, 2020. |
Includes bibliographical references and index.
Identifiers: LCCN 2019049529 | ISBN 9781476677002 (paperback) ∞
ISBN 9781476638348 (ebook)
Subjects: LCSH: New Zealand—Race relations. | Biculturalism—New Zealand.
Classification: LCC DU422.5 .M66 2020 | DDC 305.800993—dc23
LC record available at https://lccn.loc.gov/2019049529

BRITISH LIBRARY CATALOGUING DATA ARE AVAILABLE

ISBN (print) 978-1-4766-7700-2
ISBN (ebook) 978-1-4766-3834-8

On the cover: Front cover images © 2020 Shutterstock

Printed in the United States of America

*McFarland & Company, Inc., Publishers
Box 611, Jefferson, North Carolina 28640
www.mcfarlandpub.com*

To Teeli

Acknowledgments

How does one acknowledge all who have contributed to the publication of a book when the task entails so many people in so many ways? The popular metaphor of countless tributaries flowing from myriad directions down, around, and through diverse mountains to feed a stream of context appropriate depth, width, energy, and clarity is popular for a reason. In the present frame of reference it bespeaks academic influences, academic advice, religious inspirations, cultural relationships and courtesies, personal associations, and personal assistance; persons actively involved and others who did not, and do not, realize their contribution; persons who passed away before this project was ever a thought in mind, others who passed while it was in progress, and still others with whom relationships continue.

This book is the product of seven years of study and research through the Graduate Theological Foundation of Mishawaka, Indiana. I must express my deep appreciation for the encouragement and support of Dr. John H. Morgan, who supervised my doctoral thesis, which has culminated in this present work. I must also express my gratitude for and indebtedness to his keen academic perceptiveness and expertise; especially his understanding and presentation of the origins of human religious consciousness and his discernment and explication, first published in 1977, of a particular similarity in the anthropology of American anthropologist Clifford Geertz and the philosophical theology of German-American theologian and philosopher of religion Paul Tillich. In fact, in many respects this book applies Dr. Morgan's observations to a particular cultural setting.

Nevertheless, my primary acknowledgment must be to Teeli, Ms. Linda Jurd, my Kiwi friend and confidant, to whom this book is dedicated. Without her gracious invitation to visit her wonderful country; her faultless hospitality while I was there; and her delightful, discerning, and gentle friendship through the years; this project would likely never have been conceived.

Other contributors that I must mention include those providing publication advice (sometimes over lunch, coffee, or iced tea), formal education in the classroom (the United States, Great Britain, and Aotearoa/New Zealand), one-on-one education in the style of e-tutorials, assistance with travel arrangements, help with converting computer files, care for house and grounds (especially brother-in-law Gary and my late sister Pat), and management of what business there was to manage while I was away studying, researching, visiting, partying (only occasionally), and otherwise hobnobbing with virtually any hobnobbable person available.

I do, of course, take full responsibility for any and all deficiencies in the pages that follow.

Table of Contents

A Brief Guide
to Pronouncing Māori Words

This pronunciation guide is intended for readers who have had little or no exposure to the Māori language. While it is not a complete treatment and cuts corners in many ways, it should be adequate as an aid for such persons to comfortably peruse this book.

As in English, the Māori language has five vowels: *a, e, i, o,* and *u,* and each has a long and short sound. A macron appearing over a letter (*ā, ē, ī, ō,* and *ū*) indicates a long vowel; short vowels have no macron (*a, e, i, o,* and *u*). The macron is quite important because its presence sometimes indicates the plural form of a word while in other instances it differentiates between word meanings. For example, *tipuna* is "ancestor"; *tīpuna* is "ancestors"; and *tīpūna* (a word borrowed from the English language) is "teaspoon." Even though contextual usage would be an indicator of the writer's or speaker's intent, we must not undervalue either accurate spelling or proper enunciation.

The more curious and adventurous readers will find that an internet search turns up a number of resources which use English word examples for pronouncing Māori vowels; one set of words for the long vowels and a separate set for the short vowels. Those who peruse these aids should keep in mind that their authors, when speaking English, may voice their vowels somewhat differently than people from other places. Therefore, while the examples may adequately communicate proper Māori vowel sounds to persons who articulate vowels in the same way as do the authors of the aids, they may be of less help to persons who voice vowels differently. Unless the resource includes a feature which audibly sounds the vowels, the effectiveness of the examples may be less than optimum. Moreover, there appears to be a lack of consistency among some of the online resources.

Consequently, it may be advantageous for most of the readers of this book (who might not have access to either someone who speaks Māori or audible internet files) to use the following pronunciations which do not strictly differentiate between the articulation of long and short vowels except to hold the long vowel a count longer than the short vowel; specifically, "aa" as compared to "a," "ee" as compared to "e," "ii" as compared to "i," "oo" as compared to "o," and "uu" as compared to "u." But keep in mind that they are proffered by a speaker of Midwestern-Midsouthern American English.

- Pronounce "a" like "a" in "balm."
- Pronounce "e" like "e" in "egg."
- Pronounce "i" like "ee" in "beep."
- Pronounce "o" like "o" in "home."
- Pronounce "u" like "oo" in "spoon."

There are also diphthongs in the Māori language. If you pronounce them gliding the first vowel sound into the second in a way that retains the quality of each letter in the diphthong, you should be in the ballpark, e.g., pronounce "*ao*" to rhyme with "cow" and "*au*" to rhyme with toe.

The Māori language has only ten consonants: *h, k, m, n, p, r, t, w, ng*, and *wh*. Actually, two are digraphs, i.e., two letters which represent one sound. You may enunciate the consonants as you would in English with the exception of the digraphs.

- Pronounce "ng" as in "ring" (never as in "linger"), e.g., *Ringatū* (ri nga TU); and
- "wh" as "f," e.g., *whare* (FA re).

Of course, there are other nuances—for instance,

- "r" is pronounced with a slight roll, and
- "t" with a slight sibilant sound which can vary somewhat depending on the vowel which follows it.

But these utterances may require much practice to master.

For syllable stress you may follow these simple guidelines.

- Emphasize syllables with macrons, e.g., *Pākehā* (PA ke HA) or *mānu* (MA nu).
- If there are no macrons but there is a diphthong (for some speakers, prior to the end of a word) emphasize the syllable with the diphthong, e.g., *Tauranga* (TAU ra nga).
- If there are no macrons or diphthongs and the word is four syllables or fewer, stress the first syllable, e.g., *koro* (KO ro), *wahine* (WA hi ne), and *mokopuna* (MO ko pu na).
- If there are no macrons and diphthongs and the word has more than four syllables, emphasize the fourth syllable from the right and the first syllable, e.g., *kotahitanga* (KO TA hi ta nga).

Remember that this is a simplified rendition that is not intended to replace good study under qualified instructors.

The careful reader may have already noticed that all Māori syllables end with a vowel, hence, *āki* (encourage) would be divided as A ki and not AK i. This is true even for words borrowed from another language (loan words); for instance, *hama* (hammer) would be divided as HA ma and not HAM a.

There is a "causative prefix" of which the reader should be aware: *whaka* (pronounced FA ka), the force of which is "to cause something to happen." It often appears with another Māori word attached to it. For instance, the word *whakakā* (FA ka KA) is a combination of *whaka* (to cause to be) and *kā* (ablaze); it means "to cause to be ablaze," i.e., to start something (perhaps an oven) burning. Additionally, the word *whakapukapuka* (FA ka PU ka pu ka) is a combination of *whaka* (again, "to cause to be") and *pukapuka* ("book"); it means "to cause to be a book" (perhaps as a process of binding pages together).

While this guide is admittedly a gross over-simplification, it should suffice to help those unfamiliar with the language read this book.

Preface

Pivotal visits

A personal invitation to visit places 8,000 miles toward the other side of the world is a rare occurrence in Hayti, Missouri, USA, population consistently just under 3,000 persons. In fact, compared with larger communities, Hayti, excluding activities sponsored by the local primary and secondary school systems and periodic activity associated with churches, mostly Protestant, is a community without a particularly active social calendar; especially as it pertains to a short time resident about which the citizenry is still mostly suspicious. Such is often the way of borderline Midwestern-Midsouthern small towns. They can be quite enjoyable for those who do not particularly mind mildly littered streets and are content with a sleepy community where almost everyone knows almost everyone else and their business, and where family ties can extend over generations and be somewhat complicated. But for me, Hayti, which in 2006 had been my home for a mere two years following a 30-year sojourn in Kansas City, was at the time far from the most compelling place imaginable. I did not particularly care for street litter and my friend and family associations there were few. It should be no surprise that the opportunity to visit a land so near the other side of the globe and closer to Antarctica than the Equator brought to this restless Hayti resident an ample measure of excitement.

In late May 2006 a newly acquired Aotearoa/New Zealand internet acquaintance who went by the name of Teelibird, or Teeli for short, arrived in the United States to attend a weeklong gathering of 20 or 30 Middle Age Friends or MAFers as we called ourselves. MAF, in which I had taken refuge shortly after my arrival in Hayti in 2004, was an internet chat forum with an informal membership of perhaps 50 or 60 persons that, although mostly Americans and Canadians, spanned several countries. It had formed in 1999 as a mostly apolitical and areligious gathering directed toward a sort of social and cultural exchange. MAFers cheerfully and often humorously talked about their special interests and occupations, compared and contrasted various parts of the United States with one another and with other lands, exchanged recipes and different ways of getting things done, and learned how words and expressions can differ in meaning from place to place. Although a turn toward a particular partisan political loyalty would later disenchant some of the members and result in some of us leaving the group, the MAFer bond at that time was genuine and strong. Shortly after its formation, MAF began a tradition of holding a "reunion," as we called it, during the month of June somewhere in the United States, which persons from other countries would sometimes attend. Teeli had decided to be present for the 2006 meeting, the venue for which was in Springfield, Illinois. She visited MAFer friends from California to the American Southwest before flying into the Memphis, Tennessee, International Airport

3

where this curious and restless Hayti resident met her. The ensuing trip by automobile from Memphis to Springfield provided the perfect setting for a constant conversation about almost every conceivable subject as a prelude to the MAF reunion.

One characteristic of such gatherings is the sometimes serious and at other times merely courteous invitations to one another for visits to wherever it may be that the inviter resides, an activity that can sometimes leave the invitee perplexed as to the seriousness with which the invitation is delivered. But fortunately, such ambiguity was not to be an issue when it came to visiting Aotearoa/New Zealand. For Teeli, who by the end of the Springfield gathering had become my trusted friend and confidant, extended her invitation in recognition of and exchange for travel assistance in the United States. As it turned out, she had a guest room which was mostly unoccupied. However, since (at least from the perspective of a person without a lot of loose cash) a visit to Aotearoa/New Zealand is not inexpensive; my acceptance of her invitation would, of necessity, be delayed. The 2007 MAF reunion in Oklahoma City rolled around and passed into history as did the 2008 gathering in Louisville, Kentucky. Nonetheless, Teeli and I corresponded often through MAF, email, and internet chat; and fortunately, a full three years later, in 2009, although changes in MAF had by now resulted in both of us withdrawing from the group, her invitation was still open. By now, however, this invitee had managed, through a little resourcefulness and a lot of corporal moisture, to put back a few dollars and was finally in a position to say "yes" to his very gracious host. Thus began an adventure which has yet to come to an end.

Teeli's hospitable invitation was for a prolonged visit, and the Aotearoa/New Zealand summer of early January into early March 2010 provided an opportune time to travel and explore. This gracious lady, who grew from a child to a young adult as a member of the only family of white European descent (Pākehā) in a community of indigenous Polynesian tribespeople (Māori) and was thus familiar with the tribal language and customs, provided a unique perspective on the country. Her home in Kawerau, a town with a population of just under 7,000 residents, mostly Māori, in the Bay of Plenty Region on the east side of the North Island served as home base. Kawerau contrasted sharply with Hayti. It had a much more ordered way of life, streets free of debris and without grass growing in the cracks, ornately flowered foot paths (sidewalks), unspoiled natural reserves, picturesque hiking trails, and Māori carvings that commemorated some of the town's historical events. From this base, the travel route frequently included visits to the nearby coastal town of Whakatāne to the east and the geothermal community of Rotorua to the west, but broader excursions covered the land area within lines drawn from Coromandel to Waihau Bay to Taupō to Otorohanga to Auckland. Although time constraints precluded wider exploration, this range of experience sufficiently declared this nation to be quite unique.

Aotearoa/New Zealand was an incredibly beautiful place with its beaches and coastline, varied animal life, lush forests, clear streams, stunning waterfalls, scenic lakes, active and dormant volcanoes, wild and domestic plants, and geothermal power. However, there was, also, the sense of something quite distinctive about the people. At the outset this suspicion motivated an examination of such things as "coffee table" books, home wall art, yard décor, and town memorials; but soon required the ferreting out of private chats with local individuals, both Māori and Pākehā, about their communities. While they certainly articulated a measure of disagreement among themselves, these same persons also manifested a more or less normative bicultural attitude. Virtually every discussion included an expression of respect for others and a sensibility that appeared to both celebrate divergent ethnicity and support unity within the communities. Of course some localities had their provocateurs, a non-race specific phenomenon; but the vast community majority practiced robust support for and took intense pride in activities which promoted a bicultural mind-set. The possibility of a truly united bicultural nation was so intriguing as to demand an exploration of the interaction of Māori and Pākehā with a view to their achieving this remarkable result.

Mining the resources

The most difficult question to answer when considering how the very different Māori and Pākehā cultures can come together as a mutually beneficial bicultural nation has been *how* to properly mine resources pertaining to the nation's development; particularly, how to identify what is most important and to accurately and inoffensively interpret and report the findings. Clearly, the task would entail poring over a great deal of Aotearoa/New Zealand's history including Māori "traditional culture" (their tribal culture as it was before and during the first several decades after contact with the Western world in 1769) and deciding how both Māori culture and the nation as a whole have developed into what they are today. Moreover, an examination of Māori traditional culture and its development into the present would involve understanding a number of concepts and behaviors quite alien to Western people. Indeed, the colonizing Pākehā required more than a century to break through the complexity, complicatedness, and abstractness of Māori society.

Because the present task's interests are in the historical processes and conceptual differences that brought the people of Aotearoa/New Zealand to their current state of affairs, its method is not a "boots on the ground" study that employs devices such as polls and questionnaires and then processes the collected data to determine current attitudes and trends. Rather, its approach is to examine, understand, and explicate the dynamic processes behind the current cultural arrangement; and independent writers as well as those, both Māori and Pākehā, authorized by the Aotearoa/New Zealand Government have already collected and made readily available a wealth of information. While it is impossible to poll the past, it is quite appropriate to examine history in the light of these recent studies and draw fitting conclusions.

Since the interaction of Māori and Pākehā spans about two and a half centuries, there is a plethora of concepts, circumstances, and events to sort out. This necessarily entails a process of identifying and including the sources which more clearly explain the concepts and more honestly and accurately portray the circumstances and describe the events, which assemblage demands a large measure of subjectivity in its intent. Notably, the discussion which the selection process has facilitated is not intended as a compendium of Aotearoa/New Zealand history, even though it must take Aotearoa/New Zealand history into account. Neither is it a philosophical treatise even though organized around synergistic synthesis as a philosophical principle, nor is it a blueprint for all cultural interaction even though cultural dialogue and understanding are at its heart. This scrutinizing of Māori-Pākehā reciprocity and power relations is simply an inquiry which examines an extreme case of cultural exchange and attempts to learn from its success.

Understandably, over the years, Māori, as well as other indigenous groups, have developed a keen sensitivity for unwelcome prying into their affairs. Consequently, they have devoted themselves to explaining their own culture and its plight, and some have invited non-indigenous researchers to butt out. They, of course, have good reason to be suspicious of outsiders. Over the two and a half centuries of contact between Māori and Pākehā several notions have been propagated about Māori which at best have been misguided and at worst downright insulting and abusive. These have ranged from speculations that Māori are a devolved remnant of the ten lost tribes of Israel, to viewing them as so primitive as to be incapable of abstract thought, to misrepresenting them as unsavvy and incompetent seafarers who arrived in Aotearoa/New Zealand by luck, to explanations of them in terms of a form of cultural evolutionism which viewed Māori as having progressed from savages to barbarians and thus on the verge of being civilized and ready to participate in the modern world; ideas that required forcing Māori culture into hubristic Western historical, philosophical, religious, technological, and cultural evolutionist categories which then resulted in such fallacious judgments.

Nonetheless, one problem with Māori and other indigenous efforts to tell their own story, as qualified as they are to tell it and it is *their* story, is that the ethnic narrators mostly do not receive the recognition they deserve outside of their immediate sphere of influence, tantamount to "preaching to the choir"; and they have an important story to tell. Consequently, it is fitting for others, without the judgmental pomposity of imposing cultural verdicts, to examine an array of resources—including those directed to Māori customs and concepts, Aotearoa/New Zealand social, political, and religious history and thought, and Western philosophical and anthropological schemes—with the express intent of drawing as much attention as possible to Māori tribal culture and its association with the culture of Pākehā; to understand and make available the Māori worldview and ethos and how it interacts with the Pākehā way. Not because Māori people are an odd curiosity, but because their culture-mate association with Pākehā is a developing paradigm for successful cultural relations and a potential lesson for the larger world. Surely, it is possible for a researcher to tell such an important story with the admiration and respect that underpins the endeavor; to satisfy the demands of curiosity without assuming the posture of an observer overlord; to fulfill the requirements of a genuine interest without sticking an unwelcome nose into someone else's business.

The current task is not a judgmental one, but an interpretive one addressed to synergistic synthesis in cultural relations. As such, it requires an epistemological method which is at home with cultural synergy; one which promotes the expanding of cultural categories in the light of interaction with other cultures, noting similarities and differences in such a way that not only enlarges the categories but also broadens understanding and enriches lives through the experience. This falls within the realm of interpretive anthropology with which American anthropologist Clifford Geertz is commonly associated. In some ways it may be a relic of the past, but for the task at hand it is not only still viable but also perhaps the best epistemological method available. The match of the present interpretive task with the method of interpretive anthropology calls to mind the metaphor of the hand in the well-fitting glove. This approach recognizes that human action cannot be separated from its meaning, and that societies store the meaning associated with their actions in tangible, perceptible, concrete embodiments called symbols. These symbols are both proclamations of and storehouses for a society's particular view of, attitude toward, and actions in the world. What the researcher must interpret is the meaning a particular society attaches to and expresses through its lived experience and symbols.

Interpretation, of course, presupposes perspective, and the researcher's perspective determines the discipline associated with the inquiry and how it emerges from an examination of the resources. As it pertains to this current probing of the cultural interchange of Māori and Pākehā, the perspective that has surfaced as appropriate for the application of interpretive anthropology as an epistemological method is the anthropology of religion.

Regarding anthropology, at the outset of this project an examination of Māori and Pākehā associations through an anthropological lens was not a main consideration; there was simply the feeling of intrigue that the Aotearoa/New Zealand experiment could succeed. But anthropological categories evolved naturally from the subject matter. Of course, it is easy enough to understand the interpretive endeavor as an anthropological one simply because it is addressed to culture.

But how did the emphasis on religion come about? As with anthropological categories, it also emerged from the research. An examination of traditional Māori culture found that Māori tribes made no separation of culture and religion. As difficult as it might be for Westerners to comprehend, Māori culture and religion were one and the same; their society was spiritualized. This was enough to establish religion as a category, but a close look at Pākehā culture also raised the question of religion. The first Christian missionaries arrived in the country in 1814 and, even though there was no recorded baptism prior to 1825, began exerting a definite influence on the indigenous population. They established the first mission school in 1816 and by the mid–1830s Māori prophets were demonstrating the influence of Christianity on their traditional religio-culture. However, there remained yet another consideration. Pākehā religion was at that time largely secularized and remains so today. Particularly, over the past few decades more and more of this country's people have declared themselves to have no religion. Is there, then, a way to conceptualize religion that both describes Māori spiritualized society and transcends Pākehā religious secularization?

The answer emerged from an examination of fundamental human existence. According to a particular approach to religion for which German-American theologian and philosopher of religion Paul Tillich has provided a quite complete and comprehensive statement, religion is not fundamentally characterized by institutions or gatherings but rather as the dimension of depth in every aspect of human experience, both personal and corporate. Religion, from this perspective, is inescapable in any human interaction and has characterized Māori-Pākehā cultural interchange from the outset; notably not only undergirding the start of the Māori renaissance, occurring around the turn of the 19th to the 20th century and one of the greatest turning points in the history of Aotearoa/New Zealand since Captain Cook's arrival in 1769, but also buttressing the current national commitment to be a bicultural nation.

Notably, this approach to religion correlates with the epistemological method of interpretive anthropology because both understand human action as inseparable from its meaning, which meaning societies store in tangible expressions called symbols, which in turn project that meaning back on to the society. Thus emerges the application of interpretive anthropology as an epistemological method to the discipline of the anthropology of religion.

In addition to its emphasis on symbols, this book's Māori-Pākehā inquiry develops four particular themes; namely, forms of reciprocity, the operation of power, a concept of culture, and (as briefly mentioned above) the place of religion. It has indeed also been a fortunate happenstance that these notions have likewise developed rather naturally from an examination of the source materials. Therefore, forcing research findings into preconceived prejudicial, strained, and unnatural categories has not been necessary as these themes are broad enough to be fundamental to the examination of *any* cultural interaction. Although some might prefer an epistemological approach other than interpretive anthropology and its emphasis on cultural symbols, few are likely to seriously argue with the inclusion of these four broad universals of human experience.

Of course, these four themes, as do symbols, have their origin in the human drive to make sense of and order the world for the purpose of getting along in it as well as possible. While the expressions of these categories and associations between and among them can vary, sometimes radically, from society to society; in an examination of cultural interchange, these four notions are certain, at some point and in some sense, to emerge as factors. And even though the concepts may be Western in origin, their broad use in understanding and explaining a particular society requires neither forced associations nor judgmental activity.

The chapters

The first two chapters provide background data necessary for discussing Māori-Pākehā cultural interchange. Chapter One describes Aotearoa/New Zealand by taking a look at the nation's origins, some national demographics, its religious orientations, the governmental organization, the one *de facto* and two official languages, and a history in minuscule. Chapter Two discusses key Māori and Pākehā symbols. It includes a general description of symbols, shows how a symbol is born, details how the Māori *whare tipuna* (ancestral house) symbolizes Māori culture, sketches the *whare karakia* (church house) as the Pākehā analogue to the Māori ancestral house, and illustrates some results of the encounter of the two *whare* (houses).

Chapters Three through Six provide a layered analysis of four essential societal concepts and extracts some principles of cultural interchange. These four chapters are organized in a stair-step fashion. Chapter Three addresses reciprocity. It establishes a background from which to discuss the theme, examines it within the very different Māori and Pākehā societal structures, and presents bicultural reciprocity as the reinterpretation of cultural symbols. Chapter Four follows a similar pattern in considering power and its relation to reciprocity. It establishes a background from which to discuss power relations, explores the operation of power among both Māori as a spiritualized people and Pākehā as a secularized people, and examines the synergistic potential integral to cross-cultural power-related reciprocity. Chapter Five discusses culture and religion as complementary articulations of worldview and ethos and a broad context for the exercise of power-related reciprocity. It treats the themes of culture and religion separately, shows how they are interrelated, discusses them with reference to both the spiritualized Māori and secularized Pākehā, and then scrutinizes the convergence of Māori and Pākehā religio-cultural systems. Chapter Six identifies and discusses six principles of cultural exchange as derived from the preceding chapters.

Chapters Seven and Eight are wholly about the nation now. They examine some specific results of Māori-Pākehā encounter in today's Aotearoa/New Zealand. Chapter Seven views *Io* (the Māori proper name for a Supreme Deity) as a prime example of how the dynamics of cultural exchange function in "real time" and offers an answer to the question: "Is *Io* Really God?" Chapter Eight examines the nature of cultural authenticity, briefly presents three examples of Aotearoa/New Zealand's bicultural initiative and discusses the religious dimension of the examples.

Introduction

A synergistic synthesis of cultures

Aotearoa/New Zealand, the geographically small but proud island nation located about 1,000 miles southeast of Australia at the closest points, has developed as a cultural laboratory with its people conducting an "experiment" in biculturalism with important implications for other lands, peoples, and nations. It is not an experiment in the sense of a pre-thought procedure with an anticipated and predicted result, but an occurrence, as strange as it may appear at first glance, that has come about naturally and spontaneously; and over the last several decades has been perpetuated by an expectant optimism—an attempt to do something new with hopes that good things will happen.

Importantly, the aforesaid outlook does not suggest a continuously cordial give-and-take between the principal participants in the experimental activity; specifically, of Māori tribes-people (the indigenous Polynesian inhabitants of Aotearoa/New Zealand) and Pākehā colonialists (the white European settlers who arrived there little more than two centuries ago). In fact, the very mention of indigenous people interacting with colonialists has already suggested a problem. Indeed, for more than two centuries Māori-Pākehā relationships were difficult at best and today are not conflict free. But struggle has been characteristic of the interaction of cultures for millennia, to the extent that it has the appearance of something natural and spontaneous. Indeed, the dictionary definition of struggle as striving to achieve or attain something in the face of resistance appears to be woven into the fabric of existence; a fundamental aspect of reality. Such recognition does not glorify struggle, for societal groups often suffer inappropriately, sometimes to the point of extinction. Nevertheless, the potential intrinsic to struggle also has a positive aspect, and cultural interaction may engender an outcome greater than each individual culture remaining in isolation. In the case at hand, that of Aotearoa/New Zealand, there has persisted amid the difficulty an optimism, especially among Māori tribes, for an egalitarian society; a hope that is finally coming to fruition, and in so doing, is producing a nation with important lessons for the future of other peoples, lands, and nations.

As an illustration of progress in Māori-Pākehā associations, this book continues a convention, utilized in the 2004 collection of essays, *Ki te Whaiao: An Introduction to Māori Culture and Society* (*Ki te Whaiao* translates as "into the world of light"), which combined the word "Aotearoa" with the phrase "New Zealand" to indicate the name of the country as Aotearoa/New Zealand[1]—the careful reader may have already noted this usage in the paragraphs above. It does so in full awareness that maps and other resources refer to the country most often simply as "New Zealand" and on other occasions simply as "Aotearoa." "Aotearoa" is today's Māori word for the name for the country; "New Zealand" is Pākehā.

In *Ki te Whaiao* combining them as Aotearoa/New Zealand served two functions: first, the compound usage reflected the commitment of that book's editors and authors to national bilinguality; and second, it served as a differentiation from the traditional Māori use of the non-compound term, "Aotearoa," for the northernmost of the country's two main islands.[2] But moving past *Ki te Whaiao* there is a third function, one which is of paramount importance for this current book; specifically, the combination of languages in the nomenclature, Aotearoa/New Zealand, represents the movement of Māori and Pākehā toward a synergistic synthesis of cultures.

Hiwi Tauroa's musing

In today's Aotearoa/New Zealand a *marae* is an area consisting of buildings and grounds where Māori gather. It is a *Māori* meeting place and casual visitors are normally not permitted. Māori people who meet there must first extend a welcome to the visitors, and even though it may vary somewhat from tribe to tribe, a particular protocol governs interaction on the *marae*.

Shortly prior to my initial visit to Aotearoa/New Zealand in 2010, the town of Kawerau, which became the operations center for exploring the country, initiated a program to better acquaint its Pākehā citizens with Māori customs, which agenda entailed a weeknight school for learning some of the indigenous language as well as some of the customs and protocols of the *marae*. This school would then facilitate the students' welcome onto the *marae* for a series of weekend visits. The weeknight school's texts included a 2007 book co-authored by husband and wife, Hiwi and Pat Tauroa, titled *Te Marae: A Guide to Customs & Protocol*.[3] Hiwi Tauroa (1927–2018) had spent many years active in Aotearoa/New Zealand's affairs generally and Māori affairs particularly. For instance, in the 1950s he had played for the New Zealand Māori rugby team and was later a successful coach; in 1974 he was Founding Principal of Tuakau College, a secondary school which today serves the town of Tuakau and surrounding area, located less than an hour's drive south of Auckland, a position he held until 1979; from 1979 to 1986 he served as Aotearoa/New Zealand's Race Relations Conciliator; and from 1991 to 2001 he was a member of the Massey University Council. Although not a direct participant in the community program, this curious American read the book as a matter of interest and in so doing encountered a contemplation that has served as a launch point for exploring Māori-Pākehā cultural interchange; an introspection that engendered a consideration of one aspect of the larger issue of biculturalism.

In the co-authored book, Hiwi Tauroa looked back upon his life and recounted portions of his personal experience that were of paramount importance to him and his Māori heritage. He reminisced about the land of his people and Te Patunga Marae in the far north of Aotearoa/New Zealand, near Kaeo. Specifically, he meditated about the *whare tipuna* (ancestral house), the *marae-ātea* (the courtyard in front of the *whare tipuna*), and the *whare kai* (food house; dining room); he also remembered the nearby *whare karakia* (church house) which he had attended as both a child and an adult, where he and his wife were married, and where his father had preached and was interred. Regarding the *whare karakia* he wrote a line which ignited this American visitor's inquiry into associations between Māori and Pākehā; associations that can be at times humorous and at other times tragic, sometimes disturbing while at others heart-warming and reassuring; peaks and troughs perpetually homogenized on the one hand with an insuppressible desire for poetic justice and on the other hand with a fidgety longing for Māori and Pākehā to succeed in their bicultural experiment. Regarding the *whare karakia* he wrote, "I wonder whether it ever took the place of the whare tipuna."[4] The questions posed by Hiwi Tauroa's musing are clear. The *marae* is indispensable to Māori culture and the ancestral house is the focal point of the *marae*; so, did the church ever replace the ancestral house as the centerpiece of Māori culture and if so to what extent? This, of course, is only one expression of a much larger issue. For at the heart of Hiwi Tauroa's musing is the question of the survival of a proud, capable, and complex indigenous island people.

Indeed, it is difficult to imagine two groups more different than Māori and Pākehā of two centuries ago, and yet today they participate together as co-contributors in a vibrant society. The questions are how this can come about and what significance it can have. Hiwi Tauroa's musing, expressed in terms of the relationship of the Māori ancestral house and the Pākehā church, summons a consideration of the dynamics of a cultural interchange with the potential to produce a successful bicultural nation. This book, however, moves past Hiwi Tauroa's musing in suggesting that Aotearoa/New Zealand's bicultural experiment has significance for cultural dialogue and understanding in the larger world.

The emerging paradigm

Bicultural success in Aotearoa/New Zealand is measured by the voluntary integration of Māori and Pākehā ideas and practices without the sacrifice of cultural identity; the ability of two radically divergent cultures to inform one another and establish a system of self-government and mutual respect. Undeniably, the fact that Māori and Pākehā are having their current conversation is awe-inspiring. On the one hand, 19th century Pākehā were a colonizing people who were militarily superior to any group Māori tribes had previously encountered. Yet they abandoned a course of bloodshed and plunder in favor of an integration of cultures for mutual benefit. On the other hand, 19th century Māori; although keen observers, quick thinkers and learners, and capable performers who often proved a worthy match for Pākehā; lost so much population through combat, disease, and despair that many feared they would become extinct as a race. Yet they discovered avenues of interaction with Pākehā that over time have resulted in a revival of their ethnicity and a strengthening of their culture. Certainly, cultural exchange in Aotearoa/New Zealand has not been easy nor is today free from conflict, but the blending of cultures in this island nation is producing an extraordinary people. While Aotearoa/New Zealand is not a perfect model, the current success of the nation's bicultural experiment indicates that a mutually beneficial cross-cultural experience is possible and marks Aotearoa/New Zealand as an emerging paradigm for it. Indeed, both Pākehā and Māori have "come of age," in the sense of achieving their current world esteem, as a *result* of their interaction and not *despite* it.

The phrase, "our *shrinking* world," has become an all but threadbare cliché for the *expanding* development of technology, especially in communications and travel, which brings about a commensurate increase in cultural contact. Living in isolation is, in fact, becoming more and more a non-option with the likelihood of encounter bringing possibilities for both enrichment and conflict. Regrettably, the current slant is toward the latter. Today, racial purists arm themselves against those whom they consider an ethnic threat. Religious purists, motivated by what they believe to be instructions from their "God," group together and engage in military style training awaiting the day they conquer. Political purists do not stop at referring to those espousing different views as political *opponents*, but call them political *enemies*. Stronger nations exploit the culture and resources of others less able to defend themselves. Ethnic cleansing is a topic of the daily news. The internet social media pages are filled with tweets, posts, and shared posts that extoll the superiority of the group of which the one tweeting, posting, or sharing is a member as set against the perceived ignorance, dishonesty, treachery, and overall inferiority of the religion, politics, ethnicity, cultural affiliation, sex, and sexual orientation of those with different physical characteristics, cognitive outlooks, languages, and lifestyles. A common theme for all these contexts is the belittlement of the "other" groups, a degradation of their status as "beneath us." This condescending attitude and abusive behavior begs the question of a cross-cultural model which can be instructive and constructive for the advancement of fair treatment and peace both within and among the nations, an endeavor which success or failure in today's world has far reaching consequences for the welfare of the entire planet.

The sciences addressed to human society and social relationships have for a long time understood that every person on Earth has a worldview and an associated ethos. Worldview is a reference to a person's or a group's basic cosmology; it is the downright truth about the way things fundamentally are; the line of reality below which there is not another turtle. Ethos is a reference to a general attitude toward life and customary behavioral patterns which are inextricably related to the worldview. It is a reference to personality and values which includes personal and group orientation and temperament toward self, others, and the world at large. Together, worldview and ethos define the boundaries of humankind's organization into its various groups from the small association of friends to national organizations. The adages "birds of a feather flock together" and "oil and water don't mix" capture the thought from opposite perspectives; specifically, a common view of the world and similar attitudes and behavioral patterns within it strengthen society and mitigate social conflict. Of course, diverse flocks coming together can bring about predator-prey behavior and the meeting of oil and water will invariably result in a movement of one away from the other.

However, human persons are neither flock nor fluid; their reaction to different others is not confined to pure instinct or chemical reaction. People can make conscious choices. For certain, worldview and ethos profoundly influence how persons interact and, therefore, are not to be taken lightly. Every political, religious, social, and economic decision of every person on the planet is tied to a particular take on the world and how to get along well in it; and every issue of humor, common sense, art, language, justice, etc., is an expression of worldview and ethos. Nevertheless, persons can choose to expand their cultural categories when interacting with other persons. Cultural interchange, which is actually an encounter of different worldviews and ethae, has a synergistic potential, which on the one hand is personal but on the other hand can come to fruition on a scale inclusive of lands and peoples bound together in a national fashion.

The gurus of social attitudes and behavior have long known that the more persons understand about why they think, feel, and behave in particular ways, the better equipped they are to manage personal interactions of agreement and conflict and become enriched in the process. They also know the flipside to be so; that is, that persons understanding more about why others think, feel, and behave as they do can help mitigate attitudes of superiority and injurious behavior. This is no less true for entire nations as they sort out pertinent issues and solutions gain momentum. The emerging paradigm for cultural interchange in Aotearoa/New Zealand is for a synergistic convergence of worldviews and a correspondingly more inclusive temperament and deportment.

CHAPTER ONE

Aotearoa/New Zealand

Before you begin, consider...

How familiar are you with Aotearoa/New Zealand? Chances are, if you are an American, you probably know a little, but only a little, about the nation. For instance, you may know that it is part of the (British) Commonwealth of Nations; that it is located almost on the other side of the world from the United States; that it is in the South Pacific; that English is the main language; that the Lord of the Rings was filmed there; and that it is a place of periodic earthquakes which can be quite destructive. If you are a rugby fan, you might also be familiar with the All Blacks, and know that the name is a reference to their uniforms. But what about the details of the country? What is the origin of its name? How many people live there and who are they? How do they organize their day to day lives? What is their religion, if any? What is their form of government and how do they choose their leaders? Is English an official language? What are the nation's official languages? How did the nation come to be what it is today? This chapter addresses these questions. So, if you are a Kiwi (as Aotearoans/New Zealanders commonly call themselves), or a citizen of a Commonwealth nation, or otherwise knowledgeable about the country, feel free to skip ahead to Chapter Two. This current chapter is designed to answer the most basic questions about this island nation in order to provide a general orientation for those unfamiliar with "the land of the long white cloud."

Some notes on the name

Māui (pronounced like the second largest of the Hawai'ian Islands) arose early in the morning before his four brothers were awake. He, the youngest of the five, had frequently asked to go fishing with them, but invariably they had refused. Sometimes they told him that he was as of yet to small and would only be in the way, but at other times they said that he was much too large and would take up valuable canoe space that would otherwise be devoted to holding their catch. But today would be different, although none of the five knew just how different it would be.

Māui gathered his flax fishing line, which he had woven himself and over which he had chanted an incantation to make it very strong, and his fishhook, which he had fashioned from his grandmother's jawbone—ordinarily, making a fishhook from your grandmother's jawbone was in violation of a *tapu* and could bring a severe penalty, but the resourceful Māui had managed to turn it into an occasion for power. He then made his way to his brothers' fishing canoe, craftily hid himself under its floorboards, and patiently waited. As he had anticipated, his brothers soon arrived. Off they set! Out among the waves they traveled toward a place where fish were plentiful. Māui was fidgety on the inside, but outwardly he maintained his calm and remained hidden.

He waited until they were too far out to sea to simply return him to shore; and when the time was just right, he sprang from his hiding place beneath the floorboards of the canoe. Imagine his brothers' surprise! … and annoyance! But, short of throwing Māui overboard, what could they do so far out to sea? Alas, they could only find indignant ways to express their aggravation. It then fell to Māui to cleverly circumvent his brothers' annoyance. Māui asked his brothers to share their bait so he, too, could fish; but the brothers, who were unhappy with his presence, refused. So he made a fist, struck himself in the nose, and baited his jawbone hook with his own blood. Slowly he lowered his hook and line into the depths. Down, down, it went; fathom after fathom; until the most remarkable of events occurred.

A great fish took the hook; or was it that the hook snagged an extraordinary creature? Whichever the case, a tremendous struggle ensued. The canoe was tossed about, and with it, its occupants. The elder brothers shouted for Māui to cut the line lest they all drown. But Māui would not capitulate to their demand. Instead, he recited an incantation, and soon the giant fish was afloat atop the ocean water with the canoe resting on the fish's back. As the fish writhed about, the elder brothers jumped from the canoe and began chopping at it; the wriggling and hacking resulting in fleshy mountains, hills, valleys, cliffs, gorges, and the like. During the struggle the canoe slid off the fish's back and its anchor came to rest at its stern. At last the fish was subdued, and to this very day the fish, the canoe, and the anchor lie next to one another as islands in the Pacific Ocean. There are, of course, variations of this legend in the Māui corpus; and the story above is a conflation with a measure of independent expression.

Māori tribespeople call the North Island *Te Ika a Māui* (The Fish of Māui) and the South Island *Te Waka a Māui* (The Canoe of Māui). Māui's anchor is *Rakiura*, the much smaller Stewart Island, which lies just south of the South Island. The stern of the canoe is the southern end of the South Island; the bow of the canoe is at the northern end. The head of the fish is at the southern end of the North Island; the tail of the fish is at the northern end. As it pertains to the North Island, this seems to contradistinct from the way Westerner's view the world. Māori go up to the head which is actually south to us, and they go down to the tail which is actually north to us. But viewing the same phenomena from different perspectives can be an enlightening experience for those who are up to the challenge.

Aotearoa/New Zealand, the island nation located about 1,000 miles southeast of Australia at their closest points, is actually an archipelago of more than 700 islands most of which are quite small and within about 30 miles of the two main islands. A perusal of a map produced to scale will verify that this geographically small but proud island nation is long and narrow with the two main islands, the North Island and the South Island, combining for a total length of about 1,200 miles with their individual lengths roughly equal. A further look will show that the North Island's width varies from somewhat less than a mile at its narrowest point (at Ōtāhuhu) to somewhat more than 275 miles, while the South Island's width ranges from about 100 miles to about 240 miles. The North Island's land area is almost 44,000 square miles and the South Island's is slightly more than 58,000.

The designation of the country as "New Zealand" has its roots in the Dutch exploration of the 17th century and is linked to the voyages, sponsored by the Dutch East India Company, of Abel Tasman (1603–1659). Tasman and his crew first sighted the South Island on 13 December 1642. Historians credit Dutch East India Company cartographer Johan Blaeu for naming "New Zealand" after a province of the Netherlands. They also tell us that the name had been added to maps by the mid–1640s. Māori tribes had well established themselves in this land long before Tasman's arrival and considered the Dutch visit an unwelcome one. Interaction between the two groups on 18–19 December 1642, while Tasman was anchored in what maps today identify as Golden Bay, resulted in the death of four Dutch crew members and the wounding of one Māori tribesman. After Tasman's voyage, the Europeans did not return until the English expedition led by James Cook in 1769.

"Aotearoa," today's Māori name for these islands, is a combination of three Māori words: *ao, tea,* and *roa.* Māori dictionaries define *ao* as "world," "daylight," "earth" or "cloud"; *tea* as "white" or "clear"; and *roa* as "long," "tall," or "long-lasting." Over the years and according to who is doing the interpreting, these words have amalgamated for slight variations in meaning, but in today's parlance they mean "the land of the long white cloud." At the time of the English arrival, Māori used the term for the North Island only; but over time it has become a reference to the entire country.

The exact origin of the word, "Aotearoa," remains a mystery, and Māori have more than one tradition about it. For instance, some say it is based on the name of an ancestral voyaging canoe which made the journey to this land from central Polynesia at least 1,000 years ago, while others attribute it to the pre–10th century Polynesian explorer, Kupe, and his wife, Hine-te-apa-rangi. As one story goes, Kupe, his wife, other family members, and non-family voyaging crew had been at sea for many days—according to some, they were chasing an octopus that had disturbed their fishing in Hawaiki, the ancient Māori homeland. The early Polynesian voyagers had learned that clouds form over islands; and as Kupe and company traveled, such a cloud gradually came into view. When Hine-te-apa-rangi saw it she called out, *"He ao! He ao!"* (A cloud! A cloud!). Kupe named the land for his wife's exclamation: *Aotearoa,* "the land of the long white cloud."

A peek at the population

Just who are these people who occupy this island nation located below Australia? The previous topic recounted popular Māori legends about the origins of the land itself and the arrival of the first Polynesians; it also mentioned the coming of the first Europeans. But let us now describe the nation today. Of course, little if any of the information below will be news the Aotearoa/New Zealand citizenry, but people of other lands—especially in my home country of the United States—may find it a useful orientation.

Most Aotearoans/New Zealanders enjoy a very temperate climate, albeit not tropical; but it ranges from subtropical in the far north to potentially very cold winters in the far south. The terrain varies from rolling hills (mainly on the North Island) to mountains (mostly on the South Island), and no location is further than about 80 miles from the sea. The nation's economy is based on free market principles and its well-educated, healthy populace enjoys a good standard of living.

The nation's chief imports are vehicles, parts, and accessories; mechanical machinery and equipment; petroleum and petroleum products; electrical machinery and equipment; textiles and textile articles; and plastic and plastic articles.[1] The chief exports are milk powder, butter, and cheese; meat and edible offal; logs, wood, and wood articles; fruit; and wine.[2] Aotearoa/New Zealand's top suppliers of goods and services, in order by monetary value, are China, the European Union, Australia, the United States, and Japan.[3] The top receivers of Aotearoa/New Zealand's goods and services, also in order of monetary value, are China, Australia, the European Union, the United States, and Japan.[4] The unemployment rate in Aotearoa/New Zealand over the past five years has ranged from about 6 percent to about 4.5 percent,[5] and the country is successfully maintaining its inflation target of between 1 percent and 3 percent.[6]

The nation's total population passed 1,000,000 in 1908; 2,000,000 in 1952; 3,000,000 in 1973; and 4,000,000 in 2003.[7] The populace at the time of the latest census in 2013 was approximately 4,250,000[8] and is currently estimated at around 4,900,000.[9] The current number of citizens is roughly comparable to the Republic of Ireland, or Norway, or Costa Rica. Aotearoa/New Zealand's annual population growth over the last 10 years has ranged from a low of .55 percent in 2012 to a high of 2.14 percent in 2017.[10] For the past 10 year period the excess of births over deaths accounts for about 53 percent of the population increase and net migration accounts for about 47 percent; however, net migration has exceeded the natural increase for the past four years.[11]

The nation's people identify themselves with several broad ethnic groups: European, Māori, Pacific Peoples, Asian, Middle Eastern, Latin American, and African. However, identifying the number of persons for each of these categories can be somewhat problematic. On the latest census, in 2013, almost 250,000 persons did not know their ethnicity, refused to answer the question, provided an unidentifiable response, stated a response outside the scope of the question, or ignored the question altogether. Moreover, almost 500,000 identified themselves with more than one, and up to six, ethnic categories. By excluding the dissenting, unknowledgeable, and unintelligible responses and including all responses from those who self-identified with more than one ethnic group, we can project percentages which are sufficiently accurate for an overview of Aotearoa/New Zealand's ethnic constituency (see Table 1).

Table 1. Aotearoa/New Zealand's Ethnic Constituency

Ethnic Group	Percent of Population
European	66.72
Māori	13.45
Asian	10.60
Pacific Peoples	6.65
Middle Eastern/ Latin American/African	1.06
Other Ethnicity, e.g., New Zealander	1.52
Total	100.00

(Calculations derived from: Stats NZ/Tatauranga Aotearoa, 2013 Census QuickStats About Culture and Identity; Tables, [NP: Stats NZ, 2014], Table 1, http://archive.stats.govt.nz/Census/2013-census/profile-and-summary-reports/quickstats-culture-identity.aspx [accessed April 5, 2018]).

As indicated in Table 1, the two largest ethnic groups in Aotearoa/New Zealand are European, which is about 66.72 percent of the population, and Māori, which is about 13.45 percent. Together they account for more than 80 percent of the total. Interestingly, Māori as an ethnic group are much younger than the population generally; half of them are under 23.9 years old which is 14.1 years younger than the median age of the total population.[12]

For general considerations, the average number of births per woman required for a population to replace itself in the long term, exclusive of net migration, is 2.1; one to replace the mother, one to replace the father, and .1 to account for persons who die childless. According to data collected by the Aotearoa/New Zealand Government for 2017, this number for the country's total population was 1.81[13] with the mother's median age being 30.3 years.[14] This represents a downward trend from the 2013 census at which time the fertility rate was 2.02 and the mother's median age 30.05 years.[15] Over the last several decades Aotearoa/New Zealand families have on the average transitioned from relatively large to relatively small families. A statistical comparison of the peak year of 1961 with the most recent data shows the average births per woman dropping substantially. It was 4.31 in 1961,[16] but dropped, as indicated above, to 1.81 by the close of 2017. Over the past 10 years the rate has fluctuated from a high of 2.19 in 2008 to its current low of 1.81.[17]

The numbers above also indicate an aging population, a trend which is confirmed by other statistics. The median age increased from 33 in the 1996 census to 38 at the time of the latest census in 2013.[18] In fact, the number of Aotearoans/New Zealanders 65 years old and greater has increased by almost 35 percent in the current century.[19] Aotearoa/New Zealand's statistical service attributes the aging of the population to a sustained low birth rate, improvements in health care, and the movement of persons born in years with high birth rates into senior ages.[20] In other words, on the whole Aotearoans/New Zealanders are generally having fewer babies and living longer.

School education in Aotearoa/New Zealand is compulsory until age 16 and there is no official retirement age. Nevertheless, the Government views the working age population as beginning at age 15, and most people view their working career as continuing until age 65, at which time they become eligible to receive Superannuation payments from the Government. Roughly 65 percent of the nation's population is working age while children ages 14 and under are about 20.5 percent of the citizenry and seniors ages 65 and above make up approximately 14.5 percent.[21]

When it comes to males and females, the latter have a slight population advantage. Females are about 51.3 percent of the population and have a median age of about 38.9 years, while males comprise about 48.7 percent with a median age of about 36.9 years.[22] Since the turn to the 21st century the median age in Aotearoa/New Zealand has increased by 3.3 years for females and 2.9 years for males.[23] This reflects the current difference in life expectancy of 83.4 years for females and 80 years for males, which is up .2 years for females and .5 years for males over the last three years.[24]

Aotearoa/New Zealand recognizes both civil unions and same sex marriages. The Parliament's Civil Union Act 2004[25] introduced civil unions as a new form of legal relationship. Effective 26 April 2005, an opposite sex or same sex couple in which both persons are at least 18 years old, or persons 16 and 17 years old with consent from their parent(s) or guardian(s), could enter into a civil union provided they are not married to or in a civil union with another person. In 2013 Parliament took an additional step by approving the Marriage (Definition of Marriage) Amendment Act 2013[26] which clarified the definition of marriage as "between 2 people regardless of their sex, sexual orientation, or gender identity" and allowed same sex marriage effective 19 August of that year. There were 165 male and 190 female same sex marriages in 2013.[27] The following year there were 373 male and 504 female same sex marriages.[28] In 2015, of the 19,950 total marriages and civil unions, 471 were same sex[29]; and in 2016, the 20,232 total marriages and civil unions included 480 that were same sex.[30]

Of the total marriages in 2016, 71 percent were first time couplings while 29 percent were remarriages or transfers from civil unions.[31] The median age for first time marriages was 30.3 years for men and 29.0 years for women; this was up as compared to 1987 levels of 25.9 years for men and 23.7 years for women.[32] The general marriage rate (the number of marriages per 1,000 non-married population ages 16 and over), was 10.95 in 2016; significantly lower than the 29.39 rate of 35 years prior.[33] Factors possibly responsible for the decline include an increase in couples living together without legally formalizing their union (*de facto* unions) and more persons choosing to remain single, as indicated by the declining marriage rate; and a general trend towards delayed marriage as indicated by the increase in the median age for first time marriages.

Marriage dissolutions are also an issue in Aotearoa/New Zealand. The nation's family court system granted 8,169 marriage dissolution orders in 2016; this translates into a divorce rate (the number of marriage dissolutions granted per 1,000 existing marriages) of 8.7.[34] This was the lowest mark in 34 years after peaking at 17.1 in 1982.[35] Additionally, the age of those getting a divorce has steadily trended upward. The median age for divorce in 1994 was 39.8 years for males and 37.0 for females; in 2016, this had increased to 46.8 and 44.4 respectively.[36]

Finally, a snapshot of Aotearoa/New Zealand's crime statistics provides insight into the nation's quality of life. In 2014, the latest year for which statistics are available, there were 41 murders, 11 attempted murders, 3 homicide related offenses, and 11 instances of manslaughter (including driving related deaths) in the entire country.[37] Based on an estimated population for that year of approximately 4,510,000 people, this is about .15 offenses for each 10,000 people. Other violent crime numbered 43,682 instances,[38] about 97 offenses per 10,000 people. Property crime—including burglary, robbery, breaking and entering, motor vehicle and other theft, and property damage—totaled 213,829 occurrences,[39] about 474 offenses per 10,000 people.

So what do these statistics mean? While Aotearoa/New Zealand contrasts with a country like the United States in some ways—for instance, it is a geographically small island nation which largest minority is Polynesian—it is not generally atypical of countries in the English-speaking world.

A review of the religion

The definitions of "religion" and "religious" for statistical purposes are of a different species than those for theological or ecclesiastical aims. Chapter Five addresses the latter, but for now, as it pertains to the compilation of a national databank, the Aotearoa/New Zealand Government views religion as "a set of beliefs and practices, usually involving acknowledgement of a divine or higher being or power, by which people order the conduct of their lives both practically and in a moral sense"[40] and understands religious affiliation to be "the self-identified association of a person with a religion, denomination or sub-denominational religious group."[41] However, the Government's statistical service includes in its count of religions and religious people those entities that are widely considered as religions and those persons who regard themselves as religious, even if they do not fall within the scope of the strict definition.[42] The Government, which has solicited information regarding religious affiliation as a part of its national census since 1851, believes this more comprehensive classification to be of greater use in obtaining an overview of the country. While we must be careful not to consider the census data as a measuring rod for participation or commitment, we can use it to provide significant insight into Aotearoa/New Zealand's current religious configuration and direction.

The 2013 census asked persons about the particular religious group(s) with which they associate themselves, if any. Census responses about religion suffered from the same maladies and those regarding ethnicity. On the one hand, some census respondents did not know their affiliation, objected to answering the question, or simply did not reply; others supplied an answer outside the definition of religion—for instance, vegetarian; and still others gave completely unintelligible responses. On the other hand, many persons indicated more than one religious affiliation. Making allowance for the maladies yields the results shown in Table 2.

Table 2. 2013 Census: Religious Affiliations

Classification	Total People	Percent of Total
Christian (all groups)	1,911,924	50.30
No Religion	1,635,345	43.02
Hindu	89,919	2.37
Buddhist	58,404	1.54
Islam/Muslim	46,149	1.21
Other Religions (Sikh, Baha'i, Zoroastrian, etc.)	34,245	0.90
Spiritualism and New Age	18,285	0.48
Jewish/Judaism	6,867	0.18
Total	3,801,138	100.00

(Calculations derived from: Stats NZ/Tatauranga Aotearoa, 2013 Census QuickStats about Culture and Identity, Table 30.)

What can the census tell us about the spiritual direction of the country? Comparing the 2013 statistics to the previous census in 2006 yields a seven-year trend as depicted in Table 3.

Table 3. Religious Affiliations: Seven Year Trend

Classification	2006 Census Total People	Percent of Total	2013 Census Total People	Percent of Total	Difference Total People	Difference Percent of Total
Christian (all groups)	2,092,968	58.32	1,911,924	50.30	-181,044	-7.93
No Religion	1,297,104	36.10	1,635,345	43.02	+338,241	+6.92
Other Religions (all groups)	203,934	5.67	253,869	6.68	+49,935	+1.01
Total	3,594,006	100.00	3,801,138	100.00	207,132	0.00

(Calculations derived from: Stats NZ/Tatauranga Aotearoa, 2013 Census QuickStats About Culture and Identity, Table 30.)

Let us first notice that just over half of usable, positive responses to the question of religious affiliation in the 2013 census indicated an association with some form of Christianity. However, Christianity is on the decline. In terms of the percentage of affiliation, the 2013 results show a drop of almost 8 percent from seven years prior. Moreover, this drop of more than 181,000 respondents occurred against an increase in the total number of respondents of more than 207,000. For Christianity to hold its own over the seven year period, it would need to have shown an increase of more than 120,000 on the 2013 census instead of a decrease of more than 181,000.

What factors influenced Christianity's decline? The trend may be somewhat supported by an increase in people in the 2013 census indicating affiliation with non–Christian religions—in 2013 the number of these affiliates was almost 254,000, a growth of about 50,000 from the 2006 census; which is an increase from about 5.67 percent in 2006 to about 6.68 percent in 2013. However, this expansion is more likely an indication of immigration trends. The most telling statistic for the decline of Christianity is the number and percentage of "No Religion" responses. This number increased from 1,297,104 to 1,635,345 from 2006 to 2013; a growth of about 7 percent. Table 4 summarizes the "No Religion" classification by ethnic group.

Table 4. 2013 Census: "No Religion" per Ethnic Group

Ethnic Group	Percent of "No Religion" Responses	Percent of Population	Percent of Ethnic Group: Religious	Percent of Ethnic Group: Not Religious	Total Percent of Ethnic Group
European	73.30	66.72	51.99	48.01	100.00
Māori	14.24	13.45	52.75	47.25	100.00
Asian	7.49	10.60	69.17	30.83	100.00
Pacific Peoples	2.65	6.65	82.01	17.99	100.00
Middle Eastern/ Latin American African	.41	1.06	82.57	17.43	100.00
Other Ethnicity (e.g., New Zealander)	1.91	1.52	47.53	52.47	100.00
Total	100.00	100.00			

(Calculations derived from: Stats NZ/Tatauranga Aotearoa, 2013 Census QuickStats About Culture and Identity, Table 35.)

In the 2013 census the largest "No Religion" group was comprised of those who associated themselves in some way with European ethnicity, the nation's largest ethnic group. These respondents accounted for more than 73 percent of total "No Religion" responses while they comprised less than a 67 percent of the nation's population. More than 48 percent of this group, considered in itself, indicated they had "No Religion"; an increase from 38 percent in the 2006 census. Table 5 is a complete profile of this ethnicity's religious affiliations.

Table 5. 2013 Census: Religious Affiliations, European Ethnicity

Classification	Number of Responses per Christian Classification	Total Responses	Percent of Total
Christian			
Anglican	406,245		
Baptist	44,721		

Classification	Number of Responses per Christian Classification	Total Responses	Percent of Total
Catholic	347,172		
Christian—not further defined	157,359		
Latter-Day Saints	12,639		
Methodist	57,552		
Pentecostal	45,777		
Presbyterian, Congregational and Reformed	262,698		
Other Christian Religions	75,276		
Total Christian	1,409,439		
Māori Christian			
Rātana (Total responses, all ethnicities: 50,199)	8,706		
Ringatū (Total responses, all ethnicities: 15,453)	2,010		
Other Māori Christian Religions (Total responses, all ethnicities: 708)	126		
Total Māori Christian	10,842		
Total Christian & Māori Christian		1,420,281	50.25
Total All Other Religions		49,293	1.74
Total "No Religion"		1,356,816	48.01
Grand Total		2,826,390	100.00

(Percentages calculated from: Stats NZ/Tatauranga Aotearoa, 2013 Census QuickStats About Culture and Identity, Table 35.)

Māori, the second largest ethnic group and largest minority, accounted for slightly more than 14 percent of total "No Religion" responses, which is just slightly more than the percent of the population they represent (see Table 4). Of those identifying themselves as Māori, more than 47 percent indicated "No Religion." Compared to the 2006 census, this is up from 35 percent, which shows that Māori are moving toward a more secular outlook along with the Pākehā population. Table 6 profiles current Māori religious affiliations.

Table 6. 2013 Census: Religious Affiliations, Māori Ethnicity

Classification	Number of Responses per Classification	Percent of per Christian	Percent of Māori Christian	Percent of Christian & Māori Christian	Percent of Christian Grand Total
Christian					
Anglican	61,269	26.63		21.76	
Baptist	3,189	1.39		1.13	

Classification	Number of Responses per Classification	Percent of per Christian	Percent of Māori Christian	Percent of Christian & Māori Christian	Percent of Christian Grand Total
Catholic	63,996	27.82		22.74	
Christian—not further defined	32,688	14.21		11.61	
Latter-Day Saints	18,801	8.17		6.68	
Methodist	11,070		4.81	3.94	
Pentecostal	9,783	4.25		3.48	
Presbyterian, Congregational and Reformed	17,751	7.72		6.31	
Other Christian Religions	11,490	5.00		4.08	
Total Christian	230,037	100.00		81.73	41.25
Māori Christian					
Rātana (Total responses, all ethnicities: 50,199)	38,268		74.40	13.59	
Ringatū (Total responses, all ethnicities: 15,453)	12,639		24.57	4.49	
Other Māori Christian Religions (Total responses, all ethnicities: 708)	528		1.03	.19	
Total Māori Christian	51,435		100.00	18.27	9.22
Total Christian & Māori Christian	[281,472]*			100.00	[50.47]*
Total All Other Religions	12,741				2.28
Total "No Religion"	263,517				47.25
Grand Total	557,730				100.00

*This entry is the addition of the "Total Xn" and "Total Māori Xn" entries above. The brackets indicate that it is not included in the Grand Total for this column. (Percentages calculated from: Stats NZ/Tatauranga Aotearoa, 2013 Census QuickStats About Culture and Identity, Table 35.)

The Tables pertaining to religion clearly indicate that, even though religion continues to be an important influence in Aotearoa/New Zealand, the general movement of the nation's population is toward a more secular mind-set.

As stated above, in the 2013 census more than 47 percent of Māori responses indicated "No Religion"; however, historically (as Chapter Five explains) Māori religion has been synonymous with their culture. It is, therefore, appropriate to take a closer look at the formal religious groups that are specifically Māori.

Of Māori responses to the question about religious affiliation on the 2013 census (see Table 6), 41.25 percent indicated a connection with mainstream Christianity, while 9.22 percent indicated a connection with a special category labelled "Māori Christian." Thus, more than 50 percent of Māori positive responses to the religious affiliation question declared some form of Christian faith. Of these, the top categories were Catholic at 22.74 percent and Anglican at 21.76 percent, but the special "Māori Christian" group followed closely at 18.27 percent. Responses for this special category were approximately 24.57 percent Ringatū Church and 74.4 percent Rātana Church. The remaining 1.03 percent was spread over groups statistically too small for consideration. The Ringatū and Rātana groups draw particular attention because they have specifically Māori cultural origins, include Christian elements, and have figured prominently in Māori-Pākehā interchange.

The Ringatū faith dates to the 1860s and Te Kooti Arikirangi Te Turuki (1830?–1893), a Māori spiritual and military leader. The Ringatū faith is formally registered with the Aotearoa/New Zealand Government as *Hāhi Ringatū*. *Hāhi* is the Māori word for "church," "sect," or "religion." *Ringatū* is a combination of two words: "*ringa*" which means "arm" or "hand" and "*tū*" which means "to stand," "to be erect," "to be raised." The words combine to mean "the upraised hand"; hence, the phrase *Hāhi Ringatū* means "the Church of the Upraised Hand." The tradition of raising the right hand at particular times began with the founder of the Church, Te Kooti, and continues in the Church's services into the present. In the 2013 census, Ringatū received 15,453 total responses of which 12,639 (almost 82 percent) were Māori.

The Ringatū church has no special buildings dedicated to the worship of God; rather, Ringatū members meet in the main house (*wharenui*) of the grounds and facilities that Māori reserve for themselves (*marae*) and to which they restrict admittance—Chapter Two of this book discusses the *wharenui* and *marae* at length. The Church has no paid clergy. It elects its leader, called a *Pou Tikanga*, and an executive body of 12 members every two years; and each worship group has a *tohunga* (expert) who specializes in the operation of the Church. None of these officials, however, wears any form of ecclesiastical vestment. Services, which take place on the 11th and 12th of each month, are in the Māori language. The services feature prayers, songs, scripture recitations, meals, and communion. Information generally available about the services (e.g., YouTube videos) shows them as relaxed and reserved, and portrays the leaders as gentle spirited.

The Church's seal[43] includes two upraised hands between which an eagle is perched atop a belt surrounding the Old and New Testaments. The belt's buckle represents fastening on the armour of God. Around the belt and at its base is inscribed, "*TE TURE A TE ATUA ME TE WHAKAPONO O IHU*" which translates as "the law of God and the faith of Jesus." There are two additional inscriptions at the base of the seal. At the bottom left is, "*WHAREKAURI 67*," a reference to the origins of the faith in the Chatham Islands in 1867—*Wharekauri* is the Māori word for the Chathams. At the bottom right is, "*WAINUI 26*." Some interpret it as a reference to the gifting of land to the Church at Ōhiwa Harbour in 1926,[44] while others understand it as a reference to the beginnings of Church reorganization in that year[45]—*Wainui* is a place name. The eagle is a reference to a portion of "The Song of Moses" as recorded in Deuteronomy 32:11–12 which reads (NRSV), "As an eagle stirs up its nest, and hovers over its young; as it spreads its wings, takes them up, and bears them aloft on its pinions, the Lord alone guided him; no foreign god was with him."

The Rātana Church dates its origin to 1918 and takes its name from its founder, Tahupōtiki Wiremu Rātana (1873–1939).[46] The Rātana Church (*Te Hāhi Rātana*) has been formally registered with the Aotearoa/New Zealand Government since 1925, but also enjoys an Australian presence. Its website, *Te Haahi Ratana: The Official Website of The Ratana Established Church of New Zealand,* is accessible to any interested person. In the 2013 census, the Rātana Church received 50,199 responses of which 38,268 (more than 76 percent) were Māori (see Table 6).

Almost from its beginning Rātana has been a Church with a definite political agenda tied to the Labour Party. Its political mission is for the progress of Māori people in the country. It is classified as Christian, and its beliefs are Biblically based; however, the Church uses the Blue Book (a collection of hymns and prayers in the Māori language) in its services and supplements the Christian doctrine of the Trinity with belief in the Faithful Angels and the acceptance of T.W. Rātana as the Mouthpiece of God. As the designation "Mouthpiece" indicates, the Church regards its founder as a prophet. Today, the Church's leader is determined by a process of nomination and appointment. Thus far, the Church's leaders have mostly been family relations, but the power of the Church is in its collective membership and the influence it exerts throughout the country. The Church accepts other Christian denominations and is tolerant toward other faiths.

Early in his career as a spiritual leader, T.W. Rātana developed a reputation as a healer, and by 1920 a shanty village of followers developed on the family farm located on the western side of the southern half of the North Island near Whanganui; it became known as Rātana Pā. There are Rātana churches all around the country, but Rātana Pā, with its 2,000 seat Holy Temple of Jehovah, is the Church's home and a pilgrimage site for the faithful.

Today, the Church's symbol is a multi-colored five pointed star partially encircled on the bottom and sides by a blue crescent moon. The symbol may vary a bit, but generally, as the observer faces the symbol, on the left side of the moon is the letter, "A," for Alpha and on the right side is the letter, "O," for Omega. T.W. Rātana's name is sometimes inscribed in the crescent moon. Each point of the star is a different color. Often, (the observer facing the symbol) the point upward is blue representing "the Father," the point upward left is white representing "the Son," the point upward right is red representing "the Holy Spirit," the point downward left is purple representing "the Faithful Angels," and the point downward right is yellow or gold representing "the Mouthpiece (of God)." Together the moon and star represent the Kingdom of Light opposing its antithesis.

A glimpse at the government

The Aotearoa/New Zealand political system is a constitutional monarchy. It is a parliamentary system of governance about which the website of the New Zealand Parliament/ Pāremata Aotearoa provides a wealth of information.[47] The country's general population elects a House of Representatives which advises the Sovereign (the Head of State). The Sovereign and the House of Representatives comprise the Parliament. Aotearoa/New Zealand is one of the 53 nation (British) Commonwealth of Nations of which Queen Elizabeth II is head, but the country enjoys full legislative independence. The Governor-General represents the Queen for opening and dissolving Parliament and assenting to bills passed in the House of Representatives. The Sovereign appoints the Governor-General on the advice of the Prime Minister. The Governor-General is to be non-partisan and remain detached from the business of government. Even though all legal authority derives from the Sovereign, it is rare for the Sovereign (or the representative thereof) to act outside the advice of the House.

The Aotearoa/New Zealand system spreads power across three branches of government: the Parliament (the House of Representatives and the Sovereign), which makes the law; the Executive (the Ministers of the Crown, often called the Government), which administers the law; and the Judiciary (the court system), which interprets the law. Although called a constitutional monarchy, the nation has no written constitution as does the United States. The term refers to a system of government in which the power of the monarch is not absolute; rather, it is controlled by Parliament and the nation's laws, and there is no law that transcends that which the Parliament passes. The rules which direct the operation of government are present in Acts of Parliament, relevant English and United Kingdom Acts of Parliament, decisions by the court system, and some unwritten customs.

Prior to 1950 the Aotearoa/New Zealand Parliament was bicameral; the upper chamber was designated the Legislative Council and a lower chamber called the House of Representatives. Since that year it has been unicameral with only a House of Representatives. The country's citizens elect Members of Parliament (MPs), usually 120, for a term of up to three years. The Government (the Ministers of the Crown) derives its membership from elected MPs, and can retain power as long as a majority of the House of Representatives lends its support, up to a maximum of three years between elections. This arrangement is called Responsible Government. The Ministers are responsible to Parliament on two fronts; collectively as a body and individually for performing their charged responsibilities. But ultimately, all MPs are responsible to the voters.

This parliamentary form of government is considerably different from the presidential system with which we of the United States are familiar. We Americans, too, spread power over three branches of government, but do it in a way much different than the Aotearoa/New Zealand Parliamentary system. Our written Constitution separates the powers and defines the roles of each of the three branches. Perhaps the most obvious difference in Aotearoa/New Zealand's parliamentary system and the American democracy is how the American Constitution separates the legislative and executive branches. The American President cannot be a member of the country's legislature. He or she is independently elected by the people, and for better or worse, is not directly accountable to the American legislative branch for the performance of duties. The President can be removed from office only by a very difficult process that begins with impeachment in the United States House of Representatives, the lower chamber of Congress. Impeachment is only a formal statement of charges. If the impeachment is successful (tantamount to an indictment in a civil court), the matter goes to the Senate, the upper chamber of Congress, for a trial. The trial determines the success or failure of dismissal. Impeachment and removal from office can only occur in cases involving treason, bribery, or a vague something called "high crimes and misdemeanors," and is a very rare occurrence. Only two Presidents (Andrew Johnson in 1868 and Bill Clinton in 1998–99) have been successfully impeached by the House of Representatives and both were acquitted in the Senate. One President (Richard Nixon) resigned before the impeachment process was complete. This contrasts sharply with the Aotearoa/New Zealand parliamentary system in which the executive branch is an essential part of the legislature. The two branches come together in the Cabinet, a group of senior Ministers whose meetings are chaired by the Prime Minister. The Governor-General can exercise "reserved power" in order to dismiss the Prime Minister, but this happens only in the most extreme of situations. For instance, the House of Representatives may, by a majority vote, indicate that they no longer support the person (or group) in power. Such a vote signals the Head of State that the Parliament has lost confidence in the Government. The only Aotearoa/New Zealand Prime Minister to lose in a vote of no confidence was Thomas MacKenzie in 1912.

Let us now consider how Aotearoa/New Zealand handles its elections. The Electoral Commission/Te Kaitiaki Take Kōwhiri, an independent Crown entity, is responsible for the administration of Parliamentary elections.[48] The country has used the Mixed Member

Proportional (MMP) system of electing MPs since 1996; previously the nation employed the First-Past-the-Post (FPP) system. There are major differences in FPP and MMP. In the FPP system, each voter casts one vote only and the candidate with the most votes wins the election even if that person did not receive 50 percent of the vote—in some cases there may be three or more candidates. Consequently, in the days of FPP, political party representation in Parliament failed to reflect the overall Aotearoa/New Zealand spread of votes. The MMP system brings party representation more in line with the country's overall poll by allowing each elector two votes; one for the preferred political party and one for a local MP. However, since there are several active political parties in Aotearoa/New Zealand, it also creates a situation in which it is unlikely that any one party will win more than half the seats. In this case the parties must negotiate with each other in order to form a Government; that is, some of the parties must pool their election victories in order to have a majority of members, and from which to recommend a Prime Minister to be appointed by the Governor-General. In the MMP electoral system there are more seats in Parliament than those which will be filled by direct election of local MPs. The voters elect 71 members by direct vote—of these voting districts, 64 are general while seven are reserved for Māori. The remaining seats are filled from closed party lists in a way that insures that the parliamentary membership reflects the percentage of the vote that each party received. The current Parliament is the 52nd Parliament. It was elected in 2017 and consists of five parties: The Act Party (one member), The Green Party of Aotearoa/New Zealand (eight members, all from the party list), The New Zealand Labour Party (46 members, 17 from the party list), The New Zealand National Party (56 members, 15 from the party list), and The New Zealand First Party (nine members, all from the party list). The current Prime Minister is Jacinda Ardern, leader of the New Zealand Labour Party.

The nation held its first Parliamentary elections in 1853 (at that time the Parliament was styled "The General Assembly"); prior to that time, a Governor appointed by the British Crown ruled the colony (albeit, not without significant challenge from Māori). At the outset of voting, the Government decided eligibility by criteria pertaining to sex, age, nationality, and property ownership; those eligible to vote were male British subjects, at least 21 years old, who owned or leased property, and who had not been convicted (or if convicted, pardoned or completed the sentence) of treason, felony, or other serious crimes. It is noteworthy that, although Māori men were *theoretically eligible* to vote, they were *practically excluded* because Māori land ownership was communal rather than by individual title.

However, over time the country has moved toward and approved universal suffrage. In 1867, Parliament reserved four seats for Māori, and decided that *all* Māori men over the age of 21 years could vote for their representative without the restriction of property ownership. In 1879, Parliament lifted the property restriction from all adult European men. In 1893, Aotearoa/New Zealand became the first of the world's self-governing nations to extend the right to vote to all adult women. More recently, Aotearoa/New Zealand has taken additional steps to improve the vote as it pertains to age and participation. Parliament lowered the voting age in two stages; it reduced it to 20 years of age effective in 1969 and to 18 years of age effective in 1974. Finally, in 1975 Parliament determined that all permanent residents could vote with or without Aotearoa/New Zealand citizenship.

Let us now consider the local governments. Like the Parliament, the local authorities operate on an electoral basis by a vote of the citizens; but they derive their authority from Parliament. This derivation of authority from Parliament means that the nation operates on a "unitary" governmental structure; a system which is significantly different from the "federal" structure of governments such as the United States. In a federalist system a national government and several regional authorities (in the United States, we call them "states") share power. Both can take action that affects the citizenry. Recently, Americans have seen the central government and various state governments in conflict over issues such as the legalization of marijuana, the restriction of immigrants, and so-called sanctuary cities. In the United States both the central government and the state governments have the right to govern independently of the other; and when serious conflicts occur, the court system must sometimes decide which will prevail. By contrast, Aotearoa/New Zealand has a "unitary" system of governance in which all local power derives from the national level. The central government may delegate power to its local governments, but the power of the local governments always stems from the national government.

It is now apparent that the flow of power in Aotearoa/New Zealand is through a hierarchical structure. The Department of Internal Affairs/Te Tari Taiwhenua details the arrangement.[49] The nation has 78 local authorities; these include 11 Regional Councils, 54 District Councils, 12 City Councils, and one Auckland Council—Auckland is the country's largest city with almost a third of the nation's population. Of these 78 local authorities, the 54 District Councils, the 12 City Councils, and the Auckland Council comprise the 67 Territorial Authorities, of which six (the Auckland Council, one City Council, and four District Councils) have the powers of Regional Councils; these six are the Unitary Authorities.

The 11 Regional Councils and the six Unitary Authorities serve as the highest level of local government, and the 61 remaining Territorial Authorities do duty at the next level. Community Boards minister at the lowest level of local government; they are located in both urban and rural areas and currently number 110.[50] The purpose of this arrangement is to provide tiers of governance appropriate to address even the smallest concerns within each community.

Local elections occur every three years in October. They are administered not by the Electoral Commission (which handles parliamentary elections) but by the Local Councils, and may involve a number of organizations. In the case of local elections, the Electoral Commission's role is limited to maintaining accurate and up-to-date voter rolls. Whereas elections for Members of Parliament use the Mixed Member Proportional (MMP) election system exclusively, Aotearoa/New Zealand's Department of Internal Affairs recognizes two electoral systems for local authority elections: First-Past-the-Post (FPP) and Single-Transferrable Vote (STV). As already mentioned, the FPP system is a simple arrangement where each voter has one vote and the candidate with the most votes wins. The STV system is a bit more complicated. Those conducting the election establish a quota based on the number of votes available in the voting district and the number of positions to be filled. Voters rank the candidates in the order of their preference. Candidates who reach the quota of first preference votes are elected. If vacancies remain after the first count, a process of elimination determines the winner(s).

A look at the languages

According to the 2013 Aotearoa/New Zealand census, the country is home to at least 69 verbal languages, each of which is spoken by at least 1,000 residents, and many other tongues (perhaps an additional 90), each of which is spoken by a lesser number of the population.[51] The nation is also the abode of sign languages, the most prominent of which is New Zealand Sign Language (NZSL) used by more than 20,000 people.[52] Less clearly defined and not listed on the census reports is the language content of Māori carvings. Plainly, multi-ethnicity and multi-linguality are important issues which will become even more important as these social aspects develop within Aotearoa/New Zealand's borders and the country participates more and more with other nations.

Nevertheless, for most practical intra-national considerations, Aotearoa/New Zealand remains generally bicultural and trilingual; bicultural because Māori and Pākehā combine for more than 80 percent of the population and the Government actively supports biculturalism, and trilingual because the Government recognizes one *de facto* language (New Zealand English) and two official languages (Māori and NZSL). Notably, the principles of the 1840 Treaty of Waitangi, Aotearoa/New Zealand's founding document (see the topic, "A handle on the history," below), between Māori tribes and the British Government, provides the basis for biculturalism; and the Government's recognition of Māori as an official language exemplifies its support for a bicultural concept. Although there is a sense in which being trilingual extends beyond being bicultural, trilinguality is rooted in biculturalism by virtue of the fact that most of the users of NZSL are spread through the Māori and Pākehā populations. The following paragraphs examine the use of New Zealand English, NZSL, and Māori in the nation's current social design.

Interestingly, the Aotearoa/New Zealand Parliament has not determined it necessary to establish English as either *the*, or *an*, official language of the land. Rather, English remains the *de facto* language; it is "of fact" the country's primary medium of communication. This has not always been the case. Māori was with original *de facto* language; English became so as the result of colonization. Judging from responses on the 2013 census, 96 percent of the total population can converse in English.[53] Add in another 2 percent that are too young to talk,[54] and it leaves only about 2 percent of those capable of communicating in an established verbal language who cannot converse in the *de facto* tongue. Moreover, as much as 78 percent may speak English as their only language.[55] By contrast, those who speak only Māori are less than .22 percent of the population.[56] The swap of *de facto* languages represents a complete social reversal from pre and early colonial times.

There are, however, persons who cannot effectively converse audibly in any language. In response, the New Zealand Sign Language Act 2006[57] made NZSL the latest official language. As stated above, it has become a medium of communication in which more than 20,000 people can talk. We might well wonder why an Act of Parliament was necessary as the need for an inaudible language seems apparent, especially when considering the need for communications in venues such as the court system and medical facilities. According to the Aotearoa/New Zealand Human Rights Commission, and as strange as it may sound to us contemporarily, there was a time when the country actively prohibited using NZSL.[58] Misconceived notions treated sign languages generally as inferior to spoken languages and linguistically inauthentic. The misconceivers believed that it was more to the advantage of deaf people to try to speak as much as possible and to read lips.[59] Of course, the ability to use a sign language is severely limited without someone present with the ability to interpret. Fortunately, attitudes have changed. The evolution of opinions led the Office of Disability Issues to consult with the deaf community in May to June 2003; and in October of that year the Government agreed to put together a bill in favor of an official language for non-verbal communications. This bill, the New Zealand Sign Language Act, received Royal Assent in April 2006.

The New Zealand Curriculum, published by the Ministry of Education, captures the country's reversal of outlook in its description of NZSL and statement of how it is important for the country:

> ... NZSL is a complete visual-gestural language with its own grammar, vocabulary, and syntax ... [which] ... uses the hands, the body, and facial expressions (including lip patterns) to express meaning and the eyes to perceive meaning. Like any language, it is capable of communicating an infinite number of ideas.... [I]t has no written form.... There are, however, notation systems that are used for recording signs on paper....
>
> For many Deaf people, NZSL is essential for effective daily communication and interactions. New Zealand needs more people who are fluent users of the language and who have an appreciation of Deaf culture. By learning NZSL, hearing students are able to communicate with their Deaf peers and participate in the Deaf community. Skilled communicators may find career opportunities that involve working with Deaf people. As Deaf people come to have a wider circle to converse with, our society becomes more inclusive.[60]

The Māori Language Act 1987[61] declared Māori an official language of Aotearoa/New Zealand and acknowledged it to be a *taonga* (treasure). The Māori Language Act 2016,[62] which replaced the 1987 Act, reaffirms the status of Māori as an official language and a *taonga*; it also declares it the indigenous language and a language valued by the nation. However, we should keep in mind that this recognition is not an indicator of a pan–Māori language or society. There are, and have been from the outset, regional variations, albeit not so significant as to prevent cross-tribal communication. Underlying these Acts is the entire history of the language, including its ties with the 1840 Treaty of Waitangi. The online source *New Zealand History/Nga Korero a Ipurangi o Aotearoa* provides a concise treatment.[63]

Te reo Māori (the Māori language) is indigenous to Aotearoa/New Zealand, and at the beginning of the 19th century was dominant. At that time the language had no written form, but early frontierspersons found it necessary to learn it if they were to trade with Māori; and as more and more settlers arrived, the need for written communication grew. The Christian missionaries, from as early as their first arrival in 1814, made the first attempts to put the language into written form; and by the 1820s Māori were even teaching each other to read and write. As late as the 1870s it was not unusual for Government officials, missionaries, and settlers to speak Māori even though by the 1860s Pākehā were the majority population and English was the main language. Soon afterward, however, speaking the indigenous tongue fell into disrepute with the settlers. Pākehā communities officially discouraged it to the point of Māori children, as late as the early 20th century, facing corporal punishment in schools for speaking their mother tongue on school grounds. Additionally, many Māori parents, for economic reasons, encouraged their children to focus on learning English.

Nevertheless, the indigenous language persisted even though it changed considerably as a result of contact with English, the predominant language of the settlers. The cultural contact, of course, resulted in Māori borrowing English words which they altered as euphony and grammar required; and conversely, the settlers borrowing words from Māori. Even at the start of World War II most Māori still spoke their native tongue as their first language; it was the speech of the *marae*, worship, and the home. There were also newspapers and other literature written in Māori. World War II, however, brought tremendous changes to Māori society. Whereas Māori had lived mostly rural lives, they now moved to the cities for the available work. As a result, use of the indigenous tongue sharply declined; and by the mid–20th century many feared that the language would disappear. But the Government and people of Aotearoa/New Zealand, although not without difficulty, set out to preserve the indigenous way of verbally communicating and from 1975 forward have celebrated a Māori Language Week.

Perhaps the most significant development for the preservation of the indigenous speech began when the Government approved the Treaty of Waitangi Act 1975[64] which established the Waitangi Tribunal to hear Māori claims of breaches of the 1840 Treaty of Waitangi. The Tribunal's original jurisdiction could not exceed contemporary claims, but in 1985 the Government expanded the Tribunal's authority to include claims dating to the signing of the Treaty. The pertinent instrument for this change was the Treaty of Waitangi Amendment Act 1985.[65] In this first year of extended jurisdiction, Māori presented a claim that their language was a *taonga*; that is, a cultural "treasure," that required protection and nurture. After hearing the claim, the Tribunal released its recommendations that led to the Māori Language Act 1987, which declared the Māori language an official language of the land and set up the Māori Language Commission to promote it as such.

The campaign to revive *te reo Māori* has not been an easy one, but today familiarity with the language and fluency in speaking it is on the upswing. Māori language publications, which had all but disappeared, have returned. Also, there is a Māori language television station. Moreover, in the 1980s Māori language immersion schools for teaching children from the primary through the secondary level appeared. It has become quite common to hear the greeting "*kia ora*" (an informal "hello") in casual day-to-day informal personal encounters around the country.

Obviously, there are legal ramifications for official languages. Legal recognition of NZSL and *te reo Māori* fosters its use in court and other official places. For instance, the New Zealand Sign Language Act 2006 states, "Where the presiding officer in any legal proceedings is aware that any person entitled … to use NZSL in those proceedings intends to do so, the presiding officer must ensure that a competent interpreter is available."[66] The Māori Language Act 1987 used similar language to provide the same guarantee for anyone intending to speak Māori, and the 1987 Act's 2016 replacement reaffirms the right. Moreover, official recognition places a responsibility on the Government to provide official telephone and other communications in the Māori language for transacting official governmental business. All of this entails investments of time and money for personnel and other resources.

As it pertains to audible languages, with New Zealand English the *de facto* language and Māori an official language, Aotearoa/New Zealand makes her bicultural legislative frame apparent in some of her recent publications. For instance, the New Zealand Diversity Action Programme, in the *Statement on Language Policy*, recorded the following: "The outcome for language is as follows: By the bicentenary of the signing of the Treaty of Waitangi in 2040 New Zealand is well established as a bilingual nation and communities are supported in the use of other languages."[67]

Additionally, the Māori Language Commission/Te Taura Whiri i te Reo Māori stated in the Introduction to its 2012 *Annual Report*:

> This Annual Report highlights progress Te Taura Whiri i te Reo Māori has embarked on towards the achievement of the vision of Aotearoa as a true and active bilingual nation by 2028 as envisaged in by our overall vision: *ka haruru a Aotearoa tangata i tōna reo taketake—the human landscape of Aotearoa will resonate with its indigenous language.*[68]

A handle on the history

Historians and other researchers have written book after book detailing Aotearoa/ New Zealand history. In addition to the many books, two online sources sponsored by the

Aotearoa/New Zealand Government's Ministry for Culture and Heritage—*Te Ara: The Encyclopedia of New Zealand,*[69] which includes a biography section, and *New Zealand History/ Nga Korero a Ipurangi o Aotearoa*[70]—are freely available to anyone wishing to investigate the nation's development. What follows in the present discussion is only a brief introductory chronological record. It is designed as a bare bones orientation for those who have little knowledge of the country.

The first documented European contact with Aotearoa/New Zealand occurred in 1642 with Abel Tasman's Dutch expedition, and after his departure in early 1643 Europeans recorded no further contact until James Cook's British expedition of 1769. When the Dutch and British arrived, Māori were well established in the land. They had settled there centuries earlier, but did not call themselves Māori in any pan-societal sense until after the British arrived. The word, *māori*, means "normal," "natural," "ordinary"; it evolved into a reference to the indigenous people in contrast to the foreign arrivals. Some researchers estimate the population of the *tangata whenua* ("people of the land," as Māori often refer to themselves) just prior to British contact at about 100,000; others say it was possibly twice that number.

But what of Māori origins? Māori oral tradition identifies Hawaiki, which scholars believe to be located in the Southern Cook and Society Islands, as their ancient homeland. One of the more popular speculations regarding arrival from this part of the world originated with S. Percy Smith (1840–1922) and his fellow amateur ethnologists in the late 19th and early 20th centuries. According to Smith's theory, Polynesians first arrived in the land about 750 CE, but a fleet of voyaging canoes from the Tahitian region followed about 1350 CE. Māori scholar, Te Rangi Hīroa (Sir Peter Buck; 1877 or 1880–1951; of Māori-Pākehā mixed ancestry whose full Pākehā name was Peter Henry Buck) also supported this idea. Smith's notion remained popular among both Māori and Pākehā into the 1970s at a minimum, but more recent archaeological and other scientific data have refuted his idea.

Two other misconceived notions about Māori arrival are also pertinent. The first sprang from Norwegian adventurer Thor Heyerdahl (1914–2002) and the second from Aotearoa/ New Zealand historian Andrew Sharp (1906–1974). Heyerdahl, accompanied by five friends and a green parrot (which unfortunately did not survive the trip), drift voyaged from Peru to eastern Polynesia in 1947 on an 18 by 45 foot balsa wood raft, called the *Kon-Tiki* after an old name for a Peruvian sun god; his theory being that early migrants, using ocean currents, sailed or drifted into Polynesia from the east. He believed that there were two migrations into the Polynesian islands: the first around 500 CE and the second about 1100 CE. Heyerdahl believed that the earliest voyagers would have found it impossible to travel against the winds and currents from Southeast Asia directly into Polynesia. In his opinion, the first Polynesians must have sailed or drifted into these islands from the west coasts of the Americas on balsa wood rafts and that the second wave came westward to Hawai'i on much more sophisticated vessels and then traveled south.

The *Kon-Tiki* was made of balsa wood logs and equipped with sail, centerboards, and a steering oar. South American indigenous people had once used crafts such as this, and Heyerdahl set out to prove that a journey into Polynesia was possible on them. He documented his 4,300 mile trip, which lasted slightly longer than three months, in his entertaining book first published in Norwegian in 1948 as *Kon-Tiki Ekspedisjonen* and in English in 1950 as *Kon-Tiki: Across the Pacific by Raft*. A movie about the trip was released in 1950.

A short time later, in 1956, Andrew Sharp published his book, *Ancient Voyagers in the Pacific*, in which he declared that any notions of the Polynesians as great voyagers was

misinformed. He wrote a follow-up book, titled *Ancient Voyagers in Polynesia*, in 1963. In his opinion, their crafts and navigational methods were incapable of long planned ocean journeys; therefore, settlement of Polynesia must have been mostly unplanned and accidental. Although he generally differed with Heyerdahl about the Polynesian direction of arrival—Sharp allowed for occasional trips from the Americas but believed they mostly arrived from the west—he agreed with him that their coming to these islands was by chance.

In fairness to Heyerdahl, he and his crew succeeded in demonstrating that a balsa wood raft could successfully transport a crew from Peru into Polynesia; and as it pertains to Sharp, it is quite probable that the success of some journeys was more related to fate than skill. However, today, the theories of both men find little acceptance within the academic community. As it pertains specifically to Heyerdahl, linguistic, cultural, and genetic evidence remains a severe challenge to his theory of the direction of arrival; and as it pertains to both men, the navigational skills of those who would become Polynesians and the integrity of their ocean-going crafts have been strongly substantiated.[71] In particular, in 1976, Melanesian master navigator Mau Piailug (1932–2010) proved the seaworthiness of South Pacific voyaging crafts and the reliability of navigational methods which do not rely on Western instruments when he, on an expedition backed by the Polynesian Voyaging Society, used the sun, moon, stars, ocean currents, winds, etc., to successfully navigate a traditional sailing canoe roughly 2,500 miles from Hawai'i to Tahiti. Mau Piailug's accomplishment of successfully navigating without Western instruments has been repeated several times since then. The evidence strongly supports the notion that the Polynesians and their ancestors were skilled navigators of seaworthy vessels; there is little reason to conclude that their voyages into and within Polynesia were necessarily unplanned or accidental.

So from whence did Māori hail; and when? For time of arrival, research associated with kiore (Pacific rats) provides a clue. These rats were a food source which the early Polynesian voyagers took with them on their trips. Early kiore presence in Aotearoa/New Zealand has been the subject of considerable recent study. Researchers have radiocarbon dated rat-gnawed seeds and rat bones found in Aotearoa/New Zealand to approximately 1280 CE.[72] The earliest evidence for human presence provides confirmation for this dating.[73] As for the travel route, it is generally accepted that the people who would become the Polynesians migrated through Southeast Asia and into the island groups below thousands of years ago.[74] They then turned east, moving from island to island, reaching Tonga and Samoa possibly by 1000 BCE.[75] While the time of their arrival into what we today call central Polynesia is not certain,[76] a date of 300 CE is not unreasonable. From central Polynesia they moved three directions into the lands that today form what we know as the Polynesian Triangle; specifically, they moved north to the Hawai'ian Islands (perhaps by 400 CE), southeast to Rapa Nui (Easter Island; perhaps also by 400 CE), and southwest to Aotearoa/New Zealand (by 1280 CE, as mentioned above).

Turning to more recent history, from the 1770s, non–Polynesian explorers tended to use Aotearoa/New Zealand as a stopping point for more challenging quests, but entrepreneurs and settlers soon followed. Even though there were still only about 200 permanent settlers in the early 1830s, many more Europeans were in and out, exploiting such resources as seals, whales, timber, and flax.

The time from these earliest arrivals to the 1840 signing of the Treaty of Waitangi (see below) was a complex jumble of associations. First, Pākehā competed with Pākehā for Aotearoa/New Zealand resources. A description from 1834 records 30 to 35 whaling ships docked for three weeks at Kororāreka (today's Russell) in the Bay of Islands with 400 to

500 sailors on board. Second, Māori, using the newly arrived European firearm technology, sought to gain the upper hand with other Māori. The "Musket Wars" of the 1810s through the 1830s, that often involved revenge for past deeds, saw the death of thousands of Māori at the hands of other Māori. Third, Māori and Pākehā fought, especially if Māori believed that Pākehā had mistreated a person of tribal importance or tried to cheat them. In fact, an incident in 1809 (the *Boyd* incident) was so severe that it caused the Christian missionaries to delay their arrival until 1814. Fourth, after their arrival, the Christian missionaries were at odds with Pākehā behavior and fearful for the well-being of Māori. Following a conflict in 1834 (the *Harriet* affair), the Church Missionary Society (CMS) went so far as to protest British excessive use of force and unrestrained colonization; and in 1837 the CMS and the Wesleyan Missionary Society (WMS) petitioned the British Government to upscale their protection of Māori. Fifth, the association of Māori and the Christian missionaries was mixed. The missionaries recorded sparse Māori baptisms prior to 1830 but by 1842 had documented more than 3,000. From the outset, the missionaries devoted much time to teaching European farming techniques and trades. They also translated the New Testament into the Māori language and enabled Māori literacy. But some who fell out of favor found it necessary to flee for their lives. Finally, to add to the intrigue, under the right circumstances both Māori factions and Pākehā factions would unite in various ways, both intra-group and inter-group, both supporting and opposing one another, depending on the purpose of the moment, especially if it entailed the acquisition of goods or *mana* (tribal prestige).

In 1831, this jumble of violence and cooperation combined with fear that the French had intentions for Aotearoa/New Zealand incited 13 Māori chiefs to petition then British King William IV for protection. Moreover, in 1835, James Busby, the British Resident (an official title), kindled further action at a meeting in Waitangi. He drafted the Declaration of Independence of New Zealand and persuaded 34 Māori chiefs to sign it. Among other things, the Declaration asserted Aotearoa/New Zealand's independence, declared the sovereignty of the chiefs, and entreated William IV to continue to be the infant State's parent. At that time the Declaration received little serious attention and had virtually no practical effect. However, even though historians today disagree about its particular association with the Treaty of Waitangi (see below), they generally regard it as a forerunner to a formal constitutional relationship with Great Britain because it asserted indigenous rights.

Although it has not always been the case, Aotearoa/New Zealand today regards the Treaty of Waitangi, between the British Crown and Māori tribes, which initial signing took place on 6 February 1840, as the nation's founding document, even though not all Māori chiefs signed it. There were at the time and are today two versions of the Treaty, one in English and one in Māori; both versions have three articles, but they differ. As recorded in the English version, the Māori chiefs cede "sovereignty" over the land to the Queen of England (at that time, Victoria) while they retain the full and undisturbed possession of all they own. Also, should they choose to sell land, the Queen has the preemptive right to purchase such lands. In exchange, the Queen agrees to protect the tribes and to give them all the rights and privileges of British subjects. There are, however, important differences between the English and the Māori versions of the Treaty. The word "sovereignty" in the English document appears as *kāwanatanga* (governance) in the Māori text. Many Māori chiefs believed they were allowing the Queen authority over the settlers, but that Māori had the right to oversee their own affairs as well as to undisturbedly manage all their properties and other possessions. In their understanding, the Queen agreed, as is documented in the Māori version of the Treaty, that the indigenous people would have *tino rangatiratanga* (absolute authority) over all their lands, homes, and treasures. In brief, the British negotiators believed they had absorbed the land and the indigenous population as a colony while the Māori chiefs believed they would rule their own affairs and the Queen's authority would be limited to her own people. These differences both exemplify and serve as the basis for Māori-Pākehā relations even today. They underscore two issues that we should clearly understand about Māori: They are fiercely autonomous, and have an unmitigated attachment to their cultural treasures, their land, and their land's resources. The political and religious development of Aotearoa/New Zealand has provided a context for working out these issues, and an understanding of the dynamics of the encounter is what this book is all about.

The exploitation of Māori, especially the procurement of their land, was already an issue at the time of the 1840 Treaty. But after Governor William Hobson declared British sovereignty over both the North and South Islands on 21 May 1840, exploitation became an even greater problem. On the one hand, the colonial government established a Native Protectorate Department in 1841, and in 1842 land claims commissioners began investigating all land purchases made prior to the Treaty of Waitangi. But on the other hand, in 1844, Governor Robert FitzRoy acquiesced to demands by both Māori and settlers to deviate from the Treaty's land procurement provisions; and in 1846 the colonial Government decided that all Māori land must be registered and it seized Māori land deemed unused or surplus. Also, while the Government reinstated the exclusive right of the Crown to procure land, they allowed that payment at market rate was not a requirement. Additionally in that year, Governor George Grey disbanded the Native Protectorate Department. In effect, Pākehā were taking over. Through all this, there were Māori tribal conflicts; wars between Māori and Pākehā, sometimes with Māori factions siding with Pākehā; and intra-Pākehā competition for the country's resources.

To establish greater control, the (British) New Zealand Constitution Act 1852, at about the time that the indigenous and settler populations were becoming equivalent, set up a parliamentary system of government based on the model used in Britain. Aotearoans/New Zealanders elected members to the governing body in 1853, and the Parliament (at that time designated as "The General Assembly") first sat in 1854. At that time the law limited the voting right to men and based it on a system of land possession that virtually excluded Māori. In 1858 Māori responded with the *Kīngitanga* movement, an attempt to establish a Māori King who would be complementary to the British Monarch; the intent being to unite the tribes and protect the indigenous population from further loss of land and resources. However, many of the tribal chiefs would not place their *mana* (prestige) under that of another person, and the colonial government would not recognize the Māori King's authority.

The issue of land resulted in the New Zealand Wars fought between Māori and Pākehā, the main period of which began in 1860 and continued well into 1864. In order to punish Māori militants, the Aotearoa/New Zealand Government, in 1863, authorized land confiscations. There was sporadic fighting into 1882. What of the Treaty of Waitangi in all this? In 1877 the Aotearoa/New Zealand Chief Justice described it as "worthless" based on his judgment of Māori as "a group of savages"; in his opinion, the Treaty was a "legal nullity" because it had not been incorporated into domestic law. Māori sought legal redress from the British Queen, but the British Crown advised each group of petitioners that the imperial government no longer accepted responsibility for their plight.

There were, of course, more benign attempts than war to bring Māori in line. For instance, The Māori Representation Act 1867 established four seats in Parliament that Māori were to occupy, even though it should have created many more, considering the population.

It also extended universal suffrage to Māori males at least 21 years old, which right they first exercised the following year. Pākehā men remained restricted by property qualifications until legislation passed in 1879; for them, the first elections under the new arrangement were in 1881.

Although largely unsuccessful for unifying tribes and airing grievances, Māori continued to take initiatives in an attempt to stop the Pākehā advance. In addition to the King Movement mentioned above they organized several Māori "Parliaments" (*Kotahitanga*) which met from the early 1890s. Nonetheless, the decline of the tribal influence and population continued. In fact, Māori population reached an all time low toward the end of the 19th century. According to the 1896 census, only slightly more than 42,000 Māori survived in the country's total population which had reached more than 743,000. Such was the effect of European diseases, tribal disenfranchisement, and general despair.

However, toward the end of the 19th century, a change began on two fronts. First, by 1892 many Pākehā had become concerned for the survival of Māori as a race. For instance, a group spearheaded by S. Percy Smith, Elsdon Best, and Edward Tregear founded the Polynesian Society to record as much as possible about Māori and other Polynesian groups. Although Māori fortunes did not turn suddenly for the better and not all Pākehā changed their outlook, the founding of the Polynesian Society stands as a prime example of the beginning of a shift in Pākehā attitudes. Māori potential for survival and their overall destiny improved considerably toward the end and after the turn of the century. Second, a group called the Young Māori Party formed in the late 1890s. Not to be confused with a political party per se, they were an association of persons who shared the common goal of improving Māori fortunes. They set out to breathe new life into Māori culture and in the process became politically influential. The Young Māori Party gave rise to a number of leaders, such as Sir Āpirana Ngata, Sir Māui Pōmare, Te Puea Hērangi, and Te Rangi Hīroa (Sir Peter Buck), who became significant for the Māori renaissance. In fact, even though it required several decades to gain traction, the Māori renaissance originated at around the turn of the 19th into the 20th century.

Although Māori continued to experience difficulties in the 20th century, let us turn our focus to more positive developments. In 1918 the Rātana movement (see the topic, "A review of the religion," above) began, and in the 1920s developed a political arm directed toward the Treaty of Waitangi. By the mid–1930s, Rātana and the Labour Party had established an alliance, and Labour began nominating Māori candidates in the Māori electorates. By 1943 Rātana Labour candidates held all four Māori seats which strengthened the Rātana voice and thus the emphasis on the Treaty in government. Also, in 1926 a commission began an inquiry into the land confiscations of the 1860s; they judged many as excessive and recommended compensation which started in 1931. Moreover, in 1932 Governor General Lord Bledisloe, who had acquired James Busby's house in Waitangi, where the Treaty of Waitangi signing first took place, gifted it to the nation; and in 1934 Aotearoa/New Zealand formally observed the first Waitangi Day. The 1940 national centennial celebrated the signing of the Treaty of Waitangi as the nation's founding moment, and by 1945 every school and *marae* in the country displayed a copy of the Treaty. In 1947 the Government changed the word "Native" in official references to "Māori." Throughout this period, the Young Māori Party was active in rejuvenating Māori pride and prestige and helping shape the nation's political direction. Interestingly, the Government supported these Treaty activities even though it had not officially ratified the Treaty. In fact, the Government has not ratified it to date, and it is officially a part of Aotearoa/New Zealand law only insofar as Acts of

Parliament reference it. Yet the principles of the Treaty have become paramount in Māori-Pākehā relations.

After World War II, Māori urbanization presented some challenges to the survival of the culture and there was still much concern for the loss of tribal land and its resources. Māori fortunes continued to improve, but not without protests, marches, sit-ins, and legislative disagreements. Examples of legislation that caused Māori concern include the Maori Affairs Act 1953,[77] which allowed anyone who could prove to the Māori Land Court that desirable land was not in use could make application for it to be vested in trustees, and the Maori Affairs Amendment Act 1967,[78] which allowed the conversion of Māori freehold land owned by not more than four persons into general land. Māori considered these Acts an attack on their rights and tantamount to a land grab. Māori reactions to legislation and events they considered unfair included the formation in 1970 of Ngā Tamatoa (The Young Warriors), which set out to raise nationwide awareness of Māori interests with activities such as circulating petitions for recognition of the indigenous language and disrupting Waitangi Day gatherings; the 1975 march on Parliament by thousands of marchers, led by Whina Cooper, to raise awareness about the ongoing loss of Māori land; the 506 day Bastion Point (coastal land in a suburb of Auckland) occupation in 1977–78 that protested a government housing project on a former tribal reserve; the 1978 protests at Raglan (a coastal town on the west side of the North Island about 30 miles from Hamilton) over the conversion of Māori land used as a World War II airfield into a golf course instead of returning it to Māori; and the establishment in 1980 of the Mana Motuhake political party (deregistered since 2005) which pushed, as the name implies, for Māori independence and self-determination.

Positive developments we have already mentioned include the establishment of the Waitangi Tribunal in 1975 with authority to hear breaches of the Treaty going forward, its empowerment in 1985 to investigate claims dating back to 1840, how this resulted in the Māori Language Act 1987 which made Māori an official language of Aotearoa/New Zealand, and how the language's status was later affirmed in the Māori Language Act 2016 (see the topic, "A look at the languages," above). To this we add the State-Owned Enterprises Act 1986[79] which incorporated a reference to the Treaty of Waitangi and in so doing fostered recognition of the Treaty in both national and local government and the Te Ture Whenua Maori Act/Maori Land Act 1993[80] which recognized the special Treaty relationship between Māori and the Crown, affirmed the Māori right of self-determination, identified land as of special significance to Māori, promoted retention and development of land by Māori, and provided a legal mechanism for achieving these goals.

What is at stake in Aotearoa/New Zealand's move toward biculturalism is the nature of the Treaty relationship. Many believe the nation's bicultural commitment is in name only and Māori are progressively being assimilated into Pākehā culture; according to them, a proper Treaty relationship entails nothing short of the full recognition of Māori authority and the development of tribal institutions to completely handle all of the affairs of the indigenous people. At the other end of the spectrum are those who believe the nation has absolutely no special responsibility to Māori; according to them, Māori culture should receive no recognition that is not afforded to any other culture in the land. But the past cannot be erased, and the Treaty is the Treaty. If the nation is to recognize the Treaty of Waitangi as her founding document, it must acknowledge that the seeds from whence today's nation springs are planted in bicultural soil. In fact, any path to multiculturalism must pass through the nation as bicultural, as by the very nature and intent of the nation's founding document, biculturalism is Aotearoa/New Zealand's default state. Significantly, the nation appears committed in principle to a genuine biculturalism which entails the unity and social comfort of both Māori and Pākehā while recognizing and insuring the rights, contributions, and worth of the other 20 percent of the population. Nonetheless, the country is still debating the appropriate cultural model.

CHAPTER TWO

Understanding Symbols

A world of symbols

"I pledge allegiance to the flag of the United States of America…." While every country has a flag and may have various oaths of loyalty, not every country has a formal pledge of allegiance to its flag. In this, the United States is somewhat unique.

My earliest school-day recollections include the entire enrollment of the Trenton (Tennessee) Elementary School, perhaps 400 or so boys and girls in grades one through six, periodically gathering outside our school building where our teachers taught us to gaze upon the stars and stripes flag flying high above, place our hand over our heart, and recite the Pledge of Allegiance. Our government, as one built on freedom of expression including that of dissent, had no edict to force any citizen to repeat the oath, but in our case neither parents nor kids objected. This was the 1950s; a time when the recollection of World War II and the befuddlement of the Korean War were fresh in the minds of adults and developing in the minds of us kids. Our teachers were our guides whose tasks included impressing upon us the importance of the American flag as a symbol of our country. They, having lived through the events of the 1930s–40s, had experienced the flag's power and meaning as a symbol; and pledging allegiance to flag and country was among their most rousing and inspiring participatory activities. We, as children, many of us born post–World War II, were just learning.

Our class, as many others before and since that time, moved on and entered the Trenton Peabody High School where we learned about our school colors, anthem, and identity as the "Golden Tide." We thus grew in the knowledge and experience of symbols, even though we did not think about the hues, songs, and images specifically in those terms. These representations set our school apart from those of the neighboring towns. Somehow they communicated a level of acceptance, provided a certain behavioral direction, and sometimes declared our school's superiority to the surrounding ones. As with any other high school, we had our social groups and cliques which did not always peacefully coexist; but our colors, songs, and images united us on a level that transcended our differences, just as our nation's flag had united our country's various factions during the war years.

Writers discussing the nature and function of symbols have for a very long time appealed to a nation's flag as an example of such phenomena because it is such an obvious one. Moreover, the more sagacious reciters of The Pledge of Allegiance will have noted how the oath defines the nature of symbols and describes their function. "I pledge allegiance to the flag of the United States of America and to the republic *for which it stands*…." A symbol stands for something; and the flag *stands for* the country in a very obvious way just as our school colors, songs, and images stood for our school.

Some symbols, however, are more obscure. We are surrounded by symbols that rarely ascend as such to the cognitive level and yet they stand for something quite definite. Institutions, for example, are not particularly apparent as symbols, but think of what they mean. Our churches, synagogues, mosques, and other religious facilities communicate the presence, power, and impact of the invisible world; our financial institutions declare the advantages of a market based economic system; both our civic and military organizations extoll the importance of a "free" society; and the functionality (or dysfunctionality) of our homes reinforces particular social behaviors. Moreover, social behavior itself has come to be recognized as symbolic. The national flag fuses these notions with many others integral to the "American way" in its very prominent and noticeable physical betokening of the country.

Symbols operate in a special way in the performance of their task. Most persons, if they think about it, will acknowledge that symbols are at the very least, in some sense and by some process, bearers of information. However, everything we encounter in one way or the other communicates something. For instance, a blade of grass may be green, or blue, or yellow, or brown; it may be short or tall; it may be wide or narrow. Also, some items are constructed by human beings solely for informational purposes. Road signs, for example, signal us to operate a vehicle in certain ways: Stop here; do not drive faster than a particular speed; there is a curve ahead. But symbols are very much more than simple bearers of information. They are agents of a particular sort; they have a *representative* function. In fact, the revered theologian and philosopher of religion Paul Tillich observed that it is appropriate to translate the word, "symbolic," as "representative."[1] He also recognized that being "representative" had certain implications. Specifically, symbols are not that which they represent, but they bring to bear the "power and meaning" of whatever or whomever that they represent.[2] And it is this agentive function that separates symbols from non-symbolic bearers of information.

Because a symbol is not that which it represents, harming it does no immediate existential damage to that for which it stands. For instance, burning the American flag, an act currently protected under the First Amendment of the American Constitution, does not destroy the nation because the flag is not the nation; and only in the most extreme cases is the burning of the flag emblematic of abolishing the nation. Mostly, it is a protest against something extremely grievous for the perpetrators and done to make an appeal for change. In either case, absent the ability of the American flag to powerfully and evocatively represent the nation for which it stands, setting it ablaze would be meaningless except for the fun and excitement igniting any piece of patterned colored cloth can bring. Of course, such an act could be the catalyst for existential damage to the flag burners should particular nationalists witness the desecration; which once more bespeaks the power of the flag as a symbol. Again, symbols are not that which they represent, but they stand for and participate in the power and meaning of that which they represent.

Any careful thinker might ask the question of the origin and necessity of symbols. Symbols, of course, developed in the course of human evolution. Humankind evolved into a world already billions of years old; its rise occurring 64,000,000 years (give or take) after the death of the last dinosaur, as a process (or amalgamation of processes) amid all the developments in the evolution of the cosmos. It occurred as a blip on the screen of cosmic becoming and was subject to the stimuli of a ready-made world. Therefore, the development of symbols is connected to the stream of influences that undergirded both the evolution of human physical characteristics and the simultaneous rise of human mental capacities, and the necessity of symbols to humankind's inclination to and activity of organizing its experience of and in the world. The principal agency of symbols is to define reality.

The ontological make-up of human persons as a union of both "material physical" aspects and "non-material mental" aspects (some say, "matter and mind") has resulted in the propensity of human persons to recognize reality as both "this-worldly" and "other-worldly." Thus symbols broker reality in two ways. There is on the one hand a stratum that is more mundane in the sense that it has do with the casual mysteries of everyday life and on the other hand a layer at the very base of one's grasp of the nature and ground of life itself. From this, we may conclude that from the lesser depths to the deepest depths, symbols function to unveil that which is actual, genuine, and trustworthy. Furthermore, symbols are, as the celebrated American anthropologist Clifford Geertz expressed it, both "models *for*" and "models *of*" that which is real.[3] They both cache and communicate a particular view of reality. They store and declare specific understandings of the world and the larger cosmos, and connect them with attitudes toward and proper behaviors in them. In other words, symbols are storehouses for and communicators of a particular worldview and ethos.

Worldview and ethos, as terms intricately related to symbols, work in concert with one another; however, to treat worldview as merely the mental element of a society and ethos as the moral element, or worldview as the intellectual aspect and ethos as the emotive aspect, is to oversimplify the relationship. Worldview is a reference to a person's or a group's most fundamental cosmology; the existential nature of the natural world, the person, and the society at large; the absolute bedrock of human perception below which there remains nothing more to be perceived. Ethos includes both a general attitude toward life and customary behavioral patterns which are inextricably related to the worldview; it is a reference to both individual and group personality and values which includes orientation and temperament toward self, others, and the world at large. Worldview and ethos cooperate in a circular fashion to define humankind's division into and organization of its various groups from the small association of friends to national and international organizations. Not unlike elephants with trunk in tail and tail in trunk, they validate one another and delimit the group.

Symbols are marvelous practical devices relevant to getting along in the world. One way to explain their relevancy is to understand them as embodying "myths" and "rituals" as conveyers of the worldview and corresponding ethos. Myths are stories of a sort that reflect a community's self-understanding (worldview) and fundamental attitudes and values (ethos). Rituals are visible acted-out portrayals of myths. Myths and rituals encapsulate worldview and ethos and, notably, have an important association with symbols. As John H. Morgan, in his discussion of specifically religious symbols, expressed it, a symbol "is a multi-dimensional focusing of the myth-ritual complex in a phenomenal expression."[4] In other words, symbols are perceptible expressions which mediate a level of self-understanding and conjure particular emotional responses, commitments, and behaviors in a way not otherwise possible as they transmit and reinforce the particular worldview and corresponding ethos embedded in the myth-ritual complex.

A nation's flag, as mentioned at the outset of this chapter, is one exemplification of how a symbol points beyond itself to a greater reality, how it projects a particular worldview and ethos which then finds expression in myth and ritual. To make this more specific, the American flag, especially on the Independence Day celebration, embodies for the participating American populace the entire perceived experience and associated values of the United States from *her* origin to *her* present. Notably, the use of "her" in the previous sentence has a mythical function of recognizing the USA as a person; a "Grand Lady" with a noble personality; thus myth is *not falsehood*, but an expression of *perceived truth*. As a physical object the flag has qualities such as length, width, thickness, and weight; and displays particular colors in particular patterns; yet it is so much more than a physical object. For Americans it summons all the stories of sacrifice and victory in the entire experience of the nation; belief in the American way as the greatest honesty, best justice, and all-encompassing good; and desire for the perpetuation of the nation as the world's greatest hope for correcting all wrong and securing prosperity for all. This "myth" (i.e., this self-evident body of "truth") is celebrated in such rituals as patriotic speeches and music, military and civilian parades, dazzling fireworks, and emotional commemoration of battles and Americans who were wounded and others who died fighting them. These "mythic" stories and their "ritual" expressions reinforce one another within the symbol. The flag is analogous to a reverse prism that takes the many colors of the spectrum and blends them into a single white light set atop and gleaming from a tall structure in such a way that indicates global position and enables proper navigation. Like the Christian Star of Bethlehem, it guides those who follow it to the truth; and a glimpse of the truth may bring tears to the eyes of the beholders.

There are several aspects of symbolic representation to keep in mind. First, myths and rituals not only reinforce one another within the larger symbol but sometimes combine in ways to take on a symbolic quality of their own; that is, one symbol can embody another. The February 1945 photograph of marines raising the American flag on Iwo Jima is a symbol of American determination and victory even at tremendous personal sacrifice. It is a symbol in its own right, especially for the American soldiers who fought there and elsewhere, but the American flag includes it along with myriad others.

Second, a symbol can also include the perceived tyranny, cowardice, and consequent well-deserved animosity for another nation or group. In a negative way this can reinforce the superiority of the particular worldview and fundamental values of the nation or group to whom the symbol belongs. Images of the World Trade Center destruction in New York City, USA, on 11 September 2001, evoke, for many Americans, a measure of hostility toward and mistrust of persons from the Middle East (albeit most often inappropriately). But these images also communicate to Americans that the United States is a morally strong and deserving survivor and a power that will seek to carry-out a reckoning.

Third, particular factions of the larger group can share a symbol while shades of interpreted meaning can create conflict between them. In other words, the American people as a whole may agree regarding the overarching values embodied in their flag, but may disagree about the practical expression of those values. For example, one faction may emphasize the duty of every American to learn self-sufficiency, report to work every work day, and rely on no one; while a rival faction may declare the duty of those who "have" to support those who "have not." Regardless of the conflict, there exists a level at which the symbol's embodiment of an overarching reality bonds them into a larger cohesive unit.

Fourth, while not every object is in actuality a symbol, any object is potentially a symbol. For instance, immediately after the 11 September attacks, a fire-fighter's headgear stood for such things as duty, honor, sacrifice, and bravery; was ritually held aloft at patriotic events; and was specifically referenced in dignitary's speeches. However, the headgear over time and through changing circumstances, as with other symbols, may lose potency as a representation of the 9/11 attacks.

Fifth, human behavior itself has a mythic and ritualistic quality that is expressive of a worldview and associated ethos. Therefore, human action is itself symbolic in nature. It may be as simple as an adolescent wink or as complex as elite dining etiquette, but it will always reflect a particular take on and attitude toward the self, the community, and the world at large.

Of course, the world is vastly different now that when I attended elementary school.

Our current technological world was scarcely imaginable then; and we no longer live in the fear that either Martians or "moon men" will threaten the Earth—we have verified their nonreality. We also know the health effects of tobacco; consequently, our efforts are not to develop a better smoke, but to aid smokers in giving-up the habit. The images of World War II that The Pledge of Allegiance summoned in the 1950s are yielding to those pertaining to globalization. From generation to generation the world moves on; therefore, the way persons view it and respond to it must change. Even our national flag's star field has changed 26 times since the Second Continental Congress first adopted the stars and stripes design in June 1777. This refashioning of the world and our nation's place in it has required some symbols to change, others to pass into history, and new ones to develop.

The fact that symbols developed in the course of human evolution and transform with the general movement of life provides a strong basis for the use of organic metaphors to describe their coming, changing, and ceasing. Accordingly, it was the insight that symbols develop out of human experience that allowed Tillich, as an existentialist theologian, to ask "Out of what womb are symbols born?"; answer that they are born out of the womb of that which some call "'group unconsciousness' or 'collective unconsciousness';" and add that they die "in that moment in which this inner situation of the human group to a symbol has ceased to exist."[5]

A symbol is born only when it opens up a level of reality in the group collective mind in which the group understands its own being in such a depth and in such a way that whatever it may be—a national flag; a school anthem; a religious, social, or economic institution; or something else—represents the group's self-understanding and engenders its particular mood and behaviors. For this reason, no one can intentionally create a symbol with the same resolve as, for instance, creating a child. Symbols are not premeditated creations; and even when persons attempt to create them, their status as a symbol still requires unconscious group assent. But neither are symbols purely accidental. They are the spontaneous offspring engendered in the intercourse of human life in which a combination of the past and a relevant future enter and inseminate present experience; they are the product of the impregnation of human experience by life's circumstances; life's choices begat symbols.

As certainly as symbols are born naturally, they also die a natural death. It is equally impossible to either artificially inseminate life's experiences to produce a symbol or to prevent a symbol from being born. They are born in the group's collective unconsciousness in the intercourse of life's circumstances with human experience, they thrive in a particular environment that supports their life, and they die when and only when the environment which sustains them goes away. When a particular phenomenon—an object, event, word, or anything else—conjures-up the community's myths and rituals, when it embodies the group's self-understanding and fundamental values, a symbol is born; but when that phenomenon no longer calls up community myths and rituals, when it no longer embodies the group's self-understanding and fundamental values, it is dead as a symbol.

In between its birth and death a symbol has a life of its own without a predetermined life expectancy. It can endure for generations, but its content must change over time as the group's self-understanding and accompanying values change, which modification may be largely transparent to the group. Importantly, this ability to transform means that a symbol is in some measure open to manipulation. The world at the time of the American Revolution was radically different from today's world, and the American self-understanding has changed commensurately. Yet, as a symbol, the American flag mediates a continuity of development and a belief that such American values as honesty, justice, and love of liberty have always been the same as it brings to bear on Americans the stories and associated rituals that re-enact and reinforce the American way. However, the notion of what is patriotic can be gerrymandered, an act that accounts for much of today's political division in the United States.

Thus myths and rituals, as expressions of worldview and ethos, find their collective embodiment in symbols. It is a particular phenomenon's abstract association with particular myths and rituals and their expressions of truth that defines it as a symbol. The point in history notwithstanding, the telltale sign of a symbol is its ability to project a worldview and ethos and conjure-up specific myths and rituals.

The birth of a symbol

There is no more potent symbol of Māori culture than the *whare tipuna* (ancestor house). It is as powerful a symbol to Māori as the American flag is to Americans. However, full appreciation of the *whare tipuna*'s power as a symbol requires an understanding of its evolution within the historical context of the *marae*; and the cultural significance of *marae* has, for Māori tribes, very deep roots that extend to the very origin of their heritage as distinctly Polynesian people. The cultural development of the Māori *marae* literally spans centuries and includes generations of ancestors, far antedating the arrival in Aotearoa/New Zealand of the first voyaging canoes.

However, let us first scrutinize the contemporary Māori *marae*. Today, a *marae* in Aotearoa/New Zealand is an area consisting of buildings and grounds, usually fence enclosed, where Māori gather. These spaces, which number more than 800 nationally,[6] are the evolved cultural progeny of Māori villages from times before and during the 1st century and a quarter of contact with Europeans. Even though by the late-1980s all but about 20 percent of Māori had moved to town, at the end of the 1st quarter of the 20th century, about 85 percent of the Māori population still lived in rural tribal settlements.[7] Modern *marae*, as cultural centers and not places of residence, have their origin in these villages and have developed in conjunction with the revival of Māori culture which began toward the end of the 19th century; a time of heightened cultural emphasis which included both new Māori cultural constructions and restorations of old facilities, especially the all-important *whare tipuna*. The buildings and grounds where Māori previously lived and conducted their everyday affairs have become a model for cultural space dedicated to the preservation of the Māori tribal way. Today, the Māori *iwi* (tribe), *hapū* (sub-tribe), or *whānau* (extended family) to whom the *marae* belongs does not permanently live there but congregates there for various cultural purposes, which observances are always rooted in tribal mythology.

Currently, there are two *marae*-centered ceremonies that stand out to observers. The first and most important is the *tangihanga* (rites for the dead); it is briefly discussed in the last topic of this chapter. But also quite significant, and the occasion a visitor is more likely to witness, is the *pōwhiri*, the formal and potentially lengthy welcoming ceremony, conducted according to specific customs and protocols, by which the *marae* hosts receive *manuhiri* (guests) in a way similar to the way they received them in their villages in the 19th century and before. Whereas yesteryear's visitors might be mostly other tribes, today's guests, in addition to representatives of other *iwi*, might include political dignitaries, tourists, or student groups. According to Māori custom, the *pōwhiri*, as dictated by tribal mythology, is the necessary beginning to inter-group interaction on the *marae*. Of course, a *hui* (meeting; gathering) may also entail nothing more pressing or complicated than a time of sociability within the group to whom the *marae* belongs, which requires no particular welcome since it does not involve outsiders.

Although by its physical description and for legal purposes a *marae* is a complex of buildings and grounds, culturally it is so much more than *mere* buildings and grounds. Māori, not even in the case of tourists, take either the facilities or the gatherings, formal or informal, lightly. The *marae* and the style of the proceedings on it have a deep cultural significance that has grown out of a long developmental history, a brief sketch of which will prove useful for more clearly understanding both the *marae's* importance to Māori society and the place of the *whare tipuna* within the *marae*.

Māori *marae*, as a composite of buildings and grounds, are a testimony to the human need for defined space dedicated to particular activities. Societies dedicate areas for sacred pursuits or set them apart for secular purposes; even when they use the same space for both, they are apt to demarcate the usage. Human organization of the experienced world even requires the division of space within space. Today's Westerners separate the social space of their homes into places for sleeping, cooking, dining, recreating, bathing, and relieving oneself; and the sacred space of their religious houses according to their style of worship and commensurate social observances. Similarly, the ancient ocean traveling forebears of today's Māori people set aside certain spaces for particular purposes and accordingly developed a variety of styles as they island-hopped across the Pacific Ocean. *Marae* throughout Polynesia exhibit a variety of forms and uses while maintaining a thread of continuity, which is exactly according to expectation as diverse forms and contents grow out of different and changing circumstances. Māori immigrants to Aotearoa/New Zealand would have been much aware of immediate antecedent *marae*, but would have adapted the form and content of the precursors to their own needs, eliminating some features while maintaining or changing others.

Let us now turn to the developmental history of *marae* as a lead-in to exploring the symbolic character of the *whare tipuna*. The ancestors of those who would become Polynesians migrated through Southeast Asia and into the Pacific islands.[8] They traveled south and then turned east into present-day Melanesia reaching New Guinea and the Bismarck Archipelago (inhabited 30,000 years prior by Aboriginal people) by 1500 BCE.[9] By 1000 BCE they had arrived at the western edge of contemporary Polynesia.[10] It was there that migration (not necessarily exploration) stopped for about 1,000 years at which time the Polynesian culture and language, as we understand it today, had its origin.[11] But advances in sea craft construction and navigation techniques facilitated further expansion into the island groups at the core of modern Polynesia possibly by about 300 CE. From there, the culture spread north to the Hawai'ian Islands (perhaps within 100 years) and southeast to Rapa Nui (also perhaps within about 100 years) before venturing southwest to Aotearoa/New Zealand, the arrival beginning around 1280 CE.[12] These three places (Hawai'i to the north, Rapa Nui to the southeast, and Aotearoa/New Zealand to the southwest) mark the points of the Polynesian Triangle.

The various migrations entailed the development of language and required the adventurers to make adjustments to their view of the world and way of life in response to different climatic, geographical, and happenstantial conditions at each stage. Accordingly, the forerunners of today's Aotearoa/New Zealand *marae* can be traced as an institution with various incarnations along the migratory route(s). Although sites may still have cultural significance to the indigenous people and in some cases have been restored and are currently in use, most of our knowledge of them comes from historians and archeologists; which, of course, include indigenous researchers. Notably, archeologists' efforts to understand and reconstruct these sites and the indigenous population's efforts to restore use of them have, in many cases, been hampered by the early Christian missionaries' destructive activity of defacing and burning carvings, dismantling lithic structures and reusing the stones, and building churches on the sites themselves.

Today's Tonga, on the western side of the Polynesian Triangle, is a monarchy of 171 islands of which only about 45 are inhabited.[13] Historically, its *mala'e* (their word equivalent for *marae*; note the similarity in language) was an unpaved common open area in the village which the dwellers used for secular purposes.[14] Think of it as the "village green"[15]; a park or playground.

The modern nation of Samoa, also on the western side of the Polynesian Triangle, is a parliamentary republic, comprised of two main islands and several smaller islands and islets,[16] and member of the (British) Commonwealth[17]; the presidential democracy of American Samoa adds five volcanic islands and two coral atolls to the archipelago.[18] With reference to former days, the Samoan word, *malae* (their equivalent word for *marae*; again note the similarity in language), means the unpaved well-kept and shady village square or courtyard which was near the tribal chief's residence; it was a place for informal meetings.[19] It was very similar to the Tongan *mala'e*, but the Samoans conducted formal ceremonies in a house rather than on the village green.[20]

Moving more to the center of Polynesia, today's Cook Islands are a parliamentary democracy comprised of a northern group of seven coral atolls and a southern group of eight more elevated islands, the largest of which is Rarotonga.[21] The Cook Islands' official language along with English is Cook Islands Māori,[22] a language which is distinct from yet closely related to Aotearoa/New Zealand Māori.[23] Cook Islands Māori and Aotearoa/New Zealand Māori share the word "*marae*," but the spaces referenced by the word differ both as physical phenomena and in cultural use. The Cook Islands are home to a number of examples of *marae* which, in sharp contrast with the unpaved *marae* of Tonga and Samoa, feature the use of stones. Although over-zealous missionaries and time have destroyed many of the *marae*, others survive as ruins while still others have been restored.

What remains of the historical site of Marae Kainuku on the island of Rarotonga is among the most interesting.[24] This space is a rather large stone-surrounded rectangular hillside area which the people used for both religious and non-religious purposes. Religious purposes would have included rites to insure community prosperity and farewells to deceased persons; no evidence of human sacrifice has yet turned up in the Cook Islands. The site's communal social uses would have included weddings and other celebrations, open-air forums, and lodging for visiting groups. This *marae*, constructed on a hill, featured five rock terraces with a building of several rooms, built of coral, farther toward the top. At the hill's crest was another building with an earth oven for cooking; the food prepared there would be taken down and served to the gatherers.

The Society Islands, one of five groups of islands that comprise French Polynesia, are divided into an eastern group of five Windward Islands and a western group of nine Leeward Islands.[25] They are host to numerous *marae* (their word) of different sorts which served such diverse purposes as private family worship; local, intra-island, and inter-island business meetings and celebrations; healings; and industries such as canoe building and fishnet making.[26] *Marae* dimensions and construction differ here as they do throughout Polynesia, and some of the *marae* may date to the 10th century CE.

Let us first consider the island of Ra'iatea, the largest of the Leeward Islands and perhaps a beginning point for navigation to Aotearoa/New Zealand. It is home to the now restored Taputapuātea Marae complex, at the heart of which is Taputapuātea Marae itself,[27] which was dedicated to the god Oro. The complex dates to perhaps 1000 CE. The island is located at the center of the Polynesian Triangle, and its marae were the focal point of a political alliance which included most of Polynesia. Chiefs and their entourage would gather regularly at Taputapuātea. Among Taputapuātea Marae's features is a paved courtyard with stone backrests at one end, perhaps for the comfort of tribal dignitaries.

The island of Tahiti in the Windward group, the largest island in French Polynesia, may also have been a point of departure for navigation to Aotearoa/New Zealand. It, too, provides good examples, one of the most significant of which is the 15th century Arahurahu Marae.[28] It has been fully restored and is today used for the reenactment of ancient ceremonies. This open-air paved meeting place is about 65 feet long and 50 feet wide. It is enclosed by a stone wall about three feet high and a little thicker than it is tall. At the near end are stone steps for entering it. The *marae's* construction includes a three tiered pyramid-like altar at the far end from which tribal priests would conduct ceremonies. It has a kneeling stone toward the center of the enclosed area against which the tribal chief would lean, perhaps in a posture for a sort of prayer, during the ceremonies. Carved human, animal, and geometric figures are set at strategic places. Leading up to the marae and butting-up against the wall at the entrance end is a stone-paved area. There are trails leading to and from the site, and there is also evidence of buildings near the enclosed space.

The *marae* in pre–European Aotearoa/New Zealand was, like those in Tonga and Samoa, an unpaved courtyard in front of the chief's house and the focal point of the village.[29] Today, Māori refer to it as the *marae-ātea* (*marae* courtyard), and use the non-compound word, *marae*, for the entire complex of buildings and grounds. This change in reference occurred in conjunction with the Māori adaption to Pākehā style housing and their migration to population centers. It is indeed interesting that Māori *marae-ātea* have more in common with those of Samoa and Tonga, which are further removed along the migration route, than they do with those of the Cook Islands and the Society Islands, which are nearer along the path; the latter being at the heart of the migration and from whence it is widely believed that Polynesians navigated to Aotearoa/New Zealand.

Also, like those of Tonga and Samoa, *marae* in Aotearoa/New Zealand's traditional times (today's *marae-ātea*) did not host religious rites; such activities were conducted away from the village by experts in such ritual occasions.[30] Rather, people gathered in front of the chief's residence for secular meetings and social purposes.[31] If the first morning activity was greeting the sun and recognizing a new day; this space would have afforded a venue for so doing; insofar as a group's predominant concern was the production and acquisition of food, this area would have served as a rendezvous point for bands of hunters, fishers, gatherers, planters, and harvesters; and in times of combat, which were not uncommon, the village *marae* would have served as a gathering spot for war parties.[32] It would also have accommodated both children's play and the deliberations of elderly tribal people.[33] As an unpaved, more vaguely defined area used for non-religious purposes, it avoided the ruinous influence and arrogant behavior the missionaries brought to the paved and stone enclosed *marae* in other parts of Polynesia. But perhaps more significantly, especially as over time the *whare tipuna* replaced the chief's house at the head of the *marae*, it, as an institution, survived Pākehā efforts to assimilate Māori culture into that of Western society.

We may now focus our attention on the *whare tipuna*, its gestation and birth as a Māori symbol. Today, the *whare tipuna* enjoys the status as the most important structure on the *marae* (considered as the entire complex of buildings and grounds); and like the *marae*, it has a developmental history. The *wharepuni* (guest house; house for sleep) was its precursor.[34] The guest house was rectangular in shape and featured the usual Māori design of extending the roof (or recessing the front wall) to form a porch (see Figure 1 in the next topic of this chapter). Māori developed this style in reaction to the colder Aotearoa/New Zealand climate; this construction provided a sheltered out-of-doors living space in addition to the interior space of the structure.[35] This architectural testimony to their creativity dates to the early arrivals in Aotearoa/New Zealand. John Moorfield's *Māori-English English-Māori Dictionary* entries clearly convey the function of the *wharepuni*. *Whare* means "house"[36]; *puni* refers to a "camp" or "camping place."[37] The *wharepuni* was a house for camping; hence, a place for sleeping.

By the 18th century the distinctive features of the *wharepuni* were common; specifically, the extended roof which formed a porch, bargeboards slanting downward and forming the front edge of the extended roof, a ridgepole supported by interior posts (usually three, but longer ridgepoles required four) extending from the apex of the bargeboards to the rear of the structure, and carvings on the bargeboards and both the interior and exterior walls.[38] While these houses varied in size and not every Māori village had a separate guest house, by the late 18th century some of them measured 30 feet in length.[39] The arrival of Western tools enabled the upsizing of these structures, and by the 1840s Māori were building houses measuring at least 50 feet by 28 feet.[40] Māori fully decorated these structures inside and out with ancestral carvings. They adorned the interior walls between the carved side posts with woven reed panels which incorporated Māori cultural notions into the design, and embellished features such as the ridgepole and rafters with painted ornamentation which patterns also had cultural significance.[41] Māori often refer to these structures as *whare whakairo*, "carved houses." The use of these carved structures as "sleeping houses" carries over into today's *whare tipuna*. The host group will often provide mattresses on the floor of the ancestor house on which their guests may sleep overnight, provided sleep is possible amid the verbal chatter and snoring.

Importantly, it was the changing conditions brought about by the arrival of Pākehā that underlay the increasingly enriched development and significance of these edifices. At first, Māori enhanced these facilities to accommodate visitors to their land, but as Māori concern about Pākehā presence and influence elevated, they held more meetings involving more tribal representatives, which entailed building larger facilities for their own use.[42] By the mid–1850s, the dimensions had reached as much as 90 feet by 30 feet.[43] Moreover, with the New Zealand Land Wars of the 1860s came even greater recognition of carved houses as cultural and political symbols, and in the following years, as the Pākehā population and influence grew and Māori waned, Māori designers and builders incorporated more and more cultural identity and history into their work.[44]

Let us consider two examples. First, the New Zealand Wars that began in the 1860s saw the rise of the warrior-founder of the Ringatū Faith, Te Kooti Arikirangi Te Turuki of the Ngāti Maru (a sub-tribe of the Rongowhakaata).[45] Te Kooti (a transliteration of the Pākehā name "Coates") had been wrongfully imprisoned in the Chatham Islands in 1866 for allegedly spying for the Hauhaus, a group of Māori who were at war with Pākehā. Te Kooti had been educated in the mission schools, but had become something of a ne'er-do-well and a nuisance around Poverty Bay on the east coast; hence, his incarceration had more to do with his role as a community problem than as a spy. However, while in confinement, through a revelation which came to him during a feverish illness, he joined elements of Christianity with his Māori heritage, the result of which was to become known as the Ringatū faith. Te Kooti taught his revelation to his fellow prisoners; they became his first followers. In 1868, a revenge seeking Te Kooti and more than 200 adult prisoners, along with a number of children, escaped their confines in the Chathams, commandeered an ocean going vessel, and returned to Aotearoa/New Zealand, where Te Kooti proved to be an effective and elusive warrior. The resourceful Te Kooti, whom Pākehā could never capture and thus pardoned in 1883, retired from the battlefield in 1872 in the King Country. By now it was clear to him that, given the current state of affairs, Māori could not prevail militarily against Pākehā troops.[46] In response, in 1873 he built a carved house at Te Kuiti at which township it stands today.[47] In 1883, shortly before his pardon, he gifted it to the Ngāti Maniapoto (Maniapoto tribe) in appreciation for their hospitality; they named it Te Tokanganui-a-Noho.[48] His house stressed ancestral links between tribes; it was a cultural and political statement which emphasized the need for a pan–Māori tribal arrangement that he believed was necessary in order to check the advance of Pākehā society.[49]

Second, and interestingly, some Māori who cooperated and fought with Pākehā had a similar cultural vision. One such person was Major Rapata Wahawaha (1820–1897), who held a tribal grudge against Te Kooti and fought with Pākehā against him.[50] He also built a carved house, opened in 1888, named Porourangi[51] after the eponymous ancestor of the Ngāti Porou (Porou tribe). Today it stands at Waiomatatini Marae. This house would figure prominently in the revival of Māori culture.

As fortune would have it, the next decade, the 1890s, saw the formation of The Young Māori Party. Although not a political party, this group shared both a political and cultural concern, and some of the most important Māori leaders of the 20th century came out of it. Sir Āpirana Ngata (1874–1950) was one of them. In 1907, Ngata spearheaded the restoring of Porourangi and thus affirmed his own recognition of the importance of the *whare tipuna* to Māori society.[52] This act typified an already established trend of accepting the carved meeting house as the embodiment of the entire spectrum of Māori myth and ritual and thus representative of tribal pride, prestige, dignity, and honor. Ngata also drafted rules for *marae* councils which addressed such concerns as the inclusion of wood floors in carved houses as well as ventilation, heating, and refuse disposal for all *marae* facilities; and called for enclosing *marae* reserves with boundary fences, which at the time were necessary to preclude the intrusion of livestock into the area.[53] By the late 1920s, Ngata had revived the art of Māori carving which included an overhaul of other existing carved houses as well as the construction of new ones.[54] Each case was a restatement of the Māori tribal worldview and ethos and a declaration of the revitalization of Māori society. The *whare tipuna* was now unquestionably the focal point of the *marae* and the flagship of Māori culture. Thus, the Māori renaissance was underway.

The rise of the *whare tipuna* in conjunction with the development of the *marae* illustrates the gestation and birth of a symbol. The resurgence of Māori culture happened against a backdrop of renewed tribal pride and prestige most evidenced by the construction and refurbishing of these *whare tipuna*, these ancestor houses, on *marae*.

The whare tipuna *as a symbol*

Just as the Māori village of Aotearoa/New Zealand's traditional times was a place of personal and family belonging for the kinspersons who dwelt there, today's *marae*, as the offspring of those villages, is a place of community and cooperation for the persons who meet there; it is a unique place for Māori to be Māori. This is not to detract from the importance of the general Aotearoa/New Zealand communities where Māori and Pākehā live, associate, and solve problems as neighbors. Towns and cities with their various personalities are always special places for their residents; for good, for ill, or for both. They instill values and a sense of identity according to community norms. Fifty years later, many of us can still recall the streets and other features of the town in which we were reared and can still mentally walk through the houses where we grew up, recalling details of its layout and furnishings of every room. But just as important as the physical features, are the attitudes and standards of behavior that community and home implanted and nurtured; they remain to this day a powerful influence. However, for Māori, as a tribal people largely dispossessed of their land and way of life, the *marae* has come to occupy a particularly important place. It is a distinctive home and a special community. The *marae* binds its people together according to their genetic, geographical, and historical heritage. It connects Māori with one another, their land, and their tribal legacy. It reaches more than 3,000 years into the past and projects itself into the foreseeable future and beyond. It is the *kaitiaki*, the "custodian," of the Māori way.

According to the 2013 national census,[55] Aotearoa/New Zealand is home to 17 "Main Urban Areas," the largest of which is Auckland with about 1,400,000 people followed at a distance by Wellington with almost 390,000 and Christchurch with almost 370,000; the smallest by population is Blenheim with just over 30,000. There are 14 "Secondary Urban Areas" with populations ranging from just under 10,000 to about 28,000, 102 "Minor Urban Areas" with populations from 800 to 10,000, and 133 "Rural Centres" with populations from 100 to 1,400. Nonetheless, the country is mostly square mile after square mile of purely rural territory. Whether walking through the urban areas, touring the towns, or traveling the highways by bus or automobile, the casual visitor is likely to encounter a *marae*; and although each one will differ according to the area's environment and demographics, all *marae* will share a particular cultural continuity.

Some *marae*[56] are controlled by a *hapū* (sub-tribe; decent group; clan), an amalgamation of *whānau* (extended families) which are associated with a particular geographical area. A *hapū marae* is associated with the ancestor who founded it, and its facilities are available to all those who trace their lineage to that ancestor.

Other *marae* are controlled by *iwi* (tribes), which are aggregations of *hapū*. That which unites sub-tribes into an *iwi* is the ability of each *hapū* to trace its kinship past its founding ancestor to the ancestor from whom the *iwi* takes its name. Of course, genealogical associations with various *hapū* and *iwi* are today complicated by generations of tribal intermarriage, and may depend heavily on where a person or family is living at the time.

Urban *marae* stand in contrast with *hapū* and *iwi marae*. They are designed to accommodate larger groups and serve a variety of participants. These *marae* may be controlled by a cooperative arrangement of different *hapū* or *iwi*, or they may be sponsored by an agency, such as a religious organization or educational institution, which may or may not be specifically Māori. Not only may various *hapū* or *iwi* from urban large population centers share the facilities, but the *marae* leaders may also open the premises for booking by non–Māori groups looking to experience Māori culture or offer them to students as a center for study, guidance, and help in their educational endeavor.

Notably, any area can be temporarily turned into a *marae* if need be. Memorial halls, town halls, church buildings, libraries, schools, car parks, office rooms, and political chambers have at one time or another been used in this way for cultural purposes. In these venues, the primary emphasis may be specifically religious, social, educational, or political; but the sheer recognition of *marae* ceremony and decorum serves, at a very minimum, to value Māori ways.

Whether *hapū, iwi,* or urban, the *marae* as a cultural complex serves to communicate and preserve Māori culture, and one feature crucial to this function and which virtually all share is the *whare tipuna.* Almost all Aotearoa/New Zealand *marae* have an ancestor house, whether of traditional construction, doing double duty with another structure, or existing as purely provisional as in the case of those venues serving as temporary facilities. Significantly, in every instance the *whare tipuna,* which Māori usually (but not always) name for an ancestor, is the most set apart and revered feature of the premises. Māori deliberately build them as expressions of how they view reality and as statements of how they, as tribal people, fit in. Thus the *whare tipuna* provides an exceptional example of the nature of symbols and how they operate.

Worldview and ethos exist as understandings, attitudes, and behaviors that develop as a result of experience of both the physical and non-physical aspects of life. Symbols are tangible expressions of worldview and ethos which encapsulate a corresponding complex network of myths and rituals. Symbols are concrete articulations of the way societies understand the world and get along in it. Therefore, an examination of the *whare tipuna's* physical features, both inside and out, and how they fit together as a coherent representation of the Māori world, provides an understanding of how this structure functions as a Māori symbol. Figures 1, 2, and 3 detail aspects of the *whare tipuna's* exterior construction; Figures 4 and 5 depict its interior arrangement. Not all ancestor houses are as elaborately carved as the ones presented in these figures nor are they all built to the same dimensions, but all will display the same basic lay-out and essential elements.

The design of the *whare tipuna* is anthropomorphic. While this is no new revelation to Māori, it is a necessary beginning point for those unfamiliar with the indigenous culture. Even though it requires only a bit of abstraction to understand how Māori conceptualize the ancestor house as the ancestor, the depiction of a human image by the architectural design is, nonetheless, an ingenious way of conveying the way Māori envision their world.

At the very top is the *tekoteko* and *koruru* with *kōwhaiwhai* just underneath. The term *tekoteko* is usually reserved for a complete human figure situated at the apex of the building while *koruru* refers to the carved face of an ancestor. Not all ancestor houses display a *kōwhaiwhai* and not all have both a *tekoteko* and *koruru.* Figure 2 is a photograph of the *tekoteko* and *koruru* at Tamatekapua Meeting House on Te Papaiouru *marae* in Ōhinemutu, a traditional Māori village in Rotorua on the North Island. The *tekoteko* depicts Tamatekapua, the captain of the *Arawa* voyaging canoe, one of many such vessels to which Māori trace their arrival in the land.

This configuration of *tekoteko* and/or *koruru* represent the ancestor's head, but even when they are absent from the building, the apex of the *maihi* (bargeboards) is visualized as representing it. The architects of these *whare* position the bargeboards in such a way as to represent the ancestor's arms spread in a gesture of welcome. In their design the *raparapa* at the end of the bargeboards are the ancestor's fingers, the *amo* which extend vertically and attach to the bargeboards are the ancestor's legs, the *roro* (porch) is the ancestor's brain, and the *matapihi* (window) is the ancestor's eye.

Most explanations treat the *whatitoka* (doorway) as representing the ancestor's mouth;

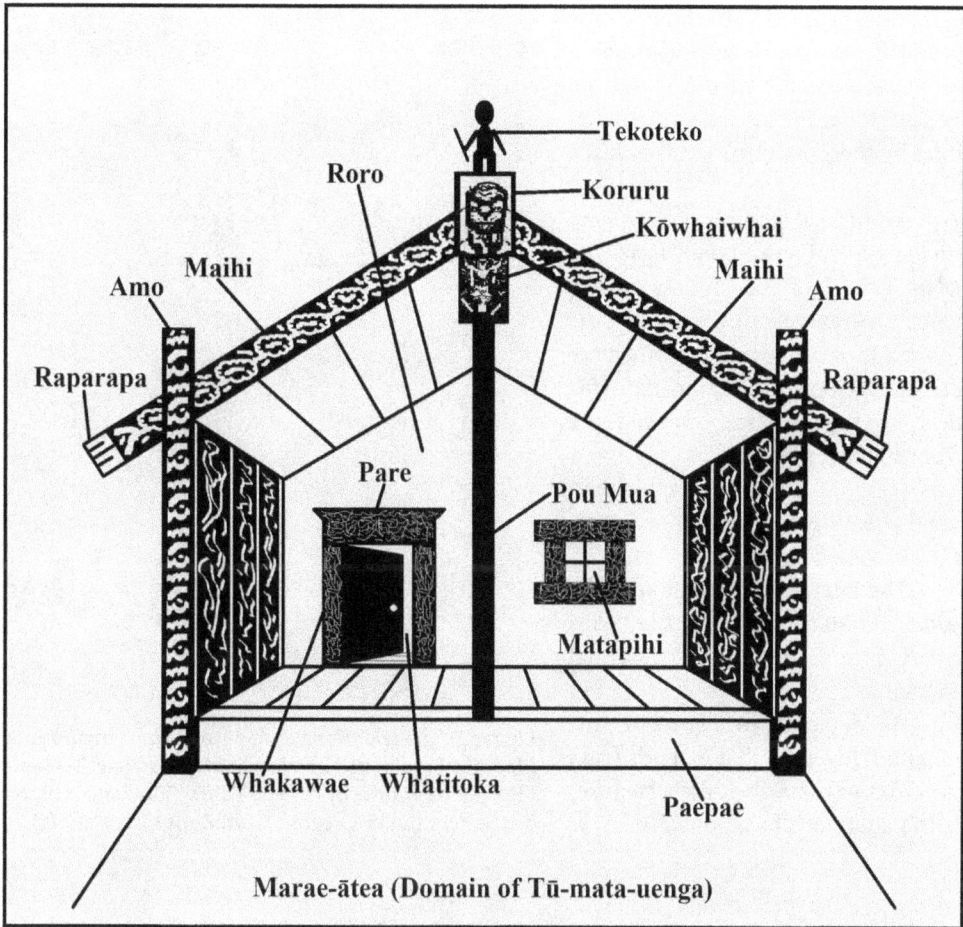

Figure 1. Features of the *whare tipuna*'s frontal exterior. (Drawn by the author.)

however, some interpret it in terms of the female anatomy, as the vagina and birth canal. This is a powerful statement of the Māori genealogical scheme. Each individual tribal person is the offspring of the ancestor who is represented by the anthropomorphic design of the ancestor house; there is a blood relationship. It is out of this ancestor, through other tribal forebears, that each person enters the world; and to them that the person returns upon death, whether by virtue of representation in a carved *poupou* (post; vertical slab; side-support pillar) or other physical depictment, or simply by way of remembrance of the dead which takes place at the outset of every *pōwhiri*.

Figure 1 also shows the *paepae* (orator's bench) where, at meetings with visitors who have been welcomed onto the grounds, those speaking on behalf of the host people would group; and the *marae-ātea*, the courtyard which is immediately in front of the *whare tipuna* where the visitors would gather. The *marae-ātea* is the domain of Tū-mata-uenga, god of conflict and war in Māori mythology. From these positions hosts and visitors would exchange orations which could be quite amiable but could also include contentious issues. It is noteworthy that Māori customs have flexibility and can vary from group to group. For instance, if the weather is rainy or extremely cold the welcome may take place inside the *whare tipuna*, in which case the *marae-ātea* becomes the space between the hosts' orators and visitors inside the house. Additionally, it is the custom of some groups to welcome visitors inside the house. However, the welcome of visitors by the hosts mostly takes place outside.

Additional features of the *whare tipuna* which Figure 1 depicts are the *whakawae* (door and window jambs), which are carved figures; and *pare* (door and window lintels), which are carved slabs over the door and window. It also shows the *pou mua*, the front support post.

Figure 3 is a photograph showing the features of the *wharenui* exterior discussed above.

The interior construction of the *whare tipuna* continues the symbol. Figure 4 identifies its essential elements.

As depicted in Figure 4, the *tāhuhu* (ridgepole that extends from the front to the rear of the structure) is the ancestor's backbone. The *heke*

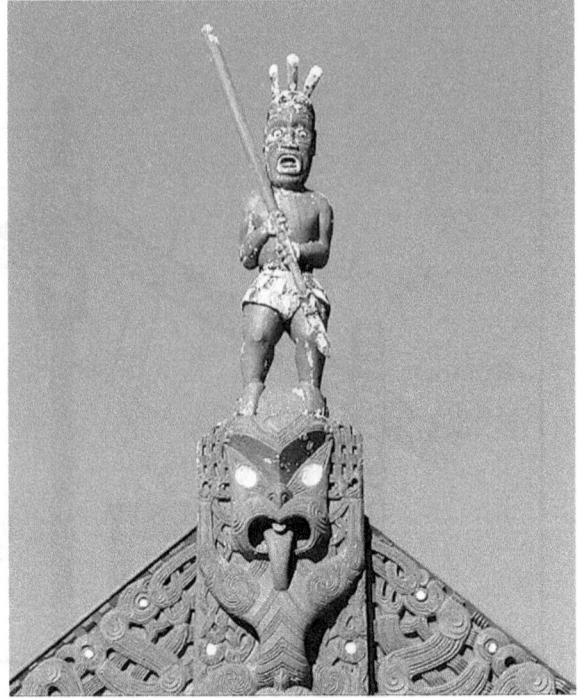

Figure 2. The *tekoteko* and *koruru* at the Tamatekapua Meeting House in Rotorua, Aotearoa/New Zealand. (The photograph is by Natalia Volna [2014] and is reproduced here under Creative Commons Licenses 2.0.)

Figure 3. The *wharenui* on the Rotowhio Marae (Maori Arts and Crafts Institute) at Te Puia in Rotorua, Aotearoa/New Zealand. (The photograph is by Bob Linsdell [2012] and is reproduced here under Creative Commons Licenses 2.0.)

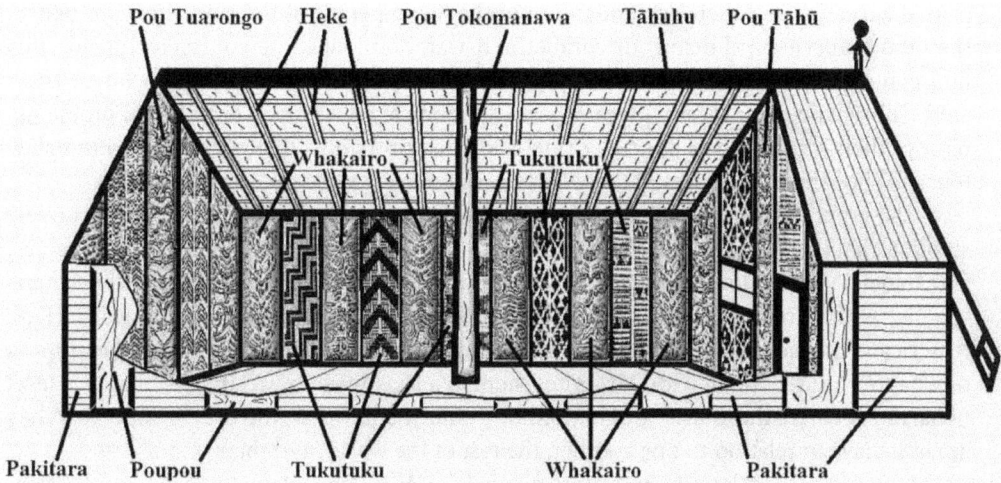

Figure 4. Features of the *whare tipuna*'s interior. (Drawn by the author.)

(rafters) are the ancestor's ribs. The *poupou* (vertical posts) form the framework for the *pa-kitara* (side walls). In this illustration, *whakairo* (carving) refers to the sculpted interior side of these posts; they mostly represent the ancestor's descendants who uphold the prestige of the tribe, but can also include gods such as Tāne and folk heroes such as Māui as forebears of the tribal ancestors. The *heke* link the *poupou* to the *tāhuhu*. This symbolically expresses the unity of the personalities depicted in the carvings with the ancestor.

The *tukutuku* panels (ornamental woven reed latticework) between the *poupou* display patterns with cultural significance. The designs may be specific to a particular tribe or represent tribal culture more generally. The more general motifs include the "flounder" pattern, based on the fish's diamond shape, which represents a time of bounty, a good season, and food storage; and the "staircase" design which is a model for higher learning, advancement, and success.[57] This latter image may be either a common single stairs moving ever upward or a double stairs pattern in which stairs rise symmetrically from each side to form a platform at the summit. Other designs stand for readiness for war, combat itself, catastrophe, and lamentation.[58]

Also as shown in Figure 4, three upright columns separate the floor from the ceiling. They are the *pou tāhū* (front wall post), the *pou tokomanawa* (center post), and the *pou tuarongo* (back post). This represents Māori creation mythology where Tāne, one of the children of Ranginui (the Sky Father) and Papatūānuku (the Earth Mother), succeeded in separating his parents thus allowing light to enter the world. The ceiling, of course, depicts Ranginui, and the floor represents Papatūānuku. The space in between is *te whaiao* (the world of light). Illumination is in the bosom of the ancestor. To enter this house is to leave the dark world and enter the light world. To enter the ancestor is to be enlightened with regard to unmitigated actuality. In some explanations the porch (see Figure 1) of the *whare tipuna* represents the predawn; it separates the world of darkness, which is the courtyard, from the world of light, which is inside the *whare*. In some cases the carved figure over the exterior side of the doorway is Hine-nui-i-te-pō (the great woman of the night, darkness, underworld). She guards the passage between the two worlds.

Virtually every detail of the *whare tipuna* bespeaks the spiritual unity of myths, gods, primal ancestors and their descendants, and the living people of the land. Tū-mata-uenga, the *atua* (supernatural being) of conflict and war, dominates the courtyard outside this house; but Rongo, the *atua* of peace, reigns in the bosom of the ancestor. This house is sacred. Those who enter it (except for those with medical issues or other practical problems) remove their shoes, and no food or drink is to pass through its doorway. Figure 5 is a photograph showing the features of the *wharenui* interior.

The point of this discussion of the ancestor house, and what should be clearly understood, is that the *whare tipuna* brings to bear upon Māori all the self-understanding, values, and associated behavior that the flag of any nation brings to its people. In a sense the American flag, with its representative stars and stripes, is the "ancestor house" of·Americans. Here, Americans go deep inside the nation. It connects them with their myths and ancestors as one nation "under" their "God." It unites them at a level where peace reigns; that is, a level of harmony where the divisions of nationhood pale. It tells them who they are and how they are to behave in relation to one another, the rest of the world, and their "God."

One of the best known and most powerful Māori concepts is the concept of *tūran-gawaewae*; it combines *tūranga* (standing place) and *waewae* (feet), to mean "a place to stand." It refers to that venue where particular persons not only have the undisputable right of physical presence but also at which they may enjoy the full freedom of their cultural expression. The *marae* is a special Māori standing place, and all *marae* activity is coordinated around the all-important *whare tipuna*. The Māori worldview and ethos begins with this

Figure 5. The interior, looking from the entrance toward the back wall, of Te Whare Rūnanga (The Meeting House) at Waitangi, Aotearoa/New Zealand. (The photograph is by cheetah100 [2012] and is reproduced here under Creative Commons Licenses 2.0.)

house and all Māori roads home lead here. At this house Māori people especially connect with one another and their tribal world. It is here that unity subsumes division. This house is the guiding star that they themselves have hung in their cultural heavens by which they navigate their cultural ocean. It projects the Māori worldview and ethos. It preserves and declares the myths and rituals of their tribal reality. The *whare tipuna*, as the centerpiece of the *marae* complex, is the predominant symbol of Māori culture for Māori people.

The whare karakia *as a symbol*

In the language of Māori tribes, *whare* (house) *karakia* (incantation; prayer) refers to *any* building where religious services are held, and Aotearoa/New Zealand is currently home for thousands of them belonging to many organizations. Nevertheless, it is Christianity that has most influenced the development of Māori spirituality and has both partnered with and opposed the political and military authorities in the shaping of the country, especially during the first 100 years or so of colonial European contact. Although Aotearoa/ New Zealand has never had an official state religion, Christianity's influence is significant enough to establish the Christian Church, viewed as an institution represented by its physical facilities, as a symbol analogous to the Māori *whare tipuna*.

Other groups, of course, have been in Aotearoa/New Zealand from the earliest European arrivals. The initial whalers and sealers in the country included persons of the Jewish faith, but the earliest records of Jewish ceremonies, either personal or communal, date from the first years of the 1840s[59]; while Māori found strong identification with the descendants of Abraham as described by the Christian Old Testament, the Jewish faith as represented by rabbis and synagogues appears to have had little impact. Muslims have been in the country since about the middle of the 19th century, but their total population likely did not exceed 100 until after the Second World War[60]; and the effect of Islam on the country has been negligible. Buddhists were also present in small numbers by the 1860s[61] and Hindus by the 1890s,[62] but their sway has been slight at best. In fact, outside Māori spirituality, there has been comparatively little religious influence in the country except for the various brands of Christianity; most importantly Anglicanism, Methodism, and Catholicism. When Hiwi Tauroa contemplated the impact of external religious societies on his Māori heritage (see this book's Introduction), he mused not about Judaism, Islam, Hinduism, or Buddhism; rather, he wondered if the Christian worship center, the Christian *whare karakia*, had ever taken the place of his beloved *whare tipuna*.

Notably, Māori were quite slow to accept initiation into Christianity. The first official missionary in Aotearoa/New Zealand was Samuel Marsden (1765–1838). He was an appointee of the Church Missionary Society (CMS), an independent evangelical faction of the Anglican Church. Marsden arrived in Aotearoa/New Zealand's Bay of Islands shortly before Christmas in 1814. Ruatara (1787?–1815), a leader of the Ngā Puhi (Puhi tribe), assisted him in conducting his first official religious service at Rangihoua Bay on Christmas Day of that same year.[63] The service was directed toward a Māori audience of perhaps a few hundred persons in hopes of gaining converts. Perchance it was because his Māori listeners could not understand what he was saying or maybe they understood at least some of it and simply chose to not accept Christianity; but they, at the conclusion of the service, went away apparently no more Christian than when they arrived. In fact, while the first Māori baptism actually occurred in 1825 and there were a few others, perhaps nine or ten, before the turn of the decade, it was not until the 1830s that Christianity gained wide formal acceptance by the indigenous population as evidenced by Māori submission to baptism.[64] By 1842 the missionaries had baptized more than 3,000 Māori, but it would be a mistake to believe that those baptized completely disconnected themselves from their tribal ways. Of necessity, they could not escape understanding the Christian Scriptures through a Māori mind.

The Māori prophets provide excellent examples of the operation of the Māori psyche as it pertained to the impact of Christianity on the traditional culture. Alongside the baptisms of the 1830s, the first of a series of Māori prophets surfaced. These prophets were persons who, even though well acquainted with the Christian Scriptures, both Old and New Testaments, and mostly recipients of Christian baptism, were not so confident about the missionaries and the direction the overall society was headed. Māori *tohunga* (spiritual experts) had exercised the power of prophecy (making predictions based on the signs of the times) long before the arrival of Pākehā, but contact with Europeans shaped the practice in special ways; the prophets of the 1830s and onward developed a sense of their tribal culture being overwhelmed by Pākehā society and sought a solution to the problem. Nevertheless, they incorporated Christian elements, which they learned from Pākehā missionaries, into their own tribal views and customs thus demonstrating the Māori propensity to be sensitive to the message and practice of the Christian Church while attempting to protect their culture and retain a sense of their own dignity and tribal spirituality. The Māori prophets represent both a reform of their traditional culture and a restatement of missionary Christianity. Each prophet, in a different way, blazed a middle trail between the two systems. The Christian message of peace and impending final justice by supernatural means became particularly attractive as Māori military options failed, but the Māori in-your-face attitude and inclination to fight back was never far removed.

Aotearoa/New Zealand historians largely regard Papahurihia (1797?–1875), who was active at least from 1833, as the first Māori prophet.[65] On the one hand, he was trained as a *tohunga* and well acquainted with his tribal traditions, while on the other hand, he was literate and knowledgeable of the Christian Scriptures. He founded the *Nākahi* (serpent) movement in the early 1830s. *Nākahi* was both a Christian Old Testament reference to the fiery serpent on Moses's rod and a Christian New Testament emblem of Jesus; in both these cases it stood for hope. However, for Papahurihia, *Te Nākahi* (the serpent) was his *ariā* (familiar or "companion" spirit). Although he converted to Christianity in 1856 (his baptismal name being Penetana Papahurihia), in previous times Papahurihia opposed Christianity and its missionary ambassadors. By the late 1830s, he had taken the name of Te Atua Wera, "the fiery God," perhaps in contrast to Jesus. Throngs of Māori turned out to hear his Biblically based messages. In particular, his identification of the Māori people with the Biblical Jews bereft of their land in his assessment of the needs of his people strongly appealed to his followers. Papahurihia exemplifies how the arrival of the new Pākehā technologies, and teaching and proclamation of the radically different Judeo-Christian view of the cosmos, placed the prophets in the unique position of blending the Pākehā world with their traditional culture in charting new directions. As prophets, much of their message pertained to an accurate critique of the developing Pākehā dominance.

Academics also recognize Aperahama Taonui (1809 to 1816–1882),[66] who had received Wesleyan baptism in 1833 and had associations with Papahurihia in the 1850s, as a prophet. Researchers acclaim him as a man of peace and vision who had a great concern for Māori loss of land and growing political impotence. It was he who persuaded Papahurihia to embrace Christianity. He had a leading role in founding the *Kotahitanga* (Oneness; Pan-Māori) movement which resulted in the Māori parliaments of the 1890s.

Additionally, scholars identify Te Hura (?–?) as a prophetess,[67] albeit in a different way. She was a senior adult in 1850 when she acknowledged visits from both her deceased child and Moses. She combined Christianity with her ancestral worldview in her healing practice (which included both steaming herbs and praying in the name of Jesus Christ) in the Hawke's Bay region on the east coast of the North Island.

There were several other prophetic leaders who either established or continued the development of brands of Māori Christianity in contradistinction to missionary Christianity. These include Te Ua Haumēne (early 1820s–1866) who founded the Pai Mārire (good and peaceful) movement in the early 1860s and his successors, Te Whiti o Rongomai III (1832?–1907) and Tohu Kākahi (1828–1907) who founded Parihaka, a community of passive resistance, on confiscated Māori land in the 1870s; Te Kooti Arikirangi Te Turuki (1832?–1893) who initiated the Ringatū (the raised hand) faith in the mid–1860s, and his successor Rua Kēnana Hepetipa (1868/69–1937) who established a peaceful community at Maungapōhatu; and Tahupōtiki Wiremu Rātana (1873–1939) who established the two pronged (spiritual and political) Rātana Church in the first quarter of the 20th century.[68] Each of these movements featured a combination of Māori and Christian beliefs and practices.

One reason why Christianity could have some appeal to Māori was because some features of the Church's teaching resonated with the worldview of their traditional culture; the "church house," as representative of Christianity, stood in some measure in an analogous relationship with the Māori ancestor house, as representative of Māori spirituality. Spatial arrangements of facilities, iconic trappings and other ornamentations, veneration of saints, and stories retold from the Christian Bible provided resonances and parallels, in one way or another, with the Māori tribal worldview. Also important would have been the roll of lineage and ancestors in the Christian faith. It is not difficult to view the recognition of Abraham as the father of the Jewish nation and the gospel report that Jesus of Nazareth could trace his ancestry through Joseph, his (supposed) father, to King David and finally to Adam as especially resonant with many indigenous folk. We have already mentioned the Māori identification with the Jews bereft of their homeland. Although the Christian message of peace and freedom was attractive to some Māori because of its *contrast* with their tribal way of life, notional harmonies such as these allowed the indigenous population to blend Christian notions into their own ideas.

Today the Christian *whare karakia* and the Māori *whare tipuna* continue their analogous relationship. To enter the *whare tipuna* is to enter the eponymous ancestor, the place where the ancestor's presence is particularly focused; to enter the church building is to enter the house of the Lord, the place where the Christian God, represented by Jesus, is particularly present. While the Māori *whare tipuna* and the Christian *whare karakia* represent two very different worldviews and ethae, the parallels and reverberations allow them to connect as symbolic analogues.

However, while an understanding of the *whare tipuna* as a symbol in Aotearoa/New Zealand is rather straight forward and while aspects of Christianity would have suggested resonate visualizations and feelings to Māori, several factors complicate an understanding of the *whare karakia* as a symbol there. Heading the list is the fact that there was incomplete Māori solidarity with regard to the early missionaries. The first CMS sponsored missionaries to Aotearoa/New Zealand established their mission station at Rangihoua, on the north end of the North Island, under the protection of Ruatara; when Ruatara died in 1815, the mission came under the protection of Hongi Hika (1772–1828), who set out to use the missionaries to obtain European technologies and products, especially muskets, for his own benefit.[69] The Methodist backed Wesleyan Missionary Society (WMS) followed CMS suit in 1822 by sending missionaries to Kaeo, also on the north end of the North Island.[70] Here they established a mission station, Wesleydale, in 1823. The selection of this site proved indeed unfortunate. It was within a few miles of Whangaroa Harbour where, in 1809, Māori, in retaliation for the ill treatment of a chief's son, massacred the crew of the sailing ship *Boyd*. Tensions were still running high five years after the missionaries' arrival. In 1827, this circumstance combined with Māori intertribal combat to force the missionaries to flee for their lives when Māori attacked the mission station. The Wesleyans were able, however, the following year to establish another mission at Mangungu, which was a considerable distance removed from their initial location; it was here that, in the 1830s, the WMS missionaries baptized their first converts. After the Methodists came the Catholics. Jean Baptiste Pompallier (1802–1871), a member of the Society of Mary and the Church appointed bishop to the area, led his group to Hokianga, again in the north of Aotearoa/New Zealand, in early 1838; they enjoyed the support of and baptized many Māori.[71] On the one hand, some Māori chiefs protected the missionaries whether CMS, WMS, or Catholic. But on the other hand, others within the loosely organized indigenous population either exploited them or found their presence undesirable.

Māori maintained a mixed attitude long after these first missionaries arrived. They were slow in embracing Christianity, but widely accepted it in the 1830s. By the 1840s political developments had undermined missionary influence. The 1850s brought a further loss of respect, and by the 1860s the missionaries had closed virtually all the mission schools and deserted the missions. After the land wars of the 1860s the missions gradually revived, but many settlers and Māori continued to see the wars as evidence of missionary failure.[72] Nevertheless, the missionaries persevered, and as recently as the 2013 national census, more than 50 percent of Māori responses to the religious affiliation question acknowledged identification with some form of Christianity.

Second, just as there was incomplete Māori solidarity with regard to the early missionaries, there was likewise no clear European solidarity with regard to Māori. The Christian faith was both fragmented and compartmentalized within Western culture; it did not permeate Pākehā society as Māori spirituality saturated their tribal organization. Europeans who arrived both before and after the first missionaries often exhibited attitudes and behaviors which included prejudices and hostilities toward Māori; and in response, the European missionaries frequently criticized their European kin. By the 1820s the seaport town of Kororāreka[73] (modern Russell) had sprung up in the Bay of Islands as a stopping place for sealing and whaling vessels. As there was no formally recognized national law in Aotearoa/New Zealand and as Māori were unable to enforce their customs in the town, the only justice was that which could be developed and imposed locally. Therefore, Kororāreka had a well-deserved reputation for decadence and lawlessness. When CMS missionary, Henry Williams (1792–1867), arrived in Aotearoa/New Zealand in 1823, he very quickly that same year established a mission station at Paihia, located only a short distance away on the opposite shore from Kororāreka. This was a direct protest to the licentious lifestyles of those dwelling in and passing through the port town. Williams developed a strong reputation among Māori partly because he had the courage to speak out against the unruly behavior of the sealers, whalers, merchants, and outlaws.

Third, and as might be expected, the missionaries failed to demonstrate unity in both their own religious belief and practice or their approach to Māori. The Anglican based CMS, sponsors of the first missionaries of 1814, believed Māori could gradually convert and organize into a Māori version of the Anglican Church[74]; and Samuel Marsden, their first missionary appointee to Aotearoa/New Zealand, believed introducing European culture was the first step toward their conversion.[75] However, the Methodist backed WMS, which sent their initial missionary team to the Aotearoa/New Zealand Northland in 1822, rejected Marsden's premise and opted for a primary goal of making converts.[76] Moreover, French Catholics, who arrived in 1838 and faced hostility from both Anglicans and Methodists, focused on baptizing converts without challenging Māori lifestyles.[77] Finally, missionaries from most of the major Christian denominations followed and each group brought its own peculiar twist to Christianity.

Fourth, Māori tribes could combatively defeat the representatives of the European "God." The early missionaries depended upon Māori for food, shelter, and protection; and sometimes acquiesced to Māori demands that were not in Māori best interest. While Hongi Hika (referenced above), the Ngā Puhi protector of the CMS missions, exhibited an interest in and a favorable attitude toward Westerners and Western culture, even visiting Britain and Australia; he did not forego the opportunity to enhance his own standing and gain an advantage in war with other Māori, sometimes negatively affecting the mission stations.[78] In 1819 he sought his own best interest by sponsoring a new CMS mission station at Kerikeri and demanding muskets in return; the missionaries supplied them thus contributing to the terrible Musket Wars (roughly, late 1810s to late 1830s) in which thousands of Māori died at the hands of other Māori. In this case, Hongi Hika sought to enhance his prestige through setting-up what he viewed as a sort of win-win situation with these CMS missionaries in order to get something that he wanted. In contrast, albeit relatedly, the Wesleyan (WMS) missionaries were caught up in the Musket War combat and were able to maintain their mission station at Wesleydale only from 1823 to 1827. In 1820 Hongi Hika had traveled to England where he received a considerable wealth of gifts. He returned home months later by way of Sydney, Australia, having arranged for considerable additional muskets and related supplies. This helped set in motion a kind of Māori arms race, and Aotearoa/New Zealand tribal conflict escalated. In late 1826 Hongi Hika, in order to both control the territory and settle issues with Ngāti Pou and Ngāti Uru, invaded the area where the Wesleydale mission was located, and in January 1827 the WMS missionaries were forced to abandon the station. Accounts differ as to what happened at Wesleydale. According to one, some of the Ngāti Uru raided the mission as they made their escape; according to another, Hongi Hika's warriors were responsible for the attack. It seems likely that Hongi Hika did not order the assault, but whatever the truth of the matter, the missionaries were fortunate to escape with their lives.

Fifth, to add to the bewilderment although also not a surprise, many missionaries, in spite of some Māori opposition and the European inter-faith disagreements, trained and developed Māori people and sought to protect their interests. They put the language of Māori tribes into written form and set up schools to teach the indigenous people to read and write.[79] Missionaries repeatedly served as peacemakers for settling disputes between Māori tribes and as go-betweens and translators for negotiations and disputes between Māori tribes and Pākehā colonialists.[80] They challenged land enterprises such as the New Zealand Company and promoted the Treaty of Waitangi, first signed in February 1840, to protect Māori land ownership.[81]

Finally, a few miscellaneous observations close this list of complications. Today, no single religious group enjoys a majority of the Aotearoa/New Zealand population, and the Government recognizes two synthesized religious denominations, the Ringatū faith and the Rātana Church, which combine Christianity with traditional Māori beliefs and practices. Also, while the country is home to many Christian religious organizations which dispatch missionaries to various places in the world including Melanesia, Asia, South America, and Africa; the nation is also host to new missionaries from other countries.[82] Moreover, Aotearoa/New Zealand appears to have no interest in establishing a state church.

Although Christianity arrived in Aotearoa/New Zealand as a Pākehā institution which was often contradictory in its approach to Māori, of which many Māori were suspicious, and which Māori could easily overcome militarily; it had some appeal through its form and message and its ability to provide goods and services which the indigenous population valued. Therefore, over time and with the support of British colonizing efforts, its most obvious expression, the Christian meeting house, emerged as a symbol there. The complications associated with Christianity's establishment in Aotearoa/New Zealand point up a symbol's potential for sending a mixed message. Those solidly within the symbol's domain, even though an amalgamation of several factions, may perceive little contradiction even though they recognize differences; but those on the fringes or who do not share the symbol are likely to have a heightened sense of the disparities. Significantly, there can also be a reverse outlook where those within the symbol possess a heightened sense of difference while those on the outside are virtually oblivious to the disparities.

In any case the Christian meeting house in Aotearoa/New Zealand conjures primarily Pākehā myths and rituals, even though they can widely vary. Hence, the "church," irrespective of denominational differences, has largely either denounced Māori beliefs and practices or reinterpreted and assimilated them. It has declared those not sharing the Christian group's core understanding as misguided, and has thus buttressed the worldview and values of its adherents. Thus the "church" often projects to both insiders and outsiders a bond between otherwise diverse Christian groups by its embodiment of an overarching reality. Christianity has a birth and a developmental history within which much of its content has changed overtime as its practitioners' self-understanding has changed. Its evolution includes numerous variations of its central message, but it survives today mediating a perceived unity in diversity through its various assemblages.

The *whare tipuna* and the *whare karakia* are analogues insofar as they share a similarity of function. While undoubtedly Māori have synthesized some Christian religious ideas with their traditional culture and the Christian Church has accepted some Māori notions into its broad theological scheme, the two *whare* still declare kinship and unity within their respective domains. From the earliest days of contact between Māori and Pākehā, the ancestor house and the Christian Church have coexisted as analogous symbolic agents.

Whare *meets* whare

A casual drive through almost any Aotearoa/New Zealand residential area is apt to turn up several staple institutions familiar to any Western nation. Grocery stores, boutiques, gift shops, liquor stores, police headquarters, fire brigades, city management facilities, etc., are typical. It is also a virtual surety that the visitor will find in the area both Christian church grounds and a *marae*. To be certain the latter is not quite as common as the former, but it is indeed not anomalous. The church grounds, with its *whare karakia* displaying its distinctive cross, steeple, or both and the *marae*, with its *whare tipuna* displaying its characteristic bargeboard apex which may include a *tekoteko* or *koruru* or both, are clear indications of the presence of both Christian and Māori notions within the same community.

Moreover, the arrangement of either or both the Pākehā and Māori grounds and facilities will sometimes display features of both cultures. The Christian Church grounds may include Māori carvings, language, and an *urupā* (Māori cemetery); while the Māori *marae* may have a *whare karakia* nearby with which it is associated, and its *whare tipuna* may include Christian and other Western themes in its carvings. Nonetheless, in Aotearoa/New Zealand the base culture of the *whare tipuna*, the "ancestor house," is decidedly Māori while the base culture of the *whare karakia*, the "church house," is Pākehā. Even in those communities where no *whare tipuna* or *whare karakia* are physically present, the ideas they represent will still be fundamental. Hiwi Tauroa (see this book's Introduction) was contemplating the interaction of these base cultures and the resultant formation of a mixed culture which included both Māori and Pākehā. It is in this context that he wondered if the church had ever replaced the ancestor house as the focal point of Māori culture.

It is also worth noting that while it is not uncommon for Māori ancestral facilities and Christian religious centers to display features borrowed from one another, not all outwardly reflect the meeting of the two cultures. Some churches, especially those attended exclusively by Pākehā, may display little or no Māori influence; and some *marae* facilities, especially those controlled by persons with a militant attitude toward Pākehā, may display no more Western influence than is absolutely necessary for addressing such issues as comfort, lighting, efficient food storage, food preparation, and sanitation. Nonetheless, as there certainly has been no shortage of associations between Māori and Pākehā, a mutual cultural influence is inescapable.

Today, monuments mark the beginnings of mission sponsored Christian activity in Aotearoa/New Zealand. A Celtic cross memorial stands where Anglican missionary Samuel Marsden preached his first official sermon at Rangihoua Bay on 25 December 1814; a cairn memorial marks the site of Wesleydale, established in 1823 as the first Methodist mission; and a globe-topped cuboidal memorial commemorates the site where stood the home of Thomas and Mary Poynton in which Catholic Bishop Pompallier held the first Mass in Aotearoa/New Zealand on 13 January 1838. These missionary endeavors began a tradition of Christian *whare karakia* in the land. As with church houses throughout the world, the architecture can greatly differ as can the nuances of the Christian message delivered in and emanating from them. Yet, the central theme remains the same; the architecture, even when it includes Māori notions, supports the message; and there is a broad similarity of activities associated with the root motif.

As for Māori, the ebb and flow of the political, social, and religious life of the country has resulted in today's more than 800 *marae* most of which feature a *whare tipuna*, each with its own emphasis as decided by the group associated with the *marae* on which stands the ancestral structure. Carvings differ and customs may vary slightly from one to the other, yet as with the Christian *whare karakia*, the central theme of the Māori *whare tipuna* is consistent; its architecture, even with the inclusion of Western ideas, underpins the theme; and there is a general agreement of activities with the core tribal idea.

However, base cultures notwithstanding, the coexistence in the communities of *marae* with their *whare tipuna* and church grounds with their *whare karakia* is indicative of much more than the mere presence of two different cosmologies, and the grounds and houses of either culture which display cross-cultural expressions stand as a testimony to a profound

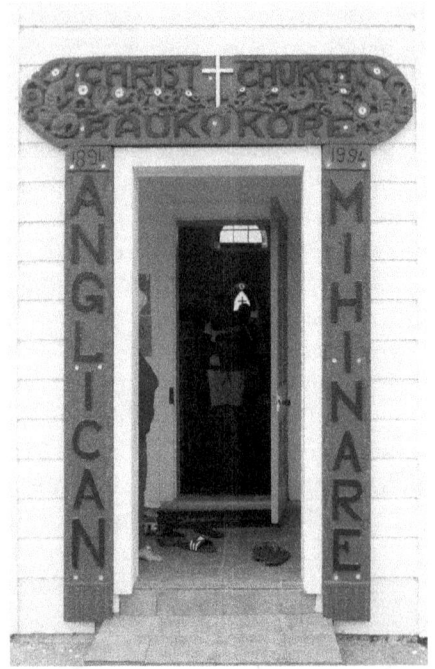

Left: Figure 6. The rural Anglican Church at Raukokore. *Right:* Figure 7. The doorway of the Anglican Church at Raukokore. (Both photographs by the author.)

influence that far surpasses the simple infiltration of beliefs. The former declares the legitimacy of alternative perspectives on and approaches to the cosmos and life; the latter indicates an interweaving of spirituality. While the core ideas regarding the Christ on the one hand and the ancestors and *atua* on the other remain unsubsumed in the encounter of the two *whare*, there has resulted a complementary mix of worldviews and ethae that extends past the bare recognition of the other group; the Christ is on the *marae* and the *atua* and ancestors are in the Church. Importantly, the meeting of the two as symbols representing and projecting very different cultural norms has affected the myth and ritual of each, and that influence is often displayed in the respective architectures and activities.

For Westerners the reciprocal effect of the *whare tipuna* and the *whare karakia* is likely to be more apparent through an examination of the latter than the former; and while Aotearoa/New Zealand has numerous *whare karakia* that express in some measure the impact of Māori-Pākehā cultural concursion, one outstanding example is the rural Anglican Church at Raukokore. This *whare karakia*, situated in a serene and picturesque area close to the sea in the Aotearoa/New Zealand Eastland, is a popular tourist destination. Thankfully, no vendors are present to either greet or bark the visitors. The photographs of the beautiful Raukokore church and its *urupā* (cemetery) presented in Figures 6, 7, 8 and 9 emphasize the confluence of Māori and Pākehā cultures.

The general architectural design depicted in Figure 6 is typical of Christian meeting houses whether exclusively Pākehā, exclusively Māori, or shared by all. However, note the Māori carving around the doorway. Figure 7 provides a close-up view.

Figure 7 is a close-up view of the doorway in Figure 6. The name for the Anglican Church in Māori is *Te Hāhi Mihinare*, "The Missionary Church." This congregation identifies itself in both the English and Māori languages. Also, note that visitors and attendees

Figure 8. The interior of the Anglican Church at Raukokore. (Photograph by the author.)

leave their shoes outside the sanctuary just as they would leave them outside the *whare tipuna*.

Figure 8 is a view of the church's interior. The carved boards at the front fit into the overall design in such a way as to be reminiscent of the bargeboards on the exterior front of the *whare tipuna* that are an expression of welcome. Also, note that the carved inscription is in the Māori language. It is a quote from Psalm 84, verse 10: *No te mea he ra kotahi i ou whare | pai atu i nga ra kotahi mano*; "Because a single day in your house | (is) better than a thousand days (elsewhere)."

Figure 9 shows the *urupā* (burial ground; cemetery). *Urupā* are often attached to church buildings, but may also occupy a completely separate area. Note the fences all around. This place is highly *tapu* (sacred); grave browsing is absolutely not permitted. The sign reads: "Please tourists and visitors to this area: This is a family urupa so only family and friends of the family are to enter. Others please remain outside the fence." Modern *urupā* illustrate how Māori burial customs have been adjusted to utilize Pākehā forms.

Figure 9 (the photograph of the *urupā*, i.e., cemetery) provides a convenient place to illustrate the encounter of the two *whare* as symbols with a brief observation regarding the *tangihanga* (rites for the dead; funeral) which takes place on the *marae*.[83] The value of this example is underpinned by the fact that Māori, without doubt, view the *tangihanga* as the most important type of *marae* gathering; it has deep mythological and spiritual roots and takes priority over all other meetings; it is the pinnacle expression of the Māori heart. As with Pākehā funerals, Māori rites for the dead express a sense of loss, display tokens of

Figure 9. The *urupā* (cemetery) at the Anglican Church at Raukokore. (Photograph by the author.)

sorrow, make expressions of love for kinfolks, support the family, and honor the deceased. Of course, funerary nuances can differ from Western practice; for example, women may wear naturally scented *kawakawa* wreaths or other greenery in their hair. This custom is a carry-over from traditional times (the period before Western influence significantly affected Māori ways) when the *tūpāpaku* (corpse) might lie in state for several days; the strong scent of the leaves would mask the odor of bodily decomposition. But it is the marriage of Māori and Pākehā funerary customs that provides the informative illustration; specifically, the *tangihanga* of traditional times included the *hahunga* (digging up; exhumation) ceremony, but contact with Western culture has resulted in the transition of the *hahunga* into the *hura kōhatu* (unveiling the stone) ritual of today. Both are acknowledgments of continued family and tribal commitments to one another and the deceased, but are much different in form. Let us take a closer look at the proceedings of each.

Although some accounts record the *hahunga* ceremony of traditional times as taking place after a period of up to four years after the initial *marae* funerary observances, by most contemporary accounts it occurred about a year or so later. After the deceased had been properly mourned and recognized the undertakers of the day would deposit the remains in a shallow grave, a cave, or a tree (sometimes a hollow tree). They kept the location secret in order to prevent enemies from desecrating the corpse. The body would decay in this undisclosed place for a period of time after which the tribal *kaitiaki*, "guardians" (in this case, of the dead), would collect the remains, remove any flesh, and wash the bones. They would then return the bones to the *marae* for display and another round of mourning and recognition. According to some records, the *kaitiaki* would prepare and exhibit the remains of more than one bone-set at a time. After the second mourning and recognition, the *kaitiaki* would take the bones to their final resting place, likely a burial cave, located in a secluded non-public space.

Māori no longer observe the *hahunga* ceremony. As hygiene became a heightened concern, they replaced it with the *hura* (uncover; unveil) *kōhatu* (rock; stone), the ceremony for unveiling the cemetery headstone. Today, after the initial mourning associated with a death, the body is buried in a cemetery like the one in Figure 9; but the headstone is not displayed at that time. A year or so later (reminiscent of the *hahunga* ceremony), there is another memorial service in which persons display photographs of the deceased along with those of other deceased relatives, celebrate and mourn the departed once again, and unveil the headstone. As did the *hahunga* ceremony of previous times, the *hura kōhatu* observance of today completes the mourning process and provides closure for the family. The deceased is afterward remembered along with other ancestors at future *marae* gatherings.

The above treatment of the interaction of Māori and Pākehā cultures is one example of how present day Māori people retain the essence of their culture although the form of cultural expression is subject to change; an idea and practice which indigenous scholars associate with the concept of *Mātauranga Māori*. The simple definition of *Mātauranga Māori* is "Māori knowledge," but the expression more broadly refers to knowledge passed down from the ancestors. Notably, even the broadened reference fails to address the full inclusivity of the expression. Sir Hirini Moko Mead was absolutely correct when he wrote of the term's complexity.[84] Over the generations, in conjunction with the processes of life, knowledge both comes to the fore and recedes into the background. In this ebb and flow it is not uncommon for circumstances to engender a relearning of something forgotten or, at a minimum, to excite a deeper search for the knowledge of the past.

Māori look to such cultural treasures as their songs, stories, and place names in their attempt to rediscover what they knew ages ago. These sources in themselves bespeak Māori inquisitiveness and innovation pertaining to their development as a people in their land. They enacted changes in their lifestyle in reaction and conformance to factors such as climate, geography, food availability, and social circumstances. Whether living on the land or voyaging on the ocean, they met challenges head on. They were not afraid to experiment or to accept something new. They noted successes and failures and were willing to alter their outlooks and practices in the light of fresh revelations. When a new arrangement proved better than the old, they adjusted their traditional practice accordingly; an ability for which Māori adjustments to the *tangihanga*, their most important gathering, stand as a testimony. Importantly, evolution of practice, whether or not precipitated by contact with other cultures, does *not* negate cultural essence; cultures can learn and borrow from one another *without* the loss of their cultural identity. The final chapter of this book addresses this issue in greater detail.

Nonetheless, there is an enormous difference in offering improvement to a culture's lifestyle or aiding its impoverished and attempting to impose a foreign worldview. British colonialists had intended to seize Māori land and resources and to assimilate Māori into a European style culture, and in many ways they were successful. It is only since the rise of the Young Māori Party in the late 19th and early 20th century and the simultaneous beginning of changes to Pākehā attitudes that a renaissance of Māori culture has occurred and an interest in biculturalism has developed.

Hiwi Tauroa (see this book's Introduction) was gazing upon the field of history after much of the smoke and dust of alliance and controversy had settled. His awareness, which entailed the encounter of symbols, was one frame of a story that is still playing out. The measure of a symbol is its momentary irreplaceability for the group to whom it belongs. How far had Māori been assimilated into Pākehā culture? How much of their culture had they retained? What processes were at work? His reflections included how one symbol can conjoin with another to unite diverse factions into an overarching unity.

Paul Tillich's observation that persons can neither deliberately of themselves create nor destroy a symbol[85] was astute. Neither a government nor a chief can simply create a symbol of conjoined cooperation within a common national setting with common national values by simply passing an Act of Parliament or making a tribal proclamation. Neither can they decide to simply do away with the symbols of resistance and resentment. Symbols must be born in a people, and they die only when the circumstances which give them life no longer exist. For Aotearoa/New Zealand biculturalism to succeed, circumstances over time must either impregnate the populace with new symbols or engender the reinterpretation of old ones. Hiwi Tauroa's contemplation (again, see this book's Introduction) raises the question of what happens when symbols collide, the question of reciprocity and power relations in a religio-cultural context. This is the question for which this book offers an answer.

CHAPTER THREE

Reciprocity

Western reciprocity

"Do unto others as you would have them do unto you." So goes the Christian Golden Rule, at least as I remember the church sponsored teachers of my childhood years quoting it. More recently, others have turned it about in order to express what they believe to be a better rendition: "Do unto others as others would have you do unto them." Of course there are also the lines from the comedies of years past: "Do unto others *before* they do unto you!" and "They did unto me, so *now* I'm doing it unto them." But no matter how you say it, with the seriousness of worship, the motivation of effective business, or comically twisted about, the Golden Rule in all its various incarnations presupposes that we do unto one another. This is precisely what reciprocity is about. Reciprocity is fundamental to all human relationships; doing unto one another is a necessary consequence of being social creatures.

However, the Golden Rule is not nearly as simple as I was taught when I was a child. First, reciprocity, according to its etymology, refers to a back (*re*) and forth (*pro*) movement of one sort or another which, in society, may entail connections which extend far past mere dyadic give-and-take to involve an entire network of associations. Second, reciprocity's back and forth behavioral characteristic possesses an agentive quality within the social dyad or network. All human behavior is symbolic, and all symbolic action inevitably represents a particular worldview and ethos. Reciprocity is a universal of human experience; but not everyone has the same take on the nature of the self, the world, and his or her place in the world or wants to be treated the same way. Reciprocity's form and structure may vary radically from group to group and person to person. When we as children first learned about reciprocity in our homes, long before we memorized the Pledge of Allegiance in our elementary school, we learned it from a particular point of view. It was not apparent to us at the time, but what we learned pertained to a particular Western social, philosophical, and theological perspective which diverse others did not share. It worked for and among us because we generally shared the same broad view of reality.

Western reciprocity is a complex theme for which a number of American social psychologists have expressed an interest, some majoring on the psychological aspect and others on the sociological. But in particular, researcher Linda D. Molm and her company of associates, whose interests appear to be slanted toward the social aspect of social psychology, have helped carry the torch for experimental research pertaining to Western style social exchange for a number of years. Their beginning point has been a particular view of reciprocity as an exchange of *benefits*. There are a number of clichés which express the idea. For instance: "One hand washes the other"; "You scratch my back, I'll scratch yours"; "I give you something; you give me something"; "You do this for me, I do that for you." These expressions also illustrate how Molm and company believed that reciprocity was not purely happenstantial but had a definite structure, and the structure for which they opted was one of Western society.

Molm and her research team of associates, David R. Schaefer and Jessica L. Collett, set out to identify different exchange forms by their structural characteristics and learn how benefits moved within the structures, how the movement of benefits within the structures produced social solidarity, and what the elements of social solidarity were. Therefore, they concocted and conducted a grand experiment to settle the questions once and for all. In their college campus venue, they put together an arrangement of computers divided into networks with three or four in each and enlisted the service of 308 undergraduate students for conducting a series of mock exchanges from which they sorted-out particular data and formulated conclusions.[1] Their models and findings, summarized by Figures 10 and 11, fairly represent the Western mind-set from which they worked; they provide an accurate portrayal of reciprocity in Western society.

Figure 10 identifies four forms of reciprocity: negotiated direct exchange, reciprocal direct exchange, chain generalized exchange, and pure generalized exchange. The structure of each is comprised of two primary factors: the directness of reciprocation and flow of benefits. Direct reciprocation bespeaks a dyadic relationship while indirect reciprocation involves other actors; the flow of benefits may be either bilateral or unilateral. *Negotiated direct exchange* means that actors reciprocate benefits directly in a bilateral flow; there are no intermediaries through which benefits move and the benefits are necessarily negotiated (e.g., a binding contract between two parties). *Reciprocal direct exchange* also means that actors reciprocate benefits directly, but the flow is unilateral; once again there are no intermediaries, but the benefits are not negotiated (e.g., two neighbors helping one another). It is the flow of benefits that determines the form of reciprocity as either negotiated or reciprocal.

Indirect reciprocation entails a group larger than a dyad within which benefits always flow unilaterally. *Chain generalized exchange* means that actors reciprocate benefits indirectly and the flow is unilateral; there are necessarily intermediaries through which benefits pass and the benefits are completely non-negotiated (e.g., a "pay-it-forward" operation in which A gives to B, B gives to C, and C gives to A). *Pure generalized exchange* is a type of exchange in which persons perform random acts for the common good (e.g., giving blood), and the general public may draw benefits from the common fund (e.g., receiving a transfusion).

Figure 11 depicts the complete Molm, Collett, and Schaefer scheme, which is very typical of the Western approach to reciprocity.

Within each of the four exchange structures there are three factors constantly at work that affect social solidarity. The *risk of non-reciprocity* recognizes the possibility of actors getting little or nothing in return for their investment; while reciprocation may occur promptly and adequately, some exchange partners may be unable to reciprocate in a timely fashion if at all, others may be unwilling to reciprocate, and still others may be oblivious to the transaction. Of course, under certain circumstances, persons may not expect reciprocation. The *expressive value* of the exchange can partially offset the risk of non-reciprocity. The exchange value per se notwithstanding, both the hope and fulfillment of reciprocity has intrinsic worth. In Figure 11, actors attach communicative value to both the act and fact of give and take. According to Molm, Collett, and Schaefer, these first two "causal mechanisms" tend to increase social solidarity. However, the third, the *salience of conflict*, tends to mitigate it; in addition to the cooperative feature of reciprocity, there is the competitive

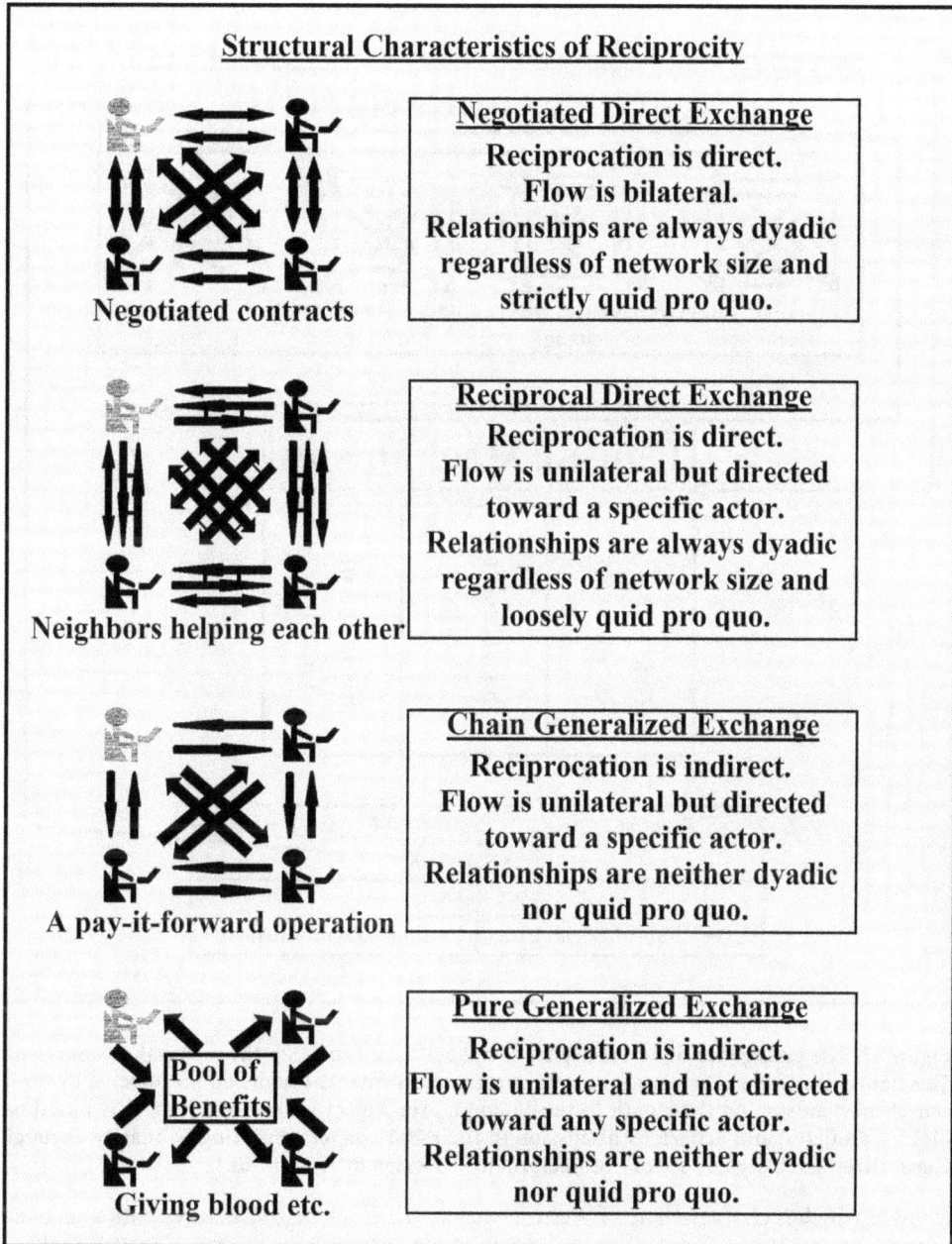

Structural Characteristics of Reciprocity

Negotiated contracts

Negotiated Direct Exchange
Reciprocation is direct.
Flow is bilateral.
Relationships are always dyadic regardless of network size and strictly quid pro quo.

Neighbors helping each other

Reciprocal Direct Exchange
Reciprocation is direct.
Flow is unilateral but directed toward a specific actor.
Relationships are always dyadic regardless of network size and loosely quid pro quo.

A pay-it-forward operation

Chain Generalized Exchange
Reciprocation is indirect.
Flow is unilateral but directed toward a specific actor.
Relationships are neither dyadic nor quid pro quo.

Giving blood etc.

Pool of Benefits

Pure Generalized Exchange
Reciprocation is indirect.
Flow is unilateral and not directed toward any specific actor.
Relationships are neither dyadic nor quid pro quo.

Figure 10. Structural characteristics of reciprocity. This illustration summarizes the four exchange forms which Molm, Collett, and Schaefer discuss in their 2007 paper, "Building Solidarity Through Generalized Exchange: A Theory of Reciprocity." The paper describes an experiment the team conducted to test the exchange forms for the production of social solidarity. The depictions on the left illustrate the flow of benefits within each exchange form; the non-ghosted images represent particular actors in the experiment while the ghosted images represent an extension of the network to an undeterminded size. The blocks to the right briefly describe the illustrations. The caption below each illustration is an example of the exchange form. (Drawn by the author.)

Structures of Reciprocity

Negotiated Direct Exchange   Reciprocal Direct Exchange   Chain Generalized Exchange   Pure Generalized Exchange

Pool of Benefits

Causal Mechanisms

Risk of Non-Reciprocity   Expressive Value   Salience of Conflict

Trust of Others   Affective Regard for Others

Social Solidarity

Perceptions of Social Unity   Feelings of Commitment

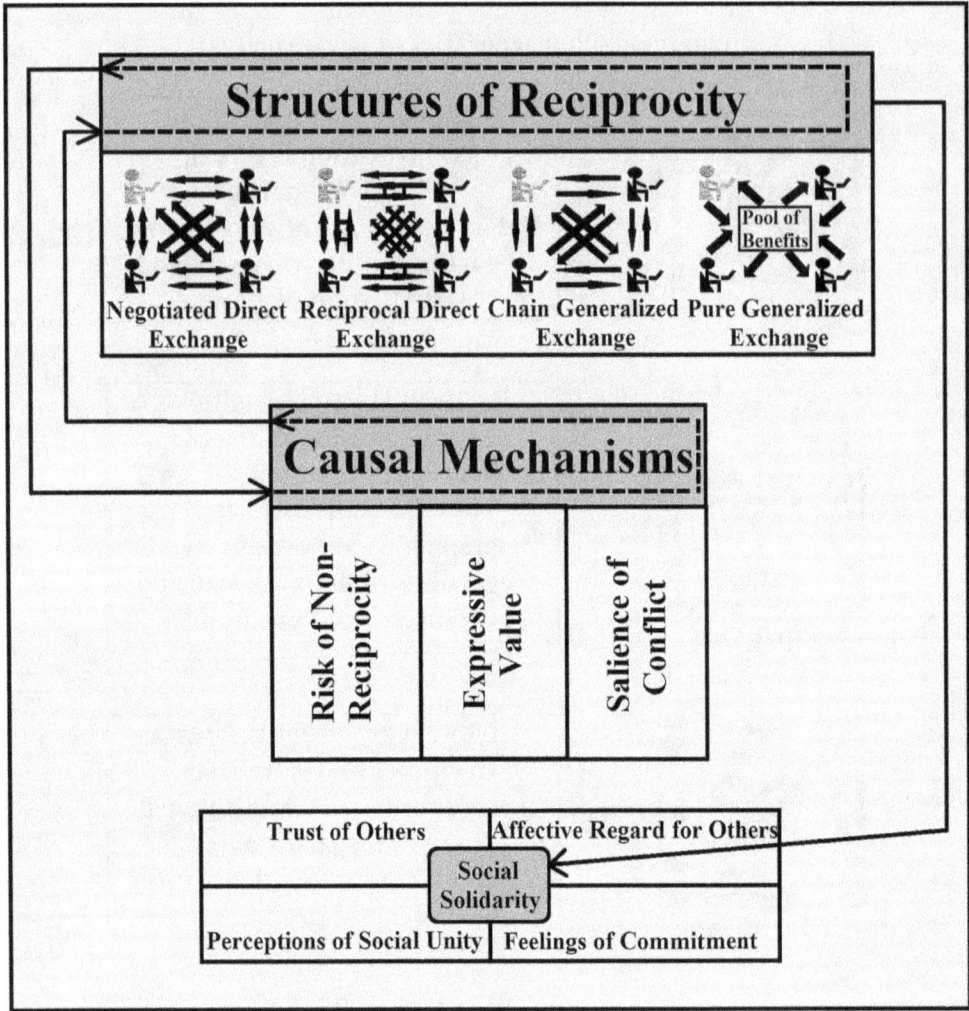

Figure 11. The emergence of a four-aspect social solidarity through three causal mechanisms. This figure illustrates how Western forms of reciprocity filter through and are affected by three causal mechanisms on their path to producing a four-aspect social solidarity. It is based on Molm's, Collett's, and Schaefer's discussion in their 2007 paper, "Building Solidarity Through Generalized Exchange: A Theory of Reciprocity." (Drawn by the author.)

element which is characteristic of Western society. The exchange structures both affect and are affected by these causal mechanisms on their path to undergirding (or dismantling) social solidarity.

In the Molm, Collett, and Schaefer scheme, which is representative of the Western world, there are four broad measures of how well a society coheres. *Trust of others* refers to an attitude by which actors anticipate kindness and/or support from others as opposed to abuse or oppression. *Affective regard for others* describes exchange partners going a step further by genuinely liking and respecting one another. *Perceptions of social unity* means that actors in various ways sense a harmony within the larger social unit. *Feelings of commitment* is a reference to actors sharing devotion to a common endeavor or enterprise. Of course, applying meaningful metrics to these four aspects can be difficult.

As might be expected, Molm, Collett, and Schaefer found, through their experiment exactly what they were looking to find. Generalized exchange forms produce the greatest social solidarity. Reciprocal direct exchange is next followed by negotiated direct exchange.

If the Molm, Collett, and Schaefer experiment seems a bit too clinical to be trustworthy, others have thought so, too. Particularly, Edward J. Lawler, who also generally accepted reciprocity as an exchange of *benefits* and acknowledged the four exchange forms and their structures, recognized that persons, in addition to thinking, experience strong feelings when it comes to give and take.[2] According to him, while human beings may have enduring sentiments, they are also subject to temporary emotions of two kinds. First, there are global emotions. These are temporary general feelings of pleasantness and unpleasantness which an individual cannot associate with any particular source. Second, there are other temporary emotions which are quite specific. For example, people associate feelings such as gratitude, anger, pride, or shame with clearly defined social objects such as organizations or other individuals. For Lawler, the key to understanding social exchange was deciding how persons tie ambiguous global emotions to definite social objects, a process by which global emotions become specific; in other words, he set out to understand the process(es) by which people interpret the cause of the global emotions of pleasantness or unpleasantness. In his opinion, the greater the association of social objects with the global emotion of pleasantness, the greater the social solidarity with those social objects.

Lawler, in his presentation, discussed a fifth exchange structure, *productive exchange*, in which actors pool their resources and coordinate their efforts for the common good. It furnishes a good illustration of his point about the importance of emotions (see Figure 12).

Figure 12 illustrates productive exchange by showing how Molm, Collett, and Schaefer each contribute to and receive benefits from their jointly authored essay, "Building Solidarity Through Generalized Exchange: A Theory of Reciprocity." For each contributor, the global feelings of pleasantness or unpleasantness become attached to their experimental

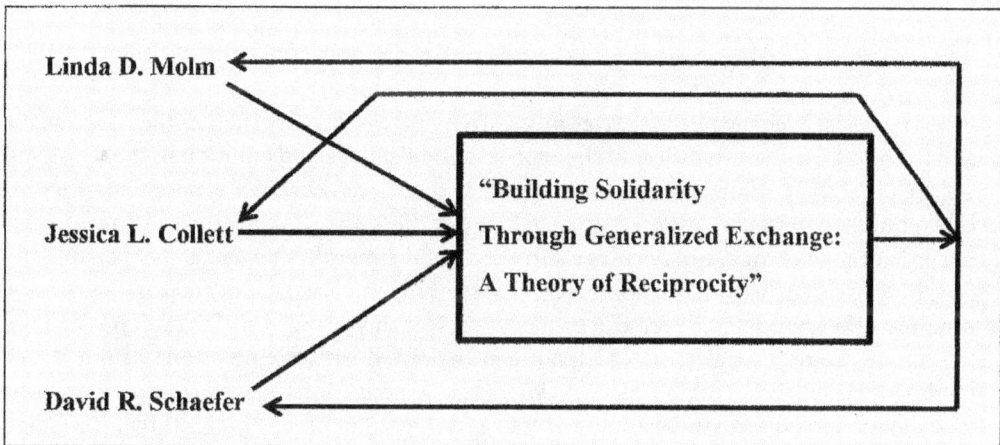

Figure 12. Productive exchange. This drawing depicts persons pooling their resources in order to facilitate a specific endeavor and receiving rewards accordingly. In the figure Molm, Collett, and Schaefer combine their talents to produce their paper, "Building Solidarity Through Generalized Exchange: A Theory of Reciprocity," and each receives benefits from both the project-in-itself and the completed product. (Drawn by the author.)

endeavor and report, thus resulting in specific emotions of, for example, pride or frustration. The resulting emotions will influence their trust of one other, affective regard for one another, perceptions of their unity as a group, and feelings of commitment to one another; that is, their social solidarity.

Lawler's work further defines the Western model of reciprocity by accounting for the role of emotions; however, his conclusions were the exact opposite of Molm, Collett, and Schaefer. According to him productive exchange produces the greatest social solidarity with negotiated direct exchange next, followed by reciprocal direct exchange, and then the forms of generalized exchange.

Of course, the two parties had a debate over the order of exchange forms in the production of societal cohesion including the method and procedures of the experiment. Obviously, there was at least one flaw in someone's thought and/or procedure, but where was it? Did the experiment adequately allow for the operation of emotions? Molm, Collett, and Schaefer said "yes"; Lawler said "no." Lawler made an attempt to explain away the differences in their conclusions by suggesting that the focus of his affect theory was on interpersonal relationships between self and other rather than less personal relationships between social units; but Molm, Collett, and Schaefer rejected his explanation. To those of us who grew up in a Western nation these approaches to reciprocity sound entirely reasonable and an ensuing debate is neither unexpected nor unfamiliar.

What is also telling is what they did *not* debate: specifically, the movement of exchange as unilateral or bilateral and direct or indirect; the various forms of exchange as productive, negotiated direct, reciprocal direct, chain generalized, and pure generalized; the causal mechanisms of social solidarity as entailing risk, trust, and awareness of cooperation and conflict; and the determinants of social solidarity as including trust of others, affective regard for others, perceptions of social unity, and feelings of commitment. The recognition of these themes as typical and the theorists' concerns as similar raise the issue of the theories' common root.

The economic bias

The social exchange perspectives of theorists and researchers such as the Molm team and Edward J. Lawler, regardless of the mix of rational choice and emotion in their systematic treatment, are rooted in a common premise which is essentially economic in nature. Market ideas dominate Western exchange theories. Both the Molm team and Lawler view reciprocity as an exchange of *benefits*. At the heart of their work is the belief that persons engage in reciprocity because they will receive something in exchange for their investment of time and other resources. There will be a pay-off. Not surprisingly, such a notion is even at the core of Western religion, in which notions associated with feelings of pleasantness and unpleasantness have a tangible reward. According to some, if you plant your seed of faith, God will grant you a commensurate harvest; and they sometimes point out that the "poor widow" gave all she had. Or to quote an outtake from the Christian Scriptures, "You have been trustworthy in a few things, I will put you in charge of many things."[3] And of course, the great payoff of devotion in both the Catholic and Protestant traditions is the escaping of the fires of hell. Out of the niceties of the Golden Rule as we learned it as a child there has developed a sort of business model which has been applied to social relationships.

Moreover, the exchange theorists, by virtue of their association with overlapping social science disciplines such as psychology, sociology, economics, and politics and the application of their work to various Western societal institutions, reveals their ambitious agenda of developing an interdisciplinary theoretical model for all social analysis. In other words, according to Western exchange theorists, people generally conduct their affairs, whether political, religious, economic, or purely social, based on a system of perceived gains and losses.[4] The potential for receiving rewards and avoiding damages is the bedrock of their agenda.

Among those who believe that most people in the West live their lives according to the simple processes of benefits and costs are those who call for a modification in approach. They attempt, through rhetoric of one sort or another, to move people from a more selfish motivation in fulfilling life's purpose(s), regardless of how it is interpreted, to one of greater altruism. But even then at the core of their presentation is the appeal to the feelings of pleasantness that are the result of such less selfish choices. Even the appeals to live by the law of love and to focus on long-term welfare of others often have a system of achievement and gain as integral to the feelings of fulfillment; fulfillment is *achieved* through *gain* which comes by giving. Their exhortations cannot escape the gravity of the market model. Milan Zafirovski well summarized the application of economic concepts to non-economic issues:

> [S]ocial exchange theorists ... transplant the concepts of supply-demand, market and just price, imper-
> fect competition, costs, profits, etc. from economic to extra-economic phenomena. They view the equi-
> librium between supply and demand as determining the exchange ratio between two non-economic
> goods by analogy to market exchange. Also, they treat the concept of elasticity of market supply and
> demand as also applicable to social relations, particularly interrelations in and structures of groups.
> Some extend the theory of imperfect and monopolistic competition, with its assumptions of market
> imperfections (e.g. product differentiation, small numbers of firms, entry constraints, incomplete infor-
> mation), to competition in status and other social rewards. Other examples of extending economic
> concepts to "non-economic situations" include (direct, fixed, variable, marginal, investment, opportu-
> nity) costs, benefits, profit, income, etc.[5]

Economics as a category for understanding human behavior has deep roots. For instance, Aotearoa/New Zealand ethnologist of Māori culture, Sir Raymond Firth (1901–2002), is recognized as a pioneer in the application of economic principles to anthropology. But significantly, he was more than a pure theorist in that he sought, as all good anthropologists do, to ground his ideas in observed, concrete social behavior. This is what separates good anthropology expressed in economic terms from purely theoretical and classroom experimental notions of exchange. Both seek to understand the meaning undergirding particular behaviors, but good anthropology always grounds its interpretation in uncontrived lived-out experience. The point at which exchange theory includes the observation and recording of actual experimentally uncontrolled human behavior is the point at which its method becomes anthropological in nature. Moreover, perhaps because of his associations with both Western European and tribal culture, Firth also understood the inappropriateness of presenting his conclusions as a complete theoretical system; he viewed work such as his own as useful for cultural analysis, but treated any attempt to develop an overarching theory with skepticism.[6]

Certainly the Western paradigms of reciprocity, based on market models, such as those produced by the Molm team and Edward Lawler, are useful for understanding the dynamics of social exchange within many environments such as the corporate, educational, or charitable institutions of secularized nations. And economic models generally are useful for understanding social interaction in other contexts insofar as the observer has a good understanding of the operation of the economy for the group(s) in question. Nonetheless, as the next topics show, exchange theories such as those proposed by the Molm team and Lawler tend to break down as testable phenomena, and therefore as a general paradigm, under the weight of exchange complexity; and as the following chapter will show, the exchange theories and the forms themselves tend to break down structurally under the weight of cultural diversity.

Māori utu

Utu is the Māori principle of reciprocity, but its full meaning can be somewhat obscure even within Aotearoa/New Zealand. The Pākehā population is more likely to associate the word with "revenge" which in traditional times often found expression in open warfare between Māori groups, sometimes more than two. There is, however, another dimension of Māori *utu* which is often overlooked. *Utu*, which finds its negative expression in feud and warfare, also has a positive expression in sociability and the exchange of gifts. Importantly, the negative and positive aspects of *utu* follow a pattern of one morphing into the other and back again. War among Māori tribes was not uncommon well into the 19th century; however, warring tribes often ended hostilities and entered into a period of social friendliness and gift exchange, which would then be followed in due course by another period of war, and so on. Notably, this oscillation of bad exchange and good exchange becomes apparent only by tracking tribal behavior over a long period of time and perhaps also by viewing it from a cultural distance.

In the United States the familiar feud between the Hatfields and McCoys in the Kentucky/West Virginia region is an American version (more or less) of *utu*. The killing phase of the feud lasted from the 1860s until close to the turn of the century, but it afterward faded. The families even appeared together on a popular television quiz show in 1979; and in 2003 both families and the Governors of Kentucky and West Virginia declared an official peace. Historians of the feud might reasonably expect any continuation of the disagreement, if any, to be settled in the American judicial system and not in terms of family raids, ambushes, and executions.

Aotearoa/New Zealand anthropologist, Dame Joan Metge (1930–), who in many respects built on the work of Sir Raymond Firth, invested much time and many resources in providing a wonderfully detailed account of a particular instance of the flow of Māori *utu*.[7] Specifically, she called upon her almost 50 year association with Māori people in the Aotearoa/New Zealand's Far North to document a history of *utu* between two tribes, Te Rarawa and Te Aupōuri. The main thrust of Metge's story begins in the last half of the 18th century with the tribes having emerged as significant political entities and living virtually as neighbors on the North Island. She describes how these two tribes have alternated between peace and hostility from then until the present. The following presentation only skims the surface of her rather detailed story.

The tribes today generally assume their relationship prior to the middle of the 18th century to have been relatively peaceful, an assumption based on the absence of stories of any conflict prior to that time and the understanding that each took its name wholly as a result of conflict with other tribes. The friendly relations began to unravel when Te Rarawa reinforced relations with a particular Te Aupōuri enemy. This created tension between Te Rarawa and Te Aupōuri, so when an incident occurred involving yet another tribe, the once friendly Te Rarawa and Te Aupōuri became bitter enemies.

The gist of the incident and resulting flow of exchange is thus. The chief of a tribe with whom Te Rarawa had friendly associations killed his Te Aupōuri mother-in-law, who was living with his tribe, because she complained about his servants stealing kūmara tubers (a sacred crop) from her storehouse. Te Aupōuri organized a war party for retaliation. Te Rarawa set out to aid the tribe whose chief had killed the mother-in-law, but the Te Rarawa chief, who was quite old, stayed home. Te Aupōuri avoided the Te Rarawa war party and killed Te Rarawa's old chief in his own home. This was not simply a death for a death, but the death of a chief for the death of a woman living outside her tribal territory. Hence, a cycle of negative *utu* was under way.

In the fighting which ensued, Te Rarawa overall outmatched Te Aupōuri. However, at the height of a particular battle, the Te Rarawa chief stopped the fighting. He drew a line in the sand to mark the boundary between the two tribes; Te Aupōuri to the north and Te Rarawa to the south. Apparently Te Aupōuri agreed, and to seal the deal gave the Te Rarawa chief a woman whom he much admired for a wife. Thus, hostile relations were reversed to peaceful ones through a magnanimous act and a marriage, and a period of positive *utu* (with gift exchange) began.

The peace lasted for years, but was not permanent. Although Te Aupōuri (who had for years secretly prepared for revenge) started the new conflict, they got the worst of it again. The decisive battle happened when Te Rarawa attacked the Te Aupōuri *pā* (a hilltop fortified village). Te Aupōuri fought bravely but lost the day including their chief and his nephew. Te Rarawa showed respect for the fallen leaders by cooking and eating some of their flesh and returning the rest of their bodies to their families along with their weapons. This ended a period of negative *utu* and positive *utu* (with gift exchange) began anew. Afterward, Te Rarawa and Te Aupōuri became allies in war and peace. Even though, now and then, there were disagreements and anxieties, they nonetheless managed to avoid war.

Over time, as Metge continues her story, tribal lines have blurred through intermarriage and mobility around the country. In fact, claims for tribal membership have become a matter of social context and place of residence. Yet periodically one of the tribes will still publically reaffirm its independence by reiterating stories about conflicts of former days and then, in accordance with the cycle of *utu*, in due course make peace once again. Of course, these days, genuine disputes are more apt to be handled through the Aotearoa/New Zealand justice system than in open combat.

Figure 13 depicts the flow of *utu*.

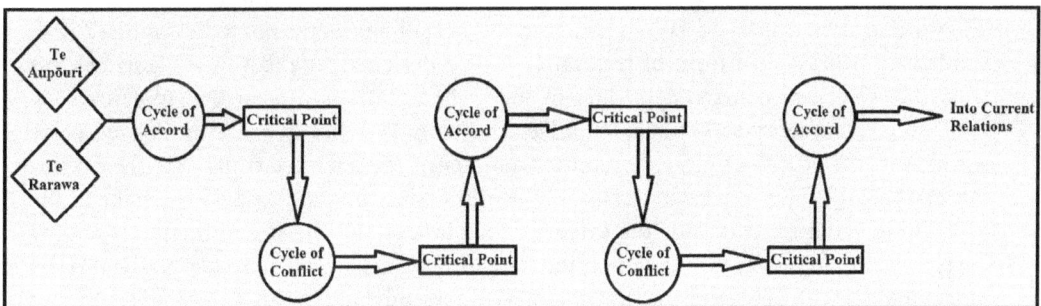

Figure 13. Ups and downs of the *utu* cycle. This illustrates Dame Joan Metge's narrative about how the exchange of "good" gifts reaches critical mass and collapses into the exchange of "bad" gifts which reaches critical mass and collapses into another exchange of "good" gifts etc. (Drawn by the author.)

Utu, as *the* principle of Māori reciprocity, was and is woven throughout the fabric of Māori society. It is fundamental to Māori tribal life. It finds its expression in conformity with the Māori worldview and ethos, which it then projects back on to the society. It both has its origins in their mythology and declares their mythology to accurately and effectively represent the way life truly is. *Utu* pervades tribal social, religious, and political order. It is a mechanism for social control including the dispensing of justice. It is a device for maintaining societal balance which is applicable to both individuals and groups.

Researchers who have spent considerable years observing Māori culture have long recognized two crucial aspects of *utu*.[8] First, the Māori principle of exchange demanded that which was returned to be at least equal to that which was received. This was true whether the context be economic, ceremonial, political, or purely social; whether the less common intra-group expression or the more common inter-group hospitality applied; and regardless of whether the swap was of the positive or negative sort. Second, *utu*, whether positive or negative, functioned to maintain an asymmetry of relations. Both the one-upmanship of exchanges in the near term and the vacillation of good and bad exchanges in the long term served to keep relationships going. In other words, it created a form of social solidarity by establishing a separation of groups while creating a sort of bond between them.

As it pertains to the positive aspect of *utu*, the researchers, particularly Joan Metge, recognize several other qualities which stand out.[9] First, the parties did not negotiate the exchange; neither its nature nor its magnitude. Second, positive expressions could include acts recognized as respectful, benevolent, forgiving, and merciful as well as tangible property. Third, in the absence of negotiation, the parties felt a cultural obligation to both accept what was offered them and to reciprocate from what they had to offer; exchanges which could become quite competitive. Fourth, the giver might return a gift different from the one received; for instance, cultivated food in exchange for fish. Fifth, the nature of the resources available for exchange meant that reciprocity might be delayed until they were available; for example, migrations of certain fish and birds took place at particular times of the year. Sixth, the nature of the relationship might require waiting for an appropriate occasion to present the return gift. Seventh, benefaction was always a display of the *mana* (pride; prestige) of the giver. The end result was a workable social system within and among tribal groups.

However, as loose as the *utu* system might appear, no system of reciprocity is without its checks and balances, and the Māori of traditional times practiced a modification of the principle of negative *utu* when it came to close kin and neighbors. They developed a form of recompense called *muru* for which retaliation and one-upsmanship was inappropriate. The word is often translated as "plunder" but this sort of plunder is not to be confused with vandalism. *Muru* was a form of restorative justice designed to effect in a Māori context what the American court system does in the United States and what the Aotearoa/New Zealand court system does in Aotearoa/New Zealand; specifically, make an injured party whole. When a person or group committed an offense, the offended could take the offending party's goods; but not before considerable discussion among those with a stake in the problem in order to determine the extent of the plunder and the size of the *taua* (raiding party). While there was no retaliation for the performance of *muru*, token physical resistance might occur. However, the drawing of blood would end the resistance.

Muru was culture specific in its indemnification for either intentional or unintentional personal injury, loss of possessions, and damage to certain social relationships. The recompense necessarily included considerations of the *mana* (prestige) and *tapu* (social set apartness) of both the injuring and injured parties; consequently, those with the greater societal position could have an advantage. Moreover, it was a sort of *ritual* compensation among relatives. *Muru* falls under the *utu* umbrella as restorative justice and a device for social control, but it is not *utu* per se. It is a negative event (from the vantage point of the "defendant") with the positive result (from the perspective of the "plaintiff") of restoring an injured party to their original state. It is a modification of the *utu* principle that protects the integrity of the social unit. It mitigates the possibility of kinship associations collapsing into chaos. It differs with *utu* per se in that it serves to maintain the balance of the group by limiting recompense to the extent of loss.

It appears indeed not uncommon for researchers, perhaps more commonly at the outset of their research, to share the experience which Joan Metge describes; that is, to view contemporary Māori culture as discontinuous with traditional Māori culture as modern Māori ways often appear far removed from their traditional roots.[10] However, as illustrated by an examination of Māori rites for the dead in the previous chapter and the operation of *utu* in this current chapter, with study of and exposure to the culture, as it also happened with Metge, this perceived disconnection resolves itself into the recognition of today's cultural expressions as transformations of past conventions and not disjunctions.[11]

Utu *and the West*

It should be apparent by now that there are several differences in Māori tribal *utu* and Western market-based reciprocity that are significant enough to preclude the strict application of Western style paradigms to Māori Polynesian culture. Several factors are easily noticeable.

First, of the forms of exchange common to the Molm team and Edward Lawler (negotiated direct, reciprocal direct, chain generalized indirect, and pure generalized indirect) and the form which Lawler added to their debate and discussion (productive exchange), *utu* more closely resembles reciprocal direct exchange insofar as it is a less formal, non-negotiated arrangement, with a unilateral flow of benefits (or consequences) within which the giver has no specific guarantees about whether or when reciprocation would occur, or the extent of reciprocation. However, none of the Western researchers viewed reciprocal direct exchange as the best producer of social solidarity. Significantly, in Māori society, *utu*, even with its modern transformations, represents the *primary* exchange structure for achieving societal unification.

Second, while persons may discuss Māori reciprocity in terms of Western forms of exchange, they must do so with the understanding that the social exchange categories are subsumed by the *utu* paradigm. Without doubt Western researchers can point to Māori tribes uniting against a common enemy in warfare as an instance of productive exchange as there was collaboration with an anticipated benefit for each of the parties. Also, they may find an example of negotiated exchange in the barter between Māori and Pākehā as there are documented bartered transactions which included the exchange of flax for tools and protection of missionaries for muskets. Moreover, they can view the general social intercourse between Māori chiefs and their followers as illustrations of the generalized forms of exchange inasmuch as the gift returned could be something different than that bestowed and could follow an indirect path to the original benefactor; for instance, procurement of particular tribal necessities and other items could result in greater *mana* for the chief. Nonetheless, all the above social exchange categories are absorbed into the *utu* model. Significantly, *all*

Māori giving, both positive and negative, includes the element of *manaaki*, which means "to display *mana*" (a spiritually based status, prestige, power, and influence). This principle is active in *all* giving and operates in accordance with the concept of *utu*, which requires receivers of benefits to return something of at least equal value and which serves to maintain an imbalance of relationships.

Third, researches can discern in *utu* the three causal mechanisms that work throughout the Western exchange forms, but these devices flow through the *utu* cycle. The strong "expressive value" of giving and receiving and the "heightened awareness" of competition in Māori society hardly require more explanation. "Risk of non-reciprocity," while also a valid category, is extremely low because returning a gift is integral to the *utu* concept. Nevertheless, experiments such as that which Molm, Collett, and Schaefer conducted is not well equipped to measure the dual aspect of Māori exchange (its positive and negative expressions), its long-term exchange cycles, or the way the exchange cycles reach critical mass and then collapse only to start again in a reverse expression.

Fourth, researchers can also usefully apply the four measures of social solidarity (trust of others, affective regard for others, perceptions of social unity, and feelings of commitment) in order to describe Māori society; but any discussion of them must take place within the context (both cognitive principle and practical operation) of the *manaaki* (the display of tribal pride and prestige) aspect of *utu*.

Finally, *utu*'s emotional aspect, while certainly a strong consideration, appears to be something different from Lawler's notion of the actor's goal being the reproduction of pleasant feelings and the avoidance of unpleasant ones. The experience of positive and negative feelings and the give and take associated with each appears integral to Māori reciprocity and social solidarity.

While the work of Western researchers and experimenters may be *useful* for Westerners to understand the operation of social transactions within a variety of contexts, both secular and sacral; their work is *not definitive* for *all* contexts. A comparison of their concepts with the Māori practice of *utu* shows how Western economic models for reciprocity tend to break down as testable phenomena under the weight of exchange complexity and both illuminates and declares the validity of the claim by cultural relativists and those with cultural relativistic tendencies that societies' diversity and complexity defy organizing social exchange into any all-encompassing theory.

The complexity of Pākehā reciprocity

There were three broad contexts for 19th century Pākehā initiated social exchange that involved Māori: the public exchange of the European style government and Māori tribes, the driving force of which was Pākehā control of Aotearoa/New Zealand; the private exchange of the European settlers and Māori persons and groups, the principal concern of which was Pākehā acquisition of Māori land; and the personal exchange of the missionaries and Māori people, the chief aim of which was Māori conversion to Christianity. All three took place against the backdrop of colonization. The first two had the motive of permanently separating Māori people from their land and its resources; the last had the motive of permanently separating Māori people from their religious beliefs and practices. Since Māori culture and religion were one and the same and inextricably linked to the land and its resources, separation entailed a complete breakdown of the Māori worldview and ethos.

The two motives combined as an attempt to assimilate the indigenous population into a British world. This three part structure of public, private, and personal exchange provides a useful framework for applying Western exchange forms in a discussion of both the secularized and sacralized incentives for Pākehā political, social, and religious transactions. The application of the exchange forms, once again, illuminates their break down as testable phenomena, and hence as a general paradigm for all societal reciprocity, in proportion to exchange complexity.

As a prelude to our discussion, let us first note the broad Pākehā attitude toward the acquisition of Māori land. Regardless of whether or not the apparent Pākehā ignorance of Māori ways was genuine, Pākehā certainly conducted their affairs as though Māori had, or should have, the same attitude toward the land as they did; a commodity to be bought and sold with little regard for its worth beyond its monetary value. They either ignored or did not understand that the land, from the Māori perspective, was sacred. Pākehā considered it good business to buy it for as little as possible and sell it for as much as anyone was willing to pay, and acted as though there was no real injustice in using questionable or deceitful tactics to carry out their agenda. This Pākehā market based attitude underlay both the public and private exchanges in colonial Aotearoa/New Zealand.

The most obvious example of Pākehā public exchange is the Treaty of Waitangi, which Aotearoa/New Zealand today acknowledges as the nation's founding document, the signing of which commenced on 6 February 1840.[12] While the parties of the Treaty are Pākehā and Māori, the Treaty was both a Pākehā idea and a Pākehā instrument. Māori tribes would soon learn, if they did not already suspect or know, just how difficult it was to beat Pākehā at their own game.

Aotearoa/New Zealand in the 1830s was Māori controlled but a land which served the British as a source for trade goods and a haven for ships and crews engaged in sealing and whaling. By the late 1830s the British Government had become concerned about the unruliness of some British subjects, the violence that would occasionally occur between the indigenous population and the Europeans, and the unscrupulousness of independent settler plans such as those of the New Zealand Company. As a result, the British took decisive action by appointing William Hobson to seek Māori agreement for the British to establish a colony in their land. He sought to carry out his mission by treaty.

The Treaty was a rushed affair. Hobson arrived on 29 January 1840. He and his secretary, James Freeman, sketched a treaty which the British Resident, James Busby, reviewed and to which he applied his input. The team issued invitations to Māori chiefs to assemble on 5 February. Anglican missionary Henry Williams and his son, Edward, hurriedly translated the treaty into the Māori language over one evening just in time for the meeting. The Treaty of Waitangi *seemingly* established a bilateral flow of benefits in a negotiated direct exchange between Pākehā and Māori, although in *actuality* the Treaty, at that time, was little more than a lure toward colonization.

Conspicuous examples of private exchange are Pākehā purchases of Māori land. These private land purchases also represent a form of Pākehā direct negotiated exchange, but sometimes include productive exchange, albeit with a twist of unproductive benefits for the indigenous population. For instance, according to historians, in 1848 a Government agent employed threats and trickery toward the South Island tribe, Kāi Tahu (also called Ngāi Tahu), in order that the New Zealand Company could acquire much of their land.[13] The resulting reduction of space and resources had devastating consequences for the tribe, but the problem was not confined to these two issues. The loss of the land was also a detachment from specific places of particular importance for the identity of the people; we might say that they lost their soul. Here a government agent combined resources with private speculators in which both received benefit (productive exchange), but the benefit's channel was a land sale agreement (negotiated direct exchange) that negatively affected Māori. It was not until the 1990s that the Government finally settled the tribe's claim which included, among other things, a formal apology, a cash settlement, rights to *pounamu* (Greenstone), and the return of their sacred mountain, Aoraki or Mount Cook.[14]

Let us now turn to the personal exchange between the Pākehā missionaries and the Māori people. The missionaries' exercise of their sacral motive provides examples of reciprocal direct and generalized indirect exchange forms in which the flow of benefits is largely unilateral; however, the lines between these exchange forms are somewhat blurred. For example, the first missionaries, sponsored by the Anglican based Church Missionary Society (CMS), arrived in 1814, and Samuel Marsden, the first missionary appointee, believed the first step toward success was introducing British culture. In these early days of association, Māori tribes had the upper hand in an unequal power situation and the missionaries (who depended upon Māori for food, shelter, and protection) were in no position to make any demands or have any expectations of the tribes. Yet they established mission stations, translated the Christian Bible into Māori, enabled Māori literacy in their own language, taught them European farming techniques and trades, and repeatedly served as peacemakers for settling disputes between Māori tribes. While this describes a unilateral flow of benefits, there exists a case for both direct and indirect return. On the one hand, the missionaries served Māori people without knowing if, when, in what form, or by whom reciprocation would come (generalized indirect exchange). Māori did reciprocate in terms of food, shelter, and protection; but the missionaries could not be certain of it, and groups that lost favor with Māori had good reason to fear for their lives. On the other hand, the missionaries' overarching expectation was that Māori, who largely received the benefits, would reciprocate in the form of accepting Christianity (reciprocal direct exchange).

What is once again apparent in the discussion above is how the categories of social exchange theory, while useful as descriptive devices and for understanding some of the dynamics of personal and group interaction, tend to break down as testable phenomena, and hence as a general paradigm for cross-cultural exchange, in proportion to cultural complexity and complicatedness. Moreover, even the experimental process itself (such as the test conducted by the Molm team), as one of making a measurement, necessarily alters that which it measures. The necessary element of control in an experiment, by its very nature, both introduces dynamics into social exchange transactions that would not otherwise be present, and eliminates some dynamics that would otherwise be present. While this does not totally negate the value of the experiments, it is a factor researchers must consider in formulating results and it certainly urges caution in judgment.

A social uncertainty principle

The above presentation makes it abundantly clear that the operation of cognition and emotion in exchange forms can vary greatly across cultures, especially when two radically divergent cultures encounter one another; and that the inter-cultural social exchange between Māori and Pākehā in Aotearoa/New Zealand has been largely in terms of virtually incompatible forms replete with misunderstanding. We may state the misunderstanding in the form of *a social uncertainty principle*: In these extreme cases persons *can* know a social exchange event is taking place, and they *can* also know *their own* rules by which such events operate; but in the encounter of radically different cultures and their associated values, the participants *cannot* definitively know the event's cross-cultural inner dynamics (i.e., how the combination of rules is operating) while the event is current. Stated differently, in the interaction of radically diverse cultures, participants can know only the *outward appearance* of an exchange and can never be certain about the transaction's *inner cross-cultural dynamics* while it is taking place. The inner dynamics must be determined by the transaction's *effect*, which requires temporal distance. Two reasons for this are that *motives* are often hidden to scrutiny of the transaction, and *balance of power* is always a variable. Importantly, the determinations also include the cognitive and emotional aspects of those making them.

One the one hand, many Māori miscalculated Pākehā intent. Two examples will suffice. First, the Pākehā motive behind the Treaty of Waitangi was colonization and assimilation while the Māori motive was to establish their full authority over their own affairs, their land, their land's resources, and their cultural treasures. Neither side understood the other at the signing of the Treaty. The motives became apparent only in the ensuing debate about its terms (an effect of the signing), which became shaped in favor of Pākehā by an imbalance of power. For Pākehā, the document which in 1840 appeared to represent an exchange for the benefit of both groups in reality represented no exchange at all; and in 1877 it was declared worthless by the Aotearoa/New Zealand Chief Justice. The Treaty of Waitangi was originally an expedient colonizing action. Only subsequent activity has given it the status of Aotearoa/New Zealand's founding document. Second, the first missionaries' (CMS) patience and sacrifice that had the appearance of a unidirectional endeavor for the good of the indigenous people had an underlying motive of displacing Māori religious beliefs and practices thus disrupting life as Māori understood it, and the Methodists (WMS) and Catholics that followed the first missionaries shared a primary intent of converting the "heathen" race. If Pākehā missionaries intended benefit for Māori people it was benefit in terms defined by Pākehā missionaries. The missionaries demonstrated concern for the survival of Māori people, but survival meant colonization and assimilation.

On the other hand, many Pākehā miscalculated Māori culture. One example will suffice. Māori *utu* was both a meaning system unto itself and a strand in a larger web of meaning. It could not be separated from the entire complex of meaning such as that communicated through and by the *whare tipuna*, and was a testimony to the *mana* and autonomy of Māori tribal groups. Also, while *utu* has a certain structure, the structure is in a very real sense a loose one; exact terms of exchange are not left to the sort of whim that characterizes pure generalized exchange, but neither are they negotiated. There is a sort of reciprocity, but any Pākehā attempt to measure it was a failed endeavor from the outset. Reasons include the unpredictability and incalculability of the sort of exchange (gift or war), the form of exchange (which gift is given/received or how war is carried out), and the intensity of exchange (giving better than was received). Moreover, the fact that *utu* happens over an extended period of time tends to conceal the complete frame of its essential features. Pākehā observers had witnessed *utu* at work, but did not understand the nature of its character and how it represented Māori pride and self-determination even *within* the tribal structure. Observation is perhaps the best tool for understanding *utu* and how it fits into the indigenous people's web of meaning. Such observation is "ethnography," but ethnography must not be judgmental. To judge the quality or morality of *utu* participants without a good understanding of the indigenous social structure, or to apply one's own social structure as the primary method of evaluating the indigenous culture, is likely to result in misinterpretation and distortion of the indigenous meaning. This was the sort of mistake that many of the early observers of Māori culture made. Such judgments led to Pākehā missing the meaning conveyed in Māori symbol systems and resulted in Pākehā condescendingly comparing themselves as "civilized" persons with Māori as "savages" and "barbarians." Such unfortunate judgments by one culture of another have been responsible for the piling-up of struggles on indigenous peoples who have not deserved the melee.

It is impossible to separate human action from its significance and difficult at best to accurately interpret human behavior. The fact that concepts such as *utu*, as practically worked out systems of meaning, only come into focus over a long period of observation and through experience with the indigenous culture should be both an incentive for patience and a caution against snap judgments and expedient social and political action when encountering cultures with different ideas and lifestyles and alternative devices for organizing and solidifying society.

The reinterpretation of culture

In the absence of any overarching theory of reciprocity how are we to understand the exchange between the radically different Māori and Pākehā cultures? The complex dynamics of social exchange transform cultures and produce social solidarity when they engender the birth of new or the redefinition of existing cultural symbols synergistically. This process is integral to both the renaissance of Māori people and Aotearoa/New Zealand's present commitment to biculturalism. Cultural symbols are the fundamental basis of social solidarity.

Uncertainty creates tension and often underlies conflict. Possible results, especially in cases of extreme power imbalance between cultures, may include either the eradication of a race by genocide or assimilation, or its banishment to the fringes of society. Also possible, however, is the societal integration and consequent reinterpretation of culture that achieves common understandings and resolves the tensions of uncertainty.

Etymologically, "assimilation" and "integration" have different roots. Assimilation derives from Latin words meaning "to make similar," "to make like," "to assume the form of," or "to absorb."[15] Integration comes from Latin words meaning "to make whole," "to bring together the parts of," or "to combine ... into a whole."[16] In cultural terms, the former entails the disappearance of one culture into another over time; that is, a culture becomes virtually invisible and essentially extinct as it is overwhelmed by and absorbed into another culture. It is included but practically eradicated in the process. The latter also carries the idea of inclusion but in the sense of complementarity; that is, a society's cultures come to complete one another. Differently stated, integration entails change, and positive change happens when cultures reinterpret themselves affirmatively as a result of their mix. In this sense, societal integration and cultural reinterpretation are interrelated, potentially synergistic, processes capable of fostering bicultural progress.

This reinterpretation of cultures is essentially the evolution of symbols. In Aotearoa/New Zealand, the symbols that were once primary to Māori and Pākehā respectively must either merge into a common national symbol or become sub-symbols within some overarching national symbol. Either way, both Māori and Pākehā must tell old stories in new ways and adjust their rituals commensurately. Thus, Waitangi Day now commemorates and annually celebrates the Treaty of Waitangi, once declared worthless by the Aotearoa/New Zealand Chief Justice, as the nation's founding document.

The evolution of a symbol essentially means the change of a worldview. The change of a worldview means persons see themselves and others in a different way. When persons view themselves and others differently, their values and behaviors change. If societal integration does not produce cultural reinterpretation (i.e., if symbols remain unaltered, if worldviews do not change, if persons do not develop a reinterpreted image of themselves and others); then integration has failed in its primary task, old values and behaviors will continue, old tensions and uncertainties will rule the day, and the risk of relegation to the fringes of society will remain. Hence, integration must be carefully devised and implemented.

The reinterpretation of cultures through proper integration is synergistic. This is so because cultures reinterpret themselves (i.e., adjust their symbols) in sensitivity to one other. On the one hand, Aotearoa/New Zealand's efforts for biculturalism reject assimilation of Māori into a Pākehā mono-cultural society. On the other hand, they extend much further than simply the establishment of parallel systems under one flag.

Notions flow from symbols through the population and return to the symbol. In the flow they filter through the properties and relevance of human experience. The quality of human experience possesses the potential to manipulate national symbols; sometimes for the reinforcement of the status quo, but at other times toward the light of a new existence thus establishing a shift in the societal paradigm to one that is not assimilationist, pluralistic, or paternalistic in nature. It mitigates the very ideas of minority status and cultural dominance in favor of cooperation for the common good. As others have pointed out, that which is at stake is not accommodation but structural change.[17] But structural change requires the evolution of symbols in such a way as to infuse the nation with new light, to alter the country's definition of self in the citizenry's subconscious assent; one possibility of which is the enabling and normalizing of bicultural associations.

Aotearoa/New Zealand's current bicultural debate is essential to the country's citizens deciding the kind of nation they want to be, fundamental to the maturing of the nation, and necessary to resolve cultural tensions and quell uncertainty. But its line of progress is not a continually upward slope; it is replete with peaks and troughs. It draws from all the experience of the past, both positive and negative, puts all considerations under the light of scrutiny, and fulfills its purpose when problem resolution occurs. The current Aotearoa/New Zealand cultural debate, which is a manifestation of symbol reinterpretation, is dynamically establishing the form and substance of bicultural reciprocity.

CHAPTER FOUR

Power

The elements of specific power

Power, broadly defined as the capacity or ability to do something or act in a particular way, does not exist in isolation. It is neither some ill-defined "stuff" floating of its own accord alighting on some while passing others by nor a particular entity unto itself endowed with some self-serving purpose. It is also not some vague psychic phenomenon. Power always has a source and at least one object which circumstance makes it contextual, but it is not merely generally contextual; its operation is always specific to particular circumstances.

For instance, the Constitution of the United States is about power. Its Preamble, which we as school kids in the 1950s-60s memorized just as we had the Pledge of Allegiance, expresses a framework very familiar to Americans:

> We the People of the United States, in Order to form a more perfect Union, establish Justice, insure domestic Tranquility, provide for the common defence, promote the general Welfare, and secure the Blessings of Liberty to ourselves and our Posterity, do ordain and establish this Constitution for the United States of America.[1]

And while, as scholars of constitutional law have pointed out, its interpreters have generally disregarded the Preamble as a conveyer of substantive power (that being reserved for the Constitution's articles and amendments), it establishes a mood and an orientation from which to read, interpret, and apply the authority of the internal document. In other words, it establishes a specific context for understanding and administering the Constitution's articles and amendments. Significantly, the American Founding Fathers developed the Constitution (signed 17 September 1787; ratified into law on 21 June 1788) as a replacement for the Articles of Confederation (adopted 15 November 1777; became effective on 1 March 1781), which had failed to provide the national government with sufficient power to adequately conduct the affairs of state; and they thought it wise to summarize the Constitution's intent in an introductory paragraph that conveys some details of power. As it pertains to the Constitution, power has a *source* and an *object*; it ultimately resides in "we the people" and is directed to governmental authority. It has a *purpose*; here, it is "...to form a more perfect Union, establish Justice, insure domestic Tranquility, provide for the common defence, promote the general Welfare, and secure the Blessings of Liberty" and thus serve the interests of the people. It has a *form*; its particular terms are expressed in the specific articles and amendments of the complete document. It has a *method*; by the Constitution's ordination and establishment by the people. It has a *duration*; there is an ongoing time element equal to the life of the Constitution. And it has a *scope*; it is specific to the United States. Within the context expressed by the Constitution, considerations of power have been integral to the debate about the kind of nation the United States is to be and how to safeguard the Union against the misuse of power, even by those with good intentions. Power, as detailed in the Constitution, is contextual, entailing at a minimum the specific elements of source, object, purpose, form, method, duration, and scope; and is relational, involving either dyadic or network associations of individuals or groups with things, concepts, other individuals, and other groups. But even though the operation of power is specific to context, researchers have scrutinized it more broadly. Let us start with a typical Western approach.

The terms of general power

As power has specific elements which are integral to all relationships, it is no surprise that the development of research in social exchange has necessarily included considerations of power as a necessary aspect of human interaction. The Constitution of the United States is an example of the operation of specific power, but can we meaningfully speak of power in more general terms? Are there terms and rules which can enlighten the operation of power across the board? Social exchange theorists say "yes," and in so doing, they extend Western principles to the study of power.

Social exchange theory as it is today, even though it does not disregard previous research, is a development dating to the 1950s, a discipline which predates Linda D. Molm (PhD, 1976) and her associates and Edward J. Lawler (PhD, 1972) by several years. One relatively early modern theorist, who greatly impacted the field of study including the work of Molm and Lawler, was Richard Marc Emerson (1925–1982). Actually, Emerson did not like to treat social exchange as a theory.[2] Rather, he saw it as a frame of reference for the interaction of various ideas about social behavior; a perspective on how items of value move through social processes.[3] It was within this framework that he developed the primary issue of his interest in social exchange; specifically, the relationship of power and dependence. Notably, in the early 1960s, Emerson added an ingredient to an already spicy recipe, the taste of which continues to infuse the social exchange stew. In 1962, he published his paper, "Power-Dependence Relations,"[4] that has proved to be a rich source for the advancement of the analysis of power relations in contemporary social exchange.

Even though social exchange theory in its modern incarnation was still relatively new in 1962 there was a considerable body of literature that discussed power both theoretically and empirically and which took into account group sizes from small to large.[5] Emerson was much aware of the literature but was of the opinion that the research up to that point was underdeveloped and under-integrated; while researchers' observations could stand scrutiny within the context of their work, the various approaches remained largely unreconciled and had not significantly surpassed the social research work of the late 19th and very early 20th centuries.[6] Therefore, he set out, at a relatively early stage in the development of modern social exchange as a field of study, to provide a systematic treatment of social power.

Emerson needed an integrating principle which he found at the very bedrock of his fellow researchers' investigations. While Emerson did not discount their work, he believed their work to be hindered by an erroneous assumption.[7] He observed that researchers were implicitly treating power as though it were an aspect of or a quality associated with an individual or a collection of individuals acting as a unit, which entities they ranked from greatest to least and then called the hierarchical arrangement the power-structure.[8] Emerson began by challenging this predominant perspective. "Power," he reasoned, "is a property of the social relation; it is not an attribute of the actor."[9] This alteration of fundamental reckoning became his integrating principle and would underlie his presentation of power-dependence relations.

As the title of his 1962 paper implies, Emerson viewed power in terms of dependence, and this fundamental switch from treating power as attributional to viewing it as relational allowed him to express his ideas as a series of formulas. Most Western persons who have been in a close romantic relationship (whether premarital, marital, extra-marital, or maritally unrelated) will immediately see his point. His classic formulation, "*Pab = Dba*,"[10] states that the *power* of actor *a* over actor *b* is directly proportional to the *dependence* of actor *b* on actor *a*. In other words, power and dependence, as societal categories, are inseparable; they require each other. The power of a social unit (say, a wife) arises from and increases, decreases, or remains constant relative to the dependence of a related social unit (say, a husband or a child); the reliance of one actor on another is a necessary condition for power and its application. Power is operational when one actor is able, in some measure, to control or influence, either negatively or positively, at least one other actor. According to Emerson's formula, where there is no relationship, there is no dependence; and in the absence of dependence, there is no power; power is always a property of the relationship and never an attribute of a social unit. Moreover, as power implies the ability of one party (or more) to influence or control at least one other party, each party has something at stake in relation to the other; therefore, although there may be mitigating circumstances, power is never absent from any relationship. While the operation of power is always relationally specific (in our example of the American Constitution, it includes the elements of source, object, purpose, form, method, duration, and scope); for Emerson, it is the tension between power and dependence that underpins relationships and thus provides a basis for the systematic treatment of and a general theory for the operation of power.

Emerson used a dual aspect formula to depict reciprocity:

$$Pab=Dba$$
$$Pba=Dab^{11}$$

He also expressed relationships as balanced and unbalanced as formulaic expressions:

A balanced relationship: *Pab=Dba*
$$\| \quad \|$$
$$Pba=Dab^{12}$$
An unbalanced relationship: *Pab=Dba*
$$\backslash/ \quad \backslash/$$
$$Pba=Dab^{13}$$

Notably, balanced relationships may be difficult to find; perhaps that is why Emerson devoted so much of his thought to operations that tend to balance them. Notably, some factions of evangelical Christianity disapprove of a relationship between a husband and wife being 50–50; 51–49 is the most they will allow. These evangelicals argue that a 50–50 relationship, by its very organization, will find a great deal of difficulty in moving forward; therefore according to them, an unbalanced relationship, where one person, by organizational structure, can guide all decision making is a much more productive arrangement. However that may be, it is important to recognize that an equal power situation does not neutralize power; power remains active even if a relationship is balanced.[14]

Obviously, an unbalanced relationship implies a power advantage of one party over another. Emerson formulated the strength of the advantage as "*Pba—Pab*"[15]; expressed in narrative form, the power relationship of the two actors is a subtraction of one from the other. In the case of a power advantage the result would not be "zero"; therefore, the relationship would not be balanced. Importantly, unbalanced power implies neither that the stronger party dominates the weaker nor that the weaker actor cannot achieve something of value, a circumstance the factions of evangelical Christianity mentioned above will be quick to point out regarding marital relationships; but it means that the weaker actors must achieve their desire at the cost of foregoing other value(s),[16] perhaps the power to perform a certain act or having a strong sense of personal worth.

For Emerson, cohesion in relationships is a function of somehow averaging the power of the actors. As cohesive, the power-dependence scheme serves to hold the actors together[17]; it provides a sort of social solidarity. He even believed it possible to view the parties as controlled by the relationship.[18] Notably, according to Emerson's formulas, regardless of power advantage or disadvantage, power flows constantly and in both directions, which means that no actor is completely powerless.

The constant flow of power in both directions indicates the presence of factors that tend to effect the balance of power relations, but there is one important factor which, according to Emerson, does not; the factor of *cost reduction*.[19] Any actor may attempt to reduce costs, but cost reduction does not necessarily affect power balance (or imbalance). For instance, a person may alter his or her behavior in a relationship in order to reduce emotional pain, but the alteration of behavior does not necessarily affect the power of the person making life painful. Emerson believed that cost reduction, even though possible in any relationship and certainly deficient in the ability to alter the power to dependence ratio, would serve to deepen and stabilize relationships.[20]

There are, however, according to Emerson, specific efforts with the ability to balance power. In his scheme, drawing from his formulaic expressions, there are *exactly* four—no more, no less.[21] The listing below expresses Emerson's balancing operations in terms of interpersonal relations:

1. The disadvantaged person may say, "I've decided I don't want to be with you any longer! It's not worth the pain!" In this example the weaker party reduces his or her motivational investment (desire for something) in goals mediated by the stronger party which decreases the power of the stronger party; one actor pulls away from the other. This is very similar to cost reduction. The difference is that cost reduction does not affect motivational investment and, hence, the balance of power.

2. The disadvantaged person may also say, "Keep your affection (or money or both); I can get it somewhere else!" In this case, the weaker party finds alternative sources for the values mediated by the stronger party which reduces the power of the stronger party.

3. The advantaged person may say, "I do want me some more o' that!" (Pick your own context.) In this scenario, the stronger party increases his or her motivational investment in goals mediated by the weaker party which increases the power of the weaker party.

4. The disadvantaged person may say, "I know what you want, but you can't have it unless you get it from me!" (Again, pick your own context.) In this setting, the weaker party, some circumstance, or other party blocks the stronger party's access to alternative sources for achieving its goals which increases the power of the weaker party.

We can as easily express the balancing operations in terms of business:

    1. In operation number one, where one party withdraws from another, the disadvantaged might say, "I've decided not to sell your product any longer. I can do just as well without it."
    2. In operation number two, in which there are other sources for the same product, the disadvantaged might say, "I can get it just as cheap somewhere else" or "I might have to pay your competitor a bit more, but there are other benefits."
    3. In operation number three, an advantaged actor in a corporate situation (say, a boss) may increase his or her own motivational investment by rewarding someone (say, a subordinate) who strokes his or her ego. "Yes, I really enjoy your companionship; why don't we go golfing this afternoon (and you tell me what a wonderful golfer I am)." The more dependent the boss is on the subordinate for ego gratification (or in another example, financial remuneration), the more powerful the subordinate is.
    4. In operation number four, the forming of a labor union might block the advantaged actor's access to alternative labor resources during a strike by establishing a boundary and carrying picket signs.

    Emerson knew his work was not the last word in research pertaining to power, but he also believed he had expressed an idea that researchers could apply to a broad range of societal structures, from dyadic interpersonal relationships to complex work associations.[22] He thought his research had near universal application including securing or making monetary loans, associations between children, relationships within families, and even the negotiation of treaties among nations.[23] In his scheme, power is always relational, unceasing active, and inseparable from some concept of dependence.
    Much has happened in the field of social exchange research since 1962. The previous chapter of this book presents a good example of the kind of work being done. Also, interested persons may find the essay, "Power, Dependence, and Social Exchange," by Karen S. Cook, Coye Cheshire, and Alexandra Gerbasi a good summary of progress post–Emerson.[24] Among other things, they point out that it was Emerson's work that served the integrative function of connecting social exchange theory with social network analysis; subsequent research, they say, has included the scope and type of network interconnections, whether they are competitive or cooperative, whether they increase or decrease exchange frequency, and how they operate to achieve results. According to them, researchers have further looked into power as a motivating factor and how balancing operations work. They have examined relational cohesion including its relation to dependence and how it can survive conflict, how types of exchange can affect commitment and trust, how classes of exchange can affect the distribution of power, and how network complexity relates to coalition formation. They have examined uncertainty in terms of unknowns such as the quality of the goods in exchange and have looked into the relationship of risk, commitment, and trust. Modern researchers know the dangers of being purely theoretical and; therefore they have sought substantive applications for their ideas. While the issues discussed by Cook, Cheshire, and Gerbasi do not exhaust social exchange research post–Emerson, they are indicative of the direction the field of study has taken. However, once again the research is from a Western perspective, and in many respects, it perpetuates a Western bias.

Power-dependence and the process of secularization

The power-dependence theory of Richard Emerson and subsequent research into power relations which have sprung from his ideas add another dimension to the social exchange forms with their causal filters which determine a four-aspect social solidarity (see the previous chapter of this book). Power relations are integral to social exchange and a consideration of them is absolutely necessary to a proper backdrop for an examination of Māori-Pākehā cultural transactions. The previous chapter demonstrates how social exchange theory's forms tend to break down as testable phenomena as cultural complexity and complicatedness increase. Let us now see how these categories, with the added consideration of power relations, break down structurally in the encounter of radically different cultures. As it pertains to relations between Māori and Pākehā, the reason for this structural collapse becomes apparent once we understand the "secularized" nature of Pākehā culture and how it contrasts which the "spiritualized" nature of Māori culture. These very different perspectives have been an underlying factor in their cultural encounter from the outset.

Secularization is a Western word developed to describe a phenomenon of the Western world; specifically, the separation of religious institutions and symbols (that once pervaded every aspect of society) from day to day political, business, and social transactions. It describes an occurrence that has had a profound effect on both the Western world and its non–Western counterpart. An example of secularization in the external world of society at large is the American separation of church and state, which the first amendment of the American Constitution addresses as a limitation on the power of the American Congress: "Congress shall make no law respecting an establishment of religion, or prohibiting the free exercise thereof…."[25] In the personal internal world, secularization is obvious in the elevation of non-religious approaches and themes to the activity of human thought and the realm of aesthetics. For instance, today, philosophy can be treated as a discipline separate from theology, and religious motifs no longer dominate the various artistic expressions as they once did. Practically speaking, secularization is the compartmentalizing of the religious perspective that was once dominant.

The underlying factor for this compartmentalization is the rise of modern science. While it has not destroyed religion, its authority has become elevated to a level at least on par with and often exceeding religious authority. The worldview of those nations affected by the rise of science, or alternatively by the demoting of religion, is one in which questions are no longer asked or quandaries spun in terms provided by religious institutions; the religious symbols which once dominated the worldview of nations have been reinterpreted in terms of or completely replaced by non-religious alternatives. The life of a symbol, including the religious sort, fades and becomes extinguished as the circumstances which give the symbol life cease to exist; hence, more and more people in the Western world now live their lives without the benefit of a religious perspective as communicated by religious institutions, and even those who call themselves religious are apt to relegate institutional religious perspectives to the personal sphere of life. Whatever a person's take on reality in the Western world, by virtue of the ascendance of science, it is likely to be a secular one.

Secularization has provided for Westerners a worldview which for them is absolutely true while simultaneously relegating other perspectives to a subordinate status, the result of which has included the criticism, mistreatment, and outright abuse of those with alternative cosmologies. It has entailed not only the idea that taking a less powerful culture's resources is acceptable because Western nations, as cultural superiors, are able to put the resources to better use; but also the notion that Western nations are justified in assimilating those who understand and live in the world differently because assimilation improves their lot in life; they enjoy a better standard of living and over time become enlightened with regard to the way things really are. Significantly, when exploited people resist, they are often critiqued as ignorant and backward.

In larger terms, the question of secularization raises the issue of which principles will permeate a society and be the main drivers of social interaction: those provided by spiritual beliefs and practices or those provided by Western science and economics. The former describes Māori tribes; the latter describes Pākehā colonialists. We may appropriately refer to Māori culture as "spiritualized" and Pākehā culture as "secularized."

The spiritualized Māori

When the British arrived in Aotearoa/New Zealand in the late 18th century Māori were a completely spiritualized people. Spiritual beliefs and practices shaped the Māori worldview and assigned tribal values. Significantly, whereas the form of Māori spirituality has evolved over time, the core ideas are still in place. An historical continuity of ideas exists between today's Māori and their ancestors, a continuity which is mediated by Māori cultural symbols.

There are three cultural concepts, in addition to *utu* (explained in the previous chapter), with which anyone wishing to understand Māori culture must come to terms; the concepts of *tapu*, *noa*, and *mana*. These three notions together with *utu* undergird all other Māori cultural ideas, are themselves interconnected, and are highly spiritual. These categories are fundamental to understanding the reciprocity of Māori power relations. Of these three additional terms, *mana* is more closely related to active power, but an understanding of *mana* requires knowledge of its association with *tapu* and *noa*. Therefore, we will first address the Māori concept of *tapu* followed by *noa* and then *mana*. Be forewarned that tribal concepts can be somewhat abstract!

The concept of *tapu* has raised observers' eyebrows from the earliest days of European contact, and not without good reason. For one thing, it was a word which Māori used in a variety of situations, sometimes pertaining to people and at other times to places and still at others to a variety of particular things both animate and inanimate. Sometimes the word appeared to refer to a prohibition of some kind, the breaking of which could have dire consequences; at other times it seemed to denote some condition of purity or impurity; still at other times it gave the impression of a state of sacredness. Early attempts to unravel the various strands of meaning and put them back together as a coherent whole without extensive experience with the indigenous population proved to be a confusing enterprise. Today's Māori dictionary entries continue to reflect the term's broad range of meaning. Among the listings are: sacred, holy, set apart, prohibited, restricted, forbidden, under the protection of deceased ancestors or supernatural beings, and a supernatural condition.[26]

Is there a common core of meaning around which the various strands of reference are wound? Perhaps the most effective explanation of *tapu* has come from Catholic priest Michael Shirres (1929–1997).[27] While Shirres did not see raw dictionary definitions of the term as inaccurate or unhelpful, he believed the dictionary format to be inadequate for conveying the term's core meaning. Consequently, he opted for a different approach; one related to his knowledge of medieval thought, particularly, that of Thomas Aquinas (1225–1274). He presented *tapu* as neither an equivocal term (a term with different meanings in different contexts, e.g., "bat") nor a univocal term (a term with the same meaning regardless of context, e.g., "animal").[28] Instead, he treated *tapu* as an analogical term,[29] a more or less middle path between the heterogeneity and homogeneity suggested by the concepts of equivocal and univocal. Simply put, an analogy, of which there is more than one type, is a device for showing how one thing is in some respects comparable to another thing. While analogies are not perfect indicators of relationships, they are built on the understanding that relationships between things can clarify meaning(s) and convey truth(s). Taking a clue from Shirres, let us examine how aspects of Thomist analogy are quite useful for illuminating the meaning of *tapu* for Westerners. As did Shirres, we begin by separating analogies into two broad categories, analogy of proportion and analogy of proportionality, and then subdividing the later into analogy of proper proportionality and analogy of improper proportionality.[30] Here we will look at analogy of proportion and the first of the two divisions of analogy of proportionality (analogy of proper proportionality) as useful for understanding *tapu* as a Māori concept. We will also briefly describe analogy of improper proportionality even though it is not necessary for understanding *tapu*.

Analogy of proportion is an analogy of reference or attribution; something has a particular meaning because of a reference or relationship to something else; or stated from the opposite viewpoint, something attributes or lends its meaning to something else. In other words, there is a primary meaning associated with one thing that gets extended to another thing.[31] A common example, and one used by Shirres, is the term "healthy."[32] The dictionary definition of healthy is a general condition or state of well-being. This is its primary meaning, but we apply the primary meaning in many secondary ways; for instance, we say that exercise is healthy or that particular foods are healthy. An understanding of the primary meaning supplies the content of each secondary meaning. We know what it means for a person to be healthy and this supplies particular content to the expressions about exercise and food. We know the secondary meaning because of its reference to the primary meaning.

We now turn to the analogies of proportionality. Again, analogy means that two or more things share a common quality. Proportionality means that a particular quality has a constant ratio to another quality. There are two sorts of analogy of proportionality: proper and improper. Proper means that the elements of comparison are actual within a particular context; those things which are being compared are in point of fact characterized by the quality in question, and the quality in question is actual within its frame of reference. For example, as Shirres points out, just as a "[m]an is 'powerful,' [so] an ant is 'powerful' and the scent of a rose is 'powerful.'"[33] The comparison functions analogically because it supplies information about one entity by making reference to another. It is proper because each is, in fact, powerful. The proportionality is that a particular quality has a constant ratio to another quality; specifically, a man, an ant, and a rose's scent is each powerful in its own way within its own context.[34]

Even though the analogy of improper proportionality[35] is not necessary to understanding *tapu*, we will, nevertheless, briefly include it here to round out the discussion. "Improper" means that the elements of the analogy are *not* referentially actual; they are actually metaphorical. In other words, the comparison under consideration is *not* in point of fact characterized by the quality in question; yet, the comparison conveys truthful information. For instance, consider Shirres's example, "the lion is the king of beasts."[36] The notion of kingship may apply literally to kings, but it applies only virtually to lions; hence, the reference is "improper." Yet the comparison functions to convey particular information about the lion as compared to other animals. The proportionality is that a particular quality has a constant ratio to another quality. But again, this type of analogy does not figure into our understanding of *tapu*.

Turning now to *tapu*, we begin by putting ourselves, as much as possible, in the position of the observers of the 18th and 19th centuries, and noting context after context for the use of the term. First, Māori spoke of *tapu* as it pertained to the personification of spiritual beings (*atua*). In Māori mythology the Sky Father (Ranginui) and Earth Mother (Papatūānuku) had six or seven (depending on tribal tradition) children, each one related to a natural phenomenon:

Atua	*Associations with natural phenomena*
Tāwhiri-mātea (Tāwhiri)	The father of the winds, clouds, rain, hail, snow, and storms
Tū-mata-uenga (Tū)	The father of humankind and *atua* of war
Rongo-mā-tāne (Rongo)	The father of cultivated food and *atua* of peace
Tangaroa	The father of the ocean/sea and its creatures
Tāne-mahuta (Tāne)	The father of forests and birds
Haumia-tiketike (Haumia)	The father of uncultivated food

A seventh offspring common to Māori creation narratives is:

Rūaumoko	The *atua* of earthquakes

Māori spoke both of the *tapu* of the *atua* and of the natural phenomena with which they associated the *atua*. They, also, spoke of both specific persons (such as a teacher, chief, or holy person) and groups of persons (such as war parties, canoe builders, or fishnet makers) as *tapu*. Moreover, particular objects (such as a cloak, a canoe, or a war club) were *tapu*; particular places (such as ancestor houses, burial areas, ritual areas, or areas under a temporary ban) were *tapu*; particular times (such as those for planting, harvesting, hunting, or gathering) were *tapu*; and certain conditions (such a woman's time of menstruation) were *tapu*. Some *tapu* could be imposed and if imposed could be lifted. Even a latrine had a certain *tapu*. It is easy enough to understand the early European confusion.

Is there a common thread running through all these examples of *tapu*, one which an application of analogy of proportion and analogy of proper proportionality can illuminate; and if so, how does it relate to power relations? Shirres was correct when he recognized that "the primary notion of *tapu*" is "being with potentiality for power"[37] or "source of power."[38] Let us refer to it simply as "potential power." In the Māori world, everything in existence is imbued with power; and not only is it always present, it may also find practical expression. But the presence and practical expression of power will always be to the degree determined by the nature of the object, entity, condition, or designation. This is not power as Westerners normally understand the term. This power has a spiritual base which is fundamental to the very nature of reality itself, which Māori express in terms of the very nature of the *atua* of their mythology; everything in existence is interrelated and *tapu* according to its nature.

How does the analogy of proportion and analogy of proper proportionality inform our understanding of *tapu* as potential power? Let us first consider the analogy of proportion; that of extended meanings. There are six instances of intrinsic *tapu* which provide primary meanings and supply content to secondary meanings or extensions. These six intrinsic *tapu* derive from the children of the Earth Mother and the Sky Father; Māori associate them with the broad categories of natural phenomena as listed above. At the broadest level, natural phenomena represent the invisible *atua*. From these, we will consider one example, the human race, to inform the application of the analogy of proportion.

Māori connect the source of this *tapu* with the *atua* named Tū-mata-uenga, the father of humankind (also, the *atua* of war). The human race is *tapu* because of its association with Tū. There are then certain things, places, and events that derive their *tapu* as extensions of the primary *tapu* of the human race. For instance, people build houses, make and wear clothes, use their hands, have babies, plant and harvest crops, and go to war. On the basis of analogy of proportion, we may apply the primary general meaning of *tapu* (having potential power) to an array of things and events as extensions of the primary meaning. The human race is *tapu* in a primary sense; but such things as hands, houses, clothes, haircuts, births, plantings, harvestings, and battles are *tapu* by extension. Māori people understand what it means for the human race to be *tapu* and this supplies particular content for what it means for hands, houses, clothes, haircuts, births, plantings, harvestings, and battles to be *tapu*. Māori know the secondary meaning because of its reference to the primary meaning.

On the basis of the analogy of proper proportionality, *tapu* (again, broadly defined as imbued with potential power), whether intrinsic or by extension, is relative to its particular context. Here we turn from our specific example of the human race to a consideration of all contexts. For instance, a place with potential power (e.g., a burial place) is different from an event with potential power (e.g., a harvest), but each possesses potential power in accordance with its own context, the strength of which is relative to its perceived importance which varies according to its category. Accordingly, the power of a funeral is different from the power of a kūmara crop (a type of potato particularly important to Māori tribes; a sacred crop), but each has power relative to its context and according to Māori understanding of its urgency. As discussed earlier, the most important event on the *marae* is the *tangihanga* (rites for the dead), but the kūmara harvest is also important and powerful in its own place, time, and way.

The sundry notions about *tapu* expressed in Māori dictionaries (such as prohibited, restricted, forbidden, and set apart) accompany the worldview that everything in existence is infused with potential power. As derivatives of this primary meaning, we may agree with Shirres that events, items, entities, etc., are not prohibited, restricted, forbidden, or set apart and therefore *tapu*; rather, they are *tapu* and therefore prohibited, restricted, forbidden, or set apart.[39] *Tapu* generates both respect and fear.

The various primary *tapu* have their origin in the offspring of the Sky Father and Earth Mother which are visually represented by natural phenomena; the *atua* are personifications of the natural world. In Māori mythology these *atua* are never static; they are dynamic and often in conflict with one another. In the natural world, the power of *tapu* becomes most apparent when the winds clash with the forests or when the winds or the sea challenge humankind. But challenges can extend even into associations with life sustaining food, both cultivated and uncultivated. Thus, *tapu* does not exist in some disjunctive realm of psychic or spiritual ambiguity; rather, it is grounded in the experiences of everyday life as a very real and present force; the potential of which each person must be aware and with which each person must contend either in its primary sense or through a secondary extension. It is significant that notions of uncleanness, defilement, contamination, or pollution are applicable only secondarily and never in a primary sense. Notably, Māori developed rites and *karakia* (incantations; ritual chants; prayers) to manage the forces of *tapu*. The associations and interactions of the various *tapu* are fundamental to Māori society.

The concept of *noa* is intertwined with the concept of *tapu* so closely that persons have sometimes treated the concepts as antonyms in defining one against the other: if *tapu* means "sacred" then *noa* means "profane." For instance, to expand an example mentioned by Shirres,[40] the kūmara (again, a type of potato particularly important to Māori tribes; a sacred crop) is intrinsically *tapu* because it is the primary phenomenal expression of Rongo-mā-tāne, the *atua* of cultivated food; just as the human race is intrinsically *tapu* because of its association with Tū-mata-uenga. Human hands are *tapu* because they are part of a human person. During the time of planting, Māori hands would contact the kūmara, and consequently, the *tapu* of the kūmara would become extended to the human hands; therefore, Māori must reconcile the *tapu* which derives from Rongo-mā-tāne (*atua* of cultivated food) with that which derives from Tū-mata-uenga (*atua* of humankind). They must remove the kūmara's *tapu* from their hands before they can use them for everyday routine activities, and consequently would perform certain procedures for that purpose. This is tantamount to and an example of maintaining proper respect and appreciation for each feature of their world, each according to its kind. These procedures would render their hands *noa*. At first glance *noa* appears to cancel *tapu* and consequently many persons have treated the two terms as antonyms.

However, treating the terms as antonyms goes a step too far. *Noa* is directly opposed only to the *extension* of intrinsic *tapu*, not to intrinsic *tapu* itself.[41] In the example of the kūmara, the human person's hands are *tapu* by virtue of being human and the kūmara's intrinsic *tapu* has been extended to human hands; however, rendering the hands *noa* does not affect either the *tapu* of the person's hands or the kūmara's intrinsic *tapu*. It affects only the *extension* of the kūmara's intrinsic *tapu*, which resulted from human contact with the plant. It is in this sense that *noa* means ordinary, unrestricted, or void. *Noa* is not an antonym to *tapu*, but its complement; a state of *tapu* normalcy, of reconciliation, of harmony. It is the absence of any conflict between and among the various *tapu*. Powers are arranged in their place and not actively contending with one another. The practical importance of *noa* is that without it no one could get on with routine daily activities.

We can now turn to a consideration of *mana* as a term more closely related to active power. Above we have presented *tapu* as potential power and have mentioned that potential power can become quite active. But how is power manifested in Māori society? *Mana* and *tapu* are closely related terms. In fact, researchers have confirmed that several 19th century Māori manuscripts treat the terms as virtually interchangeable.[42] This notwithstanding, there is, as the researchers have also understood, a difference in the meaning of the two terms, but it is one which allows for their seeming interchangeability; in other words, the difference can be quite subtle. A popular way to express this often blurred relationship is to view *mana* as the compelling and unceasingly active quality of charisma. Whereas members of Western society might be prone to understand charisma as a natural quality alone, for members of Māori society it emanates from a spiritual base; for them it is grounded in the *atua* and applicable to everything they represent. *Mana*, as the active power of charisma, complements and legitimizes *tapu* as potential power.

We owe Māori academic and Anglican priest Māori Marsden (1924–1993) a debt for his insight and ability to explain *mana* using two words from Christian Biblical Greek: ἐξουσια (exousia) and δυναμις (dunamis or dynamis).[43] However, it is helpful to somewhat expand his treatment. Ἐξουσια (exousia) is a derivative of ἐξεστι (exesti), an impersonal verb which means "it is possible," "it is permitted," "it is lawful"[44]; hence, ἐξουσια combines the ideas of potential power and approval. Persons often translate it as "authority" in the sense that it means lawful permission; in other words, delegated authority. As it pertains to *mana*, in the Māori world, as Marsden pointed out, the *atua*, as the source of power, do the delegating. The possessor of *mana* to whom or which power is delegated (i.e., gifted) is the channel for the power of the *atua*.[45] Δυναμις (dunamis or dynamis) expresses a second aspect of *mana*; specifically, power as the "strength" and "ability" to carry out a task.[46] This power to perform resides in someone or something by virtue of the nature of the person or other unit.

These two aspects of *mana* combine to produce a complete idea. *Mana* derives from the *atua* and is channeled through persons, objects, seasons, conditions, natural phenomena, etc., as delegated permission, accompanied by the ability, to act on behalf of the *atua*.[47] This is how Māori can speak of the *mana* of the land, or the sea, or a mountain, or a river, etc., in addition to the *mana* of a person. Everything in existence possesses not only potential power in accordance with its nature; it is also endowed with the permission, strength, and ability to exercise power on behalf of the *atua*. Moreover, just as *tapu* can clash with *tapu*, so can *mana* clash with *mana*, and a person's view of it as positive or negative is relative to that person's particular position in the clash.

Both *tapu* and *mana* have to do with power and are so closely related that they are sometimes seemingly used interchangeably; however, on close examination there is a difference. *Tapu* is more closely related to a condition while *mana* is more closely related to a practical force actively at work. *Tapu* is more closely associated with the condition of being set apart while *mana* is more closely associated with the activity within and among persons and things that are set apart. *Tapu* is to *mana* as potential is to expression. *Mana* takes imbuement with potential power a step further; potential power becomes active as the charisma of the existent, which then finds quite practical expressions according to the nature of the existent. Personal *mana* is often associated with prestige, pride, dignity, and honor.

If this discussion seems a bit abstract, it is because the concepts definitely are. In fact it took the European colonialists more than a century to begin to understand the abstractions. Furthermore, lest Westerners become too haughty in their judgment of such a tribal worldview, they should remember that their predominant religion understands, either literally or metaphorically, the Earth to be the battle ground of spiritual powers; those of God above in conflict with those of Satan below. They view themselves as engaged in a spiritual warfare between what they see as good and evil. They recite prayers of deliverance from evil, perform acts of penance and contrition, and participate in sacraments to ensure their right standing with God and perhaps ward-off God's chastisement sometimes delivered through natural phenomena. The difference is that Westerners tend to understand power in terms of dependence, and in their religion see themselves as unwittingly caught up in a struggle; whereas Māori view power in terms of the interrelation of the natural world, of which they are an integral part, and the *atua* which permeate it.

These three concepts of *tapu*, *noa*, and *mana* combine with the concept of *utu* to establish the four corners of a Māori worldview. Specifically, *utu*, as the primary form of Māori reciprocity, was and is a means of increasing and protecting *mana* and is thus entwined with the concepts of *tapu*, *noa*, and *mana*. Importantly, both historically and today these four notions underlie all Māori social, political, and economic interaction. These ideas are functions of a "spiritualized" culture and radically different from the exchange forms and practices dictated by the Western marketplace. For this reason, the Western reciprocity forms of the previous chapter and the view of the operation of power within and among those forms of this present chapter tend to break down not only as testable phenomena but also structurally when persons attempt to apply them to Māori culture.

The secularized Pākehā

The terms "spiritualized" and "secularized" and their derivatives characterize the way different cultures think and behave. Just as Māori as a "spiritualized" people view the world and behave within it in terms of such concepts as *tapu, noa, mana,* and *utu,* which originate with their primal "gods" and permeate and determine the course of the whole of life, Pākehā as a "secularized" people view the world as one in which spiritual concepts and institutions are compartmentalized within and sometimes removed from the main stream of their society. The Māori world is replete with spiritual beings and forces; the Pākehā world is either bereft of them or contains them in their "proper" place. The Māori world is an enchanted world. The Pākehā world is largely disenchanted.

While the underlying factor for the onset of secularization in the Western world was the rise of modern science, the decisive event(s) was the rise of Protestantism. The Protestant Reformation, which officially began in 1517, breached the unity of church and state (commonly called Christendom). Where both the religious and political institutions had once projected and reinforced one another in the same enchanted worldview, a fragmentation ensued that allowed not only for greater religious variation and tolerance but also aided the rise of science on equal footing with religion. The disenchantment of the Western world was well established by the time of Captain Cook's expeditions (his initial arrival in Aotearoa/New Zealand was in 1769) and has been apparent in Pākehā associations with Māori ever since. The European colonialists arrived in Aotearoa/New Zealand as a secularized people, with both a religious and a non-religious sphere of life.

Importantly, the processes of secularization were not limited to the non-ecclesiastical domain. They were also apparent in the arrival and activity of the Christian missionaries, the primary sign of which was Christian factions competing for resources and converts just as the businesses, which preceded and followed the missionaries' arrival, competed for resources and profits. This phenomenon is well documented throughout the interaction of Europeans and Māori, beginning with the earliest Christian groups. The Anglican based Church Missionary Society (CMS) that arrived in Aotearoa/New Zealand in 1814, the Methodist based Wesleyan Missionary Society (WMS) that followed in 1822, Roman Catholicism that came in 1838, and the other major denominations which made the trip illustrate not only the fragmentation of Christendom into various factions but also how they are overall in competition with one another, although they may cooperate under particular circumstances.

Another sign of secularization was the bureaucratic way of conducting affairs by both religious and non-religious institutions and the application of European economic principles to those ends; religious institutions conducted business using a Western business model and non-religious institutions conducted business *as* non-religious institutions. In particular, the latter is apparent in Pākehā conduct from the outset of their relations with Māori, and highly visible examples include the Treaty of Waitangi in 1840, the imposition of a parliamentary form of government in the 1850s, and the establishment of the land courts in the 1860s.

Let us again recall that the previous chapter's discussion of social exchange theory's categories and the present chapter's presentation of the operation of power as inextricable from dependence within and among those social exchange categories are descriptions of the structures and processes of a secularized society. Social exchange theorists' work draws attention to the *secularized* actor's mind-set and values in which the principles at work are

Western economic principles and in which the legitimizing processes do not extend past the marketplace. The principles of reciprocity expressed as power-dependence relations are useful for understanding Pākehā ideas about and use of power precisely because the power-dependence scheme itself is a product of a secularized worldview.

We may state the Pākehā secularized power-dependence perspective as related to Māori as follows: The power of the colonialists over the indigenous population is directly proportional to the dependence of the indigenous population on the colonialists; and reciprocally, the power of the indigenous population over the colonialists is directly proportional to the dependence of the colonialists on the indigenous population. Therefore, if the indigenous population is so independent as to deny power to the colonialists, the colonialists, if they are to have a power advantage, must find ways to make the indigenous population more dependent. As we shall see, Emerson's four basic balancing (or imbalancing) operations are useful for describing how Pākehā accomplished that purpose. Importantly, British annexation of Aotearoa/New Zealand in 1840 took place within the context of their worldwide imperialist and colonial activities with both political and economic motives. Their focus was the acquisition of the Māori resource to which they assigned a very high value, specifically, the land; and we should understand Pākehā procurement of Māori land within the context of a shifting balance of power.

For several decades after European arrival in Aotearoa/New Zealand power was decidedly tilted in favor of Māori tribes. The missionaries, the first of which arrived in 1814, were dependent on the indigenous population, even to the point of trading muskets for food, shelter, and protection. There are other examples of the power imbalance. For instance, in 1808 the crew of the *Parramatta* attempted to avoid paying Māori for goods and wounded three Māori in the process; when somehow their vessel wrecked, Māori apprehended and killed the crew.[48] Additionally, there was the *Boyd* incident of 1809,[49] in which Māori killed most of the crew of the British sailing ship and ate some of them in retribution (*utu*) for a perceived insult to a Māori chief's son. This incident caused the missionaries to delay their arrival until 1814. Even into the late 1830s, the number of European permanent settlers likely totaled not many more than 2,000,[50] a number that could easily have been extinguished by Māori warriors. Many Māori were willing to trade with the Europeans and some even welcomed them, but theft and thoughtless behavior were dangerous practices.

In terms of sheer population, Māori outnumbered Pākehā for a considerable time, but by the late 1850s this had changed. Aotearoans/New Zealanders took their first general census in 1851; it included only Pākehā and showed a population of 26,707,[51] a significant increase from the 2,000 or so of the late 1830s. They took a second general census of only Pākehā in 1854, but the results were unusable.[52] The next census came in 1858, included both Māori and Pākehā, and recorded a total population of 115,461 of which 56,049 or about 48.5 percent were Māori.[53] Significantly, this shows a steep drop in Māori population from the estimated 100,000 to 120,000 at the turn of the 18th to the 19th century.[54] Notably, Pākehā population surpassed Māori population in the 1850s. It is indeed interesting that the process of establishing a parliamentary system of government in Aotearoa/New Zealand between 1852 and 1854 happened at roughly the same time that the two populations became equal. The balance of population and the strength of organized government permanently shifted to Pākehā in the 1850s, and by 1896 the population of Māori tribes had fallen to slightly more than 42,000 in an aggregate population of a little more than 743,000,[55] which is less than 6 percent of the total. This was largely due to wars, disease, and despair.

According to Emerson, the reciprocity of power relations raises the question of balance or imbalance of power; that is, in a dyadic relationship each party has something at stake in relation to the other, in which the power of each actor presents itself as some sort of challenge to the other. Changes in power balance are actually changes in the structure of the relationship which entail two issues. The first issue is characterized by one actor having something that the other actor, in some measure, wants ("motivational investment"[56]). The second issue involves the ability of each actor to get what they value from another source (outside source "availability"[57]). Māori people valued many European goods and services such as reading and writing, farming techniques, implements of war, metal tools, and medicine; and Pākehā valued Aotearoa/New Zealand resources such as whales, seals, and greenstone, but they particularly valued the land. The conflict between the two has included other issues, such as Māori sovereignty; indeed, Māori view the issues of land and sovereignty as inextricable. But the highlight for the present discussion is the land; Pākehā wanted to take it while Māori wanted to keep it. Each actor in the dyad had a strong motivational investment in a resource for which there were no outside sources. The British could and did acquire land in other places, but they had motivational interest as Aotearoan/New Zealand colonialists in this particular land because it provided some strategic advantages; for one thing, they perceived a vested interest in keeping the French out of this part of the world.

Let us remember that Emerson discussed four possible operations that work to change the structure of power in a dyadic relationship. To briefly recount them[58]:

1. The weaker party may reduce its motivational investment in goals mediated by the stronger party which weakens the power of the stronger party.
2. The weaker party may find alternative sources for the values mediated by the stronger party which reduces the power of the stronger party.
3. The stronger party may increase its motivational investment in goals mediated by the weaker party which increases the power of the weaker party.
4. The weaker party (or some other circumstance or party) may block the stronger party's access to alternative sources which increases the power of the weaker party.

Two of the four operations involve motivational investment and two entail access to alternative resources. The lack of Pākehā access to an alternative source for this particular land and Māori lack of access to Pākehā resources, both perceived and actual, eliminate Emerson's second and fourth operations from consideration. The two operations that remain have to do with motivational investment. The first would entail a withdrawal by Pākehā (at this time the weaker party) of their motivational investment which would weaken the power of Māori (at this time the stronger party) but would also serve to deny them the Māori resource they most valued, an operation which did not occur. Instead, Pākehā stepped-up their procurement activities and committed even greater resources to the acquisition of Māori land. This strengthened their position in two ways.

First, Pākehā (at this time the weaker party) escalated their procurement activities in such a way as to increase Māori (at this time the stronger party) motivational investment in resources mediated by Pākehā; this resulted in Māori willingness to part with some of their land (Emerson's third power balancing operation). Emerson presented the operation of increasing the stronger actor's motivational investment in the context of the issues of ego-gratification and status hierarchies in *intra-group* relations. However, in this case it applies to Māori seeking to increase their *mana*. In this context, the idea of the weaker actor's increasing the motivational investment of the stronger actor is also an *inter-group* opera-tion. Second, the escalated procurement activities of Pākehā simply overwhelmed Māori by the sheer strength of Pākehā technology and civilian and military personnel which ex-ceeded the boundaries of exchange per se and entered the realm of conquest through colo-nization and assimilation.

Whereas Māori association with the land was permeated by spiritual principles, Pākehā association with the land was built on secularized strategic and economic prin-ciples. For Māori the land was sacred; for Pākehā the land was a mere commodity to be bought and sold.

Synergistic potential

Chapter Two of this book describes the interaction of Māori and Pākehā as the en-counter of symbols. Chapter Three discusses reciprocity and concludes that the encounter of symbols has a synergistic potential that becomes actual when cultures, as a result of their exchange in sensitivity to one another, either reinterpret their symbols or give birth to new ones; and that the reinterpretation of culture is essentially the evolution of symbols. This current chapter establishes a power relations perspective from which to discuss the syner-gistic evolution of symbols in Aotearoa/New Zealand, and derives its categories from a view of Māori as a "spiritualized" people and Pākehā as a "secularized" people.

From their first arrival in Aotearoa/New Zealand, the Pākehā secularized worldview has challenged Māori tribes. Conversely, from their first encounter, the spiritualized world-view of Māori tribes has confronted Pākehā colonialists. This has set the stage for a syner-gistic reinterpretation of both cultures through a synthesis of secular rational principles and spiritual recognitions. On the one hand, such a synergy entails the worldview of Māori tribes, which includes spiritual principles that bespeak the life and literal interconnected-ness of everything and everyone. The Māori viewpoint includes the recognition that every aspect of existence—past, present, and future—is bound in the same reality, and an un-derstanding of everything and everyone as set apart and possessing power in its, his, and her own way (by virtue of association with the *atua* as personifications of every aspect of the natural world), a perception which then finds expression in the treatment of all that exists with the appropriate respect and commitment. On the other hand, such a synergy entails Pākehā expansion of rational economic and scientific principles and their practical application. This synthesis presents itself as a kind of re-enchantment of the world in which respect for the life and interconnectedness of the cosmos combines with sound science. The result is a worldview in which commitment to task is so great that it demands painstaking research to find and develop increasingly better ways of caring.

We need look no further than Aotearoa/New Zealand ecology for a context from which to view this re-enchantment as a merging of Māori myth and Pākehā ritual. On the one hand, Māori mythology expresses the life and interdependence of every aspect of ex-istence. To briefly reiterate a popular version of the Māori creation narrative: Papatūānuku (the Earth Mother) and Ranginui (the Sky Father), the earth and the sky, gave birth to six children (*atua*), and each one is associated with something fundamental to Māori life. Tāwhiri has to do with atmospheric phenomenon such as the winds, clouds, rain, hail, snow and storms; Rongo with cultivated food and peace; Haumia with uncultivated food; Tanga-roa with the sea and its contents; Tāne with forests, birds, and insects; and Tū-mata-uenga, with the human race and war. The *atua*, and by extension their visual representations, have a family connection. On the other hand, Pākehā ritual, expressed through the application of science, conjures up and reinforces the stories of aliveness and interconnection. For instance, the techniques of responsible forestry that are integral to a sustainable timber industry are repeated cyclically at each timber crop's location, thus becoming a sort of ritual. In 1993, Aotearoa/New Zealand amended its Forest Act 1949[59] to end the unsustainable harvesting and clear-felling of indigenous forest.[60] The Forest Act now defines sustainable forest management as:

> management of an area of indigenous forest land in a way that maintains the ability of the forest
> growing on that land to continue to provide a full range of products and amenities in perpetuity while
> retaining the forest's natural values.[61]

This repetitive ritualistic application of scientific procedures for a sustainable timber industry summons mental images of the interdependence of all life and becomes a physical declaration of the general interconnectedness of everything and everyone and humankind's specific stake in the health of Tāne's trees.

On a cosmic level, the application of Emerson's power-dependence principle to this re-enchantment yields the following: The power of the cosmos over humankind is directly proportional to humankind's dependence on the cosmos, and the power of humankind over the cosmos is directly proportional to the cosmos's dependence on humankind. Application of this principle leads to the following conclusion: the cosmos has as many other sources for generating life as there are planets and other environments capable of spawning and sustaining it, but humankind has no alternative resource for a world to inhabit; therefore, humankind has an infinitely greater motivational investment in the nurture and maintenance of their part of the cosmos than the cosmos has in the nurture and maintenance of humankind. It is hardly necessary to spell out in detail how this principle applies nationally.

On a cultural level, the "secularized" Pākehā appear to be reinterpreting their symbols under the illumination of Māori spirituality, and conversely the "spiritualized" Māori appear to be reinterpreting their symbols in the light of Pākehā science and economics. Because the power structure in Aotearoa/New Zealand has been so strongly tilted toward Pākehā since the 1850s, this cultural synthesis currently appears as a sort of re-enchantment of the Pākehā world. This re-enchantment is not only furnishing a basis for environmental action and an approach to understanding humankind's cosmic dependence, it is also underpinning the Māori renaissance and the nation's present commitment to biculturalism.

CHAPTER FIVE

Culture and Religion

The way we are

As the Golden Rule is about reciprocity and the American Constitution is about power, so the American National Anthem is as expression of culture and religion; the association of the two terms articulated in its reference to the most obvious symbol of the United States, the American flag. Of course, compared to the one of today, the flag looked somewhat different (it had 15 stars and 15 stripes) in mid–September 1814 when, during the War of 1812, the British were bombarding Fort McHenry at Baltimore in Maryland.[1] It was at that time that Francis Scott Key penned his poem, "Defence of Fort M'Henry," which soon appeared in newspapers and gained reputation. Before the end of September of that same year it had been set to the music of a popular tune, "To Anacreon in Heaven," and not long afterward was assigned the title of "The Star-Spangled Banner." Its popularity increased throughout the 19th century, and in 1889 the United States Navy recognized it for official use, as did President Woodrow Wilson by executive order in 1916. In 1917 both the United States Army and Navy assigned it the status of "national anthem" for ceremonies, but in was not until 4 March 1931 that the song was officially recognized and designated the American National Anthem; on that morning President Herbert Hoover signed a bill making it so. Interestingly, it was the Veterans of Foreign Wars (VFW) that petitioned for "The Star-Spangled Banner" to be the American National Anthem.[2]

Most Americans are very familiar with the anthem's first verse; it is usually performed before American sporting matches[3] and may precede or conclude numerous other events. Americans commonly know that it describes the poet's anxiety about the outcome of the battle for the fort and his anticipation that the flag would still be flying over the fort come the dawn. It goes as follows:

> Oh, say, can you see, by the dawn's early light,
> What so proudly we hailed at the twilight's last gleaming?
> Whose broad stripes and bright stars, thro' the perilous fight'
> O'er the ramparts we watched, were so gallantly streaming.
> And the rockets' red glare, the bombs bursting in air,
> Gave proof through the night that our flag was still there.
> Oh, say, does that star-spangled banner yet wave
> O'er the land of the free and the home of the brave?

Many Americans, however, may not know that there are three other verses; and if they are aware of it, they are likely to be unfamiliar with the lyrics. The second verse first describes the poet's view of the fort through the sea mists at the dawn, and then gives way to his jubilance at seeing the flag still hoisted above the fort at the first light beams of the new day. Verse two goes like this:

> On the shore dimly seen, thro' the mists of the deep,
> Where the foe's haughty host in dread silence reposes,
> What is that which the breeze, o'er the towering steep,
> As it fitfully blows, half conceals, half discloses?
> Now it catches the gleam of the morning's first beam,
> In full glory reflected, now shines on the stream;
> 'Tis the star-spangled banner: oh, long may it wave
> O'er the land of the free and the home of the brave.

The third verse inquires after those attackers who would do away with the newly formed country: "Where are they?" asks the author. He replies that their blood has washed away their pollution of the land, they have no place to hide, and the flag still flies over the infant nation. Notice the line, "No refuge could save the hireling and slave...." "Hireling" appears to be a reference to British mercenaries, but what about the reference to "slave?" Some believe that it "is a direct reference to the British practice of Impressment (kidnapping American seamen and forcing them into service on British man-of war ships)," and list such conscription as a key contributor to the War of 1812.[4] Others, however, point out that "[b]y 1810, more than 15 percent of the U.S. population was enslaved, and British forces recruited escaped slaves to fight for the slaves' freedom against the American militia."[5] For these persons the reference is to black people fighting for their liberty and that of other slaves against a nation which would enslave another human being.[6] This latter view tends to bring into better focus the recent refusal of Black American athletes to stand for the performance of the American National Anthem at sporting events. Here is verse three:

> And where is that band who so vauntingly swore
> That the havoc of war and the battle's confusion
> A home and a country should leave us no more?
> Their blood has wash'd out their foul footstep's pollution.
> No refuge could save the hireling and slave
> From the terror of flight or the gloom of the grave,
> And the star-spangled banner in triumph doth wave
> O'er the land of the free and the home of the brave.

Finally, in the last verse, the poet mentions God. Here, the author expresses both intense patriotism and deep religiosity. As far as he is concerned, the new nation is a heaven rescued land preserved by transcendent power. For him, as the American cause is just (and Francis Scott Key certainly believed it was), God is on the side of Americans. According to the author, the country's motto should be "In God is our Trust." Verse four is as follows:

> Oh, thus be it ever when free men shall stand,
> Between their loved homes and the war's desolation;
> Blest with vict'ry and peace, may the heav'n-rescued land
> Praise the Power that has made and preserved us as a nation.
> Then conquer we must, when our cause is just,
> And this be our motto: "In God is our trust";
> And the star-spangled banner in triumph shall wave
> O'er the land of the free and the home of the brave.

So, what conclusions may we draw about the "culture" of the United States and its relation to "religion" from a consideration of the country's national anthem? On the one hand, the anthem is about the way Americans *perceive things to essentially be*. They generally see the nation as the gift of God and themselves as largely putting their trust in God for the national welfare. They, also, broadly believe that God will aid the country when the cause is a just one. Largely, for them, the establishment and continuance of the nation is an indication that wars about American independence and survival are just wars. For most Americans, military victory and national peace go hand in hand with their trust in God.

But on the other hand, *the national anthem is a counterpoint to the perception*; it brings to bear the judgment of history and a revelation of the way things actually are. First, "The Star-Spangled Banner" is a war song which connects American patriotism to dependence on God and both to military victory; it is about freedom through bravery in the dispensing of legal and morally justified violence. Second, the correct view of the term "slave" in verse three notwithstanding, the anthem perpetuates an attitude of haughtiness and racial superiority. According to the anthem, America is a "heaven rescued land." Expressed in the context of the 19th century throughout which the song became popular, it reflects the attitude of factions within the 19th century American Government and military establishment to continue the British practice of colonization on the North American continent through the policy, as we learned it in high school, of "Manifest Destiny."[7] The term was first used in the 1840s, but the attitude was present in Key's poem. It was obvious to the politicians and the settlers that this was a God-established land and that Providence had preordained the country to extend from coast to coast; notwithstanding that such occupation would entail the theft of the indigenous population's land, the death of thousands of indigenous people, and the relegation of the survivors to reservations, accompanied by a status of social, religious, and political inferiority. In short, even though the Constitution prevented Americans from establishing a state religion, they succeeded in connecting religion and politics; they combined extreme patriotism, greed, and a form of religiosity. The haughtiness expressed in the taken-for-granted blessings of God, which underpinned the notion of Manifest Destiny, that this land is ordained by God to be as it is, has continued through the nation's 20th century wars and into the 21st century. Third, although the anthem acknowledges God, it expresses a secular perspective on reality. It recognizes God, but not until its last verse; this is primarily a patriotic poem, not a religious one. While this does not diminish the author's religiosity, it places it in perspective within his patriotism. As in all the countries affected by the Protestant Reformation, religion is compartmentalized and often God is summoned only when necessary to make a religious, social, political, or economic point. Today, religion-backed initiatives may help the impoverished, diseased, etc.; and Americans may call upon God in times of distress, generally recognize God's power, and seek God's assistance in various matters. Nonetheless, the nation remains mostly disenchanted; American legitimizing processes are as likely to be rooted in society, politics, and economics as in religion.

So how does an analysis of the American Star-Spangled Banner inform our understanding of the nature of culture and its relation to religion? Culture refers to the way people in community essentially understand their past, perceive their present, aspire their future, and actually seek to fulfill their aspirations; and religion is a complementary aspect of culture. Concisely stated, our culture, which includes its religious expressions, is simply *the way we are.*

This book's previous chapters treat reciprocity and power separately for explanatory purposes while understanding them as inextricably related; that is, power is unceasingly operative within the structures of reciprocity irrespective of the model. The current chapter takes a similar approach to culture and religion. This chapter treats culture and religion separately, but then shows how they complement one another. It then presents the complementary relationship as the religio-cultural context for the reciprocity of power relations and a background from which we may understand the specific cultural interchange of Māori and Pākehā.

Culture

There is a sense in which anthropology, broadly defined as "the study of humankind," reaches into our kind's most distant recollections. However, let us begin our consideration of anthropology, as an academic discipline, more recently with a framework of four fields of study.[8] Archaeological anthropology studies the human species by examining the prehistoric past; it includes an investigation of human remains, evidence of human activity, and climatic, ecological, and geological processes as they pertain to the development of humankind. Biological (sometimes called physical) anthropology addresses the evolution and diversity of the human species. Linguistic anthropology looks into the development of language(s), how they are related, and how they have affected human life. And cultural anthropology examines the development and variation of human culture(s). As with the oceans of the world, these areas of interest overlap and often there is no clear division between and among them.

However, of these four groupings, the general public may largely have an adequate grasp of what doing prehistoric archaeology is about, including how climate changes and natural geological processes can affect the way people live and develop. It also may have a broad understanding of what it means to look into human evolutionary development. Moreover, the public at large certainly knows something of how important language is in the daily lives of persons and how languages can be related. But culture, even defined as the way we fundamentally are, seems to be an elusive term with a variety of contexts. We say that a person who is refined in etiquette and manners is cultured; so with a person who is knowledgeable of the arts such as music, dance, painting, and theatre (certainly not an exhaustive list). Biologists use bacterial cultures, and botanists use plant cultures. But the use of the word "culture" as it pertains to the life of the human species can indeed be difficult to firmly grasp. We can speak of culture generically; asking the question of when and how culture, however defined, initially arose and developed. But we can also relate culture to a particular group (say, ourselves as a nation) in which case, as previously mentioned, it is about the kind of people we are. Moreover, while we believe that we have a firm grasp of some features of ourselves, we acknowledge difficulties in comprehending other aspects. To intensify the problem, serious issues often pop-up when we try to come to terms with the way other groups of people are. Such is the nature of cultural anthropology.

This book uses the term anthropology as it relates to culture in a way somewhat different than simply a description of the way people live. Here is means cultural analysis; it investigates and seeks to understand and organize the various elements of the structure of that which we call culture, but it goes beyond description to include interpretation. In other words, it surpasses chronicling how a people live; it attempts to understand the meaning persons associate with their actions and how they organize that meaning into a system of symbols. This chapter addresses the following questions: At the most obvious and, of course, most familiar level, how do we *meaningfully* talk about the way we are, and at a less obvious and less familiar level, how do we *meaningfully* talk about the way others are?

We are indebted to American anthropologist Clifford Geertz for applying the expression "thick description,"[9] a term which he borrowed from Oxford philosopher Gilbert Ryle,[10] to anthropology. Geertz used this concept as the methodological thread to join together his diverse essays; it was his *modus operandi* for sorting out how people integrate their experience in and of the world in an openly observable system of symbols which makes the world and their experience understandable for them and guides their affairs. "Thin description" merely describes what the observer observes; "thick description" attempts to interpret the meaning underlying what the observer observes. While this approach does not deny the importance of individual psychologies, it views those psychologies as not confined to the private sphere of individuals; it understands them as both overtly displayed symbolic human action and set forth in a public system of symbols.[11] This is interpretive anthropology. Although some view interpretive anthropology as somewhat anachronistic,[12] we shall soon see that, while it may be dated in some respects, it remains a contemporarily suitable anthropological method; it still furnishes a viable, perhaps the most viable, perspective from which to view the interaction of diverse cultures such as Māori and Pākehā.

Human persons are hard-wired to make sense of and organize their experience in and of the world. This human propensity has undergirded the ascent of humankind in all of its aspects, including the development of religion and the rise of science. Human life is essentially the pursuit of meaning; the fundamental human task is to make sense of the world in order to make life as comfortable and fulfilling as possible and to assure, in-so-far as it is achievable, the survival of the species. To this end, human persons arrange their experience in and of the world in particular patterns which reflect their interpretation of their experience, and they store those interpreted patterns in a complex of symbols which serves to perpetuate the community. An examination of a culture is an examination of how a people corporately sort-out their experience, the analysis of a culture is essentially an attempt to understand its meaning systems, and a study of the encounter of radically different cultures (such as Māori and Pākehā) is actually an examination of how highly divergent meaning systems interact.

The organizing principle of interpretive anthropology, that which Geertz called "thick description," shifts the emphasis of cultural analysis away from a mere report of how a group of people behaves, that is, what they do and how they live (thin description), to an attempt to understand the meaning behind what they do and how they live (thick description). This interpretive task gets to the very bedrock of human existence; specifically, the obsession to give form and order to human experience. As Geertz observed, this fixation is as basic to human life as any human biological urge.[13]

Because culture (the way we are; or for that matter, the way any group is), as the imposition of form and order on human experience in fulfillment of the drive to make sense of human existence, is fundamental to the human species, culture is as old as humankind itself. John H. Morgan in his very readable book, *"In the Beginning...": The Paleolithic Origins of Religious Consciousness*,[14] discusses how, for the first human beings, "ideology and behavior" were engendered by "possibility thinking," which happened when ideas fed imagination and attitudes grew "under the light of considered opportunities."[15] Thought and behavior swirled together, the outcome of which was "the development of ideology" and "action by design."[16] Within the context of Paleolithic storytelling, Morgan describes how memory of past experience and imagination directed toward future possibilities fused together into the present moment.[17] He points out that it is in this conflation of "memory and imagination" and "ideology and action" that the human endeavor to rationally order experience in "the pursuit of a hope for the future" reside.[18] These integrated characteristics underpin humankind's interpretation of experience which gives birth to cultural symbols as expressions of the meaning of the world and how the community, which includes the role of each person individually, fits in. This gives definition to the group, and this definition is what we may understand as culture.

Put another way, within the context of the evolutionary development of the human species, culture gained shape as behaviors and ideologies, myths and rituals, worldview and ethos whirlpooled into what Morgan describes as a "vortex"[19] which spewed out answers to life's most pressing questions, and a group coalesced around these "truths" in which individuals shared common values and practiced a common lifestyle. These "truths" were self-validating in the sense of a circular reference in which the group members' experience of the world and their thought pertaining to their experience declared their actions and notions that had developed out of their experience and thought to be correct ones. Morgan amalgamated these processes into a formal definition of culture:

> Culture is a complex of behaviors and ideologies consisting of rituals and myths which appeals to an **historico-temporal legitimacy** embodying a worldview and ethos addressing the verities of life and existence conveying a dynamic level of psycho/social reality which is self-validating to the individual and community.[20]

We have a specific interest in the way Morgan constructs this definition and will return to some of its particulars later on. However, the present focus is on how diverse cultures are expressions of different interpretations of the world, and how it is within the context of these cultures as meaning systems that the reciprocity of power relations takes definite forms which both express and reinforce a group's particular interpretation of its experience.

Religion

Just as a workable view of culture can be elusive, so can a viable understanding of religion. Persons have long recognized that religion can take many forms. Among the various expressions that theologians, historians, governments, etc., generally recognize as religious are the Abrahamic faiths of Judaism, Christianity, and Islam; Eastern approaches such as Hinduism, Buddhism, and Taoism; tribal spirituality such as that of the indigenous Americans or the indigenous peoples of the Polynesian islands, and quasi-religions such as the ideological systems of fascism and communism. This, of course, begs the question of a common thread that runs through all these various expressions significant enough to underpin a notion of religion that can converse, indeed be at home with, all of them. The question is not a new one and neither is that which is perhaps the most workable solution. It comes from existentialist theologian and philosopher of religion, Paul Tillich, who viewed religion "in the largest and most basic sense of the word" as "ultimate concern."[21] The property which qualifies Tillich's understanding of religion as ultimate concern as existentialist is that its origin is rooted in an internal examination of human experience as opposed to notions which are based on some direct intervention of God or some other power into human affairs from the outside. Thus, Tillich skillfully used his existentialist perspective to develop a philosophy of religion that could meaningfully converse with *any* historical religion.

While Tillich's approach may technically be a philosophical theology, we choose it because of its close association with anthropology. Tillich explains ultimate concern by telling a story in which he personifies particular human qualities: the moral function, the cognitive function, the aesthetic function, feeling, and (of course) religion,[22] an examination of which will reveal the intimate connection of ultimate concern with anthropology. The following paragraphs present Tillich's story as the first act of a two act play. The need for a second act will become apparent, and we will proffer it close after the first act; but for now, Act I has five main characters and five scenes. The main characters are Morality, Cognition, Art, Feeling, and Religion. The overall plot is simple: the first four characters have abodes, but Religion is homeless and searching for a place to live.

Scene I finds Religion embarking on its initial quest to find a permanent dwelling place. Religion goes first to the home of its nearest relative, Morality (the personification of the human moral function), where it knocks at the door with the confidence that certainly it will be welcomed. Morality does indeed invite Religion to enter and dwell there, but in the home it treats Religion as a servant. As long as Religion keeps a tidy house by underpinning the creation of good citizens, parents, politicians, soldiers, etc., it is welcome; but when Religion makes requests and demands of its own, Morality considers it dangerous, and ushers it to the door.

Scene II opens with Religion once again in the street deciding where to look next for a home. It considers the dwelling of Cognition (the personification of the human cognitive function) because, after all, they have in common an epistemological demand and both require an imagination. Religion knocks at the door, is invited in, and dwells with Cognition for a season. However, once again, Religion finds itself a servant; a sort of Cinderella which is considered inferior to another dweller in Cognition's household, Pure Knowledge. Pure Knowledge, which has been successful in cooperating with Science, develops an indifference to Religion and points out that Religion in not significantly useful in the household. Pure Knowledge, being very influential to Cognition, is responsible for Religion once again finding itself on the street.

As the curtain opens on Scene III, Religion is standing at the door of Art (the personification of the human aesthetic function). Surely, it has a permanent place with Art. Again, Religion finds itself welcome, but only if it will surrender its identity. It can stay if it will cease to acknowledge that it has a personality of its own and will surrender all interests which are unrelated to the immediate household. These demands are too great for Religion because they encroach on Religion's other concerns; while Religion could not dwell permanently with Morality and Cognition under their terms, it certainly had interests there. So Religion once again departs.

Scene IV begins with Religion at the door of (personified) Feeling. Morality and Cognition are hopeful that Religion will find a home here because, if Religion permanently dwells with Feeling, they are relieved from any obligation to hear Religion's voice. But this is the home of *Pure* Feeling. Pure Feeling lives without admixed elements; it has no emotional object. Dwelling with Pure Feeling would strip Religion of any definite expression. So Religion is once again dismayed and leaves.

Scene V is the finale of Act I. It takes the form of a soliloquy. Religion recounts its experiences with Morality, Cognition, Art, and Feeling. And as it speaks its thoughts, Religion realizes that it does not need to seek a home. Religion is never not at home; it is at home everywhere. Religion is the dimension of depth in every aspect of the human spirit; in the most fundamental way possible, Religion is ultimate concern. Religion is at home with all its fellows. It will present itself in the home of Morality as the extreme importance of integrity. It will show itself in the home of Cognition as the ardent thirst to understand the very basis of reality. It will make itself known in the home of Art as the drive to express that which is so deep as to defy other articulations. In the home of Pure Feeling it will provide an object for emotion.

Thus Tillich develops a philosophy of religion in which religion is ultimate concern; it is the dimension of depth in every aspect of human experience. Religion so understood can engage any historical religion. Thus closes Act I.

Even though the personified Religion's wayfaring visits to the various houses of the personified aspects of the human self have stood the test of time, at first glance this treatment appears to express a view of religion that is much too broad to be meaningful because it can extend to any form and content of human experience. However, on closer examination, there is some point of distinction or Tillich could not individualize his personification of religion as one thing from his personification of morality, cognition, aesthetics, and feeling as other things. What is it that makes religion, as ultimate concern, unique? The answer is found in the complementary relationship of what humankind is in terms of its own existence and what humankind is in terms larger than itself. The correlation of these two aspects of life was the driving force of Tillich's philosophy of religion. It is at this point that Act II of our two act play becomes necessary and the association of ultimate concern with anthropology becomes apparent. What religion is cannot be separated from what religion does.

Associating Clifford Geertz's interpretive anthropology with Paul Tillich's philosophy of religion helps clarify the role of religion in human society. John H. Morgan was the first to recognize the strong similarity between Geertz's and Tillich's approach. He elucidated his insight in his 1977 essay published by The University of Chicago Press, "Religion and Culture as Meaning Systems: A Dialogue between Geertz and Tillich."[23] Morgan saw that the fundamental point of convergence between the two was the human quest to interpret (to make sense of) experience in and of the world; that is, they held compatible concepts of meaning. That which Tillich expresses as "ultimate concern," Geertz articulates as the "problem of meaning," a phrase he borrowed from social theorist Max Weber (1864–1920).[24]

The problem of meaning recognizes that some events and circumstances are simply beyond the human capacity of interpretation; they are the harbingers of meaningless existence and tend to make life chaotic. As Geertz sees it, they enter human experience at three points; at the limits of human "analytic capacities," "powers of endurance," and "moral insight."[25] He calls these experiential moments "bafflement, suffering, and a sense of intractable ethical paradox"[26]; or alternatively, "ignorance, pain, and injustice."[27] Human persons cannot avoid these three. On the one hand, human experience forces persons to recognize and affirm these issues, but on the other hand persons do not want to allow these heralds of chaos the last word for the nature of reality; hence, the problem of meaning. So, people both individually and corporately attempt to manage them, the results of which have included the recognition of numerous numinous powers and entities and the spiritual efficacy of particular practices. Thus religion developed in the evolution of humankind and continues as an address to the problem of meaning.

Herein lays the appropriateness of Act II of our play. By inventing some personifications of our own based on Geertz's anthropology, we can express the practical functions of Religion as it dwells with Morality, Cognition, Art, and Feeling; the personifications of the moral, cognitive, aesthetic, and emotive functions of the human person. Act II is in five scenes with nine main characters. Morality, Cognition, Art, Feeling, and Religion return from Act I, but there are four new characters: Bafflement, Injustice, Endurance, and a Narrator.

Scene I finds Religion in the home of Cognition. Bafflement knocks at the door and Cognition answers. Bafflement enters and attempts to establish itself by challenging Cognition at the limits of Cognition's analytic capacities; it queries Cognition about the way things essentially are. It asks, "What are the very foundations of existence, indeed of *your* being?" and proceeds from there. Whether by intent or not, its presence disrupts the order of Cognition's household. Cognition summons Religion to answer Bafflement's questions and thus return order to the house. But Religion's answers are not in terms of practical experience in the world; rather, they are in "other-worldly" terms; sometimes invoking gods, demons, and other cosmic forces of various sorts. Bafflement will ever dwell with Cognition and consequently there will forever be a conversation to sort out the "truth." But Cognition will often summon Religion's input to address Bafflement's queries.

Scene II opens with Religion dwelling in the house of Morality. This time Injustice knocks at the door. Morality answers. Injustice enters and attempts to establish itself through ethical paradox. It poses the question, "Why are people ill-treated when they don't deserve it?" and thus challenges Morality at the limits of its moral insight. Morality has no adequate response of its own and summons Religion to answer the question. Religion provides its answer once again by appealing to metaphysical purposes and influences. As Bafflement will always dwell with Cognition, so Injustice will always be with Morality. But Morality will, as does Cognition, frequently seek Religion's response to the questions of Injustice.

Scene III begins with Religion dwelling with Art. This time it is Endurance that knocks at the door, and Art answers. Endurance enters and seeks the upper hand by raising the issue of pain and suffering, which bespeaks the possibility of death and extinction. This challenge differs from that presented to Cognition in that it cuts to the very quick of experience. It entails the inability to survive, for it is here that suffering and pain find their ultimate end. Certainly, if the question of the power of the human person to endure can have keen articulation, it is through Art. Surely, from jubilance to despair, Art has something to say. Endurance's questions entail people who experience pain and die, families which go extinct, and entire cultures which disappear; but Art, even in its positive expressions, cannot escape the reiteration of Endurance's questions about pain and suffering. Where Art once attempted to absorb Religion into itself, it now summons Religion, in its own right, to reply to Endurance, to sooth the pain of human frailty. Religion responds in "other-worldly" terms.

Scene IV commences with Bafflement, Injustice, and Endurance all rapping at Feeling's door. Each, in its own way and by its own challenge, vies to become the object of Feeling's attention and thus become the usher of chaos, despair, and meaningless existence. Religion enters the conversation in order to challenge their negativity and address Feeling's confusion. Religion's task is to direct Feeling toward a view of reality, an attitude, and a behavior that makes the uncertainty presented by Bafflement, Injustice, and Endurance tolerable.

Scene V, with all the personified characters on stage, features the voice of a Narrator. The narrator summarizes the point of the play. "Whereas culture is humankind's attempt to make sense of its experience in and of the world in terms of itself, religion is the same attempt by humankind in terms larger than itself." The voice continues, "Religion, like culture, attempts to make sense of events, but does so in a unique way as it looks beyond the temporal word for enlightenment, fairness, and comfort." The narrator concludes, "It is *we* (the characters on stage) who determine what is 'real' and 'true.'"

First, our two act play dramatically demonstrates the relationship of culture and religion. Second, it shows just how strong the correlation is between Paul Tillich's philosophy of religion and Clifford Geertz's anthropology of religion. And third, it affirms just how accurate was the insight of John Morgan.

Undoubtedly, we can single out other cultural expressions in addition to religion. Geertz, who wrote the essay, "Religion as a Cultural System," also wrote essays titled "Ideology as a Cultural System,"[28] "Common Sense as a Cultural System,"[29] and "Art as a Cultural System."[30] Others have added disciplines such as those of science and law. The point is that irrespective of the topic of interest, each one, including religion, has the same overall task as culture understood as a whole: to interpret human experience in such a way as to make sense of human existence and, to the greatest extent possible, solve the problem of meaning.

The previous topic of this chapter quotes John Morgan's formal definition of culture and notes that this current topic would return to it. We do so now, but first we present his formal definition of religion; not to supersede our emphasis on Tillich's understanding of religion as ultimate concern, but to bring it into sharper focus. A comparison of Morgan's definitions of culture and religion brings out the complementarity that Tillich's approach presupposes. According to Morgan:

> Religion is a complex of behaviors and ideologies consisting of rituals and myths which appeals to a **transcendent legitimacy** embodying a worldview and ethos addressing the verities of life and existence conveying a dynamic level of psycho/social reality which is self-validating to the individual and community.[31]

Our interest in Morgan's formal definitions of culture and religion as set against those of others, now becomes apparent. Morgan defines religion as identical to culture with one exception: Whereas the legitimation of culture is connected to the historico-temporal characteristics of human experience, the legitimation of religion is associated with the transcendent aspect of human experience. What makes religion unique is *how* it attempts to answer the questions generated by human existence. It sets forth the nature of the ultimate concern. When humankind cannot find answers to its most difficult questions in terms of the natural world, it seeks other-worldly explanations. Religion arises at this point and develops its particular structures within the context of culture as a whole.

Religion has a unique relevance for culture. It develops out of the apprehension that there is that which is larger than the individual, that there is more to life than the concrete, visible world. Whether an unmoved mover, the pervasiveness of the Tao, the spirits of the ancestors, or the power and inspiration of the state, it is rooted in a sense of mystery. Communities decide the meaning behind the experience, hence, religion has an essence; and they afford it a substantive display, hence, religion has some form of systematic expression. Thus the notion of ultimate concern is not purely abstract and theoretical. It entails a network of symbols, which embody rituals and myths, which both project and perpetuate a worldview and ethos. Ultimate concern finds concrete social expression (to use Morgan's terms) in the offspring of the intercourse of "memory and imagination"; specifically, "the development of ideology," "a hope for the future," and "action by design."[32]

Our inquiry will again return to Morgan's definitions of culture and religion to make a further point later on. However, the focus at this juncture in our discussion is on how religion as ultimate concern functions as the other-worldly aspect of a culture seeking to make human experience intelligible, how its other-worldly quality is common to different cultures, and how it supplies different interpretations of the world to different cultures. As the reciprocity of power relations takes particular forms within each culture according to that culture's particular interpretation of its experience, so it operates within religious structures that participate in the culture as a whole.

The complementarity of culture and religion

Theologically speaking, in the Western world there have emerged two broad opposite approaches to religion.[33] Persons treat it as either entering the world as something imposed or gifted from the outside or as something that is wholly internal to human experience. In other words, religion either comes to humankind as something bestowed through an act of divine revelation or it comes about naturally as an internal quality in the development of the human species. We may then subdivide the latter into the question of whether religion is permanent to human development or whether it is merely transitory. Put in the form of a question: Is religion something that is temporary, serving a particular purpose in the present moment which will disappear as humankind outgrows its need for some idea of transcendent power; or is religion permanent, being rooted in some actual form of enduring transcendence?

The modern communications formats of social media and the various incarnations of television and radio provide a venue for arguments first one way and then another. Some hosts and commentators draw attention to the rise in atheism over the last several decades while others, especially of the more right-wing religious sort, who may or may not recognize the validity of the atheists' observations, challenge the conclusions which justify the move of so many to a position of atheism. Others take a more neutral position of declaring themselves spiritual but not religious, a claim that can mean virtually anything in between the extremes of classical theism and hard core atheism and often includes a good measure of agnosticism. If the various groups share anything in common, it is likely to be the view that religion serves to establish a relationship between human beings and divine beings, even if the divine beings are imaginary. This, of course, is an update of Paul Tillich's last century observations to which he applied his existential philosophy of religion.[34]

An existential approach such as Tillich's allows us to deny both theistic (belief in *a* Supreme Being that exists alongside other beings) and atheistic (denial of *a* Supreme Being that exists alongside other beings) positions. The gauntlet goes down toward the former based on the scientific observations of the latter that there is no objective evidence of any sort for the existence of a divine being. It goes down toward the latter based on the ability of the former to appeal to the limits of science in describing the various constituents of the cosmos. For existentialist philosophers and theologians, human existence is fundamental, and those such as Tillich relate human existence to a non-physical ground that they refer to as *Being* or *being* (as opposed to *a* Being/being), that underlies *a human being*, and is thus the basis of the depth dimension of human experience. Even though they run the risk of taking fire from both theists and atheists, their attempt is to establish their position in actual experience. For persons such as Tillich, religion is no more a phenomenon alongside other phenomena than God is *a* being alongside other beings. It is grounded in the realism of human experience, and as communicated in our two act play of the previous topic, religion is at home as the depth dimension in all the various aspects of human life and it functions to address the problem of meaning.

To understand religion as depth in human experience is to understand it as fundamental to human existence. When a person is experiencing depth, that person is interpreting ultimate things; seeking answers to questions that have no apparent or easy answers. The answers are beyond mundane, day to day, human experience; in fact, it is humankind's day to day exposure to and participation in the world that gives rise to the questions. The questions address such issues as why there is a humankind, why humankind is as it is, why the larger world is as it is, why human persons must suffer and die, and what happens to human persons when they die.

Ultimate questions as indicators of ultimate concerns rise in the course of human evolution. To restate John Morgan's words, religion is humankind's reaction to and participation in the deep experience of awe, wonder, and reverence.[35] Attempts to answer life's deepest questions in temporal terms do not satisfy humankind. If they did, there would be no need to seek other explanations. Therefore, humankind looks to a transcendent source for the best answers possible.

The link between culture and religion is humankind's drive to interpret, to seek meaning, to make sense out of the world and to understand its place in it. Religion, as depth in culture, assists culture's task of interpreting human experience; but culture's questions and answers are temporally based while religions questions and answers are rooted in the mystery of every aspect of human existence. As culture and religion both grow out of humankind's fundamental drive to interpret its experience in and of the world, they are complementary aspects of humankind's fundamental nature. This means, obviously, that neither the cultural nor the religious component of human life can exist without the other.

Nevertheless, in a secularized society, both the religious and secular elements attempt to establish themselves independently. A separation of religious institutions and practices from other institutions and practices occurs in which the former cannot control the latter, and in which the latter may even avoid reference to the former. This striving of both the religious and secular elements to establish themselves independently creates a gap between the two. The existentialist approach to a philosophy of religion is an address to precisely this issue; it closes the gap between the sacred and the secular because there is no aspect of culture that does not possess an ultimate concern and no ultimate concern that is not culturally based.[36]

Religion's issues, because they are generated by and within a particular culture, will always find expression in terms of the culture which generates them. Religion is the plumbing of the depths of human existence from within its particular cultural milieu. Culture fashions every religious expression and religion always reflects the culture that fashioned it. Culture and religion as an aspect of culture thus complement one another.

Māori culture and religion

Chapter Three of this book presents *utu* as the form of Māori reciprocity. Chapter Four describes *tapu*, *noa*, and *mana* as the state and operation of Māori power within the exchange form. However, anyone wishing to make sense of the Māori worldview must be familiar with how these concepts fit into the broad Māori scheme of things. Our attention now turns to that broad scheme.

Whakapapa is the broad structural principle within which Māori ideas function.[37] To apply John Morgan's thoughts (see the topic, "Culture," above), *whakapapa* is the vortex within which memory and imagination and ideology and action swirl; it is the context for possibility thinking; it is that which fuses recollections of the past and visions for the future into the present moment. It is the broadest defining Māori characteristic. *Whakapapa* describes who people are in relation to one another and the world at large and how the larger world fits together. It is the principle of interconnectedness.

However, in Aotearoa/New Zealand the mention of the word, *whakapapa*, is apt to summon, first and foremost, a mental image of a genealogical table; and this not without good reason. The term's definition includes an ancestral diagram, and historically Māori persons have demonstrated the ability to narrate their lines of descent through many reproduction cycles. For instance, one Māori litigant, Tamarau Waiari, before an 1890s land court, once recited as many as 1,400 ancestral names over 20 generations.[38] Māori also depended on memory for recalling songs, chants, incantations, etc.; but the skill of those without a written language of their own to memorize long and complicated lineages particularly amazed the early observers. Nevertheless, on this point we must be clear: such recitation is only one element of *whakapapa*.

But although it is only one aspect of the term, genealogy furnishes an illustration of the larger meaning of the concept. A family tree shows the association of persons beginning from a single person of reference; it includes individuals of different blood lines and depicts how they merge into a coherent pattern of family. It portrays how people, whether considered historically relevant or irrelevant, are related. Likewise, *whakapapa*, in its larger sense, is a framework for linking all phenomena whether a part of the natural world or perceived as an aspect of some invisible world. We may translate the term as "to place in layers,"[39] in which case it bespeaks an organized arrangement of persons, objects, and powers; whether mythological, legendary, or strictly historical. It sets everyone and everything in his, her, and its proper place and relationship. It layers one thing upon another so that each draws its definition in relation to everything else. Concisely stated, *whakapapa* is the principle of organization that makes existence coherent.

The anthropomorphic design of the *whare tipuna* (ancestor house) serves as a physical illustration of *whakapapa*. In Chapter Two of this book we examine how its construction represents the literal interconnection of everyone and everything in the Māori world. To enter this house is to leave the world of darkness and enter the world of light; *whakapapa* is the code of enlightenment. The structural details of the *whare tipuna* bespeak the unity of myths, legends, concepts, customs, protocols, the primal *atua*, phenomenal expressions of the primal *atua*, cultural heroes, the first ancestors in the land and their descendants, and the living people of the land; *whakapapa* is the principle of that coadunation.

The notion of *whakapapa*, like all major Māori cultural concepts, derives from their creation story. Māori tribes tell more than one version of their cosmogonic narrative, but all renditions include the same essential elements of the parting of earth and sky, the entrance of light, and *atua* fashioning the world.[40] The following is a general version.[41] It begins at a time long before the world became the one which human persons know today; a time when Ranginui, the Sky Father, and Papatūānuku, the Earth Mother, clung together so closely that the world had no light and was exceedingly confining. Five of their six children; Tū-mata-uenga, Tāne-mahuta, Rongo-mā-tāne, Tangaroa, and Haumia-tiketike; found this situation unbearable and sought a remedy. However, the sixth child, Tāwhiri-mātea, cautioned them that they were safe where they were and their conspiracy was shameful. Tū wanted to kill Rangi and Papa, but Tāne reminded him that they were, after all, their parents. Tāne suggested that, instead, they fling them far apart. Everyone agreed but Tāwhiri. Rongo, the father of cultivated food and peace, tried and failed; as did Tangaroa, the father of the sea; Haumia, the father of uncultivated food; and Tū, the father of humankind and war. At last it was Tāne; the father of the forest, birds, and insects that succeeded. The angry Tāwhiri, the father of the winds, angrily tore through the newly opened space, but Tāne and the other brothers looked upon their Earth Mother, and saw how the newly entered light revealed her loveliness. Tāne, who loved his parents, set out to adorn them both. The five brothers were happy in their freedom, but angry Tāwhiri sought to challenge them all and create havoc through disaster. It was Tū, the father of humankind, who not only stood firm against the storm god, but also declared his superiority to all his brothers. It was he who proclaimed that his children would not only overcome the winds but would also rule the seas, the forest, and all the land.

The first important item of notice in this narrative is the identification of the various *atua* with the environment: Ranginui, the Sky Father, and Papatūānuku, the Earth Mother, are the parents. The children are: Tāne-mahuta, the father of the forest, birds, and insects; Rongo-mā-tāne, the father of cultivated food and peace; Haumia-tiketike, the father of the uncultivated food; Tangaroa, the father of the sea and its inhabitants; Tāwhiri-mātea, the father of atmospheric phenomena; and Tū-mata-uenga, the father of humankind and war. Note that the offspring of Ranginui and Papatūānuku are both children and fathers. This is a picture of the Māori world where everything can be described as parents, children, cousins, etc. The primal parents are the cosmos where all activity takes place: Mother Earth and Father Sky. They and all that occupies a place in this earth-sky complex (the phenomena of the air, the land, the forest, and the sea and all the inhabitants thereof, including humankind) are genealogically related; another way of saying they are made of the same stuff. For example, the tree and the whale are cousins, so are the birds and fish, and humankind is cousin to all.[42] There is a sense in which humankind is above all its relatives, but it survives in the same extended family; related to everything in a genealogical way. There is a web of interconnectivity that holds all of life together. There is some aspect of everything in everything else.

Second, in Chapter Four (see the topic, "The spiritualized Māori") we take advantage of the research of Catholic priest Michael Shirres to understand how each of these primary *atua* (the offspring of Rangi and Papa, sometimes called gods) relate to intrinsic *tapu* and provide the foundation for the interfacing and interaction of humankind with both the visible and invisible worlds. The *atua* establish six fundamental *tapu*. From this we can infer that Māori recognize six basic interconnected modes of existence which they personify as spiritual forces.

Third, the creation story demonstrates the underlying basis for assertiveness among the various *tapu* (as potential power) and also of *mana* (as active power)—which underlies the *utu* system of Māori reciprocity—and, hence, requires the concept of *noa* to relax the assertions of power. These observations show how the cosmogonic narrative serves as the basis for *whakapapa* as the taxonomic framework in which all things Māori cohere.

Any person who would have an accurate grasp of the Māori worldview must clearly understand that, within this cosmic infrastructure, Māori culture and religion are one and the same. Whereas in a secularized society there may or may not be a perception of a spiritual quality in any given moment or event because religion has been institutionalized and spirituality removed from the main stream of society and relegated to the personal sphere of life; in a sacralized society spiritual forces are ever present and ever a factor with which every person must constantly reckon—there is no place, moment, or perception devoid of them. From the Māori point of view, all reality is interconnected; concepts such as *tapu*, *mana*, *noa*, and *utu* are spiritual ideas that are defined in terms of one another; and all phenomena are at once spiritual and physical.

To reshape a Tillichian existentialist notion for our purposes: just as an idea breaks through the form and content of a specific work of art, meaning breaks through the form and content of human existence. Think of form as referring to all the physical aspects of a particular painting and content as the way these physical aspects combine to express a particular subject. The two, of course, are practically inseparable in human perception. Think now of a quality of meaning that breaks through the form and content of the painting that expresses the idea intended by the artist (or perhaps some deeper understanding). Now let us allow the physical aspects of the painting to stand for the physical qualities of any worldly phenomenon, and let us permit the way these elements combine to produce a subject to stand for any particular subject in the world of subjects. The subjects themselves (as percepts) place demands on the percipient. However, there is a quality that finds expression through the subject that is beyond mere form and content, one that we may correctly call religious; not in the narrow institutional sense of the word, but as the dimension of depth in human experience. A secularized society can differentiate between meaning expressed by the subject in itself and the deeper meaning expressed through the subject. In the secularized Western world, from the Tillichian perspective, it is this quality of experience that distinguishes religion from culture. But a sacralized society not only *does not* differentiate between the two, it *cannot*. Everything is at once spiritual and physical. In the Māori world, there is no separation of awareness; all phenomena are interconnected and imbued with a spiritual quality that is ever present and can never be absent. Put another way: form, content, and life's transcendent imperatives are homogeneous in the Māori worldview; there is no deeper experience than the culture itself. The religio-culture gives content to meaning; it fills life with purpose and direction.

The Western dialectic does not apply to the Māori worldview. This is not to suggest that Māori of traditional times had no concept of opposites or that Pākehā influence has not created a Western style dialectic since first contact, but the Māori people the early Europeans describe did not separate the physical and spiritual, and today Māori descriptions of their experience inside the *whare tipuna*, where they go deep inside their traditional culture, suggest that Pākehā dialectic breaks down in that experience. Let us once again appeal to Tillich for help. After establishing religion as ultimate concern and asking, "What *does* concern us unconditionally?," he writes, "*Our ultimate concern is that which determines our being or not-being*"[43] (italics by source). For Māori people, their religio-culture *is* their ultimate concern; it is that which concerns them unconditionally; it needs no justification for its existence. Therefore, their *religio-culture* determines their being or not-being. To the extent that it continues, Māori continue. Should it cease, Māori cease. Figure 14 depicts the interconnected sacralized organization which the term *whakapapa* communicates.

As Figure 14 shows, everything takes place between the Sky Father and the Earth Mother. In Māori mythology this is the space that opened-up when Tāne, one of their six (some tribes recognize more than six) children, succeeded in separating the parents. Within this circle of existence where all activity takes place, the whole of Māori tribal life is surrounded by the primary *atua* and is permeated with their power. The influence of the *atua* is everywhere; there is no escape from it. The *atua* rule; they shape Māori society. Out of their character and their interaction, as expressed in Māori tribal mythology, comes concepts such as *tapu, mana, noa,* and *utu.* The respective personalities and interplay of the *atua* express the harmony and disharmony of Māori life, both personal and corporate. This defines the Māori tribal self and its concern for a proper life including the way by which to live it. There is no aspect of daily reality which the *atua* do not touch.

But whereas the circle of *atua* is a depiction of the separation of brothers who often contend with one another, the pyramid indicates a top down structural organization of society in which the *atua* collectively occupy the top position. The Māori concept of *mana*

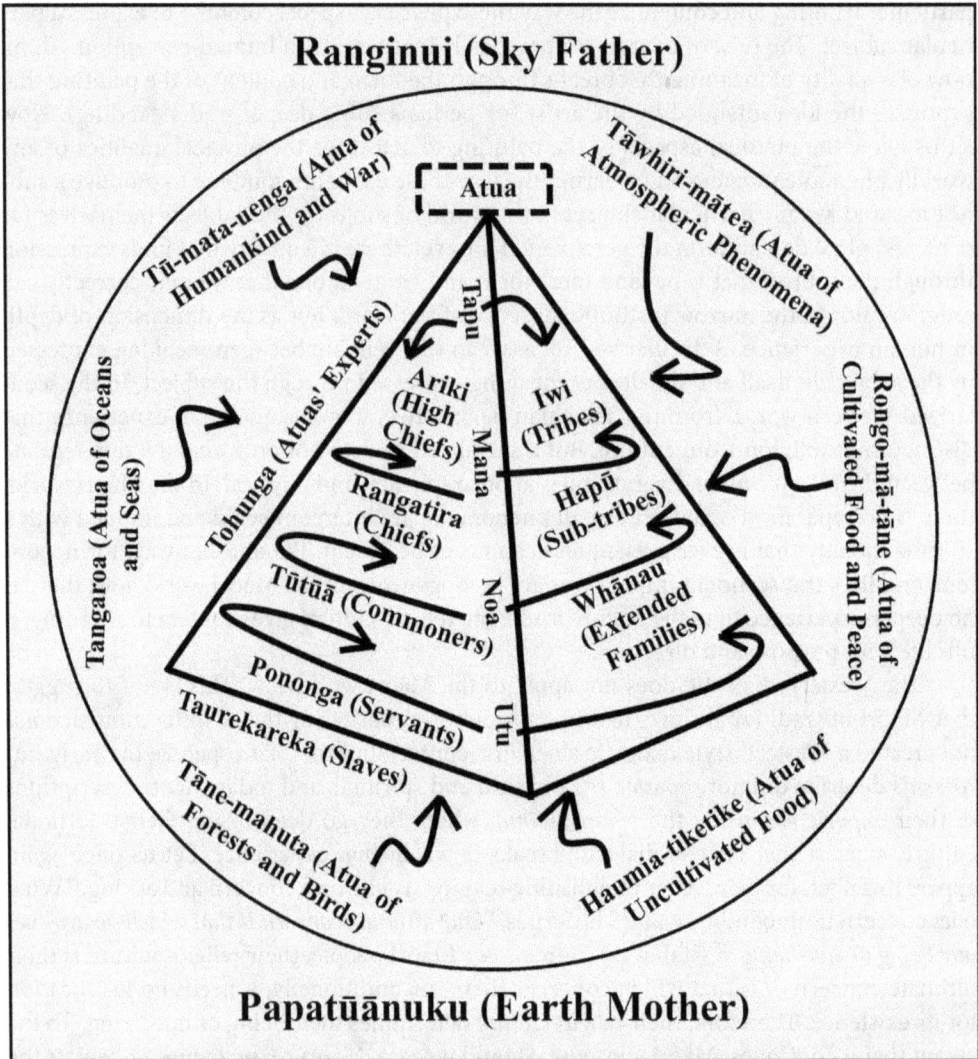

Figure 14. *Whakapapa.* **Figure 14 illustrates the interconnectedness of all existents in the Māori world. (Drawn by the author.)**

(as charisma; prestige) furnishes a good way to discuss the hierarchical genealogical social arrangement.[44] In Māori tribal life, the closer a person's line of descent is to the top of the pyramid and, hence, the *atua*, the greater the societal *mana* of that person. The top line of descent (the *tuakana* or senior line) includes those deemed genealogically closest to the *atua*. These *ariki* (high chiefs), by virtue of their *mana*, which results from their genealogical closeness to the *atua*, lead the *iwi* (tribes). The next line of descent (the *teina* or junior line) could acquire their *mana* through genealogy or by achievement. However, because these *rangatira* (chiefs) are deemed genealogically further removed from the *atua*, their *mana* usually extends over *hapū* (sub-tribes) rather than the larger *iwi*. Further down the social strata, the *tūtūā* (commoners) occupy the genealogical position of being further removed from the *tuakana* line and the *atua*, and thus relate to *whānau* (extended families). Genealogical *mana* depends on how far removed the person is from the *tuakana* (senior) line of descent and the *atua*. In traditional times the *pononga* were a servant class; to live a life of servitude to the chief and tribe could be considered an honor, and it could bestow *mana*. Also in traditional times, the *taurekareka*, who were captives of war, served as slaves and therefore possessed no *mana*. The *tohunga* (the *atuas'* specialists or experts; persons sometimes translate the word as "priest," but the societal position is not limited to that role) are set to the side of the main social structure; while there are ranks within the *tohunga* class, it is apart from the other social classes.

This, of course, is a somewhat perfected and categorical presentation of the hierarchical structure of Māori society. As a counterbalance we should keep in mind that of which cultural anthropologist Toon van Meijl reminds us. According to him,

> Any understanding of Māori socio-political organisation should ... give adequate weight to the fluid nature of the relationship between groupings. Māori kinship practices did not allow social relationships to be set in concrete. Tribal groupings mixed and divided, minor segments waxed while major segments waned, people migrated and formed fresh relationships, all causing Māori kinship groupings to be inherently flexible.[45]

Referencing the writing of Aotearoa/New Zealand historian Angela Ballera, he also pointed out that *iwi* was a highly *categorical* group comprised of a variety of groups "who thought of themselves as sharing a common identity based on descent from a remote ancestor," and that it was the *hapū* that was the *main functional* group for daily concerns including "economic affairs," "defence," etc.[46] Moreover, the word "sub-tribe" can be misleading if we ignore the fact that a particular *hapū* could be associated with more than one tribe.[47] Nevertheless, the discussion above, for our current purpose, is an adequate representation of how Māori tribal society was traditionally organized.

Figure 14, in addition to its sketch of a genealogical social structure, is also useful for understanding *whakapapa* in its wider sense. The broad point of the figure is to illustrate how everyone and everything in Māori society are literally interconnected; this *is* the principle of *whakapapa*. We have discussed personal *mana* as an example of how society fits together; however, we could have layered in other *mana*. Tānia M. Ka'ai and Rawinia Higgins mention *mana whenua* (*mana* of the land), *mana moana* (*mana* of the sea), and *mana motuhake* (*mana* of separate identity; self-determination; autonomy).[48] In our figure, we could have added concepts supplemental to *mana, tapu, noa,* and *utu* such as *kaitiakitanga* (guardianship), *tūrangawaewae* (a place to stand; place of belonging), *kotahitanga* (solidarity), and *rangatiratanga* (right to exercise authority). *Whakapapa* relates the people to one another and their cultural concepts, and through the concepts it embraces not only the people's kinship but includes their entire socialization within the very broad scheme of group associations. The concepts and socialization then provide the basis for Māori economy (the way they handle their resources). But let us not stop there. As Ka'ai and Higgins also point out, a complete view of *whakapapa* entails far more than genealogy (relations between people); it includes but extends past ecology (the relationship between people and nature) to encompass an entire cosmogony (the relationship of people to the *atua*).[49]

As Figure 14 shows, the *atua* are at once at the edge of the circle and the top of the pyramid. Their influence fills the cosmos and extends to all levels of Māori religio-culture. Concepts such as *mana, tapu, noa,* and *utu* (not an exhaustive list) are spiritual in nature; they derive from the *atua* and flow throughout and permeate the entire society. The *atua* are the source of all cultural ideas and practices. They and the concepts that emanate from them saturate every fiber of the Māori religio-cultural cloth. In the Māori worldview, all existence is interrelated; there is no division of sacred and secular. *Whakapapa* conceptualizes this cosmic interconnection and the thoroughly spiritual nature of Māori society.

Pākehā culture and religion

Up to now, this book has used the word *Pākehā* as a somewhat vague reference to the white European settlers who began their arrival in Aotearoa/New Zealand in the late 18th century. Let us now more fully identify them; just who are they? As we might expect, there has been considerable speculation regarding the origin of the term; nonetheless, the results of the inquiries have been something less than conclusive. Māori language guru, John Moorfield, in compiling his *Māori-English English-Māori Dictionary*, investigated the term's history. He found the recollections of Mohi Tūrei (c. 1830–1914) of the Ngāti Porou, an expert in the lore of his tribe, interesting enough to include in his dictionary treatment of the word. Mohi Tūrei's remembrance which caught Moorfield's attention appeared in an article published in the 1 January 1911 edition of the Māori language newspaper, *Te Pipi-wharauroa.*[50] In Moorfield's words:

> According to Mohi Tūrei … the term is a shortened form of *pakepakehā*, which was a Māori rendition of a word or words remembered from a chant used in a very early visit by foreign sailors for raising their anchor.[51]

"Others," Moorfield continues, "claim that *pakepakehā* was another name for *tūrehu* or *patupairehe*,"[52] a sort of light skinned, fair-haired, mythological fairy folk. Whatever the truth of the matter, under most circumstances, the term was not then and is not today, a derisive word.

Be that as it may, the ethnic make-up of Pākehā people was decidedly English.[53] There were other groups from that part of the world, such as the Scots and Irish, that in the 1800s also made the three to four month voyage to Aotearoa/New Zealand, and of course Americans were among the first whalers and sealers. There was also an early French presence, and Middle Easterners were there by the mid–19th century. Nevertheless, the English have been, beyond question, the largest group and most influential of the settlers.

Pākehā came to Aotearoa/New Zealand for a variety of reasons. Whalers, sealers, and traders seeking profit and adventure were there before the end of the 18th century. Missionaries with their religious agendas arrived beginning in 1814. Some persons came as the result of recruitment by businesses such as The New Zealand Company (beginning in 1840), which would often subsidize their passengers' journey. Others came in search of gold (beginning in the 1850s). Still others departed England because of dissatisfaction with the State Church and came as farm laborers (in the 1860s). There were also soldiers (especially in the 1860s) and railway contractors (beginning in the 1870s). There were philanthropists, people with commercial and political agendas, and fostered children.

Some Pākehā came as individuals, some as whole families, and some as part of organized groups. But even though certain immigrant clusters, such as the gold miners and soldiers of the 1860s, were mostly young single men, the preponderance of the new arrivals were families. At the outset, English colonization of Aotearoa/New Zealand came mostly from the south of England where agricultural skills and animal husbandry predominated. However, a shift took place in the 1890s in which regional origins of immigrants moved to the north of England; and consequently, the primary skills of the immigrants changed more to industry and mining. Along with these new arrivals came organizations pertaining to their trade; clubs, guilds, societies, cooperatives, etc.

The English settlers from both south and north set about transforming the landscape of their new home. They built railways styled after those in England; erected buildings according to English architecture; and introduced English trees (e.g., oak and beech), English domestic animals (e.g., sheep and cows), English game animals (e.g., deer and hare), English cultivated crops (e.g., carrots and cabbages), English fruit (e.g., apples and oranges), English flowers (e.g., roses and daffodils), and English clovers and grasses. They imposed an English style government, developed a legal system based on English law, and established written language and journalism. They brought English sports (e.g., cricket, rugby, and soccer), English foods (e.g., breads, cakes, puddings, cereals, beer, and English ways of preparing meats and potatoes), and English entertainments (e.g., literature of all sorts, stage plays, choral music, and Western musical instruments). This book has already discussed the arrival of English religion with its seasonal celebrations. Many of the 19th century persons who came to these islands considered Māori tribespeople ignorant and their ways inferior, and many of the missionaries of the 19th century wrote disparagingly about Māori spirituality. In all this, the colonizing Pākehā stood in stark contrast to the indigenous population.

We should keep in mind, however, that those leaving home, perhaps never to return, made important choices. While the immigrants would take much of their former way of life with them; moving to a new land, so far and so different from the one they were leaving, would require them to make changes. Without doubt the English way of life with its institutions, customs, and values has largely determined the development of Aotearoa/New Zealand; nevertheless, the English lifestyle that was so dominant before and perhaps during the ocean voyage to this land would be considerably altered in the new environment and climate. Pākehā, as their population grew, increasingly demanded that Māori adopt European ways; but with the passage of time, as this new land became home, especially as the second and successive generations were born in the new country, this demand became predicated less and less on the way of life as they remembered it in the former homeland and more and more on their current adaptation of the former way of life in Aotearoa/New Zealand. Wherever people go they construct a world for themselves.[54] The world they construct *is* their culture. Its function is to provide stability for human life, but culture changes over time. The fact of change introduces the element of instability; therefore, culture is in constant tension with itself. Pākehā set out to shape the country into a world which they found comfortable. They began with their English experience and progressively modified it to taste in an Aotearoa/New Zealand landscape.

What was the role of Pākehā religion in their colonial activity? When, in the 19th century, Pākehā judged the Māori spiritualized way of life as not worth keeping, it was not that Pākehā were without a religious influence of their own; but that their religion, its exclusivist nature notwithstanding, guided them only in a parallel and secondary way. Parallel in the sense that their religious institutions functioned *alongside* the institutions of business and government, and secondary in the sense that a rational marketplace way of thinking informed religious principles and not vice-versa. As this book discusses in Chapter Four, Pākehā were thoroughly secularized.

Secularization[55] of society manifests itself in such phenomena as the rise of science on an equal footing with religious considerations (which are defined by the religious institutions), an allowance for many religious perspectives on a par with one another and thus competing for converts and resources, and the resulting compartmentalization of religion (in its narrow institutional sense) in society. Compartmentalization means its removal from the foreground and relegation to the personal, family, and "circle of friends" aspects of daily life. As a secularized institution, religion no longer dominates the quality and conduct of life; it no longer permeates society to the extent that it is the sole or even the prime provider of a fundamental basis for understanding reality and determining conduct. Religion operating through secularized institutions may have an influence; but its influence is confined to a domain which is outside of the main stream marketplace. Market ideas dominate the culture.

Let us recall that both culture and its religious component share the task of making sense of human existence and maintaining order in human lives. However, the latter justifies its input by appealing to some form of transcendence, while the former validates its input by appealing to this-worldly considerations. In a sacralized society, such as that of Māori tribespeople, there is no separation of validation; everything is at once historico-temporal and transcendent. But in a secularized society, such as Pākehā brought to Aotearoa/New Zealand, religion is set alongside other institutions and is only one voice among many. In such an arrangement, the validation of culture with its institutionalized, and thus reduced, religious component derives mainly from human material comfort. Pākehā secularized culture was their way of creating and maintaining order and insuring societal fulfillment. Exclusivist Christianity was among its institutions as a phenomenal expression of a secular worldview. Thus Pākehā culture, including its institutional religion, was their attempt to defend their worldview from the attacks of chaos and give meaning to their way of life.

Religio-cultural synergy

While the previous topics of this chapter recognize the institutionalized nature of religion in secularized cultures, they treat religion in its broad and true sense as the dimension of depth in every aspect of the human self, irrespective of culture; in the most fundamental way possible, religion is ultimate concern. Because religion is a dimension of depth, secularization does not preclude its operation. Awareness of or reference to religious values notwithstanding, religion is always operative and inescapable.

Our two act play above (see the topic, "Religion") uses a combination of Paul Tillich's personifications of the various aspects of the human personality and Clifford Geertz's delineation of the problem of meaning in order to articulate how religion is at home as the depth dimension of human cognition, morality, and aesthetics; and how it functions to address the issues of human bafflement, moral paradox, and endurance. While religion in its narrow institutional sense may find itself banished from the domains of morality, cognition, and aesthetics; in its broad and true sense of ultimate concern religion actually dwells with them as their depth dimension, provides an object for feeling, and assists in answering life's toughest questions. To paraphrase Tillich: in terms of human cognition, religion shows itself as an insatiable hunger to discover, understand, and explain the most fundamental feature(s) of reality; in terms of human morality, religion expresses the extreme importance of sheer uprightness and decency; and in terms of aesthetics, it is on open display as an undeterrable determination to experience and articulate the profundities of existence.[56] These *are* the directional objects religion delivers to feeling. Secularization cannot exclude the operation of religion conceived in this way.

Plainly, the theoretical side is incomplete without the practical side. The ultimate concern expressed as a philosophical theology requires a concrete address to the problem of meaning within culture. As ultimate concern is common to all cultures, so is the problem of meaning; and the latter lays practical demands on culture to deal with ignorance, injustice, and pain. Human persons have their limits and constantly strive to overcome them through enlightenment, fairness, and well-being; thus they respond to the threat of chaos and the possibility of non-being. They are unwilling to give in to the limits of their capacities, which is precisely why there is a problem of meaning in the first place. Persons may be consumed by the immediate problem, but they will not accept that the immediate problem's perpetuation is how life must ultimately be. The way(s) groups deal with the issues of life defines them as specific cultures with particular religious beliefs and practices.

John Morgan demonstrated conclusively that Tillich's philosophy of religion and Geertz's anthropology are two sides of the same coin when it comes to the human quest for meaning. That which one expresses as philosophy of religion the other expresses as anthropology of religion. This book now builds upon Morgan's initial insight by specifically correlating Tillich's depth in the cognitive aspect of the human spirit to Geertz's address to befuddlement, Tillich's depth in the moral aspect of the human spirit to Geertz's address to injustice, and Tillich's depth in the aesthetic aspect of the human spirit to Geertz's address to the limits of human endurance. In this way, religion and culture are also two sides of the same coin. This correlation will now furnish a perspective from which to discuss the current bicultural conversation in Aotearoa/New Zealand.

Aotearoa/New Zealand's religio-cultural synergy springs from the fact that all human persons share common issues at the most fundamental level of life even though they deal with them in different ways. Just as theology, represented by Paul Tillich, writing as a theologian and a philosopher of religion, and anthropology, represented by Clifford Geertz, writing as an anthropologist with an interest in religion, can synergistically converse; so can the thoroughly religious Māori and the entirely secular Pākehā find common ground for meaningful dialogue. Put differently, at the most foundational level, Māori and Pākehā have the same basic issues; but because of the diversity of their worldviews, they can approach those concerns from very different perspectives. It is this difference in perspective addressed to common fundamental issues of human life that provides a basis for a tremendous synergy. Chapter Eight of this book will return to these themes in providing examples of bicultural success.

Biculturalism is Aotearoa/New Zealand's broad term for the search for meaning which includes an address to the cognitive, moral, and aesthetic aspects of the society at large. Proper cultural integration and the accompanying reinterpretation of symbols in sensitivity to others entail the development of empathy between Māori and Pākehā. The secularized Pākehā bring primarily to the table of discussion a quest for meaning in terms of humankind considered in itself, while the spiritualized Māori bring primarily a quest for meaning in terms larger than humankind. But neither is devoid of the other, and the two converge as an address to the same fundamental human desire for understanding, fair play, and comfortable survival. The synergistic potential of Aotearoa/New Zealand's biculturalism is in the depth dimension of common human experience and the application of common human concern to life's circumstances.

CHAPTER SIX

Some Principles
of Cultural Interchange

A time to reflect

The previous chapters of this book cover a lot of ground. Chapter One sketches Aotearoa/ New Zealand's origins, populace, religions, government, languages, and history. Chapter Two introduces the necessity of cultural symbols and describes not only how they express cultural essence, but also how they evolve for the preservation of cultural authenticity. Chapter Three presents various expressions of reciprocity as they pertain to different groups and shows how an encounter of different reciprocity forms can result in a reinterpretation of culture—which is actually the evolution of symbols—which brings about proper societal integration. Chapter Four details variances in ideas about power, shows how power operates in sacralized and secularized cultures, and explicates how those cultures can cooperate synergistically. And Chapter Five clarifies the association of culture and religion, explains how they combine to address the problem of meaning, and shows how the endeavor can underpin cultural synergistic synthesis.

Moreover, while this book is about the interaction of Aotearoa/New Zealand's Māori and Pākehā, it deliberately includes some American cultural expressions; specifically, the Flag, the Pledge of Allegiance, the Constitution, and the National Anthem; it also incorporates the Christian articulation of the Golden Rule. It uses these features primarily to set the stage for subsequent discussion, but not far removed is the hope that their inclusion can also serve to break down tendencies to haughtiness when considering other cultures.

As there is a time for everything between the terrestrial depths of Mother Earth and the celestial heights of Father Sky, it is now time to pause for reflection. Are there specific principles of cultural exchange which we can draw from the previous discussions that will benefit our view of cultural encounters, which may also work to mitigate our hubristic tendencies and serve to intensify respect for, and benevolence toward, different others? To that end, this chapter extracts six principles of cultural interchange from the previous chapters. They are:

1. *Cultural interaction is always dynamic and always happens in the present moment.*
2. *There is no standard way to view the world, and cultures that appear to be simple may actually be very complex and abstract.*
3. *The quest for meaning (making sense of human experience), which entails an address to the issues of befuddlement, injustice, and survival, can underpin cultural dialogue irrespective of cultural diversity.*

    4. *Cultural interaction brings about cultural reconceptualization within the com-plementary domains of sociality, religiosity, and politicality.*
    5. *Reification of culture is the basis for the synergistic synthesis of cultures.*
    6. *Reification of culture establishes rather than negates cultural authenticity.*

The dynamic encounter of meaning systems

Cultural interaction is always dynamic and always happens in the present moment.

To view cultural interaction as *dynamic* is, by dictionary authority, to understand it as characterized by constant change. More fully stated, cultural forces are unceasingly at work in humankind's attempt to make sense of and organize its experience. This continuous development involves two frames of reference: cultures (meaning systems) change in themselves, and they change in encounter with one another.

First, culture-in-itself, irrespective of its particular expression, is an *ongoing* interpretation; it is never static. It is ever changing even though its modifications may be largely transparent to those who participate in the culture. The question of cultural change, by virtue of the fact that culture arises through unconscious group assent, actually entails the deepest questions about the nature of human beings and the most penetrating observations regarding the quality of human experience. Culture as a human phenomenon justifies our use of organic models for understanding it as dynamic.

University of Oxford philosopher, Keith Ward (1938–) has provided a concise statement useful for our purposes of viewing continuing personhood as an analogy for culture-in-itself's continuous and perpetual transformation; Ward argues that "human persons are primarily chains of experience ... and actions.... But these chains are 'owned' by continuing subjects who give them their unique identity."[1] In other words, a human person constantly changes, and the changes that characterize that person are in some way connected; but a person as a collection of human processes can have no experience outside of his or her unique humanness. To approach it from a somewhat different perspective, human persons are a temporally connected conglomeration of every aspect of those things we can properly associate with human experience, whether they involve hearing, seeing, touching, smelling, tasting, remembering, imagining, anticipating, evaluating, perceiving, or any other occurrence characteristic of being human. On the one hand, the experience of an individual is unitary in a stand-alone personality as one continuous stream of integrated mental and sensory activity; that is, the various aspects of being human are blended in each person's experience. But on the other hand, there is also a separation of experience; that is, the multifarious aspects of being human are united in one person's, but *only* in one person's, experience. Within this twofold scheme, an individual's perspectives, attitudes, and behaviors change over time. The change may be gradual and indiscernible or more rapid and a topic of gossip, but the processes that bring about change are constantly at work.

There are several points of analogy between the development of human persons and culture-in-itself. To begin with, as a person is an amalgamation of processes such as hearing, seeing, touching, smelling, tasting, remembering, imagining, anticipating, evaluating, and perceiving; so is a culture a collection of human processes. Next, as human processes are united in one person, so are cultural processes a unity within the culture. Additionally, as one person cannot migrate from their unique unity into another's and back again, neither can one culture migrate from its unique unity into another's and return; cultural systems may affect one another, but change occurs within the unique identity of each culture. Finally, as a person's perspectives, attitudes, and behaviors are constantly changing; so the perspectives, attitudes, and behaviors that identify a culture as a culture also change. As cultural anthropologist Richard Handler expresses it, "...culture ... is ceaselessly emergent from ... meaningful human activity."[2]

Second, the dynamics of cultural change affect the association of one culture with another. Just as a human person can analogically represent a particular culture, so the interaction of human persons can analogically represent the interaction of cultures. For instance, persons from similar backgrounds are likely to share a similar worldview while persons from radically different backgrounds may have radically different worldviews. More specifically, perspectives, attitudes, and behaviors may be very much alike for persons who share a common social status, but extremely different for persons at opposite ends of the social spectrum. In the latter situation one group may look upon the other as intellectually or artistically inferior while the group they are judging may view them as snobs and lacking street-sense. But interaction will bring about change; particularly, it will cause either redefinition or reinforcement of perceptions, attitudes, and behaviors. Two points of analogy stand out. First, as radically different persons organize their thoughts and activities in radically different ways, so radically different cultures organize themselves and behave in radically different ways. And second, as personal interaction results in either redefinition or reinforcement of personal perceptions, attitudes, and behaviors; so will cultural interaction result in either redefinition or reinforcement of these cultural traits.

This constant movement of cultural forces in both culture-in-itself and between cultures always happens in the present moment. There exists a constant reinterpretation in the-here-and-now. In fact, the-here-and-now is comprised of recalling the past and shaping the future in compliance with present circumstances. As it pertains to the past, as Handler recognized, the link between past and present, while it may entail cultural property, is not at all physical; it is semiotic in nature.[3] Cultural treasures may serve as catalysts for reflection on the past, but reflection can only happen in the present moment and inescapably will be guided by cultural symbols. Every perception and every thought has the potential to both reinforce and reinterpret culture. Reinforcement guarantees a connection with the past, but reinterpretation underpins cultural change into the future.

Let us now apply these thoughts to Māori and Pākehā. To treat Māori culture at any point, even prior to European contact, as static, is to misperceive it. Notably, at some point in the past, human persons braved crossing the Pacific Ocean into Polynesia; they eventually arrived in Aotearoa/New Zealand and established a way of life there. However, even the activity of arrival, organization, and survival entailed interpretation and reinterpretation of each new environment and their experience within it. Their perceptions, attitudes, and behaviors were constantly in flux. Knowledge of these events is shrouded in the past, without written record; what we know of them has been passed down through oral tradition and an examination of landscapes, structures, biofacts, artifacts, and human remains. But even a written record would not render access to the dynamics-in-themselves. The most a researcher or an observer can achieve is a snapshot of cultural movement because culture is always fluid. Those in the prehistoric past lived in *their* constantly moving present.

Moreover, when Pākehā arrived in Aotearoa/New Zealand in the late 18th century, they immediately began interacting with and recording their observations of the indigenous people. The ethnography, of course, changed over time.[4] Their first observations of Māori would have been of the sort to satisfy curiosity about their tribal way of life. This "thin description" is the natural starting point for the attempt to understand a culture. The first questions were about the Māori lifestyle. How did they organize their sundry activities, their seasons of the year, and their villages (both open and fortified)? How did they build personal shelters, rivercraft and seacraft, fishing nets, bird snares, and structures to protect the food supply? How did they forage, hunt, and fish? How did they plant, harvest, and prepare food for storage? What were they saying in their strange sounding chants? How did they cure disease? What were their burial methods? Overall, how did they conduct their affairs? These "what" and "how" questions were not devoid of the "why," but the emphasis was on describing the Māori way of life. The ethnography, of course, changed over time. Whereas Pākehā had once collected data based on *observation of* the indigenous culture, especially in the early days of contact; as they gained experience in the land, their information gathering became more and more based on active *participation with* the culture.

However, it is important to note that in none of this, not even the early observations from afar, was the Pākehā scrutiny of Māori purely detached. *There was then and there is now no detached ethnography.* Not only were Pākehā descriptions merely snapshots of the moments they documented; they also included a reflection of the ethnographers' own backgrounds, interests, and attitudes toward the people and environment they were watching and chronicling. Also, Pākehā ethnographers affected the perceptions, attitudes, and behaviors of Māori which influence then became incorporated into the Pākehā record. Finally, Pākehā experience in Aotearoa/New Zealand always occurred in its own *rolling present*; it was ceaselessly flowing. Constantly flowing cultural streams, in one way or the other and to some extent, merge in the encounter of cultures; each continually reinforcing and reinterpreting itself in the process.

Without belaboring the point by reshaping the above presentation for the opposite context, let us suffice it to say that the student of culture should also keep in mind that in the present-moment dynamic encounter of meaning systems the watched is also a watcher and the judged is also a judge. Thus cultural change is constant, both within itself and in encounter with others, within an ever moving present; it happens "here and now" and can never be static.

Cultural complexity and abstractness

There is no standard way to view the world, and cultures that appear to be simple may actually be very complex and abstract.

This book's Introduction defines worldview as a person's or a group's basic cosmology; the downright truth about the way things fundamentally are; the line of reality below which there is not another turtle. Chapter Two adds that worldview is about how people perceive the existential nature of the natural world including the human individual and the society at large; one's worldview is the absolute bedrock of human perception below which there remains nothing more to be perceived. Our study, thus far, of the encounter of Māori and Pākehā should make it abundantly clear that, while diverse groups may have widely varying views of reality, one is not intrinsically superior to the other. All too often, persons have the idea that the world is one way and one way only, and that way is the way that any reasonable person should view it, especially once they have had the truth explained to them. It is difficult to overstate just how unfortunate is this temperament. It has undergirded a judgmental attitude and the ill treatment of persons who look different, sound different, adorn themselves in a different manner, and live different lifestyles.

The fact is that different cultures process reality in different ways for specific reasons. Research of some decades ago among Hopi children demonstrated that they process their indigenous language using the right hemisphere of their brain but use the left hemisphere to process English; the research then related this to the way their mentors presented the world to them.[5] Developments such as the organization of brain activity are directly related to a person's experience in the world, especially early on, to which each subsequent generation adds its input (sometimes influenced by interaction with different others) and passes it along. Differences in worldview account for differences in life's particulars such as language structure, mythology, attitudes, and daily regimen. It is indeed the height of arrogance to claim a monopoly on truth; from culture to culture, there is no standard way to view the world.

Much misunderstanding between Māori and Pākehā can be traced to the operation of the idea that human persons should share a common perception of the world and its events. Let us look at two examples; the first from treaty negotiations and the second from the interaction of society at large.

Concerning the first example, as Chapter Three of this book (see the topic, "The complexity of Pākehā reciprocity") describes, in 1839 the British Government sent William Hobson to "negotiate" for Aotearoa/New Zealand's sovereignty. From the British perspective, there was, or could be developed, a way to authoritatively bargain with the indigenous population as a whole society. The Māori idea and practice of *utu* was a then current indication to the contrary, but the British Government either did not understand or ignored its significance. The terrible Musket Wars, in which Māori fought Māori, that began prior to 1810 and continued into the early 1840s, were largely an expression of negative *utu* as the settling of old scores. While the Musket Wars were an indication to the British that the indigenous people were a very loosely organized amalgamation of numerous individual tribes and sub-tribes, the British, nonetheless, attempted to bargain with them as though they were a "pan-culture." The Māori perspective was very different from that of Pākehā. *Utu*, in both its positive and negative forms, was an expression of the interaction of *mana*, *tapu*, and *noa* on a personal, immediate family, extended family, and tribal level and an indicator of tribal pride and prestige which was absent any idea of a united Māori tribal structure. While the 1835 Declaration of Independence of New Zealand, a Pākehā document, referenced "the United Tribes of New Zealand," this reference was to only a handful (only 52 out of the hundreds of chiefs had signed the document by 1839) of tribes on the North Island, which never met again under the terms of the Declaration.[6]

Concerning the second example, taken from society at large, Chapter One (see the topic, "A handle on the history"), Chapter Two (see the topic, "The *whare karakia* as a symbol"), and Chapter Four (see the topic, "The secularized Pākehā") mention the Boyd incident. It provides an excellent example of how differing worldviews can foster misunderstanding which can lead to violence. In October 1809 the British sailing ship *Boyd* left Sydney, Australia, en route to Whangaroa Harbour.[7] Te Ara, the son of a Māori chief, secured passage on the ship in exchange for his work on board. But, when he refused orders, the Captain had him flogged and deprived him of food. In December 1809, the crew anchored the ship in the harbor, and Te Ara returned home, where he reported his treatment to his father, who then demanded revenge for the treatment of his son. So, in December 1809, when the Captain and some of his crew departed the ship for business purposes, Māori warriors captured them on shore, killed them, cooked them, and ate them. Afterward, at dusk, some Māori disguised themselves as the returning shore party while others waited for their signal to attack. Their assault was successful. Most Pākehā crewmembers were killed, although some escaped in the ship's rigging. Pākehā viewed the Māori retaliation so extreme that the first missionaries delayed their arrival in Aotearoa/New Zealand until 1814. We may glean the following from this series of events: First, the Pākehā sailors dealt with the chief's son as they would anyone who refused orders. Second, the Māori tribe considered Pākehā treatment of the chief's son a terrible insult that demanded *utu* in its most negative form. Third, both were operating within the parameters dictated by their culture, but their differing perspectives caused them to interpret events in radically different ways. Finally, these events emphasize the need for dialogue and understanding.

Not only is there no standard way of viewing the world, but each culture is primed with its own complexities and abstractions. In the past, researchers have cast doubt on the ability of Māori to think abstractly. Edward Shortland (1812–1893), a medical doctor and linguist who was among and wrote extensively about Aotearoa/New Zealand's indigenous people, described them as having "a limited notion of the abstract."[8] He wrote how they reflected "the early mental condition of man [humankind]" in that they regarded the powers of nature as "concrete objects" and "designated" them "as persons."[9] He also said that he had "seen it in print that the New Zealander [a reference to Māori people] has no sentiment of gratitude; in proof of which it was mentioned that he [a Māori person] has no word in his language to express gratitude."[10] He continued, "This is true; but the reason is that gratitude is an abstract word, and that [the] Māori [language] is deficient in abstract terms."[11] Shortland did not intend to convey that the indigenous population was ignorant of the sentiment of gratitude or unable to intelligibly express it; he was making the case that Māori people were deficient in abstract thought. Additionally, Shortland, writing about land-titles, further revealed his perspective. According to him:

> If you were to make inquiry from a New Zealander [a Māori person] as to his land-title, it would be difficult to obtain from him reliable information as to any general rules of proceeding; for he would at once consider some particular case in which he was himself personally interested, and would give an answer corresponding with his interest therein. This may be due partly to the inaptitude of the Māori to take an abstract view of anything, which has been already noticed.[12]

On the other hand, Elsdon Best (1856–1931), a farm-worker, government employee, ethnographer, and prominent member and seventh President of the Polynesian Society, took a very different view. In his discussion of Māori myths, Best wrote, "As to explanatory myths it would appear that reflection, introspective thought, must be the mental condition that produces them...."[13] He quoted the English anthropologist Edward Tylor (1832–1917) that "[n]ature myths are the most beautiful of poetic fictions," and concluded, "the mythopoetic Māori has given full play to his imagination in that direction."[14] Regarding Edward Shortland's views Best wrote, "The Māori tongue is undoubtedly lacking in words denoting abstract ideas, but it would be a serious error to believe the Māori mind to be deficient in the faculty of abstraction. That mistake was made by Shortland...."[15]

Chapter Four (see the topic, "The spiritualized Māori") points out the modern Western mind's difficulty in understanding the Māori concepts of *tapu* and *noa*, and how Westerners must appeal to such devices as a Thomist treatment of analogy to comprehend them. It also shows how *mana* makes complete sense only in its association with *tapu* and *noa*. Chapter Five (see the topic, "Māori culture and religion") describes how all Māori concepts connect and operate within the broad relational structure of *whakapapa*. The culture which Pākehā originally judged to be naïve and simple was abstract beyond their comprehension. Indeed the current conversation between the two is in some measure an exchange of abstractions. Both Māori and Pākehā worldviews are complex and complicated within themselves, and the interaction of these two radically different meaning systems has served to further complexify and complicate the respective cultures. But meaningful dialogue can facilitate cross-cultural understanding.

The beginning of cultural dialogue

The quest for meaning (making sense of human experience), which entails an address to the issues of befuddlement, injustice, and survival, can underpin cultural dialogue irrespective of cultural diversity.

Chapter Three of this book demonstrates the difficulty of Māori-Pākehā dialogue by showing how exchange forms built on Western economic principles tend to break down when we try to apply them to Māori culture, and how the dynamics behind the Māori exchange form of *utu* are not immediately apparent to the Western mind and require special research for discernibility. Chapter Four goes a step further in describing how the two cultures differ by viewing Māori as "spiritualized" and Pākehā as "secularized." However, Chapter Five declares the possibility of meaningful dialogue based on certain commonalities of human experience; specifically, the starting place for meaningful dialogue between radically different cultures is the existential experience common to both.

Chapter Five (see the topic, "Religion") uses a brief two act play in its exploration of the possibility of meaningful dialogue. Act I is based on Tillichian existentialist philosophy of religion and Act II on Geertzian interpretive anthropology. The play features characters which are personified facets of the human self. On the one hand, the personifications include the aspects of morality, cognition, and aesthetics, and on the other hand, bafflement, injustice, and human endurance. In Act II Bafflement challenges Cognition, Injustice challenges Morality, and Endurance challenges Aesthetics. This creates a problem of meaning. The former personifications must acknowledge their limits but they refuse to give in to them. They continually strive to find meaning in the midst of possible chaos. Like the "fiddler on the roof" they search for ways to maintain their balance in an unbalanced world. The play describes experience that is universally human; its setting can change without affecting its movement. Therefore, we may conclude that no matter how different cultures are in perception, thought, and expression there are three queries rooted in one common endeavor at which they may begin dialogue. The three queries are engendered by a breakdown in the qualities of reason, justice, and survival, and the one common endeavor is the urge to find meaning in life; that is, to make sense of human experience. The sheer recognition of these points implies the possibility of their antitheses as enlightenment, fairness, and well-being.

If this observation is correct, we might reasonably expect the strongest potential for meaningful Māori-Pākehā dialogue to be at the deepest moment of Māori anguish. This is because it is at this point that the common human experience of (to use Geertz's terms) "bafflement, suffering, and a sense of intractable ethical paradox,"[16] cultural context notwithstanding, is most apparent and most keenly felt. It is interesting that this is precisely the beginning point of the current Aotearoa/New Zealand commitment to biculturalism. By the turn of the 19th to the 20th century Pākehā had largely succeeded in breaking-down Māori culture. We have already noted how the population of Māori people dropped to an all-time low at the end of the 1800s through war, disease, loss of land, and despair (see the topic, "The secularized Pākehā," in Chapter Four). An air of sadness hung over the country because it viewed Māori people as doomed to extinction.[17] Pākehā had pursued a course of assimilation of the Māori population which meant, for all practical purposes, the extinction of Māori culture as forceful for shaping life in the country. For Māori tribes, the breaking up of their cultural patterns created a sense of disorder and corresponding loss of hope for survival as tribal people. They suffered physically and emotionally, and their circumstances challenged their sense of justice. However, at the time when Māori survival appeared virtually hopeless, the Māori renaissance (rebirth; reawakening) began.

The Māori renaissance has entailed activity by both Pākehā and Māori. On the one hand, about this time, Pākehā—a secular people with deep European connections, mostly English—were showing signs of breaking with their English colonialist roots. They became fearful that Māori culture would indeed become extinct. Some of them formed the Polynesian Society in 1892 to record as much as possible about Māori tribal life and other Polynesian groups. As these ethnographers set about their work, art patrons began subsidizing Māori carvers which included restoring *whare tipuna*; the pervading concern over Māori people helped generate this special interest. There developed an enthusiasm for all things Māori; consequently, many Pākehā set out to preserve Māori culture and traditions. Pākehā, as Aotearoans/New Zealanders, were in a seedling stage of developing their own views, their own cultural and spiritual principles as they deemed them proper; and contact with Māori people provided them with a unique opportunity to discover or rediscover the depth in life.

Chapter Five of this book (see the topic, "Pākehā culture and religion") briefly mentions two possible origins for the word "pākehā": the first was an anchor raising chant which some early European visitors used; the second was a reference to a mythical light skinned, fair-haired, fairy folk. Interestingly, Toon van Meijl directs our attention to Herbert W. Williams's dictionary, first published in 1844, which records another possible use of the word.[18] According to Williams, it is an adjective meaning "foreign."[19] Whatever the truth of the matter, by now Pākehā were no longer foreign in the sense of newcomers. Their family roots were in Aotearoa/New Zealand although they were not the *tangata whenua* (i.e., "the people of the land") as Māori often refer to themselves. Many Pākehā were apparently beginning to understand that the land and its resources must be shared, and this occurred when Māori faced impending chaos at the limits of their comprehension of their predicament, the limits of their sense of justice, and the limits of their endurance as a unique people.

On the other hand, as Chapter One of this book mentions (see the topic, "A handle on the history"), also toward the end of the 19th century, at the pinnacle of Māori distress, a group that became known as the Young Māori Party formed. These Young Māori came out of the Te Aute College Students' Association, an Anglican Boys College in Hawke's Bay, and drew in young men from other schools. Although not a political party in the formal sense of the word, they set about to address the destructive effect that Pākehā initiatives had brought to Māori tribal culture and Māori identity. They advocated a policy of both inclusion in and exclusion from Pākehā society; inclusion in terms of socio-economic equality, but exclusion to the extent they would have control over their own affairs and reestablish and maintain their customs and protocols.[20] Today's Aotearoans/New Zealanders call this concern and policy for maintaining tribal norms and customs within a scheme of socio-economic equality "biculturalism." Young Māori success was not immediate, but those who comprised this group became some of the most influential leaders for the proper societal integration of Aotearoa/New Zealand.

From one point of view many Pākehā feared that Māori culture would disappear and set out to preserve it. From another view, the Young Māori Party—an educated, capable, and energetic group—pushed for a bicultural integration of Aotearoa/New Zealand. Together this produced a synergy that began at the limits of Māori survival and has progressed to the current debate about the proper shape of Aotearoa/New Zealand biculturalism, that is, the most meaningful way to interpret and share life. In other words, at the point of concern about and fear of impending chaos, at the height of bafflement, a sense of injustice, and a concern for survival as a tribal people, began the discovery (or rediscovery) of essential meaning.

The terms of cultural reconceptualization

Cultural interaction brings about cultural reconceptualization within the complementary domains of sociality, religiosity, and politicality.

Cultural reconceptualization (rethinking, redefining, and reshaping one's own culture) whether a product of the movement of culture-in-itself or resulting from an encounter with others, must necessarily occur within three complementary areas of cultural activity; specifically, the domains of sociality, religiosity, and politicality. The next topic of this chapter will address the *nature* of cultural reconceptualization within these three domains, but first let us take a closer look into *the complementary aspect* of the activity within and among them. We will do so by recalling John Morgan's definitions of culture and religion from Chapter Five and adding his definition of politics. Others have offered definitions of these phenomena, and we could go to the trouble of developing our own; but Morgan's definitions have a particular appeal.

Students of anthropology will recall that Clifford Geertz developed a five-tiered definition of religion which he explicates one layer at a time.[21] Morgan, who was thoroughly familiar with Geertz's work, developed his own layered definition—seven tiers—which he also explains one at a time; however, he extends the tiered arrangement to definitions of culture and politics. In so doing, he very clearly and cleverly expresses the complementary relationship of the three.

To reiterate Morgan's first two definitions for convenience sake:

- Culture is a complex of behaviors and ideologies consisting of rituals and myths which appeals to an **historico-temporal legitimacy** embodying a worldview and ethos addressing the verities of life and existence conveying a dynamic level of psycho/social reality which is self-validating to the individual and community.[22]
- Religion is a complex of behaviors and ideologies consisting of rituals and myths which appeals to a **transcendent legitimacy** embodying a worldview and ethos addressing the verities of life and existence conveying a dynamic level of psycho/social reality which is self-validating to the individual and community.[23]

Morgan's definitions express the complementarity of culture and religion by showing that the issue of "legitimacy" is the only difference between the two; the former has a historico-temporal legitimacy—what is accepted as "true" develops out of the impact of the intelligible physical world—while the latter has a transcendent legitimacy—what is accepted as "true" develops out of the impact of the non-intelligible, non-physical aspects of human existence. In Morgan's presentation, his treatment of culture necessarily precedes his treatment of religion. This is an indicator that they complement one another in the sense that religion is a feature of culture.

This complementarity, however, generates a question. If we have accounted for physical and non-physical aspects of human life, why then do we need politics as a third category?[24] Morgan finds the answer in the further complementary relationship of the broad categories of human experience. Politics is necessary to bring the legitimacies of the first two together in such a way that the result oversees them; some quality must hold the first two together or else each will go its own way.[25] The quality must be one that extends into both culture and religion, and it must possess the ability to *harness*, to *control* them both.[26] In Morgan's words, politics "is a mechanism, self-validated, for control, for order, for pattern, for system, for process."[27] This is the quality and condition of management of power for comfort and survival; specifically, the operation of power within cultural exchange forms inclusive of a culture's religious expressions. Their interdependence notwithstanding, culture at large and its religious articulations are incomplete without the control afforded by politics; the political aspect keeps a culture with its religious features on track.[28] We may now meaningfully introduce Morgan's definition of politics. Let us notice that it differs from his definitions of culture and religion only in the matter of legitimacy.

> Politics is a complex of behaviors and ideologies consisting of rituals and myths which appeals to a **confluence of transcendent and historico-temporal legitimacy** embodying a worldview and ethos addressing the verities of life and existence conveying a dynamic level of psycho/social reality which is self-validating to the individual and community.[29]

This conflation of the historico-temporal legitimacy of culture and the transcendent legitimacy of religion establishes the three (culture, religion, and politics) as complementary characteristics of human life in the sense that, while both religion and politics fall under the umbrella of culture, each has the ability to direct the others in particular ways.

Legitimacy has to do with establishing something as real or true; it refers to the authority for and permissibility of certain attitudes and behaviors; it is the ground of a worldview and its corresponding ethos. A person need look no further than her or his fundamental epistemology (how we know what we know) for approval of what she or he perceives, feels, thinks, and does. Aside from the directedness of legitimacy (historico-temporal, transcendent, or a conflation of the two), the same elements and processes define culture, religion, and politics; but what a difference the directedness of legitimacy makes. It determines *how* people express their worldview and prevailing attitude toward the world, self, and others as cultural, religious, or political.

Let us, however, expand Morgan's observations regarding the control which politics brings to culture and religion. These three must *balance* one another or else the society through which the culture at large finds expression will founder. The legitimations of culture and religion comprise the legitimation of politics, and the dual legitimation of politics extends into both culture and religion. All three are necessary to maintain proper balance. Without balance in and among them, society, through which culture with its religious and political features finds expression, will lose its way.

The way in which sociality and culturality are related should now be apparent. Sociality refers to the association of an aggregation of persons through which cultural qualities find their expression; and as religion and politics are aspects of a culture, both religious and political expressions (religiosity and politicality) are aspects of the society at large. The impact of the temporal world considered within itself furnishes one facet of a culture's epistemology; the impact of the unintelligible, non-physical realm furnishes another; and the conflation of the two furnishes yet another—each blends with the others in seeking community articulative exhibitions. Out of the dynamics of these complementary features of a culture develops a society with particular social, religious, and political expressions. The society's overall concern is to account for and express a particular view of the physical world including its people and their place in it; to account for and express the meaning of the unintelligible, non-physical aspects of life including their imposition into the physical world; and to adequately control both for the purpose of the society's welfare and survival. Stated another way, as it pertains to society, the historico-temporal validation looks no further than physical existence in the consideration of proper peer relations and human well-being; the transcendent validation looks into the depths of human experience to make sense of the other-worldly, non-physical aspects of life and to address the deeper questions of human existence; and the conflation of transcendent and historico-temporal legitimacies taps all available validating resources, intelligible and unintelligible, physical and non-physical to insure that the society does not go awry or extinct. The reconceptualization that takes place as a result of cultural interaction is a restructuring within these domains and according to these validations. Essentially, this entails decisions about what works out best to address the issues engendered by temporal interpersonal relations, personal and corporate ultimate concerns, and the integrity and survival of the cultural community.

We may now understand how, without adequate management of power (the political aspect), the social and the religious aspects of culture become muddled in their role of providing balance to society and achieving cultural cohesion. If a transcendent legitimacy is solely influential or extremely dominant, the deeper attitudes will take precedence over personal loyalties or the well-being and survival of the community as a whole. Radical examples of the resulting behavior include the Jonestown community and the Heaven's Gate group, and more benign examples include religious hermits. Also, if a historico-temporal legitimacy is solely influential or dominant in an extreme way, personal loyalties (including loyalty to oneself) will take precedence over either deeper attitudes or the welfare and survival of the community as a whole. An example of the resulting behavior is the person willing to throw country and charity under the bus for the sake of personal advancement. Finally, if culture at large with its religious dimension does not balance politics, the quest for political power will eclipse both the physical well-being of society members and societal religious concerns. Indeed, the 20th century, in addition to numerous conflicts of a more confined scope, witnessed two wars to end all wars; and the current century is no less deadly.

However, these extremes are not the focus of our discussion. The intent here is to show that religion and politics are particular aspects of a culture, and to describe the sort of epistemology characteristic of the domains labelled culture, religion, and politics. In so doing, we have emphasized the *complementarity* of the social, religious, and political features of culture. Some persons *do* behave in extreme ways; nevertheless, most persons live out their lives well within the extremes, even though for some the transcendent aspect is more important, and for others the historico-temporal prevails. Nonetheless, because politics conflates temporal and transcendent legitimacies, it is an astonishingly powerful force. Their guise, point in time, and place in the world notwithstanding, politicians will use all available resources, including shaping and reshaping by various punditries, whether distorted or not, to insure their notion of cultural success and survival, including controlling not only the persons at the fringes but also all those well within the extremes.

As this book has pointed out repeatedly, it is difficult to imagine two groups more culturally diverse than Māori and Pākehā. Māori had a long spiritualized history of intra and inter-tribal relations before Pākehā came to Aotearoa/New Zealand. Likewise, Pākehā had developed the broad structures and interrelations of their secularized society long before their arrival there. At the start of the 19th century, power favored Māori. They were the majority population, newcomers depended on them for survival, and Māori decided permissible behavior. About mid-century power was more or less equal between Māori and Pākehā. Their respective populations were roughly equivalent, and there was a tremendous struggle over which culture would dominate and determine appropriate behavior. By the end of the 19th century power favored Pākehā; Māori were less than 6 percent of the population, and Pākehā decided acceptable behavior. Pākehā prevailed because they brought greater population and superior technology to bear.

However, management of power, with its dual legitimacy, has a potentially synergistic property which, while it certainly includes the immediate society, may look beyond it for a more fulfilling and comprehensive quality in its survival. Māori, at their lowest point, and by virtue of the dual legitimacy fundamental to the human psyche, found strength in the incomprehensible depths of their plight and the mutual support of their peers for an effort to control their own fate within a Pākehā structure. They began a reconceptualization of their culture with a strong view to its survival. At about the same time, Pākehā began a rethinking of their own culture by redefining historico-temporal processes and drawing from the depths of human empathy, and have over time distanced themselves from the strict assimilationist policies of the 19th century. The current bicultural debate between Māori and Pākehā is in terms of these cultural reconceptualizations at the social, spiritual, and political levels. It is about the interfacing of their respective meaning systems to achieve properly integrated peer relations, properly founded transcendent values, and a political system that supports both of these domestically and presents a united bicultural Aotearoa/New Zealand to the world.

The nature of cultural reconceptualization

Reification of culture is the basis for the synergistic synthesis of cultures.

Reification is the process of taking that which is abstract and regarding it as having some sort of concrete existence. Etymologically, "reify," which in the English language dates to the mid–19th century, derives from the Latin *res* which means "thing" and includes the *-fy* ending which means to "make into."[30] So, to "reify" is to make a thing of that which is not a thing; to "*thingify*"; to take that which is not tangible and consider it as though it were tangible; to present the abstract as though it were material.

We regularly engage in reification without giving a second thought to what we have done. For example, an American Midwestern family about to experience a very forceful tornado might describe themselves as "gripped by fear"; or once the storm has passed and they view the devastation, they may say that they are "in the clutches of despair"; or they may refer to someone who chooses to not seek shelter as a person who is "flirting with death"; or if the tornado simply passes over the community causing no physical damage, the family may declare that "fortune smiled upon them." We think of intangibles such as fear, despair, death, and fortune in this way to give them substance. Importantly, this does not deny the reality of non-physical phenomena; instead, it provides a way of understanding them as real. In addition to these personifications, dictionary examples of non-physical phenomena include other emotions such anger and joy, and other concepts such as liberty and justice. We cannot contain anger, joy, liberty, and justice in a physical repository; yet, each possesses its own sort of existence made more real through reification. Reification provides a greater reality in particular ways according to the nature of the reification one chooses to apply; for instance, one can be *mocked* by love as well as *consoled* by it.

The second topic of this chapter, "The dynamic encounter of meaning systems," describes culture as a "rolling present"; in other words, culture is a process of constant change. This reference includes the recognition that there is no physical substance known as culture; even physical cultural artefacts fulfill a semiotic function in an ever-rolling present. However, persons think and speak of culture as substantial because it helps them make sense of it. Additionally, the terms one chooses by which to think and speak of a particular culture as substantial influence the perception and subsequent understanding of that culture. In illustration, to speak of *the thoughtful exhibition of cultural wisdom* is quite different than to speak of *the jester-like antics of cultural foolery*; yet an observer may apply either expression to the same cultural phenomenon depending on her or his disposition. Importantly, how we perceive and understand a culture, including our own, will impact how we relate to it.

It its simplest form reification of culture refers to the everyday human perception of that which is in a constant state of change as static; persons assign to it a fixed, substantial quality in order to make sense of it and to address it according to their perception of it. However, reification of culture may have an effect beyond such daily routine processes. It may construct a type of pan-societal proto-culture for a particular group; an activity that does not necessarily entail a deliberate attempt to freeze perceptions, but is simply a possible outcome of reification. For example, at the end of the 19th century, many Pākehā decided that Māori culture was soon to be extinct and consequently became acutely interested in its defining features such as its architecture, art, artefacts, myths, and legends. They began programs to collect, restore, and record all they could about Māori while the culture was still available. One result of these efforts was the formation of an idea, based on the amalgamation of the things collected, restored, and recorded, of a "traditional" Māori culture which was more or less normative, changeless, and timeless.[31] While the accuracy of the reified image may be open to challenge on some fronts, this kind of reified construction, which had its roots in Māori cultural peril, exemplifies a normal human activity. In other words, this sort of reification of a pan–Māori proto-culture was not a pre-thought deliberate construction but an outgrowth of the concern to collect, restore, and record as much as possible about Māori culture while it was still accessible; to capture its authenticity and to preserve it as much as possible.

We would be remiss not to mention that some have taken this sort of natural reification a step too far. One example is anthropologist Allan Hanson who documented his view in his essay, "The Making of the Maori: Culture Invention and its Logic." In his paper, published in December 1989 in the *American Anthropologist*, he writes, "'Traditional culture' is increasingly recognized to be more an invention constructed for contemporary purposes than a stable heritage handed on from the past."[32] Note his use of the word "invention." He then elaborates how persons, mainly scholars, of the late 19th and early 20th centuries, "who cherished a political desire to assimilate Māoris to Pākehā culture," "constructed" an "image of Māori culture" in conformance with their assimilationist desires.[33] As for Māori, in his view, they were willing "to bolster a sense of their own ethnic distinctiveness and value" by accepting "any qualities of racial greatness that Pākehā scholars might attribute to them."[34] As Hanson understands it, in the case of Aotearoa/New Zealand, Pākehā took a tribally diverse continually developing culture and reified it into a stable traditional pan-culture in fulfillment of colonial assimilationist goals. In his opinion this "inventive process" had been ongoing for over a century and had included contributions from anthropologists and other scholars, government officials, and Māori themselves, and he sought to use this development as "an excellent context in which to frame" "fundamental questions about the nature of cultural reality."[35] He acknowledges that cultures continually shape their own traditions for purposes of their own, but then writes, "People also invent cultures and traditions for others, and then treat them as if their inventions were the actual state of affairs."[36]

Although Hanson concludes that "inventions are common components in the ongoing development of *authentic* culture..."[37] (emphasis added), he touched a sensitive Māori cultural nerve. Māori scholars and other persons objected to Hanson's use of the term "invention" and his application of it to them. They apparently understood his use of the word and the thrust of his argument as a challenge to Māori cultural authenticity.[38] Chapter Eight of this book (see the topic, "Cultural authenticity: A necessary reprise") examines in greater detail the controversy sparked by Hanson's article and its use of the word "invention" and suggests a term more appropriate for recognizing cultural authenticity amid reifying processes. But for now let us be content to briefly examine Hanson's article as it pertains to a particular aspect of reification.

Hanson's article credits Pākehā with the development of two traditions associated with Māori culture which he believes served Pākehā assimilationist purposes: the Great Fleet theory of Polynesian arrival in Aotearoa/New Zealand, which Pākehā ethnographer S. Percy Smith popularized and Māori anthropologist Sir Peter Buck (Te Rangi Hīroa) also accepted; and the *Io* tradition, a religious scheme in which a Supreme Deity, *Io*, presides over the Māori pantheon.[39] As Chapter One of this book discusses (see the topic, "A handle on the history"), the Great Fleet theory, which was generally accepted at least into the 1970s and which Hanson believed at the time of his paper (1989) to still be widely held, has been completely debunked and no longer extensively held as fact; the same chapter and topic of this book also presents an alternative version of Māori origins. The *Io* tradition, however, is another matter, and Chapter Seven of this book addresses it in some detail.

But as it pertains to Pākehā motives and their association with reification, Hanson's notion that the chief concern was the assimilation of Māori into a European-style society by the propagation of these theories is indeed unfortunate. While it is beyond question that Pākehā intent earlier in the 19th century was the absorption of Māori into Pākehā culture, a shift in motive was underway by the end of the century. The reification of a pan–Māori proto-culture in the late 19th and early 20th centuries, which included Pākehā efforts to preserve as much information as possible about Māori, was in measure a result of Pākehā reinterpretation of their own culture as distinctly Aotearoan/New Zealand and consequently inclusive of the indigenous population; and importantly, it included significant input from Māori. A dialogue between Māori and Pākehā began in the depth of Māori despair and on the brink of their eradication as a distinct people that has resulted in the continuance of Māori tribes as an unambiguous race. Put another way, the driving force of the anthropologists and ethnologists in Aotearoa/New Zealand just prior to and after 1900 was not a product of nefarious intent. Rather, their effort was a sincere, albeit sometimes misinformed, endeavor to establish for posterity a record of Māori culture as they understood it; and Māori were instrumentally collaborative in the effort to preserve the authenticity of their tribal culture. There developed a reified idea of a stable traditional pan–Māori proto-culture which was accepted as representative of Māori before and just after European contact. In this way, reifying processes have established a basis for the synergistic synthesis of cultures in Aotearoa/New Zealand as the conceptual content of the reified proto-culture has supplied ideas and language for much of the Māori-Pākehā dialogue pertaining to a bicultural society.

The act of reifying culture is most often a natural phenomenon that allows us to get on with our daily lives, and it may also entail a "snapshot" of the past. But in either case, the act of reifying culture does not necessarily entail a deliberate act; rather, it is a phenomenon integral to human mental processes. Even if persons deliberately attempt to create culture or to shape it in particular ways, the product of their efforts still requires acceptance by the target people; who, in the case of Māori, are not likely to trade their birthright for "a mess of pottage." Put in Tillichian terms, symbols must be born and they live a life of their own.

On a personal level, without reification, one could make little, if any, sense of culture, whether one's own or that of another group; and on a broader level, reification sometimes solidifies a pan-societal proto-culture through an amalgamation of traditions. Nonetheless, the reified image of culture that is formed at any level must arise from personal dispositions toward life and corporate acceptance of what is true. It is in this personal customizing of dispositions and this corporate approval of what is true that the potential for a synergistic synthesis of cultures resides. Whether we are seeking direction in our own culture or trying to understand that of others, it is the process of reification that gives shape to the result of our endeavor.

Reification and cultural authenticity

Reification of culture establishes rather than negates cultural authenticity.

While reification is natural to human experience, it does raise the issue of cultural authenticity. Put in question form: How is the process of ascribing substance to intangibles causally connected to cultural genuineness? Contemporary Māori culture provides two concepts that are helpful for addressing this issue: *Mātauranga Māori* and *Māoritanga*. These notions take us far afield from Hanson's presentation briefly sketched in the previous topic.

The first, the concept of *Mātauranga Māori* (Māori knowledge), was introduced in this book's second chapter (see the topic, "*Whare* meets *whare*"). Even though its usage among Aotearoans/New Zealanders can be very broad, and a proper understanding of that to which it refers can be quite complex,[40] this book will confine its application to three particulars. First, the expression *Mātauranga Māori* presupposes a body of knowledge, inclusive of both the established and creative aspects of culture, the nature of which one can properly call Māori; second, it implies an epistemological method for identifying that knowledge; and third, these two together presuppose such knowledge to be embedded in a broader cultural complex from which it must be extracted, reinterpreted, and given concrete social application. Looked at in this way, we might think of it as a process of Māori education.

The second concept, *Māoritanga*, has to do with the essence in which the knowledge is rooted and on which the epistemological method is based. One use of the suffix *-tanga* is "to designate the quality derived from the base noun."[41] Hence, *Māoritanga* refers to the quality of being Māori. We could easily substitute the English suffix *-ness*; hence, *Māoritanga* could be rendered *Māoriness*. In this case it refers to the *nature* of a particular knowledge; that which qualifies it as properly Māori. While in the view of some *Mātauranga Māori* "has somewhat eclipsed '*Māoritanga*' as a way of signifying the essentials of the Māori world—its values, culture and worldview"[42] (italics added); the terms (as these others may also understand) are not entirely synonymous even though inseparably related.

For our purposes, *Māoritanga* or *Māoriness* refers to that quality of being Māori which penetrates much deeper than cultural expressions such as ceremonies, carvings, and posture dances; it is a quality of the Māori heart. It signifies the intense pride that accompanies being a Māori tribesperson. It is a word that reifies the deep sense of fulfillment and worth that is integral to Māori heritage. In other words, *Māoritanga* is a reference to an essential cultural core, the essence of what it means to be Māori; an ontological quality that is specifically tied to Māori connections with *atua*, ancestors, and the land. Indeed, this sort of reification, expressed through varied physical representations such as ceremonies, carvings, weavings, songs, dances, etc., and the physical land itself and its features, gives substance to a core of continuing culture.

The terms *Māoritanga* (Māoriness) and *Mātauranga Māori* (Māori knowledge) are inseparably joined as a circular construct. On the one hand, a person must have some preliminary notion (Māoriness) of what she or he is looking for, while on the other hand, what that person is looking for (Māori knowledge) informs the looker when she or he has found it; one concept complements the other. Moreover, what a person is looking for often determines both what gets found and what gets overlooked. The two terms together include a method of searching for, identifying, interpreting, and applying that which a person to some extent already knows, and in the case of Māori people, the prevailing attitude is that they best understand what they are looking for and what to do with it; they are in a better position than anyone else to identify it, reinterpret it, and apply it to contemporary society. It takes the full application of *Māoritanga* and *Mātauranga Māori* to bring about the incessant reinterpretation of Māori culture while maintaining cultural authenticity. Both that which is there to be built upon, and that which is novel in the epistemological process, combine (indeed, are required) to reshape culture in every new drop of discovery. To apply these concepts to culture at large: cultures have a core ontological quality, an innate reified sense of self, tied to their unique past; and that cultural core continually redefines itself in conjunction with and expresses itself through forms available in the current milieu. In this way, reification of culture establishes, rather than negates, cultural authenticity.

Without doubt, both *Māoritanga* (Māoriness) and *Mātauranga Māori* (Māori knowledge) are directly related to the process of ascribing qualitative substance to intangibles. One provides a cultural core and the other allows for creative advance. The question now becomes how much room the combination of the two—as a qualitative base for a particular knowledge; the knowledge itself; and a method for discovering, extracting, reinterpreting, and applying the knowledge—allows for diversity within the unity of reification; how much from the "outside" can be brought "inside." The answer, of course, is, as much as the cultural collective consciousness is willing to allow; notably, it can reject outside elements as well as incorporate them.

Although the pan–Māori proto-culture discussed in the previous topic of this chapter, regardless of its role in the resurgence of the indigenous culture, never existed except in a reified sense, both Māori pride and the discovery and rediscovery of their knowledge embedded in the existing Aotearoa/New Zealand culture, its extraction and societal application, enthusiastically continues; and Pākehā continue to reshape their worldview in conjunction with Māori notions. The result has been an allowance for change on both fronts.

On the one hand, Māori knowledge entails the inclusion of Western ideas and practices where Māori deem them appropriate and practicable. For instance, Māori constructed the *whare tipuna*, Te Pūrengi, on the Auckland University of Technology's (AUT's) campus *marae*, Ngā Wai o Horotiu, using modern building techniques and included modern teaching aids (albeit not without some debate) as integral to its design. On the other hand, Pākehā institutions and institutional processes are including more and more Māori ideology. For example, Māori tribal pride and practice permeate AUT's educational model as exemplified by the central place the *marae* enjoys on the AUT campus. Although the limits of change and inclusion may be subject to debate, it is the potential for incorporating new ideas and ways of doing things into both Māori and Pākehā culture that undergirds the possibility of bicultural success.

Importantly, the above paragraphs are in no way a denial of or failure to consider contemporary Māori tribal diversity. In fact, Māori tribes today celebrate their differences. They have had a King Movement since the late 1850s, but there has not been, nor is there now, a single recognized leader of Māori tribes. Indeed, some even blame the lack of tribal unity for the slow progress of Māori influence in Aotearoa/New Zealand. But internal tribal diversity does not negate a reified cultural substructure which supports varied tribal identities and practices; rather, the two forms of normal non-deliberate reification discussed in previous topic of this chapter (those resulting from the daily routine of life and those resulting from active reflection on the past) combine to establish a central tribal pride within tribal diversity. Just as cultural symbols can make cultural change so transparent that today's culture appears virtually selfsame with that of yesteryear, so can they establish a core of agreement within fringe variances. In terms of the *whare tipuna* as a cultural symbol, there is a sense in which it extends itself as a symbol past the particular group to whom it belongs to embrace Māori culture as a whole; the symbol gives substance to Māori culture in both its local and pan-cultural form. Its pan-cultural form translates easily into a general sense of *Māoritanga* which complements and underlies *Mātauranga Māori*. The former reifies a general pride in being Māori while the latter allows for differences in tribal attitudes and practices, and together they may incorporate Pākehā ideas and ways of doing things thus stamping them with Māori authenticity.

As for Pākehā, as Chapter Eight of this book will show, the Aotearoa/New Zealand Government is actively seeking ways to incorporate outlooks and values which are commonly held by Māori tribes into national programs thus giving them the stamp of national authenticity. It is the synergistic combination of Pākehā and Māori cultural reification that is producing the national pride and practice of a bicultural nation without sacrificing the cultural genuineness of either group.

CHAPTER SEVEN

Io

Here an Io, *there an* Io

What *is* in a name?! The fragrance of a flower may be consistent regardless of its floral nomenclature, but selfsame nomenclature does not demand undifferentiated definition. *Io*, pronunciation (at least for the moment) notwithstanding, has several meanings depending on how persons focus their interests. Some mythologists will recall a character from Greek mythology; moviegoers may immediately think of a character from *The Clash of the Titans*; astronomers will recognize *Io* as one of Jupiter's moons; and computer enthusiasts may understand the term as an abbreviation for "input/output." However, Aotearoans/New Zealanders, most of whom will probably know the aforementioned references, also recognize an *Io* very specific to their nation. Let us now explore the extent to which *this Io* is an indicator of a synergistic synthesis of cultures.

This Māori word, pronounced "ee oh" not "eye oh," has both a non-capitalized (*io*) and a capitalized (*Io*) form. Māori use the non-capitalized form, as they do with many words in their language, as both a verb and a noun. As documented in John Moorfield's dictionary, when used as a verb, it means "to twitch," but when used as a noun it can have a variety of meanings including "sinew, muscle, nerve, nervous system"; "twitch, spasm, twinge"; "line, column"; "warp, vertical thread"; "spur, ridge"; and "strand."[1] As it pertains to the capitalized form, the word is a reference to and a personal name of a "Supreme Being."[2] While both non-capitalized and capitalized usages are important to this chapter, the focus is on the term's use as a proper noun. The Māori language includes other words often used to indicate "God" or "god(s)." The word *atua* is one example.[3] The word *ariki*, which is sometimes translated "Lord," and is thus used as a reference to a "God," is another.[4] But, as we shall see, *Io* is of particular importance.

Io, as a Māori personal name for a Supreme Being, is often found in compound forms. Several of them appear in a letter from 1908, originally written in the Māori language by a Māori tribesperson of the Ngāti Uenuku, Te Haupapa-o-Tane, to Polynesian Society co-founder, S. Percy Smith. The Polynesian Society published a translation of the letter in 1920 in its quarterly journal. The letter's author, before naming the 12 heavens (which the letter's author claimed "the learned men of old" had passed down) and singling out 12 ambassadorial spirits (which the writer said were the companions of *Io*) from their fellow representatives of these heavens, recorded a number of compound names for the "great god" as follows:

> The great god of all in our belief—that is the Maori people—above all gods, was this, Io-matua, the meaning of which is, that he was the parent of all things; in the heavens, or in the worlds. His second name was Io-mata-ngaro [Io-the-hidden-face], which name means that he is never seen by man. His

third name is Io-mata-aho [Io-seen-in-a-flash], so called because he is never seen except as in a flash of light or lightning. A fourth name is Io-tikitiki-o-rangi [Io-exalted-of-heaven], called so because he dwells in the highest and last of the heavens. A fifth name is Io-nui [Io-the-great-god], because he is greater than all the other gods that are known as dwelling in the heavens or the earth. These names will suffice [for the present] for me to tell you.[5] [Brackets by source.]

A more extensive list appears in a document which was part of a collection that Māori informant Hoani Te Whatahoro (1841–1923) gave to S. Percy Smith in 1909 and which collection Smith translated and published as *The Lore of the Whare-Wānanga—Part I, 'Things Celestial'* in 1913 and *The Lore of the Whare-Wānanga—Part II, 'Things Terrestrial'* in 1915. Over the years, the *Lore* has been reprinted several times. Te Whatahoro's enumeration is as follows:

Io-nui	Io-the-great-god-over-all
Io-roa	Io-the-enduring (or everlasting)
Io-matua	Io-the-all-parent (omniparent)
Io-te-wānanga	Io-of-all-knowledge (omnierudite)
Io-te-taketake	Io-the-origin-of-all-things (the one true god)
Io-tamaua-take	Io-the-immutable
Io-te-Toi-o-nga-rangi	Io-the-summit-of-heaven
Io-mata-putahi	Io-the-god-of-one-command
Io-mata-ngaro	Io-the-hidden-face
Io-mata-wai	Io-god-of-love
Io-mata-aho	Io-only-seen-in-a-flash-of-light
Io-te-hau-e-rangi	Io-presiding-in-all-heavens
Io-tikitiki-o-rangi	Io-the-exalted-of-heaven
Io-matua-kore	Io-the-parentless (self created)…
Io-te-waiora	Io-the-life-giving
Io-te-whiwhia	Io-who-renders-not-to-man-that-which-he-withholds[6] (parentheses by source)

Such compound forms are not uncommon in religion. For instance, persons of the Christian tradition often speak of "the God of love," "the God of peace," or "the almighty God."

Some have speculated about a relationship between the Māori word *Io* and the Jewish Tetragrammaton, יהוה (YHWH), which they transliterate as either "Yahweh" or "Jehovah." One example is Elsdon Best (previously introduced; see the topic, "Cultural complexity and abstractness," in Chapter Six of this book). In his 1922 publication, *Some Aspects of Maori Myth and Religion: Illustrating the Mentality of the Maori and His Mythopoetic Concepts*, Best divided the Māori gods into four classifications: On the bottom rung of the celestial ladder were "the spirits of dead forebears"; further up were the "tribal gods"; moving closer to the top were the "departmental gods … who preside over war, peace, the forest, winds, ocean, agriculture, etc."; but standing all alone at the top was "he who is termed Io the Parent, Io the Parentless, Io the Great, and Io of the Hidden Face."[7] Best associated the vagueness communicated by this sort of nomenclature with the Semitic practice of using descriptive names for a Supreme Being in order to avoid using the true name.[8] Interestingly, as far as Best was concerned, *Io's* occupation of the highest position on the ladder of deity smacked of "a speculative philosophy seeking a First Cause" as opposed to his elevation from the status of a primal ancestor or a phenomenon of the natural world.[9] He then wrote:

> It is just possible that the ancestors of the Māori brought the name of Io from an Asiatic home-land. In Renan's *History of the People of Israel* the author states that the name of Iahveh, or Iohoue, became contracted to Iahou, or Io. Of a verity it would be a startling discovery to find that Io is but a form of the name Jehovah. However, these far-off speculations are outside the present writer's province.[10]

Within two years Best had taken an extra step. In his *The Maori: Volume I* he writes:

> Among certain Asiatic folk the name of Jehovah assumed many forms, as Jahweh, or Iahweh, Yahweh, Iahoue. Now Renan, in his History of the People of Israel, writes: 'The holy name became contracted into Iahou or Io.' This suggests a startling theory. Has the name of Jehovah been carried westward, and that of Io eastward, from a common centre, to meet here at the bounds of the earth? This is but one of many striking Asiatic-Polynesian parallels that provide much pabulum for thinking minds.[11]

Nevertheless, today's main debate, while strongly inclusive of the origins of the name *Io*, has little if anything to do with specific Semitic associations. It is about whether there was a Supreme Deity named *Io* prior to European contact with Māori. In other words, is *Io* actually evidence of a Māori *Urmonotheismus* (a primitive monotheism) or simply a demonstration of the effect that Western ideas about God have had on the indigenous population? And if the latter is true, to what extent have those Western notions served the purpose, either deliberately (as Allan Hanson once suggested; see the topic, "The nature of cultural reconceptualization," in Chapter Six of this book) or inadvertently, of colonizing the Māori mind; that is, altering the Māori worldview so that it conforms to Western society?[12] Or to ask the question another way: To what extent, if at all, is *Io* merely a component in the reification of an unchanging, normative, "traditional" Māori culture (also see the topic, "The nature of cultural reconceptualization," in Chapter Six of this book) beginning in the late 19th century developed by both Māori and Pākehā?

The telltale twitch

Te Rangi Hīroa (Sir Peter Buck), in his work first published in 1949, *The Coming of the Maori*, has provided us with an example of the current conversation about *Io*, but some background is required in order to understand it.

Let us recall that the treatment of Pākehā culture and religion in Chapter Five of this book describes how European settlers brought with them much of the culture that was in fashion at the time of their departure from their homeland, and how they necessarily adjusted it in their new surroundings. This was no less true for the Polynesian arrivals in Aotearoa/New Zealand several hundred years prior to the Europeans. However, while researchers can document with a high degree of certainty the course of Pākehā history that led to their arrival on these islands and the content of the culture they brought with them, their reconstruction of the Māori past has proved to be a much more difficult undertaking. This is in part due to the fact that Pākehā had a written language by which they could keep records while Māori did not. Instead, the indigenous population relied upon oral tradition, carvings, geographic features, celestial arrangements, relics, heirlooms, and the like as mnemonic devices to recall ancestors, stories, events, etc., pertaining to their homeland, their arrival, and their early life in the land. Researchers of early Māori culture must and do take these into account, but they also include other evidence such as ground disturbances, skeletons, and seeds gnawed by kiore (Pacific rats that the adventurers brought with them as a food source) in their examination of early Polynesian presence. Thus investigation into the initial human inhabitance of the islands and its development lines up along two fronts: recollections handed down from generation to generation and surviving physical evidence, both natural and manufactured. Even though Māori *tohunga* (experts) held *whare wānanga* (school house gatherings) for the purpose of passing on genealogical, historical, and religious knowledge, investigators consider the physical evidence as the best evidence. As Te Rangi Hīroa writes, "…a skeleton in its original resting place surrounded by adzes, ornaments, and a blown moa egg speaks with more truth concerning the past than the living graduates of an accredited house of learning" (*whare wānanga*).[13] Scholars consider testimonial evidence selective and subject to change over time, while physical evidence, once uncovered and documented, tends to remain firm. The problem with oral evidence exacerbates when researchers who are cultural outsiders selectively embed Māori *oral* tradition in a *written* text in a *fragmentary* way and not as a *complete* narrative. The issue becomes even more augmented when these investigators attempt to translate and explain, from their own cultural point of view, the fragmentary narratives which they have selectively recorded. Moreover, in this reconstruction process, the examiners may lose sight of Māori as very loosely organized tribal groups whose narratives may vary from one to other, and thus attempt to organize their ethnography into some pan–Māori identity. From this background, our attention now moves to the specific case which exemplifies the current discussion about the identity of *Io*.

In early 1879, the Aotearoa/New Zealand Government appointed John White (1826–1891), a Pākehā civil servant, linguist, and academic, who had been in the country since 1834, to develop an official Māori history.[14] White's six volume work, titled *The Ancient History of the Maori*, was published between 1887 and 1890. Hīroa drew attention to the opening pages of Chapter I of the second volume of White's *History*.[15] White began this chapter with an "incantation chanted whilst planting the kūmara" (a type of potato and a sacred crop) in which he used the phrase "O Io" three times and appears to draw a connection between "O Io" and the expression "O god of man."[16] Although persons such as historian Jonathan Z. Smith view the repetition of *io* in the chant which White recorded to actually be a "refrain '*i-o!*' rather than a god's proper name,"[17] Hīroa recognized this *karakia* (chant) as "a Whanganui [a district on the west coast of the North Island] lament which refers to the god Io."[18] White labelled the next section of his chapter "IO," referenced the Ngāti Hau (a Māori tribe of the Whanganui district), and opened with the statements, "Io is really the god. He made the heaven and the earth."[19] White then recorded a Ngāti Hau "incantation to Io" which he said "was repeated to him [that is, repeated to *Io*] at the time that the bones of a corpse were being exhumed."[20] This is a reference to the *hahunga* ceremony, a particular bone disentombment and scraping ritual associated with Māori rites for the dead (see the topic, "*Whare* meets *whare*," in Chapter Two of this book). White also designated the next section as "IO," but referenced the Ngāti Ruanui (a Māori tribe from the Taranaki district; just north and west of the Whanganui district), and recorded some interpretations of muscular twitches, as they occur under certain circumstances and in various parts of the body, as omens.[21] As the previous topic of this chapter mentions, one meaning of *io*, in its non-capitalized form, is "a muscular twitch." However, White opened this section with the statement, "Io was a sign of good or evil. The involuntary twitching of any part of the human body was recognized as Io"[22] Note White's capitalization of the word, "*Io!*" He then listed a number of tribal interpretations of muscular twitches as omens, and in his narrative used the capitalized form of *Io* in every one of its 12 occurrences instead of its translation, "twitch."[23] For instance, instead of writing "if the *twitching* was at the extremity of the arm or leg, it was an omen of rain or wind"; he wrote "if the Io [apparently a reference to a Supreme Being] was at the extremity of the arm or leg, it was an omen of rain or wind."[24] Hīroa concluded, "Thus, White supported a page of a god Io with three pages of twitches (*io*), but capitalization does not convert a muscular twitch into a god"[25] (parentheses by source). Hīroa understood that White, who believed Māori interpreted muscular twitches as manifestations of the god *Io*, was confusing two completely different meanings of the word. Also, White appears to be conflating the ideas of separate tribes (Ngāti Hau and Ngāti Ruanui), and we may add that White seems to have ignored almost a century of Christian influence on Māori tribes.

Hīroa's presentation exemplifies the current controversy. Narrowly stated, did John White accurately record and interpret *Io* as a Māori Supreme Deity who made the heavens and the earth and sent messages through muscular twitches? or did White incorporate his own religious beliefs and cultural preferences into his work? More broadly stated, did Māori tribes have a pre–European monotheism, or is *Io* the product of Christian and other Western influences on either or both Māori and those who observed and recorded Māori?

The Polynesian Society and the search for "the historical Io*"*

In 1906 French-German physician, theologian, philosopher, and musician Albert Schweitzer (1875–1965) published his book, *Geschichte der Leben-Jesu-Forschung*, which title in its English incarnation, first published in 1910, was *The Quest of the Historical Jesus: A Critical Study of Its Progress from Reimarus to Wrede*. The "quest" to which Schweitzer refers had its roots in the Enlightenment and had been around for more than a century when his book first appeared.[26] Prior to the Enlightenment most persons considered the Christian Gospels as a purely historical record of supernatural events, but scholars influenced by the Enlightenment looked at them more rationally and with a bit more skepticism; they downplayed the supernatural element. Some set out to discern what *actually* happened and thus aimed to develop a natural history by delving beneath the supernatural history, while others treated the Gospels as neither a supernatural nor a natural history and sought to cast them as non-historical stories meant to convey "truth." Those questors who have sought to look behind the Gospel curtain, both those included in Schweitzer's book and those who have followed, have conducted their research in an attempt to learn as much as possible about the kind of person that Jesus *truly* was. Over the centuries, there has been more than one quest for the "historical Jesus," and indeed, the quests continue. Nonetheless, considering the history of the Christian Church and associated religious studies, we may generally view attitudes toward "Jesus as he truly was" as aligning along two broad fronts. The first is an uncritical pre–Enlightenment view which takes the Gospel record at face value, while the other is a critical (analytical) view with its origins in the Enlightenment and which is, at least in part, a reaction against the pre–Enlightenment approach.

Aotearoa/New Zealand has its own quest, different in some ways, similar in others, to identify the historical origins of and describe the Supreme Deity, *Io*; a mission which is on the one hand associated with a larger, more general, effort directed toward a historical understanding of Māori tribespeople and on the other hand firmly tethered to the efforts of The Polynesian Society which was officially co-founded by S. Percy Smith (1840–1922) and Edward Tregear (1846–1931) on January 8, 1892.[27] Just as there has been, in Jesus research, both an uncritical and a critical phase within religious studies circles, *Io* research has also had an uncritical and a critical phase within The Polynesian Society. In fact, we can conveniently separate The Polynesian Society's history based on these two phases, both important for understanding the current *Io* debate. The first, from 1892 to 1946, entails the collection, transmission, and interpretation of information by the first generation of Society members; while the second, from 1946 onward, involves modifications by subsequent generations of members to the methods and conclusions of the first generation. This present topic of our current chapter focuses on the first phase, and the topic below, "The higher critical school and the *Io* of faith," takes up the second phase. This discussion is not a comprehensive survey of *Io* material[28]; rather, it is an attempt to establish the prevailing attitude toward *Io* research in these respective periods.

As mentioned above, there are some differences between the quest for the historical Jesus and The Polynesian Society's quest for the historical *Io* which can help put the Society's efforts into perspective. First, while few doubt that Jesus was a historical figure, the quest for the historical *Io* has never been about a historical figure; it has been about a tribal notion of a Supreme Deity. Additionally, whereas the quest for the historical Jesus had an established body of source data to which questors applied academic tools, the initial phase of the Polynesian Society's quest for the historical *Io* was in large part a search for and receiving of source data to which the second phase of the quest applied academic tools.

As also mentioned above, there are some helpful points of similarity. First, although the searchers for the historical Jesus did not set out to reconstruct the sequence of events in Jesus's life, they did set out to determine Jesus's personal attributes and describe the kind of person Jesus actually was; likewise, those who have searched for the historical *Io* have also been quite concerned with *Io*'s personal attributes and his nature as a God. Moreover, those who have sought the historical Jesus have attempted to delve beneath the Biblical texts in order to understand Jesus in the cultural milieu of his time; comparably, those who have sought the historical *Io* have attempted to discover and interpret source data for the purpose of understanding *Io* in his original cultural context. Perhaps the greatest lesson resulting from these searches, whether for the historical Jesus or for the historical *Io*, is that the questors usually find that which they, from the outset, are looking to find.

One of the great hindrances to the *Io* quest has been, as the previous topic of this chapter states, the lack of any written Māori script prior to its development by the early Christian missionaries. This absence of a written language makes it is very difficult to establish, with a high degree of certainty, the accuracy of recollections of the past. Importantly, even a written text does not guarantee historical precision; writers always write for a reason which means that what is recorded is subject to both a process of selection and a particular interpretation of circumstances and events. And this is no less true of oral tradition; while it may be quite precise, it will likely be selective and shaped according to a particular contemporary agenda. With both written and oral tradition, the question becomes how, if it is even possible, to sort out accurate information and develop a factual picture of the past. The advantage of written script is that it provides some record often traceable to some time, place, or person(s); but credibility and dependability are issues in any case.

The question of trustworthiness, whether directed to either a written or an unwritten source, raises two important issues and some follow-up questions. First, as it pertains to the suppliers of information, how dependent are their recollections on an expediency associ-ated with a moment in the past and its development along a continuum into the present? How does this affect the information's reliability? Second, regarding the receivers of in-formation, what are their tools for sorting out the sources? Are they reliable? And are the receivers of information competent in using them? While the early *Io* searchers included physical objects, such as adzes, structures, canoes, etc., in their study of Māori culture and learned much about the indigenous folk from them; when it came to understanding Māori religious ideas and practices, they most often relied on interviews with the indigenous pop-ulation or some script either written or dictated by Māori persons. It is to these circum-stances that the ethnographers and academics of religious ideas and practices must apply their investigatory gadgets of choice.

Although the search for the historical *Io* has direct ties to The Polynesian Society, it began in some measure prior to the Society's official launching in 1892. By the time the Society was formed, academic investigators, government persons, and missionaries had amassed a considerable volume of information about Aotearoa/New Zealand's indige-nous population. Examples include Edward Shortland's (1812–1893) descriptions of Māori published in *Southern Districts of New Zealand* in 1851; some of Governor George Grey's (1812–1898) collection of Māori traditions and songs, published in *Nga Moteatea* in 1853; the work of a number of missionaries such as James Hamlin (1803–1865), William Colenso (1811–1899), Richard Taylor (1805–1873), and J.F.H. Wohlers (1811–1885); and, of course, John White's (1826–1891) six volume set of *The Ancient History of the Maori* published be-tween 1887 and 1890.[29]

Also prior to the establishing of The Polynesian Society, there are some references spe-cifically to *Io*. Māori academic Margaret Orbell documents an 1861 North Island east coast reference from the Ngāti Kahungunu; however, this *Io* seems to be related to the building of fortified villages; to date there is no reason to associate this *Io* with a High God.[30] As it pertains to a reference specifically to *Io* as a Supreme God, the earliest mention appears in an 1876 memoir by Charles Oliver Bond Davis (C.O. Davis; 1818?–1887) dedicated to Patu-one (c.1764–1872), a chief of the Ngāti Hao. According to Davis, some years earlier (he does not say how many) a Māori chief (neither does he identify the chief; but it was not Patuone) with whom he was traveling told him of a Supreme Being named *Io* whose name was so sa-cred that only a *tohunga* (holy person) could speak it at particular times and places.[31] Some, taking a clue from Davis's possible gloss of a line in an old prayer in the Māori language which he included in the Appendix of the memoir,[32] believe that he also misunderstood the old chief with whom he was traveling; that, however, is not for certain. Also prior to the founding of The Polynesian Society were John White's references to *Io* in his 1887 Volume II of his *The Ancient History of the Maori*. We have already detailed White's use of the word and recounted Te Rangi Hīroa's dispraising opinion of it (see the above topic, "The telltale twitch").

However, the founding of The Polynesian Society, which is, as it claims, undoubtedly one of the oldest learned societies south of the Equator,[33] marked a new chapter in Māori research. The Society's founding was in large part an organized thrust to create a corpus of literature about Māori and other Polynesian groups.[34] From the outset its aim has been to promote anthropological, ethnological, and philological study of the Polynesian races.[35] The Society has provided a framework for the exchange and development of ideas about Oceania in general and Māori culture in particular. From the start, the main support of that framework has been its quarterly publication, *The Journal of the Polynesian Society*.

The founders originally established *The Journal* in order to provide articles, reviews, etc., as a means of communication for its members who were separated throughout Aotearoa/New Zealand and the rest of the Pacific; the separation made it difficult to meet regularly. Many persons today, especially those of us whose homes are so remote from Aotearoa/New Zealand, are also indebted to *The Journal*. Of course, this quarterly was not the only source of information. Some Society members, as we have already noted, wrote prolifically, sometimes producing some very lengthy works, outside *The Journal*. Nonetheless, the founders established it from its beginning as a collection point and permanent record of information pertaining to Polynesian culture.

We will begin our discussion about *Io* in the first stage of The Polynesian Society with a source outside of *The Journal*; specifically the 1904 publication of *The Maori Race* authored by Polynesian Society co-founder Edward Tregear (1846–1931).[36] Persons interested in Māori religio-culture often quote from its Chapter XX which addresses "Religion and Cosmology." In this chapter, Tregear mentions *Io* rather matter-of-factly in his broad discussion of Māori gods, cosmogony, religio-cultural practices, etc., and seems to assume *Io* as the High God from whom all else emanates. Unfortunately, while his treatment is certainly interesting, it contains no concrete evidence for anything more than the robust discussion that was taking place at the time, which certainly included a number of Society members.[37] Nonetheless, Tregear's assumption of *Io* as a Supreme God, knowledge of which was shrouded in esoterity, was a harbinger of the evidence that would soon be made public by his Polynesian Society colleagues.

Indeed, in 1907 *The Journal* published a document which Society member Lieutenant Colonel Walter Edward Gudgeon (1841–1920) had received several years prior from a corresponding member of the Society, Tiwai Paraone (1847–1909) of the Marutūahu tribes.[38] Hare Hongi (1859–1944),[39] the son of a Pākehā sawyer and a woman of the Ngā Puhi who bestowed upon him the Pākehā name of Henry Matthew Stowell, translated the document into English from Māori. The *Journal* article includes both the Māori and English versions. Among other things the document claims that it was *Io* who created the heavens and the earth out of chaos, that *Io* was the engenderer of the other Māori gods, and that this knowledge was ancient and passed on by each successive tribal generation. However, our particular interest in this article extends to the attitude toward these matters which Polynesian Society President and *Journal* Editor, S. Percy Smith, plainly expresses in his introductory editor's note. He fully accepts the document's presentation of *Io* as the Prime Mover; agrees that the knowledge of *Io* was ancient, sacred, and of a highly esoteric nature; and underpins these ideas by mentioning other research not only in Aotearoa/New Zealand but also in Tahiti and Samoa.

If the year 1907 began a pivot in *Io* research, the move became complete in the years 1913 through 1915 with publications by two men whom we have already introduced. The first is amateur linguist and ethnographer S. Percy Smith, a co-founder and president (from 1904 to 1922) of The Polynesian Society and either an editor or co-editor of the Society's *Journal* for several years; professionally, Smith, among other jobs, had served as Aotearoa/New Zealand's Surveyor General.[40] The second is ethnographer and prolific author Elsdon Best, who was involved with The Society from its beginning and who also served as its president (from 1922 to 1924) after Smith's death; professionally, Best had worked in Aotearoa/New Zealand's Lands and Survey Department before becoming affiliated with the Dominion Museum.[41] He had long associations with and wrote extensively about the Ngāi Tūhoe, who resided in the Urewera, a rugged hill country toward the eastern side of the central North Island, and had developed a deep rooted appreciation for and interest in all things Māori. Smith's and Best's ideas, which met with little serious criticism until the 1930s, became the accepted belief for the topics about which they wrote, including *Io*. This lack of challenge, of course, corresponds with their influential associations with the Society—Smith was president from 1904 to the time of his death in 1922; Best was president from 1922 to 1924 but remained a force to be reckoned with until his death in 1931. While they may have privately disagreed about some matters; Smith's and Best's work publicly converged at several points. For instance, they were both heavily involved in the founding and progress of The Polynesian Society and were both ardent, if amateur, ethnographers of Māori culture. But for our present concern, the convergence of greatest importance is their understanding of *Io* as a Māori pre–European-contact Deity who was above all the other gods in the Māori pantheon and how they arrived at this conclusion in and through the less than critical phase of The Polynesian Society. Smith and Best shared a broad public ortho-doxy on the matter of *Io* and their ideas still are not completely abandoned.

There were some pertinent events after 1907 involving these two Polynesian Society leaders which led up to 1913–1915 completion of the pivot in *Io* research. First, Best, in a paper he read before the Australasian Association for the Advancement of Science in 1909, claimed that the Ngāi Tūhoe had knowledge of an ancient and high god, *Io*.[42] The Associa-tion published his paper, titled "Maori Religion: Notes on the Religious Ideas, Rites, and In-vocations of the Maori people of New Zealand," in 1910 in the *Report of the Twelfth Meeting of the Australasian Association for the Advancement of Science*. In the paper, Best comments that even though very little additional information was currently available, an informant (unnamed) had advised him of a Māori God named *Io* who was the first and principal of all the gods. According to his Māori informant, no structure was sacred enough for rites performed to *Io*, so ceremonies took place out of doors and only priests of high rank were taught the rites. According to Best, the Ngāi Tūhoe considered *Io* as a Creator and Supreme Being. Best also mentions a member (also unidentified) of the Ngāi Tahu who had told him that *Io* was the offspring of Rangi (the Sky Father) and Papa (the Earth Mother). This, of course, appears to contradict the idea of *Io* as the Supreme Creator God. So, Best surmised, "It is evident that the cult of Io was a very ancient one, and was overlaid and partially oblit-erated by the introduction of a number of inferior gods."[43]

Second, in December 1909, S. Percy Smith informed Elsdon Best of certain documents written in the Māori language which had just come into his possession from a correspond-ing member of the Society, Hoani Te Whatahoro (1841–1923), with whom Smith had been in touch for several years.[44] Te Whatahoro was the mixed race son of John Milsome Jury and Te Aitu-o-te-rangi who gave him the Pākehā name of John Alfred Jury.[45] Te Whatahoro claimed that these documents,[46] which he said dated to the early 1860s, were primarily the dictation of two men, Moihi Te Matorohanga (1804?–1884) and Nepia Pohuhu (1802?–1882), on the subject of the ancient beliefs and history of their tribal lineage. He further asserted that he had been one of two scribes appointed to record the data. The teaching conveyed in the documents which Te Whatahoro gave to Smith was divided into two parts; the first majored on tribal beliefs pertaining to "heavenly" matters including a Supreme God and some lesser gods, while the second specialized in more mundane "earthly" matters such as tribal history. Smith spent some 18 months transcribing, translating, and preparing commentary about the Te Whatahoro documents, maintaining the two-part separation. In the December 1912 edition of its *Journal*, the Polynesian Society announced the availability of the first division of the documents Smith had received from Te Whatahoro.[47] They were to be published as Volume III of the *Memoirs of the Polynesian Society* and offered for sale to Society members. Smith titled the volume *The Lore of the Whare-Wānanga or Teachings of the Maori College: Part I—Te Kauwae-Runga or 'Things Celestial.'* Te Kauwae-Runga translates as "The Upper Jaw." This brings us to the time period of 1913–1915 and the completion of the pivot in *Io* research.

In 1913 the first volume of *The Lore* was published as a public book. Smith, in his Introduction to this first volume, argues for the authenticity of the Te Whatahoro documents and against any notion that the concept of *Io* as a Supreme God presented in them was due to the influence of Christianity on Māori culture. He also summarizes that which the documents teach about *Io*. In his words, "Io [is] the supreme god, creator of all things, dwelling in the twelfth, or uppermost Heaven, where no man or god might enter except by command."[48]

Best, also in 1913, made use of the Te Whatahoro documents. In July of that year, the prestigious journal, *Man*, published by the Royal Anthropological Institute of Great Britain and Ireland, included his article, "The Cult of Io, the Concept of a Supreme Deity as Evolved by the Ancestors of the Polynesians."[49] In this article, Best demonstrates familiarity with previously published documents pertaining to a Māori Supreme Being although he does not specifically cite his sources; among them, Tregear's 1904 publication, *The Maori Race*, and perhaps Davis's *Life and Times of Patuone* published in 1876 and John White's second volume of *The Ancient History of the Māori* published in 1887. But he also shows a thorough knowledge of *The Lore* and uses it extensively, also without citation, in order to support the same views which S. Percy Smith had expressed regarding the validity of an esoteric *Io* cult; he supplements his sources with some of his own independent experience with Māori informants. In the article, Best, in solid agreement with S. Percy Smith, expresses his firm belief in an ancient esoteric cult of a monotheistic flavor which was organized around a Supreme Deity, *Io*. For Best, at the very least, the esoteric *Io* cult strongly resembled an ethical religion.

While Volume I of *The Lore* can stand on its own, Volume II enhances it; its contents were included in the documents which Smith received from Te Whatahoro, and "things celestial" are incomplete without "things terrestrial." So, beginning in March 1913 and continuing through the first half of 1915, The Society sequentially published the second volume of *The Lore* in *The Journal*. It was also published in 1915 as a separate volume titled *The Lore of the Whare-Wānanga or Teachings of the Maori College: Part II—Te Kauwae-Raro or 'Things Terrestrial.'* Te Kauwae-Raro translates as "the lower jaw."[50] The pivot was now complete. All the pieces were in place for the Pākehā reification of a pan–Māori religio-culture complete with a European style Supreme Being. Such was the orthodoxy that gripped The Polynesian Society throughout the reign of the first generation of Society members well into the 1940s, and there can be little doubt that the effect, intention and ethics notwithstanding, was to elevate Māori in the opinions of Pākehā to a people that more closely resembled the Europeans in thought and practice.

What message does this have for Māori-Pākehā relations? First, in a narrow sense, as religious studies Professor James L. Cox has pointed out, if the Pākehā improved opinion of Māori is contingent on some notion of advanced mentality as signaled by their ancient recognition of a Supreme Deity, then this is very close to a kind of discrimination built on Western cultural haughtiness.[51] And second, if Māori self-identification and self-worth depends on their acquiescence to Western models, then it does not speak well of Māori. But fortunately, the quest for the historical *Io* was a part of a larger concern to preserve and support as much of authentic Māori culture as possible and the Māori renaissance was associated with this broader interest. Nevertheless, this does not negate the impropriety of measuring the Māori (or for that matter, any other) worldview by how well it conforms to Western ideas. While having a cultural perspective is inevitable, assessing value must be done with the greatest of caution. The forcing of value standards, by one group upon another, amounts to a form of imperialism.

Chapters Three and Four of this book include a description of how some Western exchange researchers have theorized and tested models for reciprocity and power relations; and show that, while their notions have applicability within Western culture, when applied to other cultures, they tend to break down as testable phenomena under the weight of exchange complexity and structurally under the weight of cultural diversity, which diminishes their use as a general paradigm for human behavior. It should be clear by now that the position for which we opt in the pages of this book is a cultural relativism in which cultural differences should not be judged by absolute standards. Clifford Geertz once wrote that on the one hand "radical culturalism will get us nowhere" and on the other hand that "some sort of universalist tack is hardly more promising."[52] For him "a great part of what anthropology comes to" lies in the "reshaping of categories (ours and other people's…) so that they can reach beyond the contexts in which they originally arose and took their meaning so to locate affinities and mark differences."[53] However, let us be quick to add that this reshaping of cultural categories (ours and others,' which can be radically different) with a view to the discovery of ultimate meaning and positive potential is largely what the synergistic synthesis of cultures is about. From this viewpoint the synergistic synthesis of cultures is overall a constructive quality when cultural categories are expanded by the encounter of cultural differences, which are considered on their own merits and not judged by some absolute standard.

Jane Simpson connects the activity of recording reports about *Io* to the "intellectual colonization" of Māori. Her concern is "how Io is constructed through text and how a corpus is created,"[54] to which end she examines an impressive number of sources. She concludes that "the very texts that exalted and deified Io to a supreme position in the Māori pantheon at the same time dehumanized the Māori through their reductionism."[55] "The complexity of Māori religion," she writes, "was controlled through hierarchical ordering, list making, and stratification."[56] In her opinion, "Textualization [putting malleable oral tradition in concrete written form] allowed the European to complete by 1924 the intellectual colonization of the most tantalizingly elusive aspect of Māori society: their inner beliefs on ultimate questions."[57] James L. Cox connects Simpson's conclusions with his mention of possible Pākehā discrimination against Māori.[58] Whether textualization was, in effect, a tool of intellectual colonization, aided and abetted by the activity of persons such as Smith and Best, who had a passionate yearning for Māori to be more like the Europeans, is a matter of continuing discussion. Nonetheless, the indications are that this first generation of Polynesian Society colleagues absolutely believed what they propounded; and that they found honest delight in the way it challenged contemporary Pākehā society (which for decades had inappropriately disparaged the Māori mind as savage) with an elevated view of Māori mentality.

But be that as it may, what these early questors for the historical *Io*, such as S. Percy Smith and Elsdon Best, have broadly in common with the questors for the historical Jesus is that they found the *Io* for whom they were searching, whether he was there to be found or not. And where they broadly differ with the Jesus quest is in developing their opinions employing little if any historical analysis of the data; mostly they, mirroring the pre–Enlightenment approach to Jesus, took available sources at face value and fashioned their ideas with a minimum of critical inquiry.

A matter of interpretation

There is always a tension between events as they occur and events as they are interpreted, even at the time of and shortly after their occurrence; and S. Percy Smith and Elsdon Best, as it pertained to *Io* and an esoteric *Io* cult, tripled-down on a particular mode of interpretation. Although they may not have understood it in exactly this way, their hermeneutical method accepted the reliability of Māori oral tradition while glossing over both Māori and Pākehā cultural postures.

Their first interpretive risk has to do with the oral transmission of data. Māori recollections of *Io* were, as already discussed, based purely on oral transmission. There was no pre–European textual stratification against which Smith and Best could test the remembrances of Māori informants. In this situation, oral evidence before European contact was inaccessible and written evidence prior to that of the first European expeditions was nonexistent. There was no sure way to confirm the accuracy of remembrances which purportedly extended into times preceding the arrival of the Europeans.

Smith's and Best's second interpretive risk entailed the then current Māori mind-set. Māori informants had particular cultural dispositions which developed out of their cultural background which they brought to their experience and according to which they interpreted their past and relayed their oral tradition. By the time the founders established The Polynesian Society in 1892, Māori informants were several generations into contact with Europeans and their Christian religious ideas. This, of course, is no guarantee that Māori notions of *Io* were the product of European contact; historians of religion have documented the existence of esoteric tribal religious institutions and practices in other places of the world. Moreover, even though the early Christian missionaries to Aotearoa/New Zealand recorded nothing resembling an esoteric *urmonotheismus* among Māori tribes, the secret nature of such institutions and practices in and of itself makes data about them difficult to collect, understand, and explicate. Did information about the secret cult simply leak out? That appears to be the prevailing attitude among the first *Io* searchers.

Before we move to Smith's and Best's third interpretive risk, let us briefly examine the Māori persons who "leaked" the information. We do not know the identity of Best's Ngāi Tūhoe and Ngāi Tahu informants or, for that matter, those persons who enlightened Davis and Tregear. We do know that the information given to Lieutenant Colonel Gudgeon came from Tiwai Paraone and that the translator of the Paraone text, Hare Hongi, expressed some concern about the accuracy of the information therein.[59] As for Hoani Te Whatahoro (1841–1923),[60] in his early years, he was educated in the mission schools; from 1886 into 1888, he was one among others who assisted Mormon elders in translating the Book of Mormon into Māori; in the 1890s, he was affiliated with the *Kotahitanga* (Oneness) movement which promoted Māori self-government through their own Parliament; in 1900, he was baptized into the Mormon Church; and in 1907, he became a corresponding member of The Polynesian Society. We could raise the question, as some have, of the personal reliability of Te Whatahoro, but how far would that take us? Accuracy in many matters does not guarantee accuracy in all, any more than inaccuracy in many matters guarantees inaccuracy in all; and, what should be our attitude if accuracy is provably balanced between the two extremes? In this regard, S. Percy Smith appears to accept Te Whatahoro's credibility and the reliability of the documents while there is evidence that Elsdon Best had reservations.[61] Researchers have suggested reasons why Best accepted Te Whatahoro's testimony with a minimum of protest and elected not to publically challenge Smith's acceptance of it,[62] but for our purposes that is a moot point. While criticism of Te Whatahoro may *lead* to an in-dictment of his documents, it is not in and of itself an indictment of them. The indictment, if any, must come from an examination of the documents themselves.

The story of Te Whatahoro's documents[63] begins in the late 1850s in the Wairarapa, a district in the south part of the North Island on the east side. Apparently, Māori of the area became concerned about the developing political climate and the preservation of their tribal traditions. At this time, Te Whatahoro (born in 1841) was not yet 20 years old. Three *tohunga* (experts) agreed to lead an effort to record as much as they could remember. Moihi Te Matorohanga was to serve as the primary lecturer and Nepia Pohuhu and Paratene Te Okawhare were to supplement his teachings. Hoani Te Whatahoro was to be one of two scribes; the other was Aporo Te Kumeroa (?–1911). Māori constructed a special building for the lectures and teaching. It was underway at least by 1865 and continued for quite some time. Moihi Te Matorohanga and Nepia Pohuhu later, off and on over several years, provided supplemental information to Te Whatahoro. According to S. Percy Smith, "Te Matorohanga died in 1884, and Nepia Pohuhu in 1882, both being at the time of their deaths about eighty years old."[64] In 1899, Tamahau Mahupuku (1842?–1904), a Māori leader of the Ngāti Kahungunu, at a tribal meeting in the Wairarapa District suggested forming groups for the purpose of making a record of Māori ways while those familiar with them and could explain them were still around to do so. In response, Māori sent out a call for old documents and set up a committee to evaluate them. This group of evaluators, the *Tāne-nui-a-rangi* Committee, of which Te Whatahoro was a member, met between 1905 and 1910; and during this period settled on those documents tracing to Te Matorohanga, Pohuhu, and Okawhare. The committee contacted the Dominion Museum in Wellington which received the mate-rial in 1910. The originals are no longer extant, but copies are available. As a matter of note, it was in 1910 that Elsdon Best began his employment with the Dominion Museum. S. Percy Smith asserts that the documents he used for *The Lore* he copied himself from the originals and that they bore the seal of the *Tāne-nui-a-rangi* Committee and hence the approval of the most knowledgeable men available of the Ngāti Kahungunu. These documents, supple-mented by responses from Te Whatahoro to questions asked by Smith and Best, provide the bulk of data about *Io* and his esoteric cult which Smith and Best expound.

Regardless of one's opinion of the reliability of Hoani Te Whatahoro and the usability of his written materials, it is difficult to overemphasize that Māori, at and before the turn of the 19th to the 20th century, were both influenced by European ways and adjusting to Pākehā domination. Consequently, they were searching for ways to maintain links with their past and to establish their dignity in the present. This defined their mode of interpre-tation which they imposed upon their recollections and actions. Nonetheless, both Smith and Best, in the final say, opted for the reliability of the informants, and the information they provided, over the effect of European influence.

Smith's and Best's third interpretive risk entailed the then current Pākehā mind-set. Pākehā researchers, who were one step further removed from the sources, brought their own particular cultural dispositions into the interpretive process. They were a secularized people attempting the very difficult task of making sense of their observations of a spir-itualized society. The earlier missionaries—who had a vested interest in challenging the indigenous culture—while they seem to have respected Māori abilities, apparently saw no evidence of any Māori notion of a Supreme Being. One example is the Reverend Richard Taylor (1805–1873),[65] of the Church Missionary Society (CMS), who had been in Aotearoa/ New Zealand since 1836 and who advanced the idea of a degraded Semitic Māori.[66] Taylor, who viewed the indigenous population as the literal fulfillment of the parable of the prodigal son, was much aware of their qualities as a race. According to him:

> The native is not deficient in those arts which are essential to his comfort. His house is constructed with great skill and elegance, his garments with much beauty, and ornamented with a border of elaborately wrought embroidery; his little farm is tilled with the greatest care, not a weed to be seen; in fact he has carried those arts with which he is acquainted, to as much perfection, as they are apparently capable of.[67]

He also writes that "There is a degree of thought perceptible in their traditions of the creation, which mark a far more advanced state than their present. Their ideas in some respects are not so puerile...."[68] But with regard to an *urmonotheismus* he concludes:

> Properly speaking, the natives had no knowledge of a Supreme Being. They had a multitude of gods ... so mixed up with the spirits of ancestors, whose worship is entered largely into their religion, that it is difficult to distinguish one from the other.[69]

He then notes the opinion of a Māori chief:

> Speaking to Te Heuheu, the powerful Chief of Taupo, of God, as being the creator of all things, he ridiculed the idea, and said, is there one maker of all things amongst you Europeans? is not one a carpenter, another a blacksmith, another a ship-builder, and another a house-builder? And so was it in the beginning; one made this, another that: Tane made trees, Ru mountains, Tanga-roa fish, and so forth. Your religion is of to-day, ours from remote antiquity. Do not think then to destroy our ancient faith with your freshborn religion.[70]

Another example is William Colenso (1811–1899),[71] also of the CMS, who arrived in Aotearoa/New Zealand in 1834. He echoes the missionary perspective on the indigenous religion when he records that Māori

> ... had neither doctrine nor dogma; neither cultus, nor system of worship. They knew not of any Being who could properly be called God. They had no idols. They reverenced not the sun, or moon, or glittering heavenly host, or any natural phenomena. Rather, when they chose, they derided them. The three principal beings, or rather personifications,—*Tu*, *Whiro*, and *Tawhirimatea*,—(all alike malignant, and ever hated by the New Zealander, as the sole cause to them, of pain, misery, and death—in war, in peace, and in voyaging,) were certainly never loved, or reverenced, or worshipped. The New Zealander knew better than to worship them.[72]

In fact, as we have already seen, there is no record of the association of the word *Io* with the idea of a Supreme Being until C.O. Davis made one in 1876.

In contrast to persons such as Taylor and Colenso, S. Percy Smith and Elsdon Best, at the end of the 19th and beginning of the 20th centuries, when faced with the issue of a Māori Supreme Being, opted for the choice that *their* cultural dispositions dictated. While Smith's and Best's paramount resources were the Te Whatahoro manuscripts and their interviews with him, they had also conducted other personal interviews and made observations in their attempt to understand Māori culture. It is noteworthy that their work began and pinnacled at about the same time that Pākehā were coming into their own as a people; that is, they were in a process of separating from the strict assimilationist policies of colonial England. Therefore, they were looking for evidence of an intelligent Māori race that was more like themselves than some of the previous depictions had suggested. This defined their own mode of interpretation, and they found the Māori people and the *Io* that they wanted to find.

While this is not an exhaustive treatment of the first phase of the search for the historical *Io*, it establishes the uncritical attitude of the first generation of questors and furnishes sufficient background for understanding the higher critical school's rethinking of the subject in The Polynesian Society's second phase.

The higher critical school and "the Io *of faith"*

Most of The Polynesian Society's first generation members took a rather strait forward approach to understanding Māori history, customs, and belief in that they accepted the reports of Māori informants more or less uncritically. As it pertained to *Io* and an esoteric *Io* cult, in the main they, at least outwardly, dismissed the declarations by some Pākehā observers from the past that Māori had no conception whatsoever of a Supreme Being as Christianity understood the term. The work of S. Percy Smith and Elsdon Best is representative of the quest's first phase and its results; and while some persons did in private correspondence challenge the orthodoxy, little serious criticism filtered through the Society's screening processes until the 1930s.[73]

These first generation Society leaders were hard-working but lacked academic training in ethnography and anthropology and were certainly not prone to critical analysis. Smith died in 1922 and Best in 1931, and after Best's death the conflict between the amateur ethnographic tradition and a more academic approach came more into the open; however, the old view persisted for several more years—perhaps out of a combination of personal loyalty to the Society's founding fathers and sincere belief. It was not until 1946 when W.H. Skinner, a long-time supporter of the Smith-Best orthodoxy and the eighth Society president, died; and Johannes Anderson, a supporter of Smith and Best who had been either co-editor or editor of *The Journal* from 1922 into 1946, retired, that the amateur phase of the Society finally came to an end. In place of the amateur phase came a more scientifically based "higher critical school" which applied the tools of historical analysis to the *Io* question and consequently developed an entirely different idea of *Io* and an esoteric *Io* cult than did the first generation of Society members.

There were several scholars who properly belong to the higher critical school. They were professionally trained in ethnography and anthropology, and they often published outside *The Journal*. However, as it pertains to analysis of the Te Whatahoro manuscripts, our present discussion focuses on the research of David Simmons (1930–2015)[74] and Bruce Biggs (1921–2000).[75] Simmons was an ethnologist and historian who, from 1979 to 2010 except for 1992 to 1995, had served as a member of the Council of The Polynesian Society. He authored several books about Māori history and culture and enjoyed a career associated with the Otago Museum in Dunedin, the Auckland Institute and Museum, and the Auckland War Memorial Museum. Biggs had been an editor of *The Journal of the Polynesian Society* for several years in the 1960s, a member of the Council of The Polynesian Society from 1958 to 1977, and the Society's president from 1979 to 1993. He was a scholar of the Māori language and the first person appointed to teach it in an Aotearoa/New Zealand university setting—The University of Auckland beginning in 1951. The Polynesian Society awarded Simmons the Elsdon Best Memorial Medal in 1978; Biggs was the 1985 recipient. Simmons and Biggs applied the methods of historical analysis to the Te Whatahoro documents that Smith and Best used to support their ideas and which source they accepted as the dictation of Te Matorohanga and company from the 1860s; and in their *Journal* article titled "The Sources of 'The Lore of the Whare-Wānanga'" of March 1970,[76] they declared the Te Whatahoro material to be a composite.

While it was not their aim to evaluate the inclusion of authentic tribal tradition, as it pertains to the sources for Volume I of *The Lore* they conclude:

> If authentic tradition can be defined as that body of lore which is accepted as genuine by mature, well-informed members of the group concerned, *Te Kauae Runga* ["the upper jaw"; a reference to Volume I of *The Lore* subtitled *Things Celestial*, which uses the spelling "*Te Kauwae Runga*"] (with the exception of Chapter 2) can be accepted as such.[77] [Parentheses by source; brackets added.]

Significantly, Chapter 2 is the chapter containing the *Io* material.

A few pages earlier, in their chapter by chapter notes on the first volume of *The Lore* (their parenthesized numbers refer to particular manuscripts and their parenthesized roman numerals refer to materials they were unable to locate), Simmons and Biggs record:

> None of the material in chapter two is found in the extant copies of the Tāne-nui-a-rangi manuscripts (50), (51). It derives entirely from (5), Smith's copy of (xii) a book owned by Te Whatahoro, and credited to Te Matorohanga by Smith. Since this chapter contains the only primary documentation of the elaborate pantheon of gods and messengers, headed by Io-matua [*Io* the parent], the fact that this material is not found in either of (50) or (51) appears to be of great significance, and relevant to the question of whether or not the Io cult was part of Maori religious beliefs in pre-contact times.[78] [Brackets added.]

In the case of *Te Kauwae Raro* ("The Lower Jaw"; a reference to Volume II of *The Lore* subtitled *Things Terrestrial*), they conclude:

> … very little … corresponds with anything in the extant copies of the Tāne-nui-a-rangi manuscripts. On present evidence, almost all of this volume is a late compilation by Te Whatahoro from many sources. Much of it may represent authentic tradition of one area or another, but it cannot be accepted either as the teaching of any school of learning, or as authentic tradition of the Ngāti Kahungunu tribal area.[79]

While we may acknowledge the worth of Simmons's and Biggs's research for both source identification and the reliability (or lack thereof) of Hoani Te Whatahoro to produce original material, and may understand that they doubted the *Io* material's alleged connection to Te Matorohanga, we must also recognize that their work is inconclusive regarding the emergence of *Io* and beliefs about him.

At one end of the *Io* spectrum there are those who agree with the first generation of Society members that Māori belief in *Io* as a Supreme Being predates the arrival of the Europeans, but at the other end are those more modern anthropological researchers, whether Society members or not—such as Jane Simpson, Allan Hanson, and Toon van Meijl—who locate the origins of *Io* and the teaching about him at the end of the 19th and beginning of the 20th centuries. For Simpson, the *Io* sources have more to say about the colonizing Pākehā than about the colonized Māori.[80] For her, the quest for the historical *Io* by persons such as S. Percy Smith and Elsdon Best reflects, among other things, their "disaffection with missionary Christianity and a desire to discover universal religious roots."[81] She sees irony in the fact that their *Io* hunting demonstrates, in the face of their discontentment, the tenacious grip that Western religion had upon them; and concludes that, because the first generation of Society members viewed the "sect-ridden religious mores of their own society" as "spiritually bankrupt," their quest for the historical *Io* was more about their own quest for meaning.[82] Hanson ties the emergence of the *Io* tradition to an image constructed mainly by scholars, one purpose of which was the assimilation of Māori tribes into a European style culture; he believes Māori to be implicated in the development of the tradition in order to improve their societal position.[83] Van Meijl, in his discussion of *Māoritanga*, connects a similar notion of the assimilation of Māori people to the reification of Māori culture by European ethnographers of the period and the later adoption of the reified image by the Young Māori Party; he believes that such reification had helped complete the Pākehā colonization of Māori tribes.[84]

More recently, James L. Cox connects Te Whatahoro's presentation of *Io* with his association with the Mormon Church, which had arrived in Aotearoa/New Zealand in the 1880s.[85] Cox notes that Mormons had experienced severe criticism in the United States, and believes it plausible that Te Whatahoro linked Māori oppression in Aotearoa/New Zealand with Mormon suffering in America. Cox's theory is that Te Whatahoro deliberately mixed Māori notions of *Io* with the teachings of the Mormon Church in a purposeful and shrewd strategy which served the dual purpose of uplifting Māori while undermining traditional Christianity.

Interestingly, Jonathan Z. Smith's approach located the *Io* cult at neither end of the above mentioned spectrum. Instead, he placed its beginnings in the mid–19th century.[86] Smith suggests that we must understand the development of *Io* and the *Io* cult in an intersection of the Māori King Movement, which began in the late 1850s, with the Pai Mārire (good and peaceful) religious movement, which was founded in 1862 by Te Ua Haumēne (early 1820s–1866). Te Ua and Pai Mārire were introduced in Chapter Two of this book (see the topic, "The *whare karakia* as a symbol"). According to Smith, the two intersected in 1864. Smith proposes that the *Io* cult developed in order "to give Māori the possibility of direct access to Ihowa [Jehovah] without the written Bible and the Christian missionary as intermediaries."[87]

Jonathan Z. Smith's notion generates a measure of interest for the present discussion because his treatment of the rise of Te Ua and his Pai Mārire movement is a description of one instance of a Māori "prophet" making use of Christian religious ideas. As we have already noted (again, see the topic, "The *whare karakia* as a symbol," in Chapter Two), there were several other Māori prophets who have gained notoriety in Aotearoa/New Zealand.[88] In addition to Te Ua, there was Te Hura, an elderly woman in the 1850s known for her healing; Te Whiti-o-Rongomai III and Tohu Kākahi, Te Ua's successors who founded the pacifist community of Parihaka in the mid–1860s in order to peacefully resist Government surveying of confiscated land; Te Kooti Arikirangi Te Turuki, who founded the Ringatū faith in the 1860s; Rua Kēnana Hepetipa, Te Kooti's successor who, in the first decade of the 20th century, founded a pacifist community at Maungapōhatu known as the New Jerusalem; and Tahupōtiki Wiremu Rātana, who founded the Rātana Church in the 1920s. Each of these prophets, in her or his own way, has demonstrated the influence of Christianity on Māori people and their traditional beliefs and practices.

Of the ideas about the origins of *Io* listed above, Jonathan Z. Smith's notion is among the least popular. The majority opinion of more recent scholarship is that *Io* and the development of the traditions surrounding him originated in the late 19th and early 20th centuries; and as we might expect, each researcher has applied her or his own peculiar twist to the matter in formulating results. Again, what Jonathan Z. Smith's discussion establishes is the propensity of Māori to synthesize traditional Māori beliefs and practices with those of European Christianity, sometimes for the healing of diseases (many of which Pākehā brought to Aotearoa/New Zealand), but mostly as a challenge to Pākehā domination.

A common thread running throughout these various approaches to *Io* and his cult, including that of the first generation Polynesian Society orthodoxy, that of The Polynesian Society's higher critical school, and that of interested scholars outside The Polynesian Society's membership, is this: Regardless of how, when, or where researchers locate the origins of *Io* and the teaching about him, they impose their own interpretive dispositions to shape their conclusions. While the investigators discussed above may shed light on the possible motives and processes behind the development of phenomena such as *Io* and his cult, even they derive their conclusions by processing information through their own interpretive filters.

For the early Polynesian Society amateurs, the *Io* of history was ancient, predating European contact. For The Society's higher critical school and similar scholars there was no Māori Supreme Being named *Io* prior to contact with the European Christians; for them, the notions of persons such as S. Percy Smith and Elsdon Best were completely erroneous. However, all events and all history are matters of interpretation as it is integral to human experience as a rolling present. The truth of whether there was an *Io* at any time prior to European contact is difficult to establish and depends on how researchers choose to interpret the evidence. But irrespective of the *actual* origins of the *Io* traditions, just as the "Jesus of history" over time and through interpretation became the "Christ of faith," so too have the notions pertaining to a "historical *Io*," developed through the efforts of both Māori and Pākehā, through the process of the reification of culture, produced an "*Io* of faith" which is today widely accepted in Aotearoa/New Zealand.

Whereas the *Io* of faith may present a problem for many modern scholars, others, along with a good number of the general population, Māori and Pākehā alike, see no problem at all. Many firmly believe the tradition of *Io* as a Supreme Being to predate European contact which, of course, challenges Simpson's notion that *Io* is a product of Pākehā textmakers as myth creators and myth sustainers, Hanson's idea of *Io* as associated with an "invention" of culture, Van Meijl's observation that *Māoritanga* is contributing to the further colonization of Māori people, Cox's belief that Te Whatahoro took advantage of biases against traditional Christianity by his inclusion of *Io* materials in the documents he presented to S. Percy Smith, and Jonathan Smith's belief that *Io* was a Māori creation based on a synthesis of Christian and Māori traditions in the mid–19th century for the purpose of circumventing the Christian Bible and missionaries. Whatever the *truth* of the matter, the *Io* of faith, as a Māori cultural phenomenon, is today alive and doing well.

"*The* Io *of culture*"

The tension between those loyal to the view represented by the Smith-Best orthodoxy and the view of those represented by the members of the higher critical school remain unresolved, and researchers continue to lecture, produce papers, and write book chapters on the subject; however, regardless of the view taken toward the combination of Pākehā and Māori intent or whatever the truth about his origins, *Io*, today, typifies the syncretism and synergy that is producing a unique Aotearoa/New Zealand culture. The syncretism takes into account the source data and its providers, the take-it-at-face-value mind-set of the first generation of Polynesian Society ethnographers, and the analytical perspective of their higher critical school successors; and it includes both Pākehā and Māori mythopoetic expressions. The synergy is presenting itself as a reinterpretation of culture entailing on the one hand the Māori circular concepts of *Mātauranga Māori* and *Māoritanga* and on the other hand the Pākehā commitment to and movement toward biculturalism. Together they describe the rethinking and restructuring of culture—that is, the evolution of cultural symbols—in Aotearoa/New Zealand.

Let us recall how Chapter Six of this book (see the topic, "The nature of cultural reconceptualization") brings the Māori concepts of *Mātauranga Māori* and *Māoritanga* together in order to describe the ongoing reification of Māori culture, principally by Māori. The former presupposes a body of knowledge the nature of which can properly be called Māori, an epistemological method for identifying that knowledge, and a broader cultural complex in which such knowledge is embedded and from which it must be extracted, reinterpreted, and given concrete social application. The latter has to do with the essence in which the knowledge is rooted and on which the epistemological method is based. The operation of these complementary concepts allows for the inclusion of new ideas and practices while maintaining cultural authenticity. But a similar case can be made for Pākehā, just as it could for any culture.

Significantly, both Pākehā and Māori efforts are active in the current national move to be bicultural. Looking back, Pākehā of the late 19th and early 20th centuries began the development of an idealized, primordial, static view of a traditional Māori culture to which the Young Māori Party, whose members were so influential for the Māori renaissance, co-contributed; the latter saw an opportunity and used it to Māori advantage. But this objectification and essentialization—that is, reification—of culture that began in the late 19th and early 20th centuries continues to develop into the present day; and in this context, *Io*, the efforts of the higher critical school taken into account, is a prime example of the rethinking and restructuring of culture. A combination of Pākehā and Māori effort has given birth to a new understanding of a Supreme Deity, and key representatives from both groups are telling old stories in new ways.

Importantly, this is neither an affirmation nor denial of an esoteric *Io* cult that predates Māori contact with Europeans. We have already seen how some very renowned and persuasive persons from The Polynesian Society—of Māori, Pākehā, and mixed ethnicity—have been on both sides of the issue. But let us now focus briefly on two Society members from the Young Māori Party who have had opposite opinions: Sir Āpirana Ngata and Te Rangi Hīroa (Sir Peter Buck). A transcription of an informal talk with Ngata provided by John Te Herekiekie Grace records Ngata to have believed the *Io* tradition to be authentic to traditional Māori culture.[89] Ngata's discourse includes a story about Land Court Judge (from 1865 to 1876) F.E. Maning (1811/12–1883). Maning established residence in Aotearoa/New Zealand in 1833 and, in addition to some judicial decisions, is known for two books written under the penname, "A Pākehā Māori": *Old New Zealand: Being Incidents of Native Customs and Character in the Old Times* and *A History of the War in the North Against the Chief Heke, in the Year 1845*. Ngata, who believed his story to be well accredited, relates how Maning, in his early years in Aotearoa/New Zealand, had, while chasing his stray horse, stumbled upon a *tohunga* reciting a *karakia* to *Io*. Presumably because the cult was esoteric in nature, the *tohunga* gave Maning the choice of being killed or joining-up. Maning, who apparently placed a reasonably high value on his life, chose survival over extinction. Many years later, the former Judge, upon learning that he was dying of cancer, committed his knowledge of the *Io* cult to writing; but because he had taken an oath to secrecy, he became plagued by conscience. After discussing the matter with Anglican Bishop (then Archdeacon) W.L. Williams, he burned the written record. Ngata traces the *Io* cult to several tribal districts and believes that its initiates, at least for a long while, had succeeded in maintaining cult secrecy. In contrast, Te Rangi Hīroa, (Sir Peter Buck), who did not believe *Io* was authentic to traditional Māori culture, concludes:

The discovery of a supreme god named Io in new zealand was a surprise to Maori and *pakeha* alike. For years we had accepted the pattern of a number of co-equal gods, each attending to his own department. Though references to Io had been made in the literature, the extent of his claims was not fully realized until an extraordinary amount of detail was furnished by Percy Smith and Elsdon Best through the publication of copious extracts from the Matorohanga manuscript.[90]

But our interest, even though we must take the controversy into account, is more in the fusion of cultural ideas and practices; not only how Pākehā have influenced Māori, but also how Māori have swayed Pākehā. Many writers have made the argument that the Pākehā idea of a Supreme Being has profoundly affected Māori religio-culture, but let us also acknowledge that Māori traditions have entered the Pākehā Church; both Pākehā and Māori are expanding their cultural categories. The vocation and writings of the Anglican Reverend Māori Marsden (1924–1993) support this point. The Reverend Marsden was steeped in both Māori and Pākehā religious traditions and cultural milieus. In his remarks pertaining to a book of Marsden's essays, titled *The Woven Universe*,[91] Aotearoa/New Zealand musician, academic, and Māori culture expert Te Ahukaramū Charles Royal writes:

> Rev. Māori Marsden (1924–1993) was a tohunga, scholar, writer, healer, minister and philosopher of the latter part of the twentieth century…. Māori [Marsden] was both an ordained Anglican minister and a graduate of the whare wānanga…. He was uniquely placed to explore and explain the frontier between pre–Christian theology, understandings of divinity and the Māori worldview, and his Christian faith and vocation. His conclusions and perspectives on these matters are widely influential and speak meaningfully to his people whose spiritual welfare he was dedicated to.[92] [Brackets added.]

The Reverend Marsden's ordination is not an indicator of either his capitulation to Pākehā culture or his naiveté. In his essay titled "God, Man and Universe: A Maori View," he describes the work of foreign anthropologists "as seemingly facile" and declared "their attitudes, mores, and values" suspect for many Māori.[93] He was much aware of the difficulty cultural outsiders have grasping another culture; in fact, he believes the undertaking to be impossible through "abstract rational thought and empirical methods."[94] Let us not doubt that this pertains as much to the general Pākehā population and Anglican Church officials as it does to foreign anthropologists. "The grasp of culture," he writes, "proceeds not from superficial intellectualism but from an approach best articulated in poetry."[95] In other words, a person cannot fathom culture by taking it literally, as by the mere descriptiveness of "thin description"; a person can only sound its depths in resonance with it, as by the interpretive quality of "thick description." He reminds his readers that understanding a culture takes time and entails the "instilling of values, norms, and attitudes" that can only come "by experience in the cultural milieu."[96] We may add that it is this sort of activity that undergirds both temporally and transcendently based efforts to expand our cultural and religious categories to include, where deemed appropriate, the ideas and experiences of others; and that no one is ever completely excused from so doing when the opportunity is available.

Let us now note some particulars of the Reverend Marsden's essay in which this Anglican minister explores "the features of consciousness found in Māori cultural experiences."[97] In keeping with his task he describes the "religious, philosophical, and metaphysical attitudes" which characterize the Māori heart and mind.[98] In his presentation of Māori concepts, the Reverend Marsden strikes a factual tone in writing about Io as a metaphysical reality. According to him:

> In the beginning, Io existed alone in the realm of Te Korekore [realm of potential being, The Void], in his passive state…. Nothing existed before Io….
> He held intercourse within himself, between the ihomatua [mind, intellect] of his active and positive

thought, and between the ihomatua of his passive and negative self. So Io alone had a double iho ("essence")....

He was truly supreme god....

... He roused himself and stirred up his activity and communed within himself.... His essence flowed forth to fertilise Te Korekore. Then he spoke.... Thus were the essential foundations of the universe laid.

... [H]e recited (tapatapa) the names of the different foundations of things.... Thus things became differentiated and took form.

Io called into being the night realms....

Then Io illuminated the nights with soft light....

In the night regions of soft light, Io established the several Hawaiki ... in which Io chose to dwell with his divine assistants....

Having created the nights and the Hawaiki, Io brought into being the first gods, Rangi-awatea and Papa-tū-ā-nuku, the male and female principles out of which all things derived.... Out of this union sprang their first-born, Tāne and the other gods after him: Tangaroa, Rongo, Tūmatauenga, Haumia-tike-tike, Ru-ai-moko, and Tāwhiri-ma-tea....[99] [Parentheses by source; brackets added.]

The Reverend Marsden continues on describing mythical personalities, events, and places at some length.[100] These are the assertions of a dedicated, ordained, influential Anglican minister who saw no contradiction between what he understood as the traditional mythology of his Māori culture and the traditional mythology of the Anglican Church.

But the Reverend Marsden's ordination is not only a statement of his move toward Anglicanism; it is also a signal of the Anglican Church's move toward Māori culture. The "Anglican Church in Aotearoa, New Zealand and Polynesia" (as the Anglican Church in this part of the world, as an autonomous member of the worldwide Anglican community, refers to itself), in keeping with the principles of the Treaty of Waitangi and the nation's emphasis on biculturalism, is making space for Māori ideas and practices.[101] According to its website, "The 1992 Constitution of this Church provides for three partners to order their affairs within their own cultural context: Tikanga Maori; Tikanga Pakeha; Tikanga Pasefika."[102] Tikanga Māori and Tikanga Pākehā are within Aotearoa/New Zealand; Tikanga Pasefika includes Fiji, Tonga, Samoa, and the Cook Islands.[103] (The site takes "tikanga" to mean "way, style, or cultural model."[104]) The site continues, "Within Aotearoa New Zealand, Tikanga Pakeha comprises seven Dioceses, Tikanga Maori comprises five Hui Amorangi, the boundaries of which differ from those of the dioceses."[105] (Hui Amorangi means "Regional Bishoprics."[106]) The site also briefly describes the Church's periodical, *Anglican Taonga* [Anglican Treasure], as "a publication affirming the unity and diversity of the Anglican community in these islands."[107] Notably, according to the website, whereas "[t]he parliamentary procedures of Westminster were the model for debating and voting, [i]n recent years under the new constitution ... it has become customary to suspend the Westminster-based standing orders and to seek to achieve consensus for decisions after the pattern of hui [meetings] on marae."[108]

Here is both an illustration of expanding our cultural categories to include the ideas and experiences of others and an affirmation that the *Io* of faith can be at home in the expanded culture. Just as Jesus is on the *marae*, Io is in the Church. The *Io* of history has become the *Io* of faith and together they comprise the *Io* of culture.

To return for a brief moment to this book's Introduction (see the topic, "Hiwi Tauroa's Musing") and its description of Hiwi Tauroa's pondering about the relationship of the Christian house of prayer (*whare karakia*) and the Māori ancestor house (*whare tipuna*), we may now understand in greater depth what Tauroa meant when he mused about the *whare karakia*, "...I wonder whether it ever took the place of the whare tipuna."[109]

Is Io *really* God?

The Preface to this book (see the topic, "Parts and Chapters") promised an answer to the question "Is *Io* Really God?" By now the reader should be fully aware that this question is not tongue-in-cheek, a purposeful tease followed by some trite or superfluous answer; nor is it rhetorical, presented simply for effect, insinuating either an emphatic "yes" or "no" response. It is a serious question, the answer to which is rooted in the dynamic relationship of Māori tribes and Pākehā colonialists. It is now time to deliver on our promise to answer the question; however, before we can do so, we must first establish some criteria from which we can make a judgment. This entails two preliminary investigations:

• Where must we look for an answer? and
• What are the tell-tale signs of a "God?"

Regarding the first issue, there is no understanding of "God" outside of a cultural context. Let us begin our explanation of this statement by noticing how Paul Tillich brings his unique cultural perspective to his treatment of the God question. In his essay, "Religion as a Dimension in Man's Spiritual Life," he compares and contrasts notions that spring from secular scientists on the one hand and particular Christian theologians on the other in order to provide a backdrop against which he can make his point that religion is the depth aspect of the whole of human life.[110] In so doing, he brings up the question of the existence of God and writes that a God who can be the subject of the argument of existence or non-existence is a thing beside other existing things in the universe. Tillich believes that there is no evidence in support of such an entity and thus he develops an entirely different idea of God (God as ground and power of being). Nevertheless, he concludes that this question is justified and notes that those scientists who seek to refute the notion of God as a being alongside other existing things serve usefully to force theologians to rethink and restate what the powerful word "God" means. Our immediate point is that Tillich's recognition of science as an authoritative voice alongside that of theology in matters such as the existence (or non-existence) and nature of God is indicative of his Western secular perspective. He espouses an existentialist concept of religion and God in large part because he believes it diminishes the rift between the sacred and secular realms, a division which is characteristic of his Western culture. But what does bridging the gap between the sacred and the secular have to do with our query about where to look for an answer to our question about *Io*? As we shall see, it is an important step to understanding that any notion of God is shaped by culture, which then directs us to culture for an answer to our query. Let us continue.

It is at least partially in reaction to his secularized society that Tillich, in his essay, "Aspects of a Religious Analysis of Culture," establishes the close association of religion and culture[111]; that is, the religious nature of culture and the cultural nature of religion. Tillich, who is much aware of his secularized cultural perspective and knows the tendency of both the secular and the sacred elements of his society to establish their independence, has a particular take on the consequences of religion becoming "a special realm"; he, employing a Biblical trope, sees it as the clearest evidence of humankind's "fallen state."[112] He finds neither "ecclesiastical imperialism" nor the triumph of the secular desirable[113]; so, he seeks to break down the culture-religion duality and in so doing establishes their intimate connection. In Tillich's thought, there is a difference between religious packaging (which in some situations lacks intensity or can be meaningless) and in religion per se (which always supplies culture with meaning[114]). Importantly, he develops his philosophy of religion with the intent that it will presumably be adequate to engage with *any* historical religion irrespective of cultural context.[115] Tillich's solution to the question of religion as it pertains to *any* society, including his own, is to view religion as ultimate concern; the dimension of depth in every aspect of the human self (see the topic, "Religion," in Chapter Five of this book). Thus, he joins a pair of ideas, the union of which precludes establishing a strict culture-religion duality: (1) "religion is the substance of culture," and (2) "culture is the form of religion."[116] This leads him to two conclusions regarding the intimate association of culture and religion. First, "there is no cultural creation without an ultimate concern expressed in it," and second, "[e]very religious act, not only in organized religion, but also in the most intimate movement of the soul, is culturally formed."[117] Thus a person's view of and reaction to transcendent reality is necessarily in terms of that person's culture.

Tillich is not alone in taking a unique Western cultural approach to religion. Another example is British mathematician turned philosopher Alfred North Whitehead (1861–1947) who developed what he called the "philosophy of organism." Academics often refer to it as "process philosophy" or "process theism." Where Tillich is an existentialist, Whitehead is a realist; nonetheless, there are points of potential connection between the two, including the recognition of the authority of science on par with that of a certain view of religion, the resonance of their ideas with philosophical idealists, an awareness of the necessity of God, and a method for bridging the culture-religion gap. Whitehead, who also developed his thought from a Western secular perspective, expresses a complementary relationship of God and the world in which God is present in the most fundamental occasions of experience. Such a view necessarily includes God's influence in the development of all religious expressions regardless of, but in keeping with, cultural context; a perspective which is also adequate to engage the world's various religions.[118]

The impetus behind Tillich's and Whitehead's philosophies notwithstanding, secularization is not an issue in a "spiritualized" culture, such as that of Māori people, that sees everything as interconnected and having a potential for and an expression of power commensurate with its connection to everything else; nevertheless, any discussion of God is no less culture specific. There is no absolute, universal answer to the question of God. Recognition of God or gods always occurs within a particular cultural context as one aspect of the culture. Therefore, the question is always a relative one as it derives from a particular worldview and ethos. Because the question of God is a culture specific question, the answer must likewise be a culture specific answer.

Let us be perfectly clear on two points: First, there is *absolutely no* perception or understanding outside of a cultural context; and second, cultural symbols transmit the way a culture understands itself and thus establishes its values and behaviors. Even the word "God" is a symbol that transmits particular cultural information; it conjures particular ideas and images in the terms of the culture that has ownership of the symbol. Therefore, any attempt to answer the question of *Io* as God is improper and futile outside *Io*'s cultural framework. Put another way, the proper place to search for an answer to the question of *Io* is within the culture of *Io*.

We may now restate the second question, What are the telltale signs of a "God?," as "How do we recognize 'God' in culture"? Or in its more narrow form as related to our present concern: What are the telltale signs of *Io* as "God" within his culture? Astute readers will note considerable Tillichian influence in what follows.

Let us begin our answer by noting that religious symbols operate on two levels to which theologians often refer as the immanent and the transcendent.[119] To speak of immanence and transcendence is to recognize that there is, on the one hand, an immediate present reality which is, on the other hand, in some way beyond our immediate experience. As it pertains to an understanding of "God," immanence bespeaks that aspect of deity which is present in nature and is in some way accessible to human persons, while transcendence refers to that aspect of deity which either extends beyond nature or is imbedded so deeply within nature that it is, at least in part, inaccessible to humankind. All we, as human persons, ultimately have from which to make determinations about accessibility to and characteristics of God is our own experience; therefore, if there is to be a connection between that which is accessible and that which is beyond accessibility, our experience must be the point of connection. While our experience is limited, it allows us to ascertain certain information even though other information remains outside our purview. Because of the boundaries of our experience, we develop analogous language, based on our personhood and our perception of the natural world, to describe what we believe we know about that which, at least in part, is unknowable. The use of analogous language means that our descriptions are symbolic; they are not descriptions of transcendence-in-itself. Those who take analogous language as literal descriptions are vulnerable to the onslaught of absurdity. For instance, as it pertains to power, who has not heard questions such as, "Can God build a wall so high that he cannot cross over it?" or "Can God build an object so heavy that he cannot lift it?" Understanding our descriptions to be symbolic tends to break down this sort of paradox.

This, of course, shows us the value of symbolic descriptions. No one could have any notion of God except for our ability to create symbols. Moreover, insofar as we develop our symbols of ultimate reality as a result of our experience as "persons," it should be no surprise that many tend to speak of God as the biggest and best (and for some, the "baddest") "person" in existence. In effect, when we speak of God, we take that which is, in itself, beyond our clear comprehension and express it in terms we can understand. Once again, the process of reification gives substance to that which is insubstantial. While this can be beneficial as a point of reference, it must never lapse into literalness; we must constantly reaffirm the symbolic nature of our understanding of God. Basically, we take that which is irreducible and beyond description (being as being, existence itself) and endow it with the characteristics of a perfect "person." Symbolic usage allows us on the one hand the denial of God as a being alongside other existents in the universe, while on the other hand the affirmation of God through the analogy of personhood.

This assigning of human descriptions to God brings three broad issues into play when determining the telltale signs of a "God": qualities, enterprises, and purpose(s). First, we use human qualities to express the qualities of God and must make a choice for particular ones. Traditional Christianity has selected traits it finds pleasing and comforting such as love, mercy, patience, faithfulness, knowledge, and power. Other groups under the Christian religious umbrella modify these characteristics somewhat, especially the ideas of omniscience (What does God know, and when does God know it?) and omnipotence (How much power does God have, and how and when does God use it?) in an attempt to address "the problem of evil" (Why do people, especially "good" people, suffer?). But regardless of the selections we make, our experience informs our choices. Because the specifics of human experience differ from culture to culture, the worldview and ethos that grows out of experience may vary from culture to culture. Therefore, the qualities of ultimate reality that one culture may consider as proper and making perfect sense (e.g., *tapu*, *mana*, *noa*, and *utu*) another may consider improper and nonsensical.

Second, the description of enterprises as they pertain to ultimate reality may also vary. Let us consider cosmogonic narratives, incarnations, and the general experience of "other-worldliness." It is the drive, fundamental to human experience, to make sense of and order the world for survival and comfort that provides substance to each of these. Regarding cosmogonic narratives, Pākehā Christianity has its two creation accounts of Genesis (1:1–2:4a and 2:4b-25, NRSV). Māori culture has a cosmogonic narrative (which varies somewhat from tribe to tribe), but it (even with the inclusion of *Io*, which tends to soften the disparity) contrasts sharply with its traditional Christian counterparts even though both are an attempt to explain the ordering of the experienced world. Regarding incarnations, for Pākehā Christians, Jesus is the paramount representative and bearer of the holy, while for Māori traditional culture, the *atua* are the principal representatives and bearers of *tapu*; once again, very different expressions of the very broad idea. In fact, as others have noted, incarnations are quite easy in cultures such as that of Māori tribes which do not differentiate between the transcendent and the immanent. As it pertains to the experience of "other-worldliness," for secularized Pākehā Christians such experience may entail miracles, supernatural guidance, the presence of the holy in formal sacraments, etc., while Māori sacralized society is never without the mystery of transcendence.

Third, let us consider the idea of purpose(s) as transmitted by the word "God." How may we meaningfully describe the functions of a God with particular attributes who is engaged in particular enterprises? We have previously made use of Clifford Geertz's anthropology (see the topic, "Religion," in Chapter Five of this book), to show that there are three fundamental points where meaningless existence becomes a serious threat: at the point where, through the sustained intensity of life's challenges, our analytic capacity, our power of endurance, and our moral insight break down. It is here that chaos threatens our ability to cope with life's circumstances. As Geertz understood, the resulting anxiety contributes greatly to belief in a "God" or "gods." It is the function of that God or those gods to make life comprehensible, to supply a sense of justice, and in one way or the other to undergird human well-being. A God or gods, in addition to inspiring awe, wonder, and reverence (to borrow John Morgan's terms), function(s) to address a culture's needs at its most fundamental level; and the two combine in determining efficacy. But let us focus on *Io*. If *Io* is really God, he, as a cultural symbol, should inspirationally explain those things that baffle the human mind, provide comfort for human pain, and offer hope against injustice. This is not an all or nothing affair. He may address bafflement, comfort pain, and provide hope in varying degrees of intensity and for some while not for others; however, the extent to which *Io* functions in this way within the culture of Aotearoa/New Zealand is the extent to which he is real as God within that culture. Put another way, *Io* is really God insofar as he fulfills his cultural function.

While some Aotearoans/New Zealanders are partial to names such as "Yahweh" or "Adonai" for a Supreme Being (or Ultimate Reality), others like the ordained Anglican minister, Māori Marsden, may prefer *Io*. *Io* is a Māori name, and Māori present concern is primarily to maintain continuity with their past and live with dignity and comfort in a shared land. But the Reverend Marsden used the name *Io* in the context of the Anglican Church that came to Aotearoa/New Zealand as exclusively Pākehā. Pākehā have made a commitment to a bicultural Aotearoa/New Zealand, and the Anglican Church has made room for *Io*. The extent to which *Io*, as a cultural symbol, expresses this bicultural intent and functions to bring it about is the measure of *Io* as an Aotearoa/New Zealand God. The Aotearoa/New Zealand 2013 census indicated that the population is currently moving away from identifying themselves with specific religious categories. However, this does not preclude the operation of spiritual principles in the depths of the various aspects of the national culture, and insofar as *Io* is recognized as the ground of those principles is the extent to which *Io* is really God.

Whether *Io*, as a Supreme Deity, predated European contact, originated in the land wars of the 1860s, or bloomed in the work of The Polynesian Society; he functions today as meaning bearer for many, and serves as a prime example of cultural synergistic synthesis in Aotearoa/New Zealand. As the earlier discussion in this chapter shows, one cannot determine conclusively where either Māori or Pākehā influence on his development begins and ends, but one can clearly identify strains associated with each culture. From one point of view, a tribal deity holds the position of the Universal Creator of the cosmos which processes included specific Māori *atua*. From another view, the God that Pākehā have in some measure excluded or compartmentalized is beginning once again to permeate and inform culture in terms of life-honoring principles. The *Io* of today is in some measure a product of the cultural encounter of Māori and Pākehā, and just as biculturalism rejects both cultural assimilation and parallelism, so *Io* rejects assimilation while refusing the role of a parallel God. To paraphrase Tillich, all symbols are born as the offspring of specific circumstances, and they die only when the conditions which gave them their existence have come to an end.

CHAPTER EIGHT

The Up Over
of the Down Under

Cultural authenticity: A necessary reprise

An analysis of culture must account for two things: coherence and change; that is, how culture holds together and how it transforms. Academics, with that in mind, have suggested several ways of describing culture. Examples include culture as a sand pile, culture as a spider's web, culture as a human web, culture as an octopus, culture as a text, and culture as an iceberg. Of particular significance for our current topic is the use of the term *invention* as a trope to project a particular image of culture. As we would expect, each representation requires an explanation; and each explanation, while it addresses some principal issue(s) of change and coherence, may not address all and may raise other questions.

We, of course, can argue back and forth about how well each depiction represents the issues of stability and change. Let us briefly look at some of the above examples beginning with Clifford Geertz's octopus model.[1] It appears that Geertz selected it because he found the ungainliness of the octopus in its getting along with its life accurate for describing culture, but we could counter that cultures may not appear to be particularly awkward to their participants. Be that as it may, organic models do seem to account for continuity amid change (and vice-versa) well enough. In the same paragraph that he briefly described how culture is like an octopus, Geertz expressed his dislike for both the sand pile and the spider's web models. We can speculate a reason why they did not work as well for him as did the octopus. As Richard G. Fox points out, the pile of sand can account for the accretion of cultural traditions and in some instances can account for cultural change brought about by the shifting winds of the times, but there is nothing intrinsic to a sand pile to hold it together.[2] As for the spider's web model, as Fox also recognizes, once in place the web does not easily change short of, at least to a certain extent, breaking apart.[3] Geertz did espouse a web as a model of culture, but the spinner of the web he championed was a human group,[4] and the web's strands were not as easily discerned as those of arachnoid construction.[5] But let us move on.

The task of selecting a way to properly describe culture that maintains the balance between cultural coherence and cultural change has not proved to be an easy one. In fact, this issue was at the heart of a discussion about the alleged "invention" of culture and the notion of cultural "authenticity" in Aotearoa/New Zealand. Whereas the pile of sand and spider's web models of culture, briefly mentioned above, have issues in dealing with cultural change; judging from reports of Māori objections to Allan Hanson's article, "The Making of the Maori: Culture Invention and its Logic" published in 1989, in the *American*

Anthropologist (see the topic, "The nature of cultural reconceptualization," in Chapter Six of this book), the notion of "invention," certainly as it pertains to Māori culture, has the problem of accounting for cultural coherence. This is especially problematic when a substantial measure of cultural coherence is viewed as necessary for cultural authenticity. Apparently, for many Māori, Hanson's description of culture as an invention loaded much baggage onto the word; particularly when he suggested that the colonizing British invented a culture for the colonized Māori and then, as a good advertising firm might do, presented it in such a way—that is, clothed it "with such an aura of factuality" (to borrow an expression from Geertz[6])—that the people for whom the culture was invented bought the product.

Let us briefly delineate Hanson's article and consider the stir it caused. Hanson noted how historians and anthropologists had come to view "traditional culture" as unstable and something people constantly "invent" for whatever their purposes are at the time. He explained that these academics have come to understand culture and tradition as far from an unchanging something which gets passed on through the generations, and in making his point he quoted American Professor of Anthropology Lamont Lindstrom that tradition is "'an attempt ... to read the present in terms of the past by writing the past in terms of the present'"[7] Hanson not only repeatedly used the terms "invent" and "invention," he also upped the ante in his usage. The controversy that developed hinged on how he applied these words in describing the current state of Māori society. Hanson wrote, "Those contemporary purposes [which underpin the 'invention' of culture] vary according to who does the inventing. When people invent their own traditions, it is usually to legitimate or sanctify some current reality or aspiration...."[8] But he continued, "People also invent cultures and traditions for others, and then treat them *as if their inventions were the actual state of affairs*" (emphasis added).[9] According to him, in this latter case, which he believed to be the situation in Aotearoa/New Zealand, "[w]hen the inventors are politically dominant ... the invention of tradition for subordinate peoples is part of a cultural imperialism that tends to maintain the asymmetrical relationship of power."[10]

In his discussion, Hanson drew attention to two periods in Aotearoa/New Zealand history. The first was at the turn of the 19th to the 20th century when, according to him, Pākehā intended to assimilate the indigenous population into a European style society. The second was the current period (Hanson's article was published in 1989) in which Māori fervor was directed toward maintaining their identity as a distinct people and establishing for themselves a more powerful societal position. According to Hanson, although these two periods have the common goal of securing for Māori a favorable place in the nation, the two images are very different. The former, he says, was one which pertained to the development of a European style monoculture, and he points out that the work of persons such as S. Percy Smith, which emphasized similitudes between Māori and Pākehā, helped serve this goal. The latter he characterizes as one of a bicultural society, which was different in that it emphasized the unique contributions which Māori had made to the nation and how they were as important as those made by Pākehā. Whereas the first historical period emphasized similarities, the second pointed up contrasts. In the latter, Māori culture was the counterbalance to that of Pākehā.

Although the terms "invent" and "invention" were not new to anthropology (e.g., Roy Wagner's 1975 book, *The Invention of Culture*[11]), a controversy developed around them once Hanson's article reached Aotearoa/New Zealand readers. Many Māori took exception to the particular way Hanson applied the terms to their culture. Some have argued that particular Aotearoa/New Zealand newspapers, which reported on the subject, could have done a better job in titling their articles,[12] but titling notwithstanding, some Māori scholars reacted negatively toward what Hanson actually had to say. In particular, Māori academic Ranginui Walker took Hanson's use of the word "invention" as a challenge to Māori cultural authenticity; he saw it as a claim that Māori culture was something falsified or counterfeit.

Hanson took the criticism seriously enough to respond. He explained that his intent was not "anti–Māori," and charged the readers of his work who took it to be so with a measure of responsibility in understanding his argument. Nevertheless, he also recognized that he had a responsibility to successfully communicate his intent. He acknowledged that Māori and others were understandably offended by his article and apologized for the offense. According to Hanson, the controversy led him "to the conclusion that *invention* when applied to culture and tradition is a systematically misleading expression that should not be perpetuated."[13]

On the one hand, the terms "invent" and "invention" when used in particular ways to describe culture are not objectionable as long as their use is properly qualified. For instance, Roy Wagner views cultural "invention," which he understands as "the interpretive elicitation of meanings," to stand in a dialectic relationship with cultural "convention"; for him "the dialectic of invention and convention is a plausible ground for cultural meaning and motivation…."[14] But on the other hand, there is a problematic potential that accompanies the use of the terms; specifically, they may suggest, as exemplified by the controversy outlined above, that culture is, in some way, a made-up or falsified phenomenon with dubious genuineness. Therefore, because of the potentially troublesome capacity of these descriptors, in the following paragraphs we suggest a term we believe to be more appropriate.

Up to now we have treated culture as "a rolling present" in an effort to succinctly describe it as a continuous reinterpretation of symbols that may be largely transparent to the group; it requires continuity between the present and the past, albeit with a view to a relevant future. In other words, John Morgan's "possibility thinking" is constantly operative, pulling the past and future into the present moment. The present moment is always fluid and the cultural landscape is constantly changing. One problem with the expression "rolling present" is its focus on the present moment. Although we have sought to make plain the phrase's inclusion of both the past and a relevant future, one criticism might be that it appears to have insufficient regard for those aspects of the present moment.

This begs the question of whether there is another term which more adequately describes the ever-changing quality of culture while satisfactorily accounting for its coherence. In our search for such a word, the term "re-creation" (which we view as actually synonymous with "rolling present") comes to mind as fulfilling these requirements. Re-creation of culture is an expression that recognizes the contribution of past experience in the development of the present moment and acknowledges a view toward a relevant future. It declares the development of culture to be a continual process with a core of authenticity. As it pertains particularly to Aotearoa/New Zealand, it is both consistent with the complementary concepts of *Mātauranga Māori* (Māori knowledge) and *Māoritanga* (Māoriness) and compatible with Aotearoa/New Zealand's national commitment to become a bicultural nation. Let us recall that *Mātauranga Māori* presupposes a body of knowledge the nature of which can properly be called Māori, that it implies an epistemological method for identifying that knowledge, and that together these two presuppose such knowledge to be embedded in a broader cultural complex from which it may be extracted, reinterpreted, and given concrete social application; and that *Māoritanga* has to do with the cultural essence in which the knowledge is rooted and on which the epistemological method is based (see the topic,

"Reification and cultural authenticity," in Chapter Six of this book). Thus the term, re-creation, accounts for both change and coherence in culture. In terms of Māori culture, the aspect of change is more consistent with *Mātauranga Māori* while the aspect of coherence is more consistent with *Māoritanga*; but the two overlap, and it is impossible to have one without the other.

Re-creation is not *creatio ex nihilo*; it is not an "out of nothing" operation. It presupposes the full complexity of cultural movement which Sir Hirini Moko Mead describes in his essay "Understanding *Mātauranga Māori*" (see the topic, "*Whare* meets *whare*," in Chapter Two of this book), and today's form and content of Māori culture provides an example of cultural re-creation. Mead well understood that culture and its knowledge are in a state of constant development, but he also knew that there is the continuity of a particular distinctiveness of experience that qualifies certain knowledge as properly belonging to a particular culture. For him *Mātauranga Māori* included, on the one hand, efforts to recapture knowledge from the past that is culturally specific to Māori people, entailing such items as the songs of traditional times, names of places, and names of people; but, on the other hand, innovations throughout Māori history, up to and including the present day. In traditional times ideas and practices evolved according to the then contemporary occasions, and today, changes occur in the context of present ideas and applied science. As Mead, speaking of Māori people wrote, "[W]e have never been slow to grasp new ideas and use them."[15] Continuity with the past insures present genuineness and authenticity, the future is always relevant to the present moment, and cultural symbols are the point of union between an authentic past and a relevant future.

It is, however, reasonable to ask to what extent symbolic construction challenges the notion of a core identity as it is defined by a collection of cultural traits. For instance, as Richard Handler and Jocelyn Linnekin have asked, if the core cultural personality evolves, does it not become something completely different?[16] Also, while organic metaphors (such as the octopuses and human persons mentioned in the opening paragraphs of this topic) provide a solution, do they not, considering that the boundaries of personal identity are indistinct, bring their own quandary?[17] Our contention is that the symbolic construction of cultural traditions does not negate a natural cultural essence. We hold that a certain continuity of experience—including genetic, geographical, and historical aspects—furnishes a core quality that holds a culture together. Stated another way, we maintain that a complex continuity of experience is that which determines the core essence around which cultural webs form and reshape and cultural symbols cluster and change. Our position is that symbolic creation and re-creation does not negate the naturalness of cultural essence any more than a human person's constant symbolic re-creation of a worldview and ethos negates the natural recollection which that person has of his or her past, regardless of how distinct or indistinct it may be. Indeed, the symbolic re-creation of culture is proportionately no less distinct than the development of a human life. We may accept a measure of indistinctness as integral to the process of handing down customs and beliefs and therefore an aspect of culture. Importantly, indistinct does not mean absent, wholly indiscernible, or inconsequential. Both symbols and essence evolve, but do so within the continuity of cultural experience. Furthermore, without doubt, the contact of cultures and the blending of cultural symbols in today's world affect the sorting out of the various cultural strands, but such interweaving becomes an aspect of the respective cultures. For instance, the marriage of a Māori person to a Pākehā person does not negate the entire Māori *whakapapa* (genealogy); the marriage is simply included in its recitation.

The genuineness and authenticity of every cultural tradition has a beginning, somewhere at some time, even though it may at times be difficult and at other times virtually impossible to ascertain the where and the when. At some point a custom or belief may (indeed, it often does) accrete enough popularity—that is, resonate so strongly with the group—that it qualifies as a genuine and authentic expression of that group's worldview and ethos. It then takes its place in the entire complex of the coming and going of cultural symbols. This is precisely a description of the birth of a symbol, and genuineness and authenticity accompany the birth. The *whare tipuna* represents one process by which a symbol is born (see the topic, "The *whare tipuna* as a symbol," in Chapter Two of this book); *Io* represents another (see Chapter Seven of this book). Over time, many symbols die when the circumstances that give them life no longer exist; but the influence of the symbol can linger as it has affected other symbols. The symbolic construction of cultural reality does not negate a core cultural essence.

Hanson, in his discussion of culture as an "invention," is correct that what is at stake here is the very "nature of cultural reality."[18] He, also, correctly understands that the current culture in Aotearoa/New Zealand is not the product of only one group, and that the boundaries of each group's contribution overlap. However, the separation of the contributions of the various factions may be a bit more blurred than he presented. Let us recall that, according to Hanson, there are two historical moments of cultural "invention" that stand out. According to him, the first occurred at the turn of the 19th to the 20th century when the prime Pākehā motive was assimilation of Māori; the second is the present day (again, his article appeared in 1989) when Māori are keen to establish themselves in equality with Pākehā. Our argument, as it pertains to Hanson's first historical moment, is that the turn of the 19th to the 20th centuries was a time when Pākehā were breaking from Mother England and putting together what it meant to be a unique culture in the world; and they, in contrast to Hanson's notion of the invention of traditions for purposes of colonization, began to develop a genuine regard for the indigenous population. By the end of the 19th century Māori were so defeated that Pākehā would have had little trouble in eliminating Māori culture as a driving force in the nation (much as the indigenous population of the United States was relegated to a subordinate status), but they chose a different path. Our argument pertaining to Hanson's second historical moment is that even though Māori pride was never completely extinguished, its fires were on the wan; and some extraordinary Māori leaders (again, beginning in the late 19th and early 20th centuries) fanned the cultural embers thus igniting a blaze of tribal pride and prestige that became successful in conjunction with Pākehā changing attitudes toward Māori. In other words, the motives of the various factions in Aotearoa/New Zealand may not have been so different.

Let us recall that the previous chapter of this book presents *Io* as a prime example of the re-creation of culture in Aotearoa/New Zealand; it describes how processes, such as those that have come to be represented by the complementary concepts of *Māoritanga* and *Mātauranga Māori*, employed by such distinguished persons as the Reverend Māori Marsden, re-create culture. While the chapter does not challenge the view that Māori of traditional times recognized a Supreme Deity, it acknowledges that there is no historical record of *Io* as a Supreme Deity prior to European contact. But it also recognizes that despite all the studies that researchers have conducted using the tools of textual and historical analysis, there is no common agreement about *Io*'s origins. What is clear is that in the current state of affairs, *Io* and the Christian God are at least quite similar and may often be construed as one and the same. The paths that lead to this state of affairs are overgrown and difficult to discern; but wherever the paths' source(s) is/are located, and regardless of the particular route(s), today's convergence is an example of the re-creation of culture out of the materials handed down from the past and an illustration of the highly synergistic potential inherent in the encounter of cultures.

But there are other ways in which Aotearoans/New Zealanders are re-creating their culture. This entails blazing new trails and having debates, sometimes heated, about national directions. There will never be a for-ever-more crystalized outcome because Aotearoans/New Zealanders, as with every national group, must constantly re-create their culture. However, the following three examples describe in part what Aotearoans/New Zealanders are re-creating and how they are going about it. Let us note how these examples are rooted in the nation's history, and how they establish a continuity of experience and quality of spirit for both Māori and Pākehā, inclusive of both positive and negative aspects of life, into the present day; issues which are contributing to the genuineness and authenticity of a bicultural nation. The three examples below derive from the convergence of Tillich's philosophy of religion and Geertz's anthropology of religion[19] as they address the "problem of meaning" at the points where meaninglessness or chaos attempt to break in on humankind. Specifically, they are, to use Tillich's descriptions, the cognitive, moral, and aesthetic functions of human life[20]; or to use Geertz's descriptions, human analytic capacities, moral insight, and powers of endurance.[21] We shall combine the two sets of imageries as: the cognitive function and the address to education, the moral function and the address to injustice, and the aesthetic function and the address to endurance.

The cognitive function and the address to education

The first example of cultural re-creation and bicultural progress in Aotearoa/New Zealand is the national recognition of the validity of Māori educational principles and academic design. The drive to educate is, without doubt, rooted in the human compulsion to make sense of and get along well in the world. In colonial days, Pākehā, of course, brought their educational methods, including their schoolhouse model, with them and adapted them for the new environment. As for Māori, in traditional times, they addressed education and training in various ways tailored to their society.[22] It began before birth when the expectant mother would chant to the unborn child. Later, the gaining of knowledge and developing of practical skills was integral to home and community life; in addition to hands-on instruction, it entailed games, songs, proverbs, stories of various sorts, aesthetics, genealogy, etc. And when the society deemed it appropriate, training was formal as in the *whare wānanga* (the Māori "school of higher learning"). But our attention just now is on the present national arrangement and how Māori principles are informing it.

The current Aotearoa/New Zealand educational structure[23] requires children to attend school between the ages of six and 16, but most begin about age five and may continue well past the mandatory age. There are 13 years of education below the tertiary level in the Aotearoa/New Zealand system. Education begins at the primary level, which covers the first eight years if the school is a "full" primary school and the first six years if it is a "contributing" primary school. In the latter case the next two years are classified as the intermediate level. Years nine through 13 are the secondary level. State primary and intermediate public schools are co-educational as are many secondary schools; but some secondary schools, usually in higher populated locations where there are several secondary school options, are single sex.

There are state funded educational opportunities available outside these public schools which teach the Ministry of Education's *New Zealand Curriculum*. Some of these alternatives are organized around special purposes; these include correspondence schools for those children who reside a far distance from or for medical reasons are unable to attend a conventional institution and schools that are equipped to teach disabled students. There are other special schools that are eligible for government funds. Charter schools set their own curriculum and determine their own qualifications, but they receive government funds and are free to students. They are responsible to their sponsors for their performance; the sponsors are, in turn, held accountable for the school meeting its charter objectives. State integrated schools are institutions of a special character; in particular, they may employ distinctive education methods or include a religious curriculum. These schools were once private and still maintain their own buildings and grounds but have joined with the public education system; they receive money from the Government which they supplement with fees paid by or on behalf of the students. Homeschools, conducted by parents and caregivers, may receive a cost of learning materials subsidy upon approval of an application for such. However, in addition to these opportunities, there are private schools that receive no government financial assistance; these institutions set their own curriculum and collect fees from attendees.

There are other educational choices which have grown out of the Māori renaissance and are based on the Māori worldview. These "Māori approach schools" teach entirely in the Māori language or are working toward that goal and are organized according to Māori pedagogical principles. Today, they are classified as state schools and receive government financial support. As these educational endeavors are of particular interest for our purposes, let us explore how these have developed.

We begin by noting the importance of the revitalization of the Māori language for survival of the tribal culture, accurate communication of tribal knowledge, and the proper application of tribal educational methods. Without doubt, one of the most significant advances in the recent history of Māori-Pākehā national associations is the establishment of the Waitangi Tribunal in 1975 to hear Māori claims for breaches of the Treaty of Waitangi (now recognized as the nation's founding document) and make recommendations for resolution (see the topics, "A look at the languages" and "A handle on the history," in Chapter One of this book). At first the Tribunal could only look into claims going forward, but in 1985 the Government expanded the Tribunal's scope of inquiry to include claims dating to the Treaty's inception in 1840. Under the Treaty, Māori are entitled to the protection of their cultural "treasures," and one of the claims presented in 1985 as a breach of the Treaty maintained that the Māori language was a cultural treasure for which the Government had violated the requirement of protection. After hearing the claim, the Tribunal, in 1986, recommended that the Government recognize the Māori language as an official language of the land. The following year the Government passed the Māori Language Act 1987 not only for that purpose, but also to establish the Māori Language Commission to promote and expand the use of the language as both a spoken and written medium of communication.[24] These landmark events were in large part a culmination of previous indigenous endeavors which were tied to a concern not only for the survival of the language but also Māori culture generally. Māori understood full well the importance of the language for the survival of their tribal culture and the perpetuation of their worldview. Accompanying appeals for the revival of the language was a new emphasis on the Māori way and its preservation through the application of its unique pedagogical principles.

Let us now move our focus to the arena of education and some key events associated with the claim Māori made to the Waitangi Tribunal in 1985 and its resolution in 1987. Although Bruce Biggs had been teaching the Māori language on the tertiary level since the early 1950s and as early as the 1960s there were some strong indications of a national move toward bicultural education (some resulting from Māori underachievement in the prevailing Pākehā system), we shall set our first milestone for modern Māori educational initiatives in 1982 when the first *kōhanga reo*[25] (preschool "language nest") opened in Wainuiomata, near Wellington. The goal of these "nests" was to educate Māori children through immersion in the indigenous language.

We shall set another marker in 1985 when the first *kura kaupapa Māori*[26] (a formal designation for Māori emersion schools past the preschool level) began operation as a primary school at Hoani Waititi Marae at Glen Eden, a suburb of Auckland; in 1993 the backers would expand it to include a secondary school. At the outset, these were community-based initiatives which sprang from a concern to revitalize the Māori language and preserve Māori culture, but are now recognized by State legislation. It was the success of the *kōhanga reo* that led the Māori founders to establish the *kura kaupapa Māori*. *Kaupapa Māori* translates as "Māori ideology" or "Māori principles"[27]; the addition of the word *kura* (school) simply provides a particular context for their presentation and practice.

Finally, further up the educational ladder from the secondary schools, *wānanga*[28] (tribal learning centers which also employ Māori methods of teaching) had been in existence since 1981. Nevertheless, we shall place a third milepost in 1990 when the Education Amendment of that year formally acknowledged these educational endeavors as tertiary institutions. The first attainment of *wānanga* status occurred in 1993 when the Government officially recognized Te Wānanga-o-Raukawa and Te Wānanga-o-Aotearoa. Notably, in 2004 Te Whare Wānanga o Awanuiārangi achieved accreditation to teach courses to the PhD level.

While these initiatives, which have had their ups and downs, are encouraging, the educational landscape has not always been so. Let us now briefly review some events associated with Pākehā arrival which made these aforementioned programs necessary. The first Pākehā schools were the mission schools which Christian missionaries organized beginning in 1816.[29] Although the missionaries included a certain amount of religious indoctrination and "being civilized" in the studies, Māori apparently considered the schools to have some benefit. Indeed, in those early years of European contact, if Māori had objected to education by the missionaries, they would have shut it down; apparently, Māori saw value in the teachings the schools provided. Perhaps overall the tribal leaders viewed the mission schools as an inroad to understanding Pākehā society, but they appear to have particularly valued the ability to read and write. By 1840 Māori had extensively organized their own village schools to teach skills they learned from Pākehā and as many as half of the indigenous population was literate to some degree. But this positive aspect was soon to change.

After the signing of the Treaty of Waitangi in 1840, once the colonial Government became involved, assimilationist notions and policies that were in embryo form prior to government participation in education began to bloom. A significant turn took place in 1847; the Education Ordinance of that year, in effect, allowed the Pākehā authorities to supervise the mission schools.[30] The school system would receive funding, but would be managed by persons approved by the Pākehā authorities and subject to their inspection to insure that the schools were adhering to certain mandatory requirements as decided by the authorities. The Ordinance specifically required religious education (although there was a provision exempting some attendees), industrial training, and instruction in the English language. These requirements were assimilationist in nature. The authorities intended that English would replace the indigenous tongue and that Māori would occupy the position of a working class in a European style society.

On the one hand, rules for schools do not automatically extend in every respect into the home, even though they have the potential to create a hiatus between the two; and the Māori language remained the primary language for Māori for a long time to come.[31] Moreover, if teachers were to be effective in the classroom and community, they must have some knowledge of the indigenous language and culture; and this can, at least in part, mitigate any potential rift between school and home. But on the other hand, the attitudes embedded in the Education Ordinance would prevail for decades. In fact, in the early 1900s, at the same time we have evidence for changing attitudes by some Pākehā, such as those represented by members of The Polynesian Society, away from assimilation; others with a different outlook were corporally punishing Māori children for speaking the indigenous tongue on school grounds. Still, at the outset of World War I an estimated 90 percent of Māori school children still spoke Māori. The years between World War I and World War II were a time when many Aotearoans/New Zealanders were adamant to rejuvenate Māori culture and a good number of teachers desired to include Māori culture and language in the curriculum; nevertheless, the prevailing government attitude was still one of assimilation. As it pertained to the language, the authorities considered its natural disappearance as no real loss.

During and after World War II the style of Māori life changed as they migrated to the cities to obtain employment. If people are to live with a desired measure of comfort, they require appropriate food, clothes, shelter, and both large and small gadgets. This increasingly meant being gainfully employed, and the practicality of getting and maintaining a job meant that Māori must effectively communicate in the English language. Whereas at the beginning of World War II the indigenous language was still the primary language of the indigenous people, by the 1960s those fluent in the Māori language had dropped to about 25 percent. Along with the increasing urbanization of Māori came the heightened influences of Western culture, one result of which was the further predominance of the English language among Māori people. But as pendulums swing, within a few years there emerged a growing concern among Māori that the indigenous language would be lost and, along with it, the indigenous culture. By the 1980s Māori were pushing to establish educational institutions that would protect their culture and language, and in 1987 the Government recognized their language as official. The Māori renaissance, which began at the turn of the 19th to the 20th century, was now in full swing. Today, Māori culture and language are taught and celebrated at all levels of national life, and there are several Māori radio stations and a Māori television station.

But aside from the language what is it about Māori educational philosophy that makes it distinctive? Māori educational philosophy is often represented by the *poutama* (stepped) weaving pattern common to the *tukutuku* (latticework) panels of the *whare tipuna* (ancestor house). Indeed, the Faculty of Māori and Indigenous Development at Auckland University of Technology (AUT) is designated as *Te Ara Poutama* (The *poutama* path; way; route). Figure 15 is a photograph of the *poutama* pattern as displayed in the AUT Student Services Building; this particular pattern is overlaid with a Māori carving. Although the stair step pattern in the figure ascends from both right and left directions, important for us is its stair step quality. Think of looking at a stairs from a side view. There is both a horizontal and a vertical movement. Both have significance for the Māori educational model.[32]

Figure 15. The *poutama* weaving pattern, showing the *poutama* weaving pattern overlaid with an artful Māori carving. (Photograph by the author taken in the Auckland University of Technology Student Services Building, 2014.)

As we would expect, the significance of this pattern for education has its roots in Māori mythology. Let us recall that in our generic version of the Māori cosmogonic narrative it was Tāne-mahuta that succeeded in pushing Mother Earth and Father Sky far apart thus allowing light to enter the world. Soon afterward, Tāne made the first human being and brought her to life. Later, Tāne (in some versions it is Tāwhaki, and there is more than one rendition of the story) decided to ascend to the 12th and highest heaven in order to retrieve the three baskets (*kete*) of knowledge for humankind.[33] After much peril he succeeded in obtaining and returning with *te kete tuatea*, *te kete tuauri*, and *te kete aronui*. There is more than one take on the specific contents of each basket; but regardless of rendition, the baskets, considered together, represent the sum total of all knowledge. One approach translates *te kete tuatea* as "the basket of light," *te kete tuauri* as "the basket of darkness," and *te kete aronui* as "the basket of pursuit"; and treats them as knowledge we currently have, knowledge we do not yet possess, and knowledge we are presently pursuing.[34] The *poutama* pattern depicts Tāne's (or Tāwhaki's) stair-step ascent to the highest heaven to attain the baskets of knowledge and his return to the land with them.

Importantly, the contents of the baskets, in one way or another, address every aspect of and every existent in human life. Thus, the journey and the baskets taken together express the approach Māori take to education. They model how each learner follows his or her own holistic path; one which is difficult, but not impossible.[35] The vertical lines of the pattern depict the up and down movement of education; the model includes both the ascent of student achievement and the descent of teachers (who have already achieved) in assisting others. The horizontal lines depict the time necessary at each stage. Each person and particular contents from each basket have a place on the stairs appropriate to the requirement of each level. All teaching and learning is contextual. Education is in the Māori language, which is essential for the accurate communication of Māori *tikanga* (customs; lore, practices, traditions, conventions, and protocols that embody values). At each level the teacher assists the student in grasping the knowledge transmitted in the context of the appropriate *tikanga*. The lessons here are not vague but are made clear by context. The student must succeed at his or her current level before progressing to the next. Learning is developmental, and teaching is learner centered. As it is a journey into the heavens, learning does not end with the school day or the school term. This is a commitment to broad-based, life-long development; and as such, it extends the development of competencies far past the classroom into the home, the community, and the society at large.

This holistic approach to education is also expressed through *whakapapa* (see the topic, "Māori culture and religion," in Chapter Five of this book for a discussion of *whakapapa*). In the genealogical sense the word refers to a family tree, but in the comprehensive sense the concept includes the entire natural world, both animate and inanimate, with its spiritual aspects; indeed, all relationships are at the same time physical and spiritual. The Māori philosophy of education is all inclusive. It is a holistic, *tikanga* centered, educational model that involves the entire personality of the student including his or her physical health, intellectual ability, individual creativity, personal intuition, processing of emotions, spiritual perceptions and practices, and social integration.

If, as Professor Tānia M. Ka'ai writes, "Pākehā reaction to the Māori language is a mirror of Pākehā attitudes to the Māori people,"[36] then we may conclude that significant social progress is underway. And if she is also correct that the schools springing from Māori pedagogical initiatives are strong indicators of Māori people regaining their political and social self-determination under the terms of the Treaty of Waitangi,[37] then we may view Pākehā, who have in the past been a hindrance to effective Māori education, as more recently, albeit in measure, partners in a growing success.

The moral function and the address to injustice

The second example of cultural re-creation and bicultural progress in Aotearoa/New Zealand is the endeavor to include Māori principles in the system of justice. The issues of right behavior and consequences for behavior considered inappropriate have for a very long time been a national worry for both Māori and Pākehā, and a matter we must consider from both perspectives. Prior to Pākehā dominance, Māori had their own systems of social control and justice, but with the advance of Pākehā came the imposition of their structures. The previous chapters of this book have introduced some aspects of the Māori way (in particular, see the topics, "Māori *utu*," in Chapter Three and "The spiritualized Māori," in Chapter Four), and the following paragraphs will include a more complete discussion. But let us begin with an overview of the Aotearoa/New Zealand justice system as developed by Pākehā.

The Aotearoa/New Zealand Ministry of Justice was formed in 1872, well within the years of strong assimilationist attitudes.[38] Today, it not only provides advice regarding justice and legal issues to the Government's Ministers, it leads the entire justice sector which includes the Ministry of Justice, the Police, the Department of Corrections, the Crown Law Office, the Serious Fraud Office, and the Oranga Tamariki-Ministry for Children. It insures that people understand what acceptable behavior is and is not and what the penalties for unacceptable behavior are. It is also responsible for enforcing the rules. Overall, the Ministry of Justice sees itself in the positive role of ensuring the rights of the citizens and protecting their freedoms; however, it was and remains a Pākehā construct.

The Ministry of Justice has evolved in significant ways since its inception. Over the years it has come to recognize that in its policy and advice it must not neglect the Māori tribal dimension. Two issues have contributed to the changed attitude: the national emphasis by both Māori and Pākehā on the Treaty of Waitangi as the nation's founding document and the apparent disproportionate number of Māori who pass through the justice system.[39] The Ministry has come to understand that honoring Māori views, customs, and protocols is highly important for the peace and progress of the nation. With a view to this end, the Ministry broke new ground in 2001 when it published *He Hīnātore ki te Ao Māori, A Glimpse into the Māori World (Māori Perspectives on Justice)* to both provide a record of its attempt to understand Māori tribal practices and to enhance the nation's ability to find solutions to pressing social problems. Although this document is now approaching two decades old, it is still often referenced in books, academic papers, and government related materials as a source document. As indicated by its title, the study aimed to gain some insight into Māori cultural values including tribal processes and comportments for resolution of disputes and violation of behavioral norms; and, as implied in the title, to more fully understand specific ways that the Pākehā Government had transgressed on those values. The long range goal was to gain appreciation of Māori customs, traditions, and practices and to find ways of incorporating them into the institutions and processes of justice which affected Māori.

This 232-page document, while it necessarily does not include every Māori perspective, derives from Māori persons and is an attempt to generally gain insight into the Māori point of view. The Ministry, from the outset, understood that its study would be rudimentary and that much additional work would be required; therefore, it did not present it as a definitive source but as an introductory guide and resource document. Indeed, a perusal of statistical data from 2001 to 2016 shows very little progress in the Māori population of Aotearoa/New Zealand's prisons; in 2001 Māori were about 53 percent, and in March 2016 they were still about 51 percent. Nevertheless, at the very least, this document represents an acknowledgment by the Aotearoa/New Zealand Government that its approach to justice is in need of adjustment.

Throughout this book we use the Māori word *tikanga* which translates as "custom," "practice," "protocol," "convention,"[40] etc. *Tikanga* is built on the word *tika* which can cover an entire range of meanings including "correct, true, upright, right, just, fair, accurate, appropriate, lawful, proper, [and] valid."[41] So, the word, *tikanga*, bespeaks a connection between Māori customs, practices, protocols, and conventions and what the tribal society considers as correct, true, upright, right, just, fair, accurate, appropriate, lawful, proper, [and] valid. Transgression on tribal customs and protocols is a violation of tribal society. The ways in which assimilationist ideas and practices—that is, the demand that Māori fit comfortably into a European style society—are, from the Māori point of view, an attack on their social controls hardly require further explanation.

In a very broad sense, the Māori and Pākehā models of justice have something in common. They are both build on precedent.[42] The various divisions of English law which accompanied the initial colonization of the country, and have developed since, are an outgrowth of English common law dating to the Middle Ages—at least to the 1066 Norman Conquest. The common law was an amalgamation of customs and practices which were common to communities.[43] Similarly, the initial Polynesian population of Aotearoa/New Zealand—dating to between 800 and 1300 CE; probably closer to 1300 CE—who brought their customary procedures for remedying disputes and addressing inappropriate conduct with them from Central Polynesia, refined their customary system once they were in the new land. Nevertheless, there are two significant differences in the English and Māori ideas of justice. First, Māori captured and organized their ideals in oral traditions while the English textualized their ideals into books of law; and second, the Māori system was value based and as such adhered to broad principles whereas the Pākehā system was a fine-tuned set of specific rules.[44]

As previous chapters of this book have pointed out, there is no separation of the sacred and secular in the Māori worldview. It is based on the broad principle of *whakapapa* (a principle of interconnectedness) and permeated with potential and active power (*tapu* and *mana*) accordingly, which plays out in terms of such practices as *utu* and *muru*. However, these aspects of Māori culture, which are integral to Māori justice, grow out of something yet more fundamental; they derive from the *kōrero tawhito*, the "old stories" or "myths and legends."[45] Māori myths include such narratives as the Māori creation story (see the topic, "Māori culture and religion," in Chapter Five of this book for a popular version) which accounts for the entrance of light into the world and the associations of the various personifications of nature including humankind. They are the bedrock of Māori notions of proper behavior and justice; they first illustrate such concepts as *utu*, *mana*, and *tapu*. Māori legends include stories of heroes such as Māui (see the topic, "Some notes on the name," in Chapter One of this book) which are set in ancient days and include such tales as the physical origins of Aotearoa/New Zealand. Māui is a folk-hero and demigod who is especially known, among other adventures, for fishing up the North Island from the sea. Māori often refer to the Aotearoa/New Zealand North Island as *Te Ika a Māui*, "the Fish of Māui" and the South Island as *Te Waka a Māui*, "the Canoe of Māui" from which he fished up the North Island. Those who choose to examine the physical contours of Aotearoa/New Zealand's two main islands will, indeed, notice how one resembles a fish and the other a boat. Legends such as the Māui stories emphasize intelligent resourcefulness, courageousness, and quickness of thought and action; and legendary characters such as Māui serve as examples of correct behavior. Māori people derived their principles and values from their myths and legends which developed out of their tribal experience, and they orally passed them on to each succeeding generation. Today, of course, these narratives are textualized in books and reports, but let not forget that each tribe maintains its own version.

The Ministry's 2001 study is in three parts. The first part records traditional Māori concepts and how they derive from myths and legends; it is essentially an examination of dominant tribal social controls. The second part presents eight case studies of dispute resolution in order to illustrate how Māori have applied the concepts to justice issues; the case studies are based on interviews with Māori *kaumātua* (elders) who had life-long exposure to tribal customs, possessed the ability to fluently speak the Māori language, and exhibited a deep understanding of Māori society. The third part is a rather extensive collection of Māori behavioral, philosophical, emotional, and other cultural terms and sayings, both positive and negative, which are embedded in the myths, legends, songs, chants, etc., that communicate tribal values and expected behavioral patterns; the corporate authors selected them because they believed they provide at least a glimpse into the Māori mind.

The Ministry's study, among other findings, documents how Māori built their society around collective responsibility. There was no separation of individual rights from those of the *whānau* (extended family), *hapū* (sub-tribe) and *iwi* (tribe). This is another expression of the complete and total interconnectivity of everyone and everything expressed in the concept of *whakapapa*, and is in stark contrast to the Pākehā notion of individual responsibility. This arrangement applied group pressure to curtail irresponsible behavior that might harm another person or another person's goods, as well as to discourage deliberate offences.

The Ministry's study also identified, as especially important, some quite complicated issues surrounding the land and its resources. Neither did Māori separate individual rights to the occupation and use of the land from the rights of the group as Pākehā did. Nor was land merely a commodity to be bought and sold; the Māori connection was deeply spiritual. The land was a source of identity and provided genealogical continuity from ancestors through the current generation to the unborn. It is quite apparent how Māori ideology pertaining to the land was virtually incompatible with Pākehā laws of land titling. Practically, a tribal group based its right to land on certain claims which found support in the tribe's occupation of it. Some of these were discovery, conquest, gifting of land, and the recitation of genealogy as a validating device. However, continued use of the land was only guaranteed by the ability of the group to protect it and supervise the use of it. Typically and practically speaking, three generations of control were required to solidify a claim; but ideologically, Māori not only lived on the land, they had a spiritual connection with the land.

While, on the one hand, the 2001 endeavor by the Department of Justice to understand Māori tribal ways and include Māori principles in the structure of the justice system is commendable, on the other hand, it does not appear to have yet produced significant fruit. As already mentioned, the Māori percentage of the nation's prison population in 2016 was virtually the same as it was in 2001.

Whereas the study conducted by the Ministry of Justice focuses on reducing the Māori prison population, there is another view which advocates doing away with the prison system altogether and replacing it with something different and better. Māori indigenous studies expert and constitutional lawyer, Moana Jackson, has asked a critical question about traditional times: "Why did Māori never have prisons?" "Why did they not deal with harm by locking people up?"[46]

As he sees it, there is a sense in which the social attitudes of younger Māori relate directly to an unfair image of Māori culture forced upon them by Pākehā. It is one of violence and war that is a product of Pākehā reification of Māori tribal culture. He relates the depiction directly to the colonization of Aotearoa/New Zealand. According to him, one way colonizers have justified their theft of land and its resources is to portray the indigenous population as warlike and inferior. In other words, Pākehā used race to justify dispossessing Māori; they invented the idea of a "warrior race" as sufficient cause to deprive Māori people of their land and its resources and to assimilate their culture. According to Jackson, the 1994 film, *Once Were Warriors*—an almost unbearable to watch portrayal of Māori domestic violence, based on the 1990 bestselling novel by the same name—has, regardless of intent, had the effect of showing Māori to be a "gang race." Jackson believes that many Māori have largely bought into the violent image and modeled their behavior accordingly, and that this along with a general undertow of systemic racism accounts in large part for the disproportionate representation of Māori in the prison system.

Moreover, Jackson believes that prisons per se are not the answer to social misconduct. He points out that not every culture has dealt with harm by locking people up. Before the arrival of the Western Europeans, Māori had no word in their language for prisons. He takes issue with those who think that Māori did not need prisons because they would simply kill and possibly eat gross offenders, and he advocates an accurate understanding of the Māori worldview and ethos, the bedrock of which is *whakapapa* (the principle of inter-connectivity), as a strong clue for achieving justice. He, then, offers an alternative to Pākehā prisons based on what he believes was Māori practice during traditional times. He proposes a type of *whare mārie* (house of calm or peace) where offenders can achieve reorientation to society and reconciliation with those whom they have offended, and thus discover or be restored to their place in society. This is restorative justice as opposed to punitive justice. He notes that certain other countries are moving away from a system of prisons and believes Aotearoa/New Zealand can learn much from their achievements. His premise is that there was a time when there were no prisons in Aotearoa/New Zealand, and that it would be ben-eficial to explore those times for what they can teach about correcting those who would do harm, helping those who are harmed, and restoring harmed relationships.

Jackson sees Aotearoa/New Zealand as a treaty nation and believes that the Treaty of Waitangi provides an adequate framework for addressing wrongdoing. He points out that Māori never surrendered their sovereignty to the Crown; rather, Māori retained their authority in the land, and one of the fundamental powers of that authority is the right to administer justice for Māori tribespeople. He encourages debate over the shape of a future justice system; and sees the outcome as one in which Māori have much more influence and a much larger role than they do today. He connects the future reduction of Māori currently passing through the justice system, and the ultimate elimination of prisons, with the aboli-tion of colonizing attitudes and the mitigating of social and economic disparity. He is opti-mistic for the future of the country but understands that lasting solutions will take time. He thinks 2040 is a reasonable goal for fundamental change, including the replacing of prisons with something indigenous to Aotearoa/New Zealand.

The point of conversation between persons such as Moana Jackson and the Ministry of Justice is the belief that an effort to address injustices of the past and to understand and appreciate the Māori way can provide a solid foundation on which to establish a positive future for the nation. Both Māori and Pākehā have thus made a loud and clear call for jus-tice for all of the nation's people. It is certainly reasonable to conclude that the long period of colonization is at the heart of the problem. If this is so, it is not unreasonable to speculate that the more Māori and Pākehā partner together in the development of the country, in-cluding the system of justice, the more Māori engagement with the justice system, whatever its future form, will lessen.

In their 2001 study, the Ministry of Justice acknowledges that Māori are still grieving their losses at the hands of Pākehā, and it seems to understand that the effort toward healing must be genuine.[47] It has specifically called for the Aotearoa/New Zealand Government to mend the wounds, especially those caused by Māori loss of land.[48] Nonetheless, if the Māori prison population in Aotearoa/New Zealand's prison system is any measure of repairing the past, then the work has barely begun.

The aesthetic function and the address to endurance

The third example of cultural re-creation and bicultural progress in Aotearoa/New Zealand is the national acknowledgment of Māori aesthetics. Even though philosophical and psychological factors are integral to aesthetics, we shall confine our presentation to the country's practical address, through its national arts program, to what Clifford Geertz, borrowing from Max Weber, labelled "the problem of meaning." This raises two issues:

- How do we define aesthetics?
- How do Aotearoa/New Zealand's aesthetics engage the problem of meaning?

Our definition of aesthetics is very broad. It refers to any construction of imaginative inventiveness; a creation in which the adjectives of aesthetics—such as beauty, truth, sublimity, surprise, shock, clarity, wonder, grandeur, magnificence, etc., and their antitheses—that the perceiver of such may experience in his or her encounter, apprehension, description, and interpretation of the construction's form and content, are "in the eye the beholder." To borrow Tillich's language, it includes any creative thing that expresses an ultimate concern; it is anything indicative of life's deepest desire to express ultimate meaning.[49] For our purposes, aesthetics is synonymous with art; and as sketched by *The New Zealand Curriculum*, particularly inclusive of movement, sound, and image; which *The Curriculum* then broadly divides into dance, drama, music-sound arts, and visual arts.[50] But generally speaking, anything considered as a construction of imaginative inventiveness is an aesthetic expression.

Let us now consider how Aotearoa/New Zealand's aesthetic expressions address the problem of meaning. In so doing, we must be careful about limiting the country's artistic creativity to include only Māori and Pākehā; the nation's art has many sources including immigrants from other Pacific islands, Asia, and European countries. Moreover, there are various arts organizations and museums which contribute to the address: notably, the Auckland War Memorial Museum, which was officially opened in 1929 and has roots well into the 19th century,[51] and Te Papa Tongarewa, the national museum in Wellington, which was opened in 1998 but which predecessor dates to 1865.[52] Nonetheless, the Treaty association of Māori and Pākehā allows us to focus on their dyadic relationship in answering our second question. We must never forget that art is far more than some abstract expression or an alternative way of making a statement; it is invariably tied to a particular worldview and ethos. It expresses the identity and experience of those to whom it belongs, and it is precisely in this way that art addresses the problem of meaning. It is an indicator of and an agent for being and non-being. With this in mind, we will now examine the national program for arts education as the most telling perspective from which to consider the country's aesthetics because it has a mostly bicultural focus which is strongly directed toward Aotearoa/New Zealand's youth.

Let us put Aotearoa/New Zealand's art education into historical perspective by considering it in relation to the nation's broader education program. As mentioned above (see the topic, "The cognitive function and the address to education"), the first Pākehā schools in Aotearoa/New Zealand were the mission schools, but with its Education Ordinance 1847, the colonial government, by "legal" authority, effectively seized control of the mission schools and began using them as a tool to break down Māori culture in anticipation of the tribespeople's full assimilation into a European style society. On the whole, the Pākehā Government, at this time, had little respect for Māori ways and set out to separate the indigenous population from its roots and to mold Māori people into an order of working class citizens. An important move was the attempted, and not altogether unsuccessful, indoctrination of the indigenous children. As the Government's intent found expression in the education system broadly, it was integral to its program for the arts.

In the early 1850s, Aotearoa/New Zealand underwent an administrative reorganiza-tion. Up to that time, the colony had been managed by a Governor appointed by the British. But in 1852 the United Kingdom's Parliament passed The Constitution Act 1852: An Act to Grant a Representative Constitution to the Colony of New Zealand, which inaugurated a representative government; there would be a General Assembly consisting of the Governor, a Legislative Council, and a House of Representatives. It also allowed for the country to be divided into six Provinces, which occurred in 1853 (others were added later).[53] Among the functions of each of the Provinces was the establishment and oversight of public schools which were separate from the Native Schools (mission schools which had come under Pākehā supervision pursuant to the Education Ordinance 1847). As we shall see, these state schools would eventually be the nucleus of a secular central-government-mandated edu-cational system. Māori children could attend these Provincial schools if they so chose; but whether they chose these schools or the Native Schools, they would be subject to assimila-tionist intents including art education.

The tensions and conflict of the New Zealand Wars fought between Māori and Pākehā from the mid–1840s into the early 1870s, mostly confined to the North Island, caused most of the North Island's schools to be closed by the 1860s. However, heading into the 1860s, even though Māori school attendance had dropped significantly and much of the teaching in the Native Schools continued to be in the Māori language,[54] the Government passed The Native Schools Act 1858, which rather lengthily describes itself as "AN ACT to grant the annual sum of seven thousand pounds for a term of seven years from the 30th June, 1858, in aid of Schools for the education of the Aboriginal Native Race."[55] Its purpose was to rein-force the assimilationist policies of the Education Ordinance 1847. The 1858 Act detailed its own arrangements for funding and inspection of school facilities. It also stated that every school which received aid under the Act must exist in connection with and be managed in concert with some religious body; it specifically addressed the managerial continuance of schools that were currently connected to the Church of England, the Society of Wesleyan Methodists, and the Church of Rome. Additionally, the Act continued the requirements that instruction should be in the English language and that every school would provide industrial training. It specifically stated that the topics of instruction would be those of primary English education. In order to be in compliance, art instruction must fit into this broad assimilationist scheme.

Many of the schools which had closed because of the New Zealand Wars reopened as the conflicts wound down, and toward the end of the wars, the Government passed the Native Schools Act 1867—full title, "AN ACT to regulate and provide Subsidies for Maori Schools"—as a repeal of the Ordinance of 1847 and the Act of 1858.[56] The 1867 Act estab-lished a national system of Māori primary schools, under a centralized Native Affairs de-partment. It involved the local tribal residents in designating their area as a School District for the education of the children; the schools were, however, open to all local children re-gardless of ethnic background.[57] Those tribal groups wishing to establish a school agreed to provide at least an acre of land; contribute to the construction cost, operation and mainte-nance of the facilities; and help pay the teacher's salary (these latter two requirements were eliminated in 1871). The Government would provide a subsidy and a governmental appoin-tee would inspect the schools. The legislation also provided some money for indigenous children in European schools. Importantly, there is no mention in this Act of working in concert with religious groups; this Act did not abolish schools sponsored by religious orga-nizations but changed the relationship with national government. In effect the Government was exerting greater control over education. Moreover, the Government again continued the requirement that teaching would be as far as practicable in the English language and that the curriculum would be the subjects of primary English education. Art education, as a part of the curriculum, would continue to conform to Pākehā standards. In effect, 19th century schooling, as far as it touched Māori people, was a device for "civilizing" them; and it was under this educational umbrella that assimilationist dispositions shaped art education. The educational policies were not simply secular in nature; they were an attack on the spiritual basis of the indigenous culture. For the indigenous population, what was at stake was their survival as a distinct race.

Let us now move forward to the Education Act 1877—full title, "AN ACT to make further Provision for the Education of the People of New Zealand."[58] We should keep in mind that the Government, under a centralized Native Department, had supported a school system for Māori that was separate from the public schools and that this Act did not abolish the Māori school system; in fact, nothing in this Act was binding on any Māori. It did, however, establish a national system of education that provided a framework for the eventual elimination of the Native Schools, as the Māori attendees succumbed to assimilation. This view is supported by the fact that in 1879 the 57 Native Schools were transferred from the Native Department to the Department of Education which the 1877 Act established.[59] Prior to the 1877 Act, as mentioned above, a system of provincial governments,[60] a sort of federalist arrangement, had managed the public schools, but the provincial governments, which began in 1853, ended in 1876. This 1877 Act, in conjunction with the abolition of the provincial system of government, consolidated control of the public schools nationwide in a centralized government under the control of the Department of Education. Whereas education in the Provincial public schools was not previously compulsory and often not free because schools did not always meet certain requirements for funding,[61] public education would now be without direct cost to the public and, with a few exceptions, attendance would be mandatory for certain age groups. Also, instruction would be organized around secular themes as opposed to entailing religious literature and beliefs. As already noted, Māori could attend the public schools if they wished, but they were not required to do so; it was not until after World War II, when Māori flocked to the cities, that the number of indigenous children in the public schools greatly surpassed those in the Māori schools. Importantly, education in the public schools would be utilitarian in nature with the subjects of instruction being reading, writing, arithmetic, English grammar and composition, geography, history, elementary science and drawing, object lessons, and vocal music. Subjects designed specifically for girls would include sewing and needlework and the principles of domestic economy. The practical intent, of course, in both the Native Schools and the public schools was to develop the skills necessary to earn a living and move the country forward economically, but the economy was that of Pākehā. This utilitarian approach also carried over into art education in both systems.[62] The model for aesthetics was particularly British as it relied on materials brought in from Britain. Indigenous art was discouraged, which was an assault on Māori culture. No matter which schools in the nation Māori children attended and notwithstanding the quality and usefulness of the skills learned from the teachers, the nation's curriculum insured a thorough indoctrination into Pākehā ways.

Although the emphasis on developing occupational skills was paramount, there was some division in the country between utilitarian arts and the fine arts; however, education in the fine arts was mostly available to only the wealthier European settlers. Most of the country's youth learned art for practical reasons such as the production of maps of all sorts, various types of publications, and methods of advertising. While no art is ever completely devoid of imaginative inventiveness, the emphasis was not on art for art's sake or understanding its development in a historical context; it was on its utilitarian application and how it could contribute to a good European style citizenry and economy. This attitude and approach was dominant for many decades to come.

Let us now recall how attitudes toward the preservation of Māori culture began to change in the late 19th and early 20th centuries. A concern to perpetuate Māori culture developed and along with it came a renewed emphasis on Māori art, especially in the refurbishing of existing, and the building of new, *whare tipuna* (ancestor houses). This was the period of the Smith-Best orthodoxy in the Polynesian Society with its emphasis on elevating Māori in the opinions of the nation's Pākehā citizenry. It was also a time when Māori rekindled their tribal pride and upped their fervor for their culture. Although the Smith-Best influence in the Polynesian Society waned in the 1940s, the Māori passion continued. The ember once ignited could not be extinguished.

In 1946, the innovative, resourceful, and visionary Arthur Gordon Tovey (1901–1974)[63] became the first National Supervisor of Art and Crafts. He developed a scheme for and promoted the inclusion of Māori aesthetic traditions in the Native Schools, an endorsement which would prove transformative. He backed the implementation of programs that included Māori patterns in arts and crafts and the use of Māori songs, dances, and legends. The schools for the indigenous students continued until the last of them came under the control of regional education boards in 1969. Significantly, by the 1960s the Department of Education had charged its arts and crafts branches with the task of developing a program for teaching Māori arts and crafts to *all* pupils. By the late 1960s and early 1970s, as the Māori renaissance was coming into its own, art educators began suggesting the study of art for art's sake. While this may not have gone far enough toward the recognition of the social, historical, and moral contexts for particular constructions of imaginative inventiveness, it was certainly a move past art's purely utilitarian aspect.

Today, *The New Zealand Curriculum* recognizes the power and value of aesthetics in contributing to the nation's bicultural and multicultural character. It views the art of the nation's various groups, through its various communicative conventions and layered meanings, as enriching the lives of all the country's people. *The Curriculum* specifically embraces Māori performing, musical, and visual art in both its customary and contemporary forms along with those of Pākehā. It recognizes the commercial value of art and its practical value in problem solving, but does not limit aesthetics to utilitarian standards. Rather it acknowledges the ability of art to engage the human mind, senses, and feelings in creativeness, in both expression and interpretation.

Presently, many in the country believe that indigenous art is still positioned on the back burner behind European forms, which would mean that Māori culture is still considered inferior to that of Pākehā; nonetheless, the movement of the country's attitudes from those of the 19th century to those of today is quite apparent. The inclusion of Māori art in today's educational curriculum, as not only something with a significant social and historical context but also an expression with intrinsic value, is far removed from the haughty colonial practice of disparaging it and discouraging its production. A culture's aesthetic expression is tied to its unique identity, and its vigor is indicative of the health of the culture. The rejuvenation of Māori art in Aotearoa/New Zealand is representative of the rejuvenation of the tribal worldview and ethos; it has been an address to the pain of attempted assimilation and thus the endurance of Māori as a distinct people. It is indeed difficult to overstate the importance of art for defining culture. Today, the nation officially recognizes that the art, which once expressed only the worldview and ethos of the indigenous population and was largely disdained by Pākehā society, now contributes to the definition of the nation as a whole. It stands as a reminder of the journey thus far, not only of Māori people but also of Pākehā. It is a reminder of the common experience of all human persons and the obligation of each to sustain the other.

The religious dimension

A striking feature of the three examples above is how entangled the disciplines of education, justice, and aesthetics are with cultural structures of reciprocity and the operation of power for social, religious, and political purposes. There is no practical separation. Humankind plumbs the depths of its experience to make sense of its existence and to build a world that is at the same time intelligible and comfortable; but this takes place within the inseparability of the social, religious, and political domains. The way a government constructs, interlocks, and administers its policies pertaining to education, justice, and aesthetics is powerful to determine the interaction of its citizens and the direction of the nation.

But what is the proper attitude to take regarding the synergistic quality of education, justice, and art? Here the Māori concept of *Mātauranga Māori* is once again helpful. Let us recall that it allows for the inclusion of new ideas and practices within the bounds of cultural authenticity. It grows out of a central cultural core (*Māoritanga*) but enables—indeed, it sanctions—the development of that core according to new experience including contact with other cultures. It is possible to establish a spectrum on which reside the various themes of culture included in its political, religious, and social aspects—particularly, as in the case at hand: education, justice, and art. At one extreme the themes are so broad that they defy any consideration beyond very abstract notions of human universals, and at the other extreme they are so narrow that they can never escape some black hole of the culture that gives them concrete expression. But neither extreme allows for the synergistic synthesis of new experience and practice; it may permit synthesis of a sort, but not of the synergistic kind that can result from the real-life encounter of cultures. What the Māori concept of *Mātauranga Māori* communicates is not confined to Māori culture. The dynamics which the notion expresses are applicable to any culture, including Pākehā. It refers to the expectation of expanding cultural categories in concert with new knowledge; the acceptance of new ways of looking at things and the adoption of new practices; the evolution of cultural symbols; the dynamic development of worldview and ethos. It entails (to slightly modify Geertz's idea) persons looking both within and beyond their own cultural contexts—other contexts sometimes entailing radically different cultural expressions—to discover ultimate meaning and positive potential. Such is a good start toward a synergistic synthesis of cultures.

The pages of this book have largely presented Māori and Pākehā as idealized units in the sense of being united within themselves. But the reality is that, even though there are some characteristics which each group broadly holds in common—for instance: ethnicity, history, social norms, and structures of reciprocity and power—both Māori and Pākehā are a collection of factions. Along with the many who accept the broad tenets of biculturalism, there are in the Pākehā camp some who retain an assimilationist mentality, rallied around particular issues of cultural orthodoxy, which may engage in heated clashes with idealistic progressives. And among Māori there are persons with a militant attitude who, driven by their own ethnic concerns, are contemptuous toward Pākehā culture and stand as a challenge to tribespersons who embrace biculturalism. On the one hand, the various factions within each culture may move each general population toward a more standard outlook, attitude, and practice; but on the other hand and importantly, each faction is a separate voice within the national debate. In other words, the debates internal to both Māori and Pākehā not only have the potential to move each culture, respectively, toward some ideal; they also contribute to the conversation between the two, and therefore, can move the nation toward its goal of biculturalism. This would indeed reveal the religious dimension in human cognition, justice, and endurance in its broadest and truest sense of ultimate concern.

Postscript

Our anthropological examination of the ideas and practices of Aotearoa/New Zealand's Māori and Pākehā populations and how their interchange is tending toward a bicultural nation has taken the form of a winding-path journey. The undertaking's preparation included a look at Aotearoa/New Zealand's origins, history, people, religion, government, and languages (Chapter One) and the nation's two historically primary religious symbols: the *whare tipuna*, the Māori "ancestor house," and the *whare karakia*, the "house of prayer," in this case the Christian church house (Chapter Two). The expedition wound through a close examination of the differences in Māori and Pākehā reciprocity (Chapter Three), power relations (Chapter Four), and religio-cultural contexts (Chapter Five); and produced some broad principles of cultural interaction (Chapter Six). The trek ended with an in-depth treatment of the *Io* question as an example of the dynamics of cultural synergistic synthesis (Chapter Seven); and, after a statement regarding the perpetuation of cultural genuineness and authenticity through the re-creation of culture, a look at some practical outcomes of the nation's bicultural conversation, specifically, the attempt to incorporate Māori cultural ideals into the national education system, justice program, and strategy for aesthetics (Chapter Eight).

By the end of the 19th century, Pākehā, through their colonialist and assimilationist activities, were well on their way to eradicating Māori culture as a significant social, political, and religious force in the land; but around the turn of the 19th to the 20th century, Pākehā made a significant break from their English colonialist assimilationist roots and Māori began a reawakening of their cultural pride. Abstract thought and the ability to answer life's deepest questions have characterized Māori people, as a confederation of tribes and not as a pan-culture, from the outset; however, it was not until the turn of these centuries that Pākehā largely understood the depth and value of the Māori mind and quality of the tribal way of life. Pākehā cultural enlightenment and Māori tribal revival produced a reified form of Māori culture which both Māori and Pākehā generally recognized as a traditional pan-culture, a notion that has not yet been completely abandoned; but the reification of a Māori traditional pan-culture notwithstanding, both cultures were then and are now unceasingly re-creating themselves in relation to one another in a way that preserves a core continuity of experience which validates each as genuine and authentic while incorporating new ideas and practices. The focus of this bicultural re-creation has been the address to life's deepest questions; and although efforts have largely been characterized and shaped by the activity of struggle, they have engendered an effort to establish a nation of mutual respect and cooperation. This book does not glorify the conflict, sanction colonialism, or support racism in any form; rather, it simply acknowledges the role of struggle in the complicated and complex entwined history of Aotearoa/New Zealand's principal populations.

An observer might wish for a different historical movement in associations; but no matter how often the history gets revisited or how many alternative paths get plotted, the outcome remains as it is. Hence, Māori and Pākehā are currently engaged in a dialogue to determine and perpetuate the best of each culture's distinguishing qualities as they establish themselves both internally as *Aotearoans/New Zealanders* and externally as a unique country in the world. By definition, Aotearoa/New Zealand's bicultural initiative is the voluntary integration of Māori and Pākehā ideas and practices without the sacrifice of cultural identity and authenticity.

Over the last several decades there has been considerable progress toward the broad goal of biculturalism. The advancements include the recognition of the Treaty of Waitangi as the nation's founding document, the establishment of the Waitangi Tribunal to hear Māori claims about breaches of the Treaty and make recommendations for resolution, the extension of the Tribunal's power to address issues dating back to 1840 when the Treaty was first signed, the identification of the Māori language as a treasure to be protected, a recognition of Māori principles of education as valuable for the national education program, a view of Māori conventions of justice as beneficial for the nation's justice system, and a cognizance of Māori art forms as important to the national identity. Without doubt, a different 19th century European attitude toward the indigenous population may have resulted in Māori, even after the signing of the Treaty of Waitangi, deciding how to include Pākehā culture into their way of life; but that was not how events unfolded. Instead, it was Pākehā military dominance and the arrival of an overwhelming number of settlers that controlled the development of the country and serves as the backdrop for the current state of affairs with its commitment to biculturalism.

Looking ahead, the nation understands very well that it is far from attaining its goal. Among its stated objectives for bicultural accomplishments are all Aotearoans/New Zealanders valuing the Māori language and having a common awareness of its need for protection by 2028 and Aotearoa/New Zealand being, in terms of verbal languages, well established as a bilingual nation by the bicentenary of the signing of the Treaty of Waitangi in 2040; but the nation appears to have no clear idea of how to determine when it has succeeded in becoming bicultural. Perhaps the issue may never be completely settled, inasmuch as culture can never be static. By its very nature, it is in constant flux; persons and groups continually striving to increase their power are strong reminders of the condition of change. Nonetheless, it is not unreasonable to speculate that at some future date the population may experience a "dawning" that they are truly a bicultural nation.

To add to the complexity, some Aotearoans/New Zealanders have already begun discussing the issue of multiculturalism. The nation is currently working out the details of the structure and content of its future through interaction in local communities as well as through the various ministries of government; and alongside the bicultural goal is Aotearoa/New Zealand's commitment, as once stated by the Human Rights Commission, to "affirm a sense of belonging for all people in New Zealand through the development of an inclusive national identity that embraces.... Māori, Pākehā, Pacific, Asian and many other community identities."[1]

What happens next can only occur in relation to previous events; any future can only be a relevant future because it is unavoidably limited by what has preceded; possibilities grow out of a concretized past and can never be more than the past will allow. The negative effects of colonialism in Aotearoa/New Zealand cannot be erased, but they can be overcome to the nation's future advantage. Events build upon events and possibilities upon possibilities, but intent and choice are critical for which possibilities get realized and what events come to fruition. Agreement in principle may at times seem trivial and arguably sometimes is; but when it is a genuine expression of a joint willingness for something good to occur, intent provides, at the very least, a broad goal and a general direction for its achievement. Metaphorically speaking, traversing an unknown landscape can be fraught with frustrations and require reversal of steps when those traveling encounter swamps, quagmires, and impasses. And the journey must be managed one step at a time; whether the movement is a small step or a giant leap, the measure is necessarily a single unit. But with positive aspirations, unswerving resolve, and integrous cooperation those traveling together can arrive at their agreed-upon destination.

In the specific case of Aotearoa/New Zealand, the target is the achievement of biculturalism; but that which their goal represents is the hope of diverse others. Unfortunately, while respect and cooperation are widely touted in the world, the appeal for such is often connected with the victory of one particular ideology and the subordination or eradication of others. In a global economy, short of the unattractive and undesirable outcome of world conquest and a resulting thorough indoctrination of every person on earth who survived the conflict, a complete triumph of ideology is an extremely unlikely scenario. The days of sustainable national isolation are past and a new paradigm is required. In a world in which people from different cultural backgrounds, with their religious and political aspects, are continually drawn into closer contact, it becomes more and more imperative that each group develop a respect for the beliefs and ways of others. This does not require an apology for or abandonment of one's own culture, but it does necessitate respect for other worldviews, empathy with others at the most fundamental levels of human experience, and a joint will and activity for peace and understanding.

Aotearoa/New Zealand's cultural interchange has not been easy or free from conflict, and even though there has been much progress over the last several decades, Aotearoa/New Zealand is not today a perfect model for biculturalism. But what is also abundantly clear is that Aotearoans/New Zealanders are a capable people, and Aotearoa/New Zealand's bicultural course is not purely happenstance. Since the late 19th century, Māori and Pākehā have been engaged in a grand experiment in search of a grand bargain as a *result* of considered opportunities not in *spite* of random circumstances. Aotearoans/New Zealanders have established for themselves a mandate to be a bicultural nation, and they have a unique opportunity to offer the rest of the world the much-needed lesson that cultural syncretistic synergistic success is both desirable and achievable. To sum the message of this book in a single sentence: We can, indeed we must, learn to put, and become committed to putting, basic human need and common human decency ahead of social, religious, and political differences; and Aotearoa/New Zealand is developing as a helpful model for so doing. To restate a popular Māori proverb to capture its meaning for our purposes: *He waka eke noa*, "We all voyage in the same canoe."

Appendix A:
Maps for Aotearoa/
New Zealand's World Location

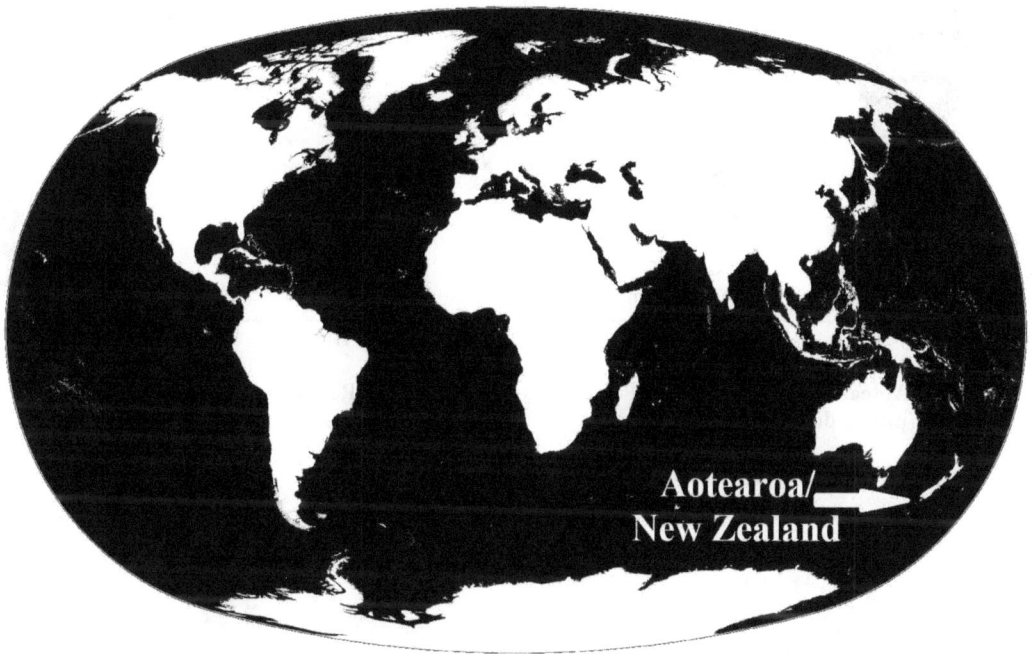

Map 1. Aotearoa/New Zealand's World Location (public domain).

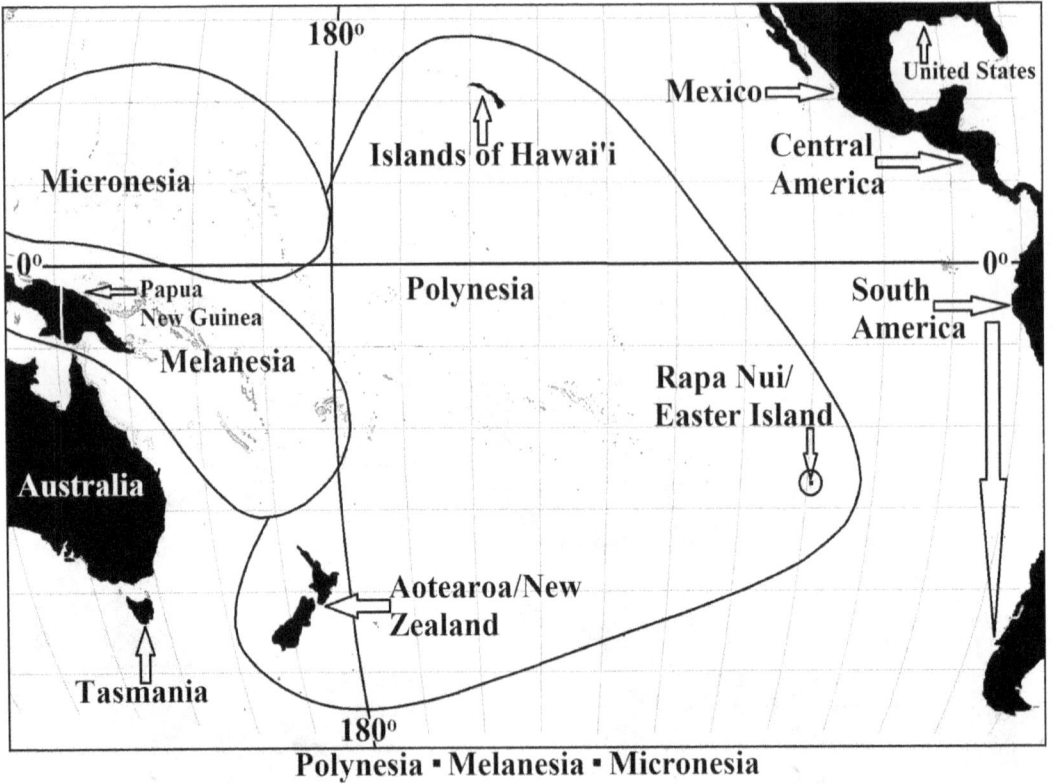

Map 2. Aotearoa/New Zealand in Polynesia and Polynesia in Relation to Micronesia and Melanesia (public domain).

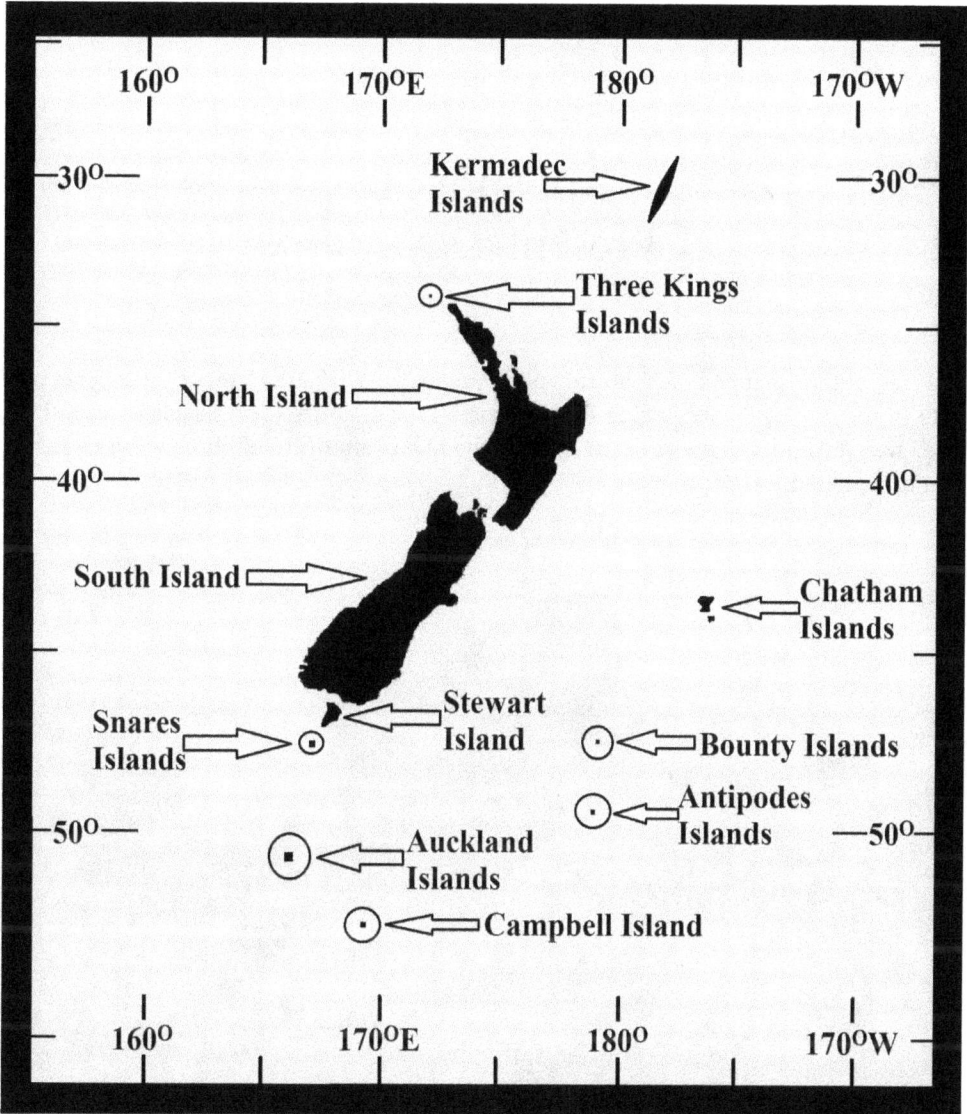

Map 3. Aotearoa/New Zealand's Territorial Sea Limits by Island Group (*Source*: Land Information New Zealand [LINZ] and licensed by LINZ for re-use under the Creative Commons Attribution 4.0 International licence).

Appendix B:
A Present-Day *Marae*

The author snapped the following photographs of Whakaue Marae at the town of Maketu in the Bay of Plenty Region of Aotearoa/New Zealand's North Island in early 2010. They were taken from the street in front of the *marae* after careful observation to ensure that no function was in progress.

The entrance to the Māori *marae*. Note the pavilion where visitors gather awaiting their welcome onto the grounds. Directly in front of the pavilion is the *whare tipuna* (ancestor house), sometimes called the *wharenui* (great house), *wharehui* (meeting house) or *whare whakairo* (carved house). The courtyard directly in front of the *whare tipuna* is called the *marae-ātea*.

The pavilion at the *marae* entrance, the *whare tipuna*, and the *marae-ātea*. Visitors gather at the pavilion but do not enter the *marae* until welcomed onto it.

A building on the *marae* complex.

Beautiful, intricate carvings on the *marae* complex such as these have deep cultural significance for the people who meet here.

Rich, intricate art work at the *whare tipuna*.

Appendix C:
New Zealand Bill
of Rights Act 1990

See the following 12 pages.

Appendix C

**Reprint
as at 1 July 2013**

New Zealand Bill of Rights Act
1990

Public Act	1990 No 109
Date of assent	28 August 1990
Commencement	see section 1(2)

Contents

Note

Changes authorised by section 17C of the Acts and Regulations Publication Act 1989 have been made in this reprint.

A general outline of these changes is set out in the notes at the end of this reprint, together with other explanatory material about this reprint.

This Act is administered by the Ministry of Justice.

An Act—

(a)   to affirm, protect, and promote human rights and fundamental freedoms in New Zealand; and

(b)   to affirm New Zealand's commitment to the International Covenant on Civil and Political Rights

1   Short Title and commencement

(1)   This Act may be cited as the New Zealand Bill of Rights Act 1990.

(2)   This Act shall come into force on the 28th day after the date on which it receives the Royal assent.

Part 1
General provisions

2   Rights affirmed

The rights and freedoms contained in this Bill of Rights are affirmed.

3   Application

This Bill of Rights applies only to acts done—

(a)   by the legislative, executive, or judicial branches of the Government of New Zealand; or

(b)   by any person or body in the performance of any public function, power, or duty conferred or imposed on that person or body by or pursuant to law.

4   Other enactments not affected

No court shall, in relation to any enactment (whether passed or made before or after the commencement of this Bill of Rights),—

(a)   hold any provision of the enactment to be impliedly repealed or revoked, or to be in any way invalid or ineffective; or

(b)   decline to apply any provision of the enactment—

by reason only that the provision is inconsistent with any provision of this Bill of Rights.

5   Justified limitations

Subject to section 4, the rights and freedoms contained in this Bill of Rights may be subject only to such reasonable limits prescribed by law as can be demonstrably justified in a free and democratic society.

3

6   Interpretation consistent with Bill of Rights to be preferred

Wherever an enactment can be given a meaning that is consistent with the rights and freedoms contained in this Bill of Rights, that meaning shall be preferred to any other meaning.

7   Attorney-General to report to Parliament where Bill appears to be inconsistent with Bill of Rights

Where any Bill is introduced into the House of Representatives, the Attorney-General shall,—

(a)   in the case of a Government Bill, on the introduction of that Bill; or

(b)   in any other case, as soon as practicable after the introduction of the Bill,—

bring to the attention of the House of Representatives any provision in the Bill that appears to be inconsistent with any of the rights and freedoms contained in this Bill of Rights.

Part 2
Civil and political rights

Life and security of the person

8   Right not to be deprived of life

No one shall be deprived of life except on such grounds as are established by law and are consistent with the principles of fundamental justice.

9   Right not to be subjected to torture or cruel treatment

Everyone has the right not to be subjected to torture or to cruel, degrading, or disproportionately severe treatment or punishment.

10   Right not to be subjected to medical or scientific experimentation

Every person has the right not to be subjected to medical or scientific experimentation without that person's consent.

11   Right to refuse to undergo medical treatment

Everyone has the right to refuse to undergo any medical treatment.

Democratic and civil rights

12   Electoral rights

Every New Zealand citizen who is of or over the age of 18 years—

(a)   has the right to vote in genuine periodic elections of members of the House of Representatives, which elections shall be by equal suffrage and by secret ballot; and

(b)   is qualified for membership of the House of Representatives.

13   Freedom of thought, conscience, and religion

Everyone has the right to freedom of thought, conscience, religion, and belief, including the right to adopt and to hold opinions without interference.

14   Freedom of expression

Everyone has the right to freedom of expression, including the freedom to seek, receive, and impart information and opinions of any kind in any form.

15   Manifestation of religion and belief

Every person has the right to manifest that person's religion or belief in worship, observance, practice, or teaching, either individually or in community with others, and either in public or in private.

16   Freedom of peaceful assembly

Everyone has the right to freedom of peaceful assembly.

17   Freedom of association

Everyone has the right to freedom of association.

18   Freedom of movement

(1)   Everyone lawfully in New Zealand has the right to freedom of movement and residence in New Zealand.

(2)   Every New Zealand citizen has the right to enter New Zealand.

(3)   Everyone has the right to leave New Zealand.

(4)   No one who is not a New Zealand citizen and who is lawfully in New Zealand shall be required to leave New Zealand except under a decision taken on grounds prescribed by law.

Non-discrimination and minority rights

19   Freedom from discrimination

(1)   Everyone has the right to freedom from discrimination on the grounds of discrimination in the Human Rights Act 1993.

(2)   Measures taken in good faith for the purpose of assisting or advancing persons or groups of persons disadvantaged because of discrimination that is unlawful by virtue of Part 2 of the Human Rights Act 1993 do not constitute discrimination.

Section 19: substituted, on 1 February 1994, by section 145 of the Human Rights Act 1993 (1993 No 82).

20   Rights of minorities

A person who belongs to an ethnic, religious, or linguistic minority in New Zealand shall not be denied the right, in community with other members of that minority, to enjoy the culture, to profess and practise the religion, or to use the language, of that minority.

Search, arrest, and detention

21   Unreasonable search and seizure

Everyone has the right to be secure against unreasonable search or seizure, whether of the person, property, or correspondence or otherwise.

22   Liberty of the person

Everyone has the right not to be arbitrarily arrested or detained.

23   Rights of persons arrested or detained

(1)   Everyone who is arrested or who is detained under any enactment—

(a)   shall be informed at the time of the arrest or detention
of the reason for it; and

(b)   shall have the right to consult and instruct a lawyer without delay and to be informed of that right; and

(c)   shall have the right to have the validity of the arrest or
detention determined without delay by way of *habeas
corpus* and to be released if the arrest or detention is
not lawful.

(2)   Everyone who is arrested for an offence has the right to be
charged promptly or to be released.

(3)   Everyone who is arrested for an offence and is not released
shall be brought as soon as possible before a court or competent tribunal.

(4)   Everyone who is—

(a)   arrested; or

(b)   detained under any enactment—

for any offence or suspected offence shall have the right to
refrain from making any statement and to be informed of that
right.

(5)   Everyone deprived of liberty shall be treated with humanity
and with respect for the inherent dignity of the person.

24   Rights of persons charged

Everyone who is charged with an offence—

(a)   shall be informed promptly and in detail of the nature
and cause of the charge; and

(b)   shall be released on reasonable terms and conditions
unless there is just cause for continued detention; and

(c)   shall have the right to consult and instruct a lawyer; and

(d)   shall have the right to adequate time and facilities to
prepare a defence; and

(e)   shall have the right, except in the case of an offence
under military law tried before a military tribunal, to the
benefit of a trial by jury when the penalty for the offence
is or includes imprisonment for 2 years or more; and

(f)   shall have the right to receive legal assistance without cost if the interests of justice so require and the person does not have sufficient means to provide for that assistance; and

(g)   shall have the right to have the free assistance of an interpreter if the person cannot understand or speak the language used in court.

Section 24(e): amended, on 1 July 2013, by section 4 of the New Zealand Bill of Rights Amendment Act 2011 (2011 No 92).

25   Minimum standards of criminal procedure

Everyone who is charged with an offence has, in relation to the determination of the charge, the following minimum rights:

(a)   the right to a fair and public hearing by an independent and impartial court:

(b)   the right to be tried without undue delay:

(c)   the right to be presumed innocent until proved guilty according to law:

(d)   the right not to be compelled to be a witness or to confess guilt:

(e)   the right to be present at the trial and to present a defence:

(f)   the right to examine the witnesses for the prosecution and to obtain the attendance and examination of witnesses for the defence under the same conditions as the prosecution:

(g)   the right, if convicted of an offence in respect of which the penalty has been varied between the commission of the offence and sentencing, to the benefit of the lesser penalty:

(h)   the right, if convicted of the offence, to appeal according to law to a higher court against the conviction or against the sentence or against both:

(i)   the right, in the case of a child, to be dealt with in a manner that takes account of the child's age.

26   Retroactive penalties and double jeopardy

(1)   No one shall be liable to conviction of any offence on account of any act or omission which did not constitute an offence

by such person under the law of New Zealand at the time it occurred.

(2)   No one who has been finally acquitted or convicted of, or pardoned for, an offence shall be tried or punished for it again.

27   Right to justice

(1)   Every person has the right to the observance of the principles of natural justice by any tribunal or other public authority which has the power to make a determination in respect of that person's rights, obligations, or interests protected or recognised by law.

(2)   Every person whose rights, obligations, or interests protected or recognised by law have been affected by a determination of any tribunal or other public authority has the right to apply, in accordance with law, for judicial review of that determination.

(3)   Every person has the right to bring civil proceedings against, and to defend civil proceedings brought by, the Crown, and to have those proceedings heard, according to law, in the same way as civil proceedings between individuals.

Part 3
Miscellaneous provisions

28   Other rights and freedoms not affected

An existing right or freedom shall not be held to be abrogated or restricted by reason only that the right or freedom is not included in this Bill of Rights or is included only in part.

29   Application to legal persons

Except where the provisions of this Bill of Rights otherwise provide, the provisions of this Bill of Rights apply, so far as practicable, for the benefit of all legal persons as well as for the benefit of all natural persons.

Contents

Notes

1 *General*

This is a reprint of the New Zealand Bill of Rights Act 1990. The reprint incorporates all the amendments to the Act as at 1 July 2013, as specified in the list of amendments at the end of these notes.

Relevant provisions of any amending enactments that contain transitional, savings, or application provisions that cannot be compiled in the reprint are also included, after the principal enactment, in chronological order. For more information, *see* http://www.pco.parliament.govt.nz/reprints/.

2 *Status of reprints*

Under section 16D of the Acts and Regulations Publication Act 1989, reprints are presumed to correctly state, as at the date of the reprint, the law enacted by the principal enactment and by the amendments to that enactment. This presumption applies even though editorial changes authorised by section 17C of the Acts and Regulations Publication Act 1989 have been made in the reprint.

This presumption may be rebutted by producing the official volumes of statutes or statutory regulations in which the principal enactment and its amendments are contained.

3 *How reprints are prepared*

A number of editorial conventions are followed in the preparation of reprints. For example, the enacting words are not included in Acts, and provisions that are repealed or revoked are omitted. For a detailed list of the editorial conventions, *see* http://www.pco.parliament.govt.nz/editorial-conventions/ or Part 8 of the *Tables of New Zealand Acts and Ordinances and Statutory Regulations and Deemed Regulations in Force.*

4   Changes made under section 17C of the Acts and Regulations Publication Act 1989

Section 17C of the Acts and Regulations Publication Act 1989 authorises the making of editorial changes in a reprint as set out in sections 17D and 17E of that Act so that, to the extent permitted, the format and style of the reprinted enactment is consistent with current legislative drafting practice. Changes that would alter the effect of the legislation are not permitted.

A new format of legislation was introduced on 1 January 2000. Changes to legislative drafting style have also been made since 1997, and are ongoing. To the extent permitted by section 17C of the Acts and Regulations Publication Act 1989, all legislation reprinted after 1 January 2000 is in the new format for legislation and reflects current drafting practice at the time of the reprint.

In outline, the editorial changes made in reprints under the authority of section 17C of the Acts and Regulations Publication Act 1989 are set out below, and they have been applied, where relevant, in the preparation of this reprint:

- omission of unnecessary referential words (such as "of this section" and "of this Act")
- typeface and type size (Times Roman, generally in 11.5 point)
- layout of provisions, including:
  - indentation
  - position of section headings (eg, the number and heading now appear above the section)
- format of definitions (eg, the defined term now appears in bold type, without quotation marks)
- format of dates (eg, a date formerly expressed as "the 1st day of January 1999" is now expressed as "1 January 1999")

11

- position of the date of assent (it now appears on the front page of each Act)
- punctuation (eg, colons are not used after definitions)
- Parts numbered with roman numerals are replaced with arabic numerals, and all cross-references are changed accordingly
- case and appearance of letters and words, including:
  - format of headings (eg, headings where each word formerly appeared with an initial capital letter followed by small capital letters are amended so that the heading appears in bold, with only the first word (and any proper nouns) appearing with an initial capital letter)
  - small capital letters in section and subsection references are now capital letters
- schedules are renumbered (eg, Schedule 1 replaces First Schedule), and all cross-references are changed accordingly
- running heads (the information that appears at the top of each page)
- format of two-column schedules of consequential amendments, and schedules of repeals (eg, they are rearranged into alphabetical order, rather than chronological).

5 *List of amendments incorporated in this reprint (most recent first)*

New Zealand Bill of Rights Amendment Act 2011 (2011 No 92)

Human Rights Act 1993 (1993 No 82): section 145

Wellington, New Zealand:
Published under the authority of the New Zealand Government—2013

Chapter Notes

Introduction

1. Tānia Ka'ai, John C. Moorfield, Michael P.J. Reilly, and Sharon Mosley, ed., *Ki te Whaiao: An Introduction to Māori Culture and Society* (Auckland: Pearson Education New Zealand, 2004), viii.

2. *Ibid.*

3. Hiwi and Pat Tauroa, *Te Marae: A Guide to Customs & Protocol* (Auckland: Reed Publishing [NZ], 2007).

4. *Ibid.*, p. 29.

Chapter One

1. Stats NZ/Tatauranga Aotearoa, *Overseas Merchandise Trade: February 2018*, Tables (NP: Stats NZ, 2018), Table 6, https://www.stats.govt.nz/assets/Uploads/Overseas-merchandise-trade/Overseas-merchandise-trade-February-2018/Download-data/overseas-merchandise-trade-february-2018-tables.xlsx (accessed April 4, 2018).

2. *Ibid.*, Table 5.

3. *Ibid.*, Table 4.

4. *Ibid.*, Table 3.

5. Stats NZ/Tatauranga Aotearoa, *Key Graph Data*, Tables (NP: Stats NZ, 2018), Table: Employment and Unemployment, https://www.rbnz.govt.nz/statistics/key-graphs/ (accessed April 4, 2018).

6. Reserve Bank of New Zealand/Te Pūtea Matua, "Monetary Policy: Inflation," *Reserve Bank of New Zealand/Te Pūtea Matua*, 2018, https://www.rbnz.govt.nz/monetary-policy/inflation (accessed April 4, 2018).

7. Statistics New Zealand/Tatauranga Aotearoa, *New Zealand in Profile 2011: An Overview of New Zealand's People, Economy, and Environment* (NP: Statistics New Zealand/Tatauranga Aotearoa, 2011), History sec., http://archive.stats.govt.nz/browse_for_stats/snapshots-of-nz/nz-in-profile-2011.aspx (accessed May 12, 2018).

8. Stats NZ/Tatauranga Aotearoa, *2013 Census QuickStats About Culture and Identity*, Tables (NP: Stats NZ, 2014), Table 1, http://archive.stats.govt.nz/Census/2013-census/profile-and-summary-reports/quickstats-culture-identity.aspx (accessed 5 April 2018).

9. Stats NZ/Tatauranga Aotearoa, *Population Clock*, current date http://archive.stats.govt.nz/tools_and_services/population_clock.aspx?url=/tools_and_services/population_clock.aspx (accessed May 8, 2018).

10. Stats NZ/Tatauranga Aotearoa, *Estimated Total Population by Sex, Year Ended 31 December 1926–2017 and 30 June 1937–2017*, Tables (NP: Stats NZ, 2018), Table 2, http://archive.stats.govt.nz/browse_for_stats/population/estimates_and_projections/historical-population-tables.aspx (accessed April 5, 2018).

11. *Ibid.*, Table 3.

12. Stats NZ/Tatauranga Aotearoa, *2013 Census QuickStats About National Highlights*, Tables (NP: Stats NZ, 2013), Table 6, http://archive.stats.govt.nz/Census/2013-census/profile-and-summary-reports/quickstats-about-national-highlights.aspx (accessed April 5, 2018).

13. Stats NZ/Tatauranga Aotearoa, *Births and Deaths: Year Ended December 2017*, Tables (NP: Stats NZ, 2018), Table 1, https://www.stats.govt.nz/information-releases/births-and-deaths-year-ended-december-2017 (accessed April 5, 2018).

14. *Ibid.*, Table 4.

15. Stats NZ/Tatauranga Aotearoa, *Age-specific Fertility Rates by Ethnicity*, Tables (NP: Stats NZ, 2013), http://archive.stats.govt.nz/browse_for_stats/population/births/births-tables.aspx (accessed April 5, 2018).

16. Stats NZ/Tatauranga Aotearoa, *Births and Deaths: Year Ended December 2014*, Commentary (NP: Stats NZ, 2015), http://archive.stats.govt.nz/browse_for_stats/population/births/BirthsAndDeaths_HOTPYeDec14/Commentary.aspx (accessed April 5, 2018).

17. Stats NZ/Tatauranga Aotearoa, *Births and Deaths: Year Ended December 2017*, Table 1.

18. Stats NZ/Tatauranga Aotearoa, *2013 Census QuickStats About National Highlights*, Table 3.

19. *Ibid.*

20. Stats NZ/Tatauranga Aotearoa, *Population Aging in New Zealand*, Tables and Commentary (NP: Stats NZ, 2000), http://archive.stats.govt.nz/browse_for_stats/people_and_communities/older_people/pop-ageing-in-nz.aspx (accessed May 8, 2018).

21. Stats NZ/Tatauranga Aotearoa, *2013 Census QuickStats About National Highlights*, Table 3.

22. *Ibid.*

23. *Ibid.*

24. Stats NZ/Tatauranga Aotearoa, *New Zealand Abridged Period Life Table: Provisional)*, Commentary (NP: Stats NZ, 2018), https://www.stats.govt.nz/information-releases/new-zealand-abridged-period-life-table-201517-provisional (accessed April 6, 2018).

25. "Civil Union Act 2004, No. 102," *New Zealand Legal Information Institute*, http://www.nzlii.org/nz/legis/hist_act/cua20042004n102166 (accessed August 21, 2018).

26. "Marriage (Definition of Marriage) Amendment Act 2013, No. 20," *New Zealand Legal Information Institute*, http://www.nzlii.org/nz/legis/consol_act/momaa2013343 (accessed August 21, 2018).

27. Stats NZ/Tatauranga Aotearoa, *Marriages, Civil Unions, and Divorces: Year Ended December 2014*, Tables (NP: Stats NZ, 2015), Table 7, http://archive.stats.govt.nz/browse_for_stats/people_and_communities/marriages-civil-unions-and-divorces/MarriagesCivilUnionsandDivorces_HOTPYeDec14.aspx (accessed April 6, 2018).

28. *Ibid.*

29. Stats NZ/Tatauranga Aotearoa, *Marriages, Civil Unions, and Divorces: Year Ended December 2015*, Tables (NP: Stats NZ, 2016), Table 8, http://archive.stats.govt.nz/browse_for_stats/people_and_communities/marriages-civil-unions-and-divorces/MarriagesCivilUnionsandDivorces_HOTPYeDec15.aspx (accessed April 6, 2018).

30. Stats NZ/Tatauranga Aotearoa, *Marriages, Civil Unions, and Divorces: Year Ended December 2016*, Tables (NP: Stats NZ, 2017), Table 8, http://archive.stats.govt.nz/browse_for_stats/people_and_communities/marriages-civil-unions-and-divorces/MarriagesCivilUnionsandDivorces_HOTPYeDec16.aspx (accessed April 6, 2018).

31. *Ibid.*, Table 1.

32. *Ibid.*, Table 2.

33. *Ibid.*, Table 1.

34. *Ibid.*, Table 3.

35. *Ibid.*

36. *Ibid.*, Table 4.

37. National Police Headquarters, *New Zealand Crime Statistics 2014: A Summary of Recorded and Resolved Offence Statistics*, Tables (NP: National Police Headquarters, 2015), p. 2, http://www.police.govt.nz/sites/default/files/publications/crime-stats-national-20141231.pdf (accessed April 6, 2018).

38. *Ibid.*

39. *Ibid.*, pp. 2–4.

40. Stats NZ/Tatauranga Aotearoa, "Statistical Standard for Religious Affiliation," *Religious Affiliation* (NP: Stats NZ, n.d.), Glossary sec.: Religion, http://archive.stats.govt.nz/methods/classifications-and-standards/classification-related-stats-standards/religious-affiliation.aspx (accessed April 6, 2018).

41. *Ibid.*, Definition sec.

42. *Ibid.*, Glossary sec.: Religion.

43. See "The Ringatū Seal," *The Journal of the Polynesian Society* (Wellington: The Polynesian Society [Inc.], March 1942), Vol. 51, No. 1, p. 81, http://www.jps.auckland.ac.nz/document/Volume_51_1942/Volume_51%2C_No._1/The_Ringatu_seal%2C_p_80/p1 (accessed May 8, 2018).

44. Ministry for Culture and Heritage/Manatū Taonga, "The Seal of the Ringatū Church," 20 December 2012, *New Zealand History/Nga Korero a Ipurangi o Aotearoa (Ministry for Culture and Heritage/Manatū Taonga)*, https://nzhistory.govt.nz/media/photo/seal-ringatu-church (accessed May 8, 2018).

45. "The Ringatū Seal," p. 81.

46. For a concise discussion of the Rātana Church see Keith Newman, "Rātana Church: Te Haahi Rātana," 14 March 2017, *Te Ara: The Encyclopedia of New Zealand*, https://teara.govt.nz/en/ratana-church-te-haahi-ratana (accessed May 8, 2018).

47. *New Zealand Parliament/Pāremata Aotearoa*, n.d., https://www.parliament.nz/en/ (accessed May 12, 2018).

48. Electoral Commission/Te Kaitiaki Take Kōwhiri, *Elections*, n.d., http://www.elections.org.nz/ (accessed April 7, 2018).

49. Internal Affairs/Te Tari Taiwhenua, "Local Government in New Zealand: Local Councils," *Internal Affairs/Te Tari Taiwhenua*, n.d., http://www.localcouncils.govt.nz/lgip.nsf/wpg_url/about-local-government-index (accessed April 7, 2018).

50. We Are. LGNZ., "Community Boards," *We Are. LGNZ.*, 31 October 2018, http://www.lgnz.co.nz/nzs-local-government/community-boards/ (accessed February 6, 2019).

51. Stats NZ/Tatauranga Aotearoa, "*2013 Census QuickStats About Culture and Identity*," Table 19.

52. *Ibid.*

53. *Ibid.*, Table 24.

54. *Ibid.*, Table 19.

55. *Ibid.*, Table 24.

56. *Ibid.*

57. "New Zealand Sign Language Act 2006, No. 18," *New Zealand Legal Information Institute*, http://www.nzlii.org/nz/legis/hist_act/nzsla20062006n18248 (accessed August 21, 2018).

58. Human Rights Commission/Te Kāhui Tika Tangata, "History of the New Zealand Sign Language Act," *Ministry of Social Development/Te Manatū Whakahiato Ora*, n.d., sec. Introduction, https://www.hrc.co.nz/your-rights/people-disabilities/your-rights/new-zealand-sign-language-act/ (accessed April 7, 2018).

59. *Ibid.*

60. Ministry of Education/Te Tāhuhu o te Mātauranga, "The New Zealand Curriculum/Official Languages," *The New Zealand Curriculum Online*, 8 December 2017, http://nzcurriculum.tki.org.nz/The-New-Zealand-Curriculum (accessed February 16, 2019).

61. "Māori Language Act 1987, No. 176," *New Zealand Legal Information Institute*, http://www.nzlii.org/nz/legis/hist_act/mla19871987n176159 (accessed August 20, 2018).

62. "Māori Language Act 2016, No. 17," *New Zealand Legislation*, http://www.legislation.govt.nz/act/public/2016/0017/latest/whole.html#DLM6174509 (accessed February 4, 2019).

63. Ministry for Culture and Heritage/Manatū Taonga, "Te Wiki o te Reo Māori-Māori Language Week: History of the Māori Language," *New Zealand History/Nga Korero a Ipurangi o Aotearoa (Ministry*

for Culture and Heritage/*Manatū Taonga*), 10 October 2017, https://nzhistory.govt.nz/culture/maori-language-week/history-of-the-maori-language (accessed May 9, 2018).

64. "Treaty of Waitangi Act 1975, No. 114," *New Zealand Legal Information Institute*, http://www.nzlii.org/nz/legis/hist_act/towa19751975n114226 (accessed August 20, 2018); also see *New Zealand Legislation*, http://www.legislation.govt.nz/act/public/1975/0114/latest/whole.html?search=ts_act_treaty+of+waitangi+act_noresel&p=1#DLM435368 (accessed August 20, 2018).

65. "Treaty of Waitangi Amendment Act 1985, No. 148," *New Zealand Legal Information Institute*, http://www.nzlii.org/nz/legis/hist_act/towaa19851985n148306 (accessed August 20, 2018).

66. "New Zealand Sign Language Act 2006, No. 18," Part 2, Item 7 (3).

67. New Zealand Diversity Action Programme, *Languages in Aotearoa New Zealand/Te Waka Reo: Statement on Language Policy* (NP: New Zealand Human Rights Commission, 2008), p. 7, https://www.hrc.co.nz/files/3414/2388/3771/25-Aug-2008_11-45-14_Language_Policy_Aug_08.pdf (accessed April 7, 2018).

68. Māori Language Commission/Te Taura Whiri i te Reo Māori, *Annual Report for the Year Ended 30 June 2012*, Commentary (Wellington: Māori Language Commission, 2012), p. 8, http://www.tetaurawhiri.govt.nz/assets/Uploads/Corporate-docs/Annual-reports/Annual-Report-2012-English.pdf (accessed April 7, 2018).

69. Ministry for Culture and Heritage/Manatū Taonga, *Te Ara: The Encyclopedia of New Zealand*, n.d., https://teara.govt.nz/en (accessed May 12, 2018).

70. Ministry for Culture and Heritage/Manatū Taonga, *New Zealand History/Nga Korero a Ipurangi o Aotearoa*, n.d., https://nzhistory.govt.nz/ (accessed February 18, 2019).

71. For a discussion of the early arrivals see Geoffrey Irwin, *The Prehistoric Exploration and Colonization of the Pacific* (Cambridge: Cambridge University Press, 1994).

72. Janet M. Wilmshurst, Atholl J. Anderson, Thomas F.G. Higham, and Trevor H. Worthy, "Dating the Late Prehistoric Dispersal of Polynesians to New Zealand Using the Commensal Pacific Rat," Patrick V. Kirch, ed., *Proceedings of the National Academy of Sciences of the United States of America (PNAS)*, Vol. 105, No. 22, 3 June 2008, p. 7676.

73. *Ibid.*

74. Geoff Irwin, "Pacific Migrations," *Te Ara: The Encyclopedia of New Zealand*, 8 February 2017, Story Summary, https://teara.govt.nz/en/pacific-migrations (accessed May 9, 2018).

75. *Ibid.*, p. 3.

76. *Ibid.*, p. 4.

77. "Maori Affairs Act 1953, No. 94," *New Zealand Legal Information Institute*, http://www.nzlii.org/nz/legis/hist_act/maa19531953n94152 (accessed August 20, 2018).

78. "Maori Affairs Amendment Act 1967, No. 124,"

New Zealand Legal Information Institute, http://www.nzlii.org/nz/legis/hist_act/maaa19671967n124232 (accessed August 20, 2018).

79. "State-Owned Enterprises Act 1986, No. 124," *New Zealand Legal Information Institute*, http://www.nzlii.org/nz/legis/hist_act/sea1986 1986n124301 (accessed August 20, 2018).

80. "Te Ture Whenua Maori Act/Maori Land Act 1993, No.4," *New Zealand Legal Information Institute*, http://nzlii.org/nz/legis/hist_act/ttwmmla 19931993n4326/ (accessed August 21, 2018).

Chapter Two

1. Paul Tillich, "The Nature of Religious Language," Chap. V in *A Theology of Culture*, by Paul Tillich, Robert C. Kimball, ed., pp. 53–67 (New York: Oxford University Press, 1964), p. 56.

2. *Ibid.*

3. Clifford Geertz, "Religion as a Cultural System," Chap. 4 in *The Interpretation of Cultures*, by Clifford Geertz, pp. 87–125 (New York: Basic Books, 1973), p. 93.

4. John H. Morgan, "Theology and Symbol: An Anthropological Approach," Chap. Five in *Being Human: Perspectives on Meaning and Interpretation (Essays in Religion, Culture and Personality)*, 2nd ed., by John H. Morgan, pp. 93–105 (South Bend: Cloverdale Books, 2006), p. 101.

5. Tillich, "The Nature of Religious Language," p. 58.

6. University of Otago/Te Whare Wānanga o Ōtākou, "The Marae and Its Place," *University of Otago/Te Whare Wānanga o Ōtākou*, n.d., https://www.otago.ac.nz/profiles/themaraeanditsplace.html (accessed May 9, 2018).

7. Ian Pool and Tahu Kukutai, "Taupori Māori–Māori Population Change: Māori Urbanization," *Te Ara: The Encyclopedia of New Zealand*, 5 May 2011, https://teara.govt.nz/en/graph/31326/maori-urbanisation (accessed May 9, 2018).

8. Geoff Irwin, "Pacific Migrations," Story Summary.

9. *Ibid.*, pp. 3–4.

10. *Ibid.*

11. *Ibid.*

12. Janet M. Wilmshurst, et al., "Dating the Late Prehistoric Dispersal of Polynesians to New Zealand," p. 7676.

13. Central Intelligence Agency, "Australia-Oceania: Tonga," *The World Factbook*, 2018, https://www.cia.gov/library/publications/the-world-factbook/geos/tn.html (accessed May 10, 2018).

14. Ranginui J. Walker, "Marae: A Place to Stand," in *Te Ao Hurihuri: Aspects of Maoritanga*, Michael King, ed., pp. 15–27 (Auckland: Reed Publishing [NZ], 1992), p. 15.

15. *Ibid.*

16. Central Intelligence Agency, "Australia-Oceania: Samoa," *The World Factbook*, 2018, https://www.cia.gov/library/publications/the-world-factbook/geos/ws.html (accessed 10 May 2018).

17. The Commonwealth, "Member Countries," *The Commonwealth*, 2018, http://thecommonwealth.org/member-countries (accessed May 10, 2018).

18. Central Intelligence Agency, "Australia-Oceania: American Samoa," *The World Factbook*, 2018, https://www.cia.gov/library/publications/the-world-factbook/geos/aq.html (accessed May 10, 2018).

19. Walker, "Marae, a Place to Stand," p. 15.

20. *Ibid.*

21. Central Intelligence Agency, "Australia-Oceania: Cook Islands," *The World Factbook*, 2018, https://www.cia.gov/library/publications/the-world-factbook/geos/cw.html (accessed May 10, 2018).

22. *Ibid.*

23. Carl Walrond, "Cook Islanders," *Te Ara: The Encyclopedia of New Zealand*, 25 March 2015, p. 3, https://teara.govt.nz/en/cook-islanders (accessed May 10, 2018).

24. The description of Marae Kainuku is from Vic Stefanu-World Travels and Adventures, "Cook Islands, Exploring a Historic, Religious, and Sacred Site (Marae Kainuku in Rarotonga)," *YouTube*, 18 October 2015, https://www.youtube.com/watch?v=iNvAd0acUCQ (accessed May 10, 2018).

25. Central Intelligence Agency, "Australia-Oceania: French Polynesia," *The World Factbook*, 2018, https://www.cia.gov/library/publications/the-world-factbook/geos/fp.html (accessed May 10, 2018).

26. Walker, "Marae, a Place to Stand," p. 16.

27. The description of Taputapuātea is from the United Nations Educational, Scientific and Cultural Organization, "Taputapuātea," *United Nations Educational, Scientific and Cultural Organization*, 2017, http://whc.unesco.org/en/list/1529 (accessed May 10, 2018).

28. The description of Arahurahu Marae is from Vic Stefanu-World Travels and Adventures, "Tahiti, Exploring the Ancient Sacred Religious Sites (Marae), Pacific Ocean," *YouTube*, 16 December 2015, https://www.youtube.com/watch?v=wxvV1qxjm0w (accessed May 10, 2018).

29. Walker, "Marae, a Place to Stand," p. 17.

30. *Ibid.*

31. *Ibid.*

32. *Ibid.*

33. *Ibid.*

34. *Ibid.*, p. 18.

35. *Ibid.*

36. John C. Moorfield, "whare," in *Te Aka: Māori-English English-Māori Dictionary*, n.d., http://maoridictionary.co.nz (accessed February 22, 2019).

37. Moorfield, "puni," in *Te Aka*.

38. Walker, "Marae, a Place to Stand," p. 18.

39. *Ibid.*

40. *Ibid.*

41. *Ibid.*, pp. 18–19.

42. *Ibid.*

43. *Ibid.*, p. 19.

44. *Ibid.*

45. For a presentation of Te Kooti Arikirangi Te Turuki see Chap. 3 (pp. 17–28) in William Green-wood, "The Upraised Hand or the Spiritual Significance of the Rise of the Ringatū Faith," *The Journal of the Polynesian Society* (Wellington: The Polynesian Society [Inc.], March 1942), Vol. 51, No. 1, pp. 1–80, http://www.jps.auckland.ac.nz/document.php?wid=2250&action=null (accessed May 10, 2018).

46. Walker, "Marae, a Place to Stand," p. 19.

47. *Ibid.*

48. Kerryn Pollock, "King Country Region-Arts, Culture and Heritage," *Te Ara: The Encyclopedia of New Zealand*, 30 March 2015, https://teara.govt.nz/en/photograph/34923/te-tokanganui-a-noho-wharenui (accessed May 10, 2018).

49. Walker, "Marae, a Place to Stand," pp. 19–20.

50. *Ibid.*, p. 20.

51. *Ibid.*

52. *Ibid.*

53. *Ibid.*

54. *Ibid.*

55. Population data extracted from Stats NZ/Tatauranga Aotearoa, *Urban Area Population Projections, by Age and Sex, 2013(base)-2043 Update*, Table (NP: Stats NZ, 2017), https://www.stats.govt.nz/information-releases/urban-area-unit-population-projections-2013base2043-update-nz-stat-tables (accessed May 11, 2018).

56. For a concise discussion of marae types see Tauroa, *Te Marae*, pp. 138–143.

57. Walker, "Marae, a Place to Stand," p. 21.

58. *Ibid.*

59. Paul Morris, "Diverse Religions," *Te Ara: The Encyclopedia of New Zealand*, 13 February 2017, p. 7, https://teara.govt.nz/en/diverse-religions (accessed May 11, 2018).

60. *Ibid.*, p. 5.

61. *Ibid.*, p. 3.

62. *Ibid.*, p. 2.

63. For a presentation of the First Christmas Service in Aotearoa/New Zealand see Zana Bell, "Marsden's First Christmas," *New Zealand Geographic*, No. 077, January-February 2006, https://www.nzgeo.com/stories/marsdens-first-christmas (accessed May 11, 2018).

64. Malcolm Falloon, "The Night That Transformed a Mission and Established a Church," *NZCMS*, 3 December 2014, http://www.nzcms.org.nz/our-story-the-night-that-transformed-a-mission-and-established-a-church (accessed May 11, 2018).

65. For a biographical sketch of Papahurihia see Judith Binney, "Papahurihia, Penetana," *Dictionary of New Zealand Biography (Te Ara: The Encyclopedia of New Zealand)*, June 1990, https://teara.govt.nz/en/biographies/1p4/papahurihia-penetana (accessed May 11, 2018).

66. For a biographical sketch of Aperahama Taonui see Judith Binney, "Taonui, Aperahama," *Dictionary of New Zealand Biography (Te Ara: The Encyclopedia of New Zealand)*, 1993, https://teara.govt.nz/en/biographies/2t7/taonui-aperahama (accessed May 11, 2018).

67. For a short sketch of Te Hura see John Sten-

house and Lachy Paterson, "Ngā Poropiti Me Ngā Hāhi: Prophets and the Churches," Chap. 16 in *Ki te Whaiao: An Introduction to Māori Culture and Society*, Tānia M. Ka'ai, John C. Moorfield, Michael P.J. Reilly, and Sharon Mosley, ed., pp. 171–180 (Auckland: Pearson Education New Zealand, 2004), p. 173.

68. For a short sketch of these prophets see *Ibid.*, pp. 173–178.

69. Peter J. Lineham, "Missions and Missionaries," *Te Ara: The Encyclopedia of New Zealand*, 13 March 2017, pp. 2–3, https://teara.govt.nz/en/missions-and-missionaries (accessed May 11, 2018).

70. This brief account of the Wesleyan Missionary Society (WMS) is from Peter J. Lineham, "Missions and Missionaries," p. 4; and Ministry for Culture and Heritage/Manatū Taonga, "Missionaries: Wesleyans and Catholics," *New Zealand History/Nga Korero a Ipurangi o Aotearoa (Ministry for Culture and Heritage/Manatū Taonga)*, 6 June 2017, https://nzhistory.govt.nz/culture/missionaries/new-arrivals (accessed May 11, 2018).

71. Rory Sweetman, "Catholic Church," *Te Ara: The Encyclopedia of New Zealand*, 3 February 2017, p. 1, https://teara.govt.nz/en/catholic-church (accessed May 11, 2018).

72. For a brief sketch of the decline of the missionary influence see Lineham, "Missions and Missionaries," p. 6.

73. For the missionary address to Kororāreka see: Bernard John Foster, "Kororareka," *An Encyclopedia of New Zealand 1966*, 1966, https://teara.govt.nz/en/1966/kororareka (accessed May 11, 2018); Robin Fisher, "Williams, Henry," *Dictionary of New Zealand Biography (Te Ara: The Encyclopedia of New Zealand)*, 1990, https://teara.govt.nz/en/biographies/1w22/williams-henry (accessed May 11, 2018); and Ministry for Culture and Heritage/Manatū Taonga, "A Frontier of Chaos?: Kororāreka," *New Zealand History/Nga Korero a Ipurangi o Aotearoa (Ministry for Culture and Heritage/Manatū Taonga)*, 13 January 2016, https://nzhistory.govt.nz/culture/missionaries/kororareka (accessed May 11, 2018).

74. Lineham, "Missions and Missionaries," p. 1.

75. *Ibid.*, p. 2.

76. *Ibid.*, p. 4.

77. *Ibid.*

78. For a brief sketch of Hongi Hika see Angela Ballara, "Hongi Hika," *Dictionary of New Zealand Biography (Te Ara: The Encyclopedia of New Zealand)*, 1990, https://teara.govt.nz/en/biographies/1h32/hongi-hika (accessed May 11, 2018).

79. Lineham, "Missions and Missionaries," p. 3.

80. *Ibid.*, pp. 1, 5.

81. *Ibid.*, p. 5.

82. *Ibid.*, p. 7.

83. For a brief discussion of the *tangihanga* see Rawinia Higgins and John C. Moorfield, "Tangihanga: Death Customs," Chap. 8 in *Ki te Whaiao: An Introduction to Māori Culture and Society*, Tānia M. Ka'ai, John C. Moorfield, Michael P.J. Reilly, and Sharon Mosley, ed. (Auckland: Pearson Education New Zealand, 2004), pp. 85–90; also see Elsdon Best, "Maori Eschatology: The Whare Potae (House of Mourning) and Its Lore; Being a Description of Many Customs, Beliefs, Superstitions, Rites, &c., Pertaining to Death and Burial Among the Maori People, as Also Some Account of Native Belief in a Spiritual World," Article XXV in *Transactions and Proceedings of the Royal Society of New Zealand 1868–1961: Volume 38, 1905*, A. Hamilton, ed. (Wellington: John Mackay, Government Printing Office, 1906), pp. 148–239, Available from the "National Library of New Zealand/Te Puna Mātauranga o Aotearoa": http://rsnz.natlib.govt.nz/volume/rsnz_38/rsnz_38_00_002700.html (accessed May 12, 2018).

84. Sir Hirini Moko Mead, "Understanding Mātauranga Māori," in *Conversations on Mātauranga Māori*, Haemata, Professor Taiarahia Black, Daryn Bean, Waireka Collings, Whitney Nuku, ed. (NP: New Zealand Qualifications Authority/Mana Tohu Mātauranga o Aotearoa, 2012), pp. 9–14, http://www.nzqa.govt.nz/assets/Maori/ConversationsMMv6AW-web.pdf (accessed August 1, 2018).

85. Tillich, "The Nature of Religious Language," p. 58.

Chapter Three

1. See Linda D. Molm, Jessica L. Collett, and David R. Schaefer, "Building Solidarity Through Generalized Exchange: A Theory of Reciprocity," *American Journal of Sociology*, Vol. 113, No. 1, July 2007, pp. 205–242, http://www3.nd.edu/~jcollet1/pubs/2007-113.pdf (accessed April 20, 2018).

2. Edward J. Lawler, "An Affect Theory of Social Exchange," *American Journal of Sociology*, Vol. 107, No. 2, September 2001, pp. 321–352, http://www.uvm.edu/~pdodds/files/papers/others/2001/lawler2001b.pdf (accessed April 20, 2018).

3. Michael D. Coogan, ed., *The New Oxford Annotated Bible with the Apocrypha*, New Revised Standard Version (New York: Oxford University Press, 2010), the Gospel According to Matthew, 25:23.

4. Milan Zafirovski provides a helpful examination of social exchange theory's use of an economic model, including the occasional plea for rehabilitation, in "Social Exchange Theory Under Scrutiny: A Positive Critique of Its Economic-Behaviorist Formulations," *Electronic Journal of Sociology*, 2005, http://citeseerx.ist.psu.edu/viewdoc/download?doi=10.1.1.454.7467&rep=rep1&type=pdf (accessed April 20, 2018).

5. *Ibid.*, p. 5.

6. Raymond Firth, *Essays on Social Organization and Values: School of Economics Monographs on Social Anthropology* (London: Athlone Press, 1964), p. v.

7. Joan Metge, "Returning the Gift—Utu in Intergroup Relations: In Memory of Sir Raymond Firth," *The Journal of the Polynesian Society*, Judith Huntsman, ed. (Auckland: The Polynesian Society [Inc.], December 2002), Vol. 111, No. 4, pp. 311–338, http://www.jps.auckland.ac.nz/document.php?wid=5182&action=null (accessed April 21, 2018).

8. See *Ibid.*, and Raymond Firth, *Economics of the New Zealand Maori*, Second ed. (Wellington: Government Printer, 1959).

9. *Ibid.*

10. Metge, "Returning the Gift," pp. 311–312.

11. *Ibid.*

12. For a concise discussion of the Treaty of Waitangi see Claudia Orange, "Treaty of Waitangi," *Te Ara: The Encyclopedia of New Zealand*, 20 June 2012, https://teara.govt.nz/en/treaty-of-waitangi (accessed May 26, 2018).

13. For a concise discussion see Jean E. Rosenfeld, *The Island Broken in Two Halves: Land and Renewal Movements Among the Maori of New Zealand* (University Park: The Pennsylvania State University Press, 1999), pp. 70–73.

14. Te Rūnanga o Ngāi Tahu, "The Settlement," *Te Rūnanga o Ngāi Tahu*, n.d., http://ngaitahu.iwi.nz/ngai-tahu/the-settlement/ (accessed May 26, 2018).

15. Douglas Harper, "assimilation," *Online Etymology Dictionary*, n.d., https://www.etymonline.com/word/assimilation (accessed May 26, 2018).

16. Douglas Harper, "integration," *Online Etymology Dictionary*, n.d., https://www.etymonline.com/word/integration (accessed May 26, 2018).

17. See Ian Culpitt, "Bicultural Fragments: A Pākehā Perspective," *Social Policy Journal of New Zealand*, No. 2, July 1994, http://www.msd.govt.nz/about-msd-and-our-work/publications-resources/journals-and-magazines/social-policy-journal/spj02/02-bicultural-fragments.html (accessed April 22, 2018).

Chapter Four

1. "America's Founding Documents: The Constitution of the United States," *The U.S. National Archives and Records Administration*, 13 September 2017, https://www.archives.gov/founding-docs/constitution (accessed May 28, 2018).

2. Richard M. Emerson, "Social Exchange Theory," *Annual Review of Sociology*, Vol. 2, 1976, pp. 335–362, http://www.jstor.org/stable/2946096 (accessed April 23, 2018), p. 336.

3. *Ibid.*

4. Richard M. Emerson, "Power-Dependence Relations," *American Sociological Review*, Vol. 27, No. 1, February 1962, pp. 31–41, https://www.jstor.org/stable/2089716 (accessed February 16, 2019).

5. *Ibid.*, p. 31.

6. *Ibid.*

7. *Ibid.*

8. *Ibid.*

9. *Ibid.*, p. 32.

10. *Ibid.*, p. 33.

11. *Ibid.*

12. *Ibid.*, p. 34.

13. *Ibid.*

14. *Ibid.*

15. *Ibid.*

16. *Ibid.*

17. *Ibid.*

18. *Ibid.*

19. *Ibid.*, pp. 34–35.

20. *Ibid.*, p. 35.

21. *Ibid.* See pp. 35–37 for Emerson's discussion of his four balancing operations.

22. *Ibid.*, pp. 40–41.

23. *Ibid.*, p. 33.

24. Karen S. Cook, Coye Cheshire, and Alexandra Gerbasi, "Power, Dependence, and Social Exchange," Chap. Nine in *Contemporary Social Psychological Theories*, Peter J. Burke, ed., pp. 194–216 (Stanford: Stanford University Press, 2006).

25. "America's Founding Documents: The Bill of Rights: A Transcription," *The U.S. National Archives and Records Administration*, 26 June 2017, https://www.archives.gov/founding-docs/bill-of-rights-transcript (accessed May 28, 2018).

26. Moorfield, "tapu," in *Te Aka*.

27. Michael P. Shirres, "Tapu," *The Journal of the Polynesian Society*, Geoffrey Irwin, ed. (Auckland: The Polynesian Society [Inc.], March 1982), Vol. 91, No. 1, pp. 29–52, http://www.jps.auckland.ac.nz/document.php?wid=3806&action=null (accessed April 24, 2018).

28. *Ibid.*, p. 33.

29. *Ibid.*

30. *Ibid.*, pp. 33–34.

31. *Ibid.*, p. 34.

32. *Ibid.*

33. *Ibid.*

34. See *Ibid.*, pp. 34–35 for Shirres's discussion of the analogy of proper proportionality.

35. See *Ibid.*, p. 35 for Shirres's discussion of the analogy of improper proportionality.

36. *Ibid.*

37. *Ibid.*, p. 29.

38. *Ibid.*, p. 46.

39. *Ibid.*

40. *Ibid.*, p. 42.

41. *Ibid.*, p. 29.

42. Tānia M. Ka'ai and Rawinia Higgins, "Te Ao Māori: Māori World-View," Chap. 2 in *Ki te Whaiao: An Introduction to Māori Culture and Society*, Tānia M. Ka'ai, John C. Moorfield, Michael P.J. Reilly, and Sharon Mosley, ed., pp. 13–25 (Auckland: Pearson Education New Zealand, 2004), p. 15; and Shirres, "Tapu," p. 32–33, 46.

43. Māori Marsden, "God, Man and Universe: A Maori View," pp. 117–137 in *Te Ao Hurihuri: Aspects of Maoritanga*, Michael King, ed. (Auckland: Reed Publishing [NZ], 1992), pp. 118–119.

44. *The Analytical Greek Lexicon*, Sixth Printing (Grand Rapids: Zondervan Publishing House, 1970), p. 146.

45. Marsden, "God, Man and Universe," pp. 118–119.

46. *The Analytical Greek Lexicon*, p. 107.

47. Marsden, "God, Man and Universe," p. 119.

48. Ministry for Culture and Heritage/Manatū Taonga, "Frontier of Chaos?: Overview," *New Zealand History/Nga Korero a Ipurangi o Aotearoa (Ministry for Culture and Heritage/Manatū Taonga)*, 13 January 2016, https://nzhistory.govt.nz/culture/maori-

europeanontactefore840verviewaccessed8208inistryorultureeritageat

european-contact-before-1840/overview (accessed May 28, 2018).

49. Ministry for Culture and Heritage/Manatū Taonga, "Frontier of Chaos?: The Boyd Incident," *New Zealand History/Nga Korero a Ipurangi o Aotearoa (Ministry for Culture and Heritage/Manatū Taonga)*, 11 March 2014, https://nzhistory.govt.nz/culture/maori-european-contact-before-1840/the-boyd-incident (accessed August 9, 2018).

50. Ministry for Culture and Heritage/Manatū Taonga, "Population, Population Trends, and the Census," *An Encyclopedia of New Zealand 1966*, A.H. McLintock, ed., 1966, https://teara.govt.nz/en/1966/population (accessed April 26, 2018).

51. Ministry for Culture and Heritage/Manatū Taonga, "The Census," *An Encyclopedia of New Zealand 1966*, A.H. McLintock, ed., 1966, https://teara.govt.nz/en/1966/population/page-2 (accessed April 26, 2018).

52. *Ibid.*

53. Stats NZ/Tatauranga Aotearoa, *Demographic Trends 2010*, Tables and Narrative (Wellington: Stats NZ, 2011), p. 19, http://archive.stats.govt.nz/~/media/Statistics/browse-categories/population/estimates-projections/demographic-trends/2010/Demographic%20Trends%202010.pdf (accessed February 8, 2019).

54. Ministry for Culture and Heritage/Manatū Taonga, "Overview of NZ in the Nineteenth Century: *New Zealand History/Nga Korero a Ipurangi o Aotearoa (Ministry for Culture and Heritage/Manatū Taonga)*," 4 August 2014, https://nzhistory.govt.nz/classroom/ncea3/19th-century-history-overview (accessed April 26, 2018).

55. Stats NZ/Tatauranga Aotearoa, *Demographic Trends 2010*, p. 19.

56. Emerson, "Power-Dependence Relations," pp. 32–33.

57. *Ibid.*

58. *Ibid.*, p. 35.

59. "Forest Act 1949, No. 19," *New Zealand Legal Information Institute*, http://www.nzlii.org/nz/legis/hist_act/fa19491949n19143 (accessed August 20, 2018).

60. "Forest Amendment Act 1993, No. 7," *New Zealand Legal Information Institute*, http://www.nzlii.org/nz/legis/hist_act/faa19931993n7223/ (accessed February 6, 2019).

61. See *Ibid.*: item "2. Interpretation," "Sustainable Forest Management"; and Forest Act 1949, No. 19, *New Zealand Legislation*, http://www.legislation.govt.nz/act/public/1949/0019/latest/whole.html#DLM255632 (accessed February 6, 2019), item "2 Interpretation," "Sustainable Forest Management."

Chapter Five

1. For a brief discussion of the Star Spangled Banner artifact and the origin and development of the American National Anthem see the Star-Spangled Banner Project: National Museum of American History, Behring Center, in Cooperation with Public Inquiry Services, Smithsonian Institution, "Star-Spangled Banner and the War of 1812," *Smithsonian*, n.d., https://www.si.edu/spotlight/flag-day/banner-facts (accessed May 28, 2018).

2. Herbert M. Mason, "National Anthem Celebrates 78 Years, Thanks to VFW," *VFW: Veterans of Foreign Wars*, 3 March 2009, https://www.vfw.org/media-and-events/latest-releases/archives/2009/3/national-anthem-celebrates-78-years---thanks-to-vfw (accessed May 28, 2018).

3. For a brief discussion of the association of the "Star-Spangled Banner" with American sports culture see Caroline Bologna, "The History of the National Anthem in Sports: How 'The Star-Spangled Banner' Became a Part of American Sports Culture," *HuffPost*, 21 May 2018, https://www.huffingtonpost.com/entry/history-national-anthem-sports_us_5afc9bcfe4b06a3fb50d5056 (accessed May 29, 2018).

4. Linda Alchin, "Star Spangled Banner Lyrics," *Siteseen Limited*, 1 July 2017, http://www.american-historama.org/1801-1828-evolution/star-spangled-banner-lyrics.htm (accessed May 29, 2018).

5. Martenzie Johnson, "Let's Take the National Anthem Literally, and the Songwriter at His Word: A Deeper Look at the Song, the Man Who Wrote It—and the History Attached," *The Undefeated*, 30 August 2016, https://theundefeated.com/features/lets-take-the-national-anthem-literally-and-the-songwriter-at-his-word/ (accessed May 29, 2018).

6. *Ibid.*

7. For a concise discussion of Manifest Destiny see Jeanne T. Heidler and David S. Heidler, "Manifest Destiny," *Encyclopaedia Britannica*, n.d., https://www.britannica.com/event/Manifest-Destiny (accessed May 29, 2018).

8. For a brief introduction to anthropological fields of study see Paul A. Erickson and Liam D. Murphy, *A History of Anthropological Theory*, Fourth ed. (North York: University of Toronto Press, 2013), pp. xix–xxi.

9. Clifford Geertz, "Thick Description: Toward an Interpretive Theory of Culture," Chap. 1 in *The Interpretation of Cultures*, by Clifford Geertz, pp. 3–30 (New York: Basic Books, 1973).

10. *Ibid.*, p. 6. for Geertz's references see Gilbert Ryle, "Thinking and Reflecting," Chap. 36 in *Collected Papers, Volume 2: Collected Essays 1929–1968*, by Gilbert Ryle, pp. 479–493 (New York: Routledge, 2009.); and Gilbert Ryle, "The Thinking of Thoughts: What Is 'le Penseur' Doing?," Chap. 37 in *Collected Papers, Volume 2: Collected Essays 1929–1968*, by Gilbert Ryle, pp. 494–510 (New York: Routledge, 2009).

11. For a brief discussion of Geertz's interpretive anthropology see Paul A. Erickson and Liam D. Murphy, *A History of Anthropological Theory*, 122–124.

12. *Ibid.*, p. 123.

13. Clifford Geertz, "Ethos, World View, and the Analysis of Sacred Symbols," Chap. 5 in *The Interpretation of Cultures*, by Clifford Geertz, pp. 126–141 (New York: Basic Books, 1973), p. 140.

14. John H. Morgan, *In the Beginning...": The Paleolithic Origins of Religious Consciousness* (South Bend: Cloverdale Books, 2007).

15. *Ibid.*, pp. 41–42.

16. *Ibid.*, p. 41.

17. *Ibid.*, p. 43.

18. *Ibid.*, p. 44.

19. *Ibid.*, p. 41.

20. *Ibid.*, p. 68.

21. Paul Tillich, "Religion as a Dimension in Man's Spiritual Life," Chap. 1 in *Theology of Culture*, by Paul Tillich, Robert C. Kimball, ed., pp. 3–9 (New York: Oxford University Press, 1964), pp. 7–8.

22. *Ibid.*, pp. 6–7.

23. John H. Morgan, "Religion and Culture as Meaning Systems: A Dialogue Between Geertz and Tillich," *The Journal of Religion*, Vol. 57, No. 4 (October 1977), pp. 363–375.

Morgan's essay is also available as Chap. Two in *Being Human: Perspectives on Meaning and Interpretation (Essays in Religion, Culture and Personality)*, by John H. Morgan (South Bend: Cloverdale Books, 2006), pp. 17–33.

24. Geertz, "Religion as a Cultural System," p. 104.

25. *Ibid.*, p. 100.

26. *Ibid.*

27. *Ibid.*, p. 108.

28. Clifford Geertz, "Ideology as a Cultural System," in *Ideology and Discontent*, edited by David E. Apter, pp. 47–76 (New York: The Free Press of Glencoe, a Division of the Macmillan Company, 1964). It is also available as Chap. 8 in *The Interpretation of Cultures*, by Clifford Geertz, pp. 193–233.

29. Clifford Geertz, "Common Sense as a Cultural System," *The Antioch Review*, Vol. 33, No. 1 (Spring 1975), pp. 5–26. It is also available as Chap. 4 in *Local Knowledge: Further Essays in Interpretive Anthropology*, by Clifford Geertz, pp. 73–93 (New York: Basic Books, 1983).

30. Clifford Geertz, "Art as a Cultural System," *MLN* (Johns Hopkins University Press), Vol. 91, No. 6 (December 1976), pp. 1473–1499. It is also available as Chap. 5 in Geertz, *Local Knowledge*, pp. 94–120.

31. Morgan, *"In the Beginning...,"* pp. 51–52.

32. *Ibid.*, pp. 41, 44.

33. For a concise presentation see Tillich, "Religion as a Dimension in Man's Spiritual Life."

34. *Ibid.*

35. Morgan, *"In the Beginning...,"* p. 45.

36. See Paul Tillich, "Aspects of a Religious Analysis of Culture," Chap. IV in *Theology of Culture*, by Paul Tillich, Robert C. Kimball, ed., pp. 40–51 (New York: Oxford University Press, 1964), pp. 40–43.

37. For a concise discussion of *whakapapa* see Rāwiri Taonui, "Whakapapa-Genealogy," *Te Ara: The Encyclopedia of New Zealand*, 1 July 2015, https://teara.govt.nz/en/whakapapa-genealogy (accessed June 9, 2018).

38. *Ibid.*, p. 4. for a brief biography of Tamarau Waiari see Wharehuia Milroy, "Tamarau Waiari," *Dictionary of New Zealand Biography (Te Ara: The Encyclopedia of New Zealand)*, 1993, https://teara.govt.nz/en/biographies/2t6/tamarau-waiari (accessed June 9, 2018).

39. Moorfield, "whakapapa," in *Te Aka*.

40. For a concise discussion of the Māori treatment of creation, see Te Ahukaramū Charles Royal, "Māori Creation Traditions," *Te Ara: The Encyclopedia of New Zealand*, 8 February 2005, https://teara.govt.nz/en/maori-creation-traditions (accessed July 12, 2018).

41. The rendition presented here is based on that of A.W. Reed, *Maori Myths & Legendary Tales*, 1999 ed. (Auckland: New Holland Publishers [NZ], 1999), pp.11–21; also, see Michael P.J. Reilly, "Te Tīmatanga Mai o Ngā Atua: Creation Narratives," Chap. 1, in *Ki te Whaiao: An Introduction to Māori Culture and Society*, Tānia M. Ka'ai, John C. Moorfield, Michael P.J. Reilly, and Sharon Mosley, ed., pp. 1–12 (Auckland: Pearson Education New Zealand, 2004).

42. See Te Taru White, "A Maori Point of View," *YouTube*, 13 March 2007, https://www.youtube.com/watch?v=WkoR8qBSUtY&feature=youtu.be (accessed March 15, 2019).

43. Paul Tillich, *Systematic Theology: Three Volumes in One* (Chicago: The University of Chicago Press, 1967), p. 14.

44. For a brief presentation of Māori social structure see Ka'ai and Higgins, "Te Ao Māori," pp. 14–16.

45. Toon van Meijl, "Changing Property Regimes in Māori Society: A Critical Assessment of the Settlement Process in New Zealand," *The Journal of the Polynesian Society*, Judith Huntsman, ed. (Auckland: The Polynesian Society [Inc.], June 2012), Vol. 121, No. 2, pp. 181–208, http://www.jps.auckland.ac.nz/document/Volume_121_2012/Volume_121%2C_No._2/Changing_Property_Regimes_in_Maori_Society%3A_A_Critical_Assessment_of_the_Settlement_Process_in_New_Zealand%2C_by_Toon_Van_Meijl%2C_p_181-208 (accessed June 25, 2018), p. 190.

In this article Van Meijl includes a discussion of how the fluid hierarchical structure of Māori society became a rigid model for Pākehā. Especially, see the topic "The Codification of Māori Property Categories," pp. 196–198.

46. *Ibid.*, pp. 198–199.

47. *Ibid.*, p. 201.

48. Ka'ai and Higgins, "Te Ao Māori," pp. 14–15.

49. *Ibid.*, p. 15.

50. For the full article, see Mohi Tūrei, "He Aha Tatou I Kiia Ai He Maori," *National Library of New Zealand/Te Puna Mātauranga o Aotearoa, Papers Past, Te Pipiwharauroa* (Newspaper), 1 January 1911, pp. 4–5, https://paperspast.natlib.govt.nz/periodicals/pipiwharauroa/1911/01/01/4 (accessed June 11, 2018).

51. Moorfield, "pākehā," in *Te Aka*.

52. *Ibid.*

53. For a concise discussion of the English settlers see Terry Hearn, "English," *Te Ara: The Encyclopedia of New Zealand*, 25 March 2015, https://teara.govt.nz/en/english (accessed June 11, 2018).

54. For a discussion of world-building see Peter L. Berger, "Religion and World-Construction," Chap. 1 in *The Sacred Canopy: Elements of a Sociological Theory of Religion*, First ed., by Peter L. Berger (Garden City: Doubleday, 1967).

55. For a classic discussion of "secularization" see

Berger, *The Sacred Canopy: Elements of a Sociological Theory of Religion*.

56. Tillich, "Religion as a Dimension in Man's Spiritual Life," p. 8.

Chapter Six

1. Keith Ward, *More Than Matter? Is There More to Life Than Molecules?* (Grand Rapids: William B. Eerdmans Publishing Co., 2011), p. 64.

2. Richard Handler, "Cultural Property and Culture Theory," *Journal of Social Archaeology*, Vol. 3, No. 3 (October 2003), pp. 353–365, see p. 354, http://web.williams.edu/AnthSoc/IJCP/Handler2003.pdf (accessed February 7, 2019).

3. *Ibid.*, p. 355.

4. For a concise discussion of the changing ethnography in Aotearoa/New Zealand, see Toon van Meijl, "Historicising Maoritanga: Colonial Ethnography and the Reification of Maori Traditions," *The Journal of the Polynesian Society*, Ray Harlow, ed. (Auckland: The Polynesian Society [Inc.], September 1996), Vol. 105, No. 3, pp. 311–346, http://www.jps.auckland.ac.nz/document.php?wid=4939&action=null (accessed June 22, 2018).

5. Barre Toelken, *The Dynamics of Folklore*, Revised and Expanded ed. (Logan: Utah State University Press, 1996), p. 263. See Chap. 7 (pp. 263–313) for his discussion of "Folklore and Cultural Worldview."

6. For a brief discussion of the Declaration of Independence of New Zealand see Basil Keane, "He Whakaputanga: Declaration of Independence," *Te Ara: The Encyclopedia of New Zealand*, 20 June 2012, https://teara.govt.nz/en/he-whakaputanga-declaration-of-independence (accessed June 23, 2018).

7. For a discussion of the *Boyd* incident see Ministry for Culture and Heritage/Manatū Taonga, "A Frontier of Chaos?: The Boyd Incident."

8. Edward Shortland, *Maori Religion and Mythology* (Auckland: Upton and Co., 1882), p. 5, available from "The New Zealand Electronic Text Collection:" http://nzetc.victoria.ac.nz/tm/scholarly/tei-ShorMaor.html (accessed June 23, 2018).

9. *Ibid.*

10. *Ibid.*

11. *Ibid.*

12. *Ibid.*, p. 88.

13. Elsdon Best, *The Maori: Volume* I (Wellington: Board of Maori Ethnological Research for the Author and on Behalf of the Polynesian Society, 1924), p. 129, available from "The New Zealand Electronic Text Collection:" http://nzetc.victoria.ac.nz/tm/scholarly/tei-Bes01Maor.html (accessed July 3, 2018).

14. *Ibid.*

15. *Ibid.*

16. Geertz, "Religion as a Cultural System," p. 100.

17. Van Meijl describes the despondency and its association with the reification of a Māori proto-culture in "Historicising Maoritanga."

18. *Ibid.*, p. 314.

19. Herbert W. Williams, *A Dictionary of the Maori Language*, Sixth ed. (Wellington: Government Printer, 1957, original work by William Williams published in 1844), p. 252, available from "The New Zealand Electronic Text Collection:" http://nzetc.victoria.ac.nz/tm/scholarly/tei-WillDict.html (accessed February 7, 2019).

20. Van Meijl includes a brief discussion of the role of the Young Māori Party in changing the course of Māori fortunes. See "Historicising Maoritanga," pp. 330–338.

21. Geertz, "Religion as a Cultural System," pp. 89–123.

22. Morgan, "*In the Beginning...*," p. 68.

23. *Ibid.*, pp. 51-52.

24. For Morgan's discussion of politics see *Ibid.*, pp. 83-100.

25. *Ibid.*, p. 84.

26. *Ibid.*

27. *Ibid.*

28. *Ibid.*

29. *Ibid.*

30. Douglas Harper, "reify," *Online Etymology Dictionary*, n.d., https://www.etymonline.com/word/reify (accessed June 26, 2018).

31. Van Meijl discusses the reification of a Māori proto-culture. See "Historicising Maoritanga."

32. Allan Hanson, "The Making of the Maori: Culture Invention and Its Logic," *American Anthropologist*, Vol. 91, No. 4, pp. 890–902 (December 1989), p. 890, https://www.jstor.org/stable/681587 (accessed June 26, 2018).

33. *Ibid.*, p. 897.

34. *Ibid.*, p. 893.

35. *Ibid.*, p. 890.

36. *Ibid.*

37. *Ibid.*, p. 899.

38. Hanson acknowledges and responds to the controversy in "Reply to Langdon, Levine, and Linnekin," *American Anthropologist*, Vol. 93, No. 2 (June 1991), pp. 449–450, http://www.jstor.org/stable/681308 (accessed June 27, 2018); also see Jocelyn Linnekin, "Cultural Invention and the Dilemma of Authenticity," *American Anthropologist*, Vol. 93, No. 2 (June 1991), pp. 446–449, http:///www.jstor.org/stable/681307 (accessed August 1, 2018).

39. Hanson, "The Making of the Maori," pp. 891–893.

40. For a presentation of *Mātauranga Māori* see Te Ahukaramū Charles Royal, *Mātauranga Māori and Museum Practice: A Discussion*, David Green, ed., National Services Te Paerangi, Museum of New Zealand Te Papa Tongarewa (Wellington: National Services Te Paerangi, Museum of New Zealand TePapa Tongarewa, 2007), https://static1.squarespace.com/static/5369700de4b045a4e0c24bbc/t/578e13812994cafd4eaabde3/1468928943167/Matauranga+Maori+and+Museum+Practice+-+a+discussion.pdf (accessed February 16, 2019).

41. Moorfield, "-tanga," in *Te Aka*.

42. Royal, *Mātauranga Māori and Museum Practice*, p. 9.

Chapter Seven

1. Moorfield, "io," in *Te Aka*.
2. *Ibid.*
3. Moorfield, "atua," in *Te Aka*.
4. Moorfield, "ariki," in *Te Aka*.
5. Te Haupapa-o-Tane, "Io: The Supreme God and Other Gods of the Maori," *The Journal of the Polynesian Society* (New Plymouth: Thomas Avery, September 1920), Vol. 29, No. 115, pp. 139–143, http://www.jps.auckland.ac.nz/document.php?wid=1683&action=null (accessed July 3, 2018). See p. 141.
6. H.T. Whatahoro, *The Lore of the Whare-Wānanga; or Teachings of the Maori College on Religion, Cosmogony, and History*, S. Percy Smith Trans. (Lexington: Forgotten Books, 2008; original work published in New Plymouth in 1913 by Thomas Avery as *The Lore of the Whare-Wānanga: Part I.-Te Kauwae-Runga, or 'Things Celestial.'*), p. 54.
7. Elsdon Best, *Some Aspects of Maori Myth and Religion: Illustrating the Mentality of the Maori and His Mythopoetic Concepts* (Wellington: W.A.G. Skinner, Government Printer, 1922), p. 19, available from the Internet Archive: https://archive.org/details/someaspectsofmao01bestuoft (accessed July 3, 2018).
8. *Ibid.*, p. 20.
9. *Ibid.*
10. *Ibid.*, p. 21.
11. Best, *The Maori: Volume I*, p. 90.
12. Jane Simpson asks this question in "Io as Supreme Being: Intellectual Colonization of the Māori?," *History of Religions*, Vol. 37, No. 1 (August 1997), pp. 50–85, http://www.jstor.org/stable/3176563 (accessed July 3, 2018).
13. Te Rangi Hīroa (Sir Peter Buck), *The Coming of the Maori*, Second ed. (Wellington: Whitcombe and Tombs, 1950), p. 2, available from "The New Zealand Electronic Text Collection:" http://nzetc.victoria.ac.nz/tm/scholarly/tei-BucTheC.html (accessed July 3, 2018).
14. For a brief biography of John White see Michael P. J. Reilly, "White, John," *Dictionary of New Zealand Biography (Te Ara: The Encyclopedia of New Zealand)*, 1990, https://teara.govt.nz/en/biographies/1w18/white-john (accessed July 3, 2018).
15. Hīroa, *The Coming of the Maori*, p. 532.
16. John White, *The Ancient History of the Maori, His Mythology and Traditions (Volume II of VII): Horo-Uta or Take-Tumu Migration* (Wellington: Whitcombe and Tombs, 1950; original work published in Wellington in 1887 by Government Printer), pp. 1–2, available from "The New Zealand Electronic Text Collection:" http://nzetc.victoria.ac.nz/tm/scholarly/tei-Whi02Anci.html (accessed July 3, 2018).
17. Jonathan Z. Smith, "The Unknown God: Myth in History," Chap. 5 in *Imagining Religion: from Babylon to Jonestown*, by Jonathan Z. Smith, pp. 66–89 (Chicago: The University of Chicago Press, 1982), p. 75.
18. Hīroa, *The Coming of the Maori*, p. 532.
19. White, *The Ancient History of the Maori (Volume II)*, p. 2.

20. *Ibid.*
21. *Ibid.*, pp. 2–3.
22. *Ibid.*, p. 2.
23. *Ibid.*, pp. 2–3.
24. *Ibid.*, p. 2.
25. Hīroa, *The Coming of the Maori*, p. 532.
26. Bart Ehrman briefly summarizes the quest's history in *Jesus: Apocalyptic Prophet of the New Millennium* (New York: Oxford University Press, 1999), pp. 21–40.
27. For a concise history of the Polynesian Society see the Polynesian Society, "A Short History of the Polynesian Society (Abridged from M.P.K. Sorrenson's *Manifest Duty: The Polynesian Society Over 100 Years* with an Update to 2011)," *The Polynesian Society*, n.d., http://www.thepolynesiansociety.org/history.html (accessed July 4, 2018).
28. Jane Simpson surveys the *Io* material in "Io as Supreme Being." Also see James L. Cox, *The Invention of God in Indigenous Societies* (Durham: Acumen Publishing, 2014), pp. 35–66; and J.Z. Smith, "The Unknown God."
29. D.R. Simmons lists a number of sources in "A New Zealand Myth: Kupe, Toi and the 'Fleet,'" *The New Zealand Journal of History* (Auckland: Department of History at the University of Auckland, April 1969), Vol. 3, No. 1, pp. 14–31, http://www.nzjh.auckland.ac.nz/document.php?wid=1620&action=null (accessed July 4, 2018).
30. Margaret Orbell, *The Illustrated Encyclopedia of Māori Myth and Legend* (Christchurch: Canterbury University Press, 1995), pp. 72–73.
31. C.O. Davis, *The Life and Times of Patuone, the Celebrated Ngapuhi Chief* (Christchurch: Capper Press, 1974, original work published in Auckland in 1876 by J.H. Field), pp. 13–14, available from "The New Zealand Electronic Text Collection:" http://nzetc.victoria.ac.nz/tm/scholarly/tei-DavLife.html (accessed July 4, 2018).
32. *Ibid.*, pp. 132–133.
33. The Polynesian Society, "About the Polynesian Society," *The Polynesian Society*, n.d., http://www.thepolynesiansociety.org/about.html (accessed July 4, 2018).
34. *Ibid.*
35. For the intent and organization of the Polynesian Society including the origin of its *Journal* see the Polynesian Society, "A Short History of the Polynesian Society."
36. Edward Tregear, *The Maori Race* (Whanganui: A.D. Willis, 1904), available from "The New Zealand Electronic Text Collection:" http://nzetc.victoria.ac.nz/tm/scholarly/tei-TreRace.html (accessed July 4, 2018).
37. J.Z. Smith, "The Unknown God," p. 74.
38. Tiwai Paraone, "A Maori Cosmogony," *The Journal of the Polynesian Society* (New Plymouth: Thomas Avery, September 1907), Vol. 16, No. 3, pp. 109–119, http://www.jps.auckland.ac.nz/document.php?wid=695&action=null (accessed July 4, 2018).
39. For a brief biography of Hare Hongi (Henry Matthew Stowell) see P. J. Gibbons. "Stowell, Henry Matthew," *Dictionary of New Zealand Biography (Te*

Ara: The Encyclopedia of New Zealand), 1996, https://teara.govt.nz/en/biographies/3s38/stowell-henry-matthew (accessed July 4, 2018).

40. For a brief biography of S. Percy Smith see Giselle M. Byrnes, "Smith, Stephenson Percy," *Dictionary of New Zealand Biography (Te Ara: The Encyclopedia of New Zealand)*, 1993, https://teara.govt.nz/en/biographies/2s33/smith-stephenson-percy (accessed July 4, 2018).

41. For a brief biography of Elsdon Best see Jeffrey Sissons, "Best, Elsdon," *Dictionary of New Zealand Biography (Te Ara: The Encyclopedia of New Zealand)*, 1993, https://teara.govt.nz/en/biographies/2b20/best-elsdon (accessed July 4, 2018).

42. Elsdon Best, "Maori Religion: Notes on the Religious Ideas, Rites, and Invocations of the Maori People of New Zealand," *Report of the Twelfth Meeting of the Australasian Association for the Advancement of Science* (Brisbane: Anthony James Cumming, Government Printer, 1910), sec. F., 2., pp. 457–464, available from the Smithsonian Institution Website: https://www.biodiversitylibrary.org/item/52764#page/1/mode/1up (accessed July 4, 2018). See p. 460.

43. *Ibid.*, p. 461.

44. Simpson, "Io as Supreme Being," p.71.

45. For a brief biography of Hoani Te Whatahoro (John Alfred Jury) see M.J. Parsons, "Jury, Hoani Te Whatahoro," *Dictionary of New Zealand Biography (Te Ara: The Encyclopedia of New Zealand)*, 1990, https://teara.govt.nz/en/biographies/1j6/jury-hoani-te-whatahoro (accessed July 5, 2018).

46. S. Percy Smith explains this source material in his Introduction to and notes scattered throughout H.T. Whatahoro, *The Lore of the Whare-Wānanga*.

47. The Polynesian Society, "Volume III: Memoirs of the Polynesian Society: The Lore of the Whare-Wānanga," *The Journal of the Polynesian Society* (New Plymouth: Thomas Avery, December 1912), Vol. 21, No. 4, p. 181, http://www.jps.auckland.ac.nz/document/Volume_21_1912/Volume_21%2C_No._4/Volume_III._Memoirs_of_the_Polynesian_Society._The_lore_of_the_whare_wananga%2C_p_181?action=null (accessed July 5, 2018).

48. S. Percy Smith, "Introduction," in *The Lore of the Whare-Wānanga or Teachings of the Maori College on Religion, Cosmogony, and History*, by H.T. Whatahoro, S. Percy Smith Trans., pp. 1–18. (Lexington: Forgotten Books, 2008; original work published in New Plymouth in 1913 by Thomas Avery as *The Lore of the Whare-Wānanga: Part I.-Te Kauwae-Runga, or 'Things Celestial'*), p. 15.

49. Elsdon Best, "The Cult of Io: The Concept of a Supreme Deity as Evolved by the Ancestors of the Polynesians, *Man*, Vol. 13 (1913), pp. 98–103, https://www.jstor.org/stable/pdf/2787812 (accessed July 5, 2018).

50. For a broad description of *Things Terrestrial* see S. Percy Smith, "The Lore of the Whare-Wānanga: Introduction," *The Journal of the Polynesian Society* (New Plymouth: Thomas Avery, March 1913), Vol. 22, No. 85, pp. 1–2, http://www.jps.auckland.ac.nz/document/Volume_22_1913/

Volume_22%2C_No._85/The_lore_of_the_whare_wananga._Introduction%2C_p_1-2?action=null (accessed July 5, 2018).

51. Cox, *The Invention of God*, p. 65.

52. Clifford Geertz, "Introduction," in *Local Knowledge: Further Essays in Interpretive Anthropology*, by Clifford Geertz, pp. 3–16 (New York: Basic Books, 1983), p. 12.

53. *Ibid.*

54. Simpson, "Io as Supreme Being," p. 54.

55. *Ibid.*, p.85.

56. *Ibid.*

57. *Ibid.*

58. Cox, *The Invention of God*, p. 65.

59. See "Translator's Notes" in Paraone, "A Maori Cosmogony."

60. For a brief biography of Hoani Te Whatahoro see Parsons, "Jury, Hoani Te Whatahoro."

61. Simpson quotes Elsdon Best's biographer, Elsdon W.G. Craig, in her statement, "Best's biographer showed that he was 'caught between two stools in his relationship with Whatahoro.' He made no secret of the fact that he doubted the credibility of the Tohunga...." See "Io as Supreme Being," p. 76. Simpson cites E.W.G. Craig, *Man of the Mist: A Biography of Elsdon Best* (Wellington: A.H. & A.W. Reed, 1964), pp. 148, 149.

J.Z. Smith also quotes Elsdon W.G. Craig in his statement, "Most interesting is the quotation from Best: 'a matter of great importance is the way in which questions are put to the native. In this respect, one has to be extremely cautious for you can get any information required from a native if you can put certain leading questions in a certain way ... by asking the same questions within intervals of some months between questionings, I have got totally different answers from Whatahoro.'" See "The Unknown God," p. 147, fn. 26. Smith cites E.W.G. Craig, *Man of the Mist: A Biography of Elsdon Best* (Wellington, 1964), p. 150.

62. For instance, Simpson, "Io as Supreme Being," pp. 75–76; and Cox, *The Invention of God*, p. 60.

63. See *Ibid.*, and S. Percy Smith, "Introduction," to H.T. Whatahoro, *The Lore of the Whare-Wānanga*.

64. S. Percy Smith, "Introduction," to H.T. Whatahoro, *The Lore of the Whare-Wānanga*, p. 2.

65. For a brief biography of the Reverend Richard Taylor see J.M.R Owens, "Taylor, Richard," *Dictionary of New Zealand Biography (Te Ara: The Encyclopedia of New Zealand)*, 1990, https://teara.govt.nz/en/biographies/1t22/taylor-richard (accessed July 7, 2018).

66. Rev. Richard Taylor, *Te Ika a Maui or New Zealand and Its Inhabitants* (London: Wertheim & MacIntosh, 1855), p. 8, available from "The New Zealand Electronic Text Collection": http://nzetc.victoria.ac.nz/tm/scholarly/tei-TayTeik.html (accessed July 7, 2018).

67. *Ibid.*, p. 6.

68. *Ibid.*, p. 14.

69. *Ibid.*, p. 13.

70. *Ibid.*

71. For a brief biography of William Colenso see David Mackay, "Colenso, William," *Dictionary of*

New Zealand Biography (Te Ara: The Encyclopedia of New Zealand), 1990, https://teara.govt.nz/en/biographies/1c23/colenso-william (accessed July 7, 2018).

72. William Colenso, "On the Maori Races of New Zealand," *Transactions and Proceedings of the New Zealand Institute-Volume 1, 1868* (Wellington: James Hughes, May 1869), pp. 1–75 (Essays sec., essay 10 of 10, p. 43; Page numbers repeat for each essay). Available from the National Library of New Zealand/Te Puna Mātauranga o Aotearoa: http://rsnz.natlib.govt.nz/volume/rsnz_01/rsnz_01_00_002170.html (accessed February 1, 2019).

73. For a brief history of the transition from the first to the second phase of the Polynesian Society see the Polynesian Society, "A Short History of the Polynesian Society."

74. For a tribute to David Simmons see Richard A. Benton, "David Simmons, MBE (1930–2015) Obituary," *The Journal of the Polynesian Society*, Melinda S. Allen, ed. (Auckland: The Polynesian Society [Inc.], December 2016), Vol. 125, No. 4, pp. 339–340, http://www.jps.auckland.ac.nz/document/Volume_125_2016/Volume_125%2C_No._4/David_Simmons%2C_MBE_%281930-2015%29_Obituary%2C_by_Richard_A._Benton%2C_p_339-340?action=null (accessed July 9, 2018).

75. For a tribute to Bruce Biggs see Andrew Pawley, "Obituary: Bruce Grandison Biggs 1921–2000," *The Journal of the Polynesian Society*, Judith Huntsman, ed. (Auckland: The Polynesian Society [Inc.], December 2000), Vol. 109, No. 4, pp. 341–346, http://www.jps.auckland.ac.nz/document//Volume_109_2000/Volume_109%2C_No._4/%5BFront_matter%-5D_p_337-346/p1 (accessed July 9, 2018).

76. David Simmons and Bruce Biggs, "The Sources of 'The Lore of the Whare-Wānanga,'" The Journal of the Polynesian Society, Mervyn McLean, ed. (Wellington: The Polynesian Society [Inc.], March 1970), Vol. 79, No. 1, pp. 22–42, http://www.jps.auckland.ac.nz/document.php?wid=4356&action=null (accessed July 9, 2018).

77. *Ibid.*, p. 41.

78. *Ibid.*, p. 36.

79. *Ibid.*, p. 41.

80. Simpson, "Io as Supreme Being," p. 84.

81. *Ibid.*, p. 85.

82. *Ibid.*

83. Hanson, "The Making of the Maori."

84. Van Meijl, "Historicising Maoritanga."

85. Cox, *The Invention of God*, pp. 152–154.

86. J.Z. Smith, "The Unknown God," pp. 81–87.

87. *Ibid.*, p. 85.

88. For a brief discussion of the Māori prophets see Stenhouse and Paterson, "Ngā Poropiti Me Ngā Hāhi."

89. A.T. Ngata, "The Io Cult-Early Migration-Puzzle of the Canoes," Transcript, *The Journal of the Polynesian Society* (Wellington: The Polynesian Society [Inc.], December 1950), Vol. 59, No. 4, pp. 335–346, http://www.jps.auckland.ac.nz/document/Volume_59_1950/Volume_59%2C_No._4/The_Io_Cult_-_early_migration_-_puzzle_of_the_canoes%2C_by_A._T._Ngata%2C_p_335-346?action=null (accessed July 12, 2018).

90. Hīroa, *The Coming of the Maori*, p. 526.

91. Māori Marsden, *The Woven Universe: Selected Writings of Rev. Māori Marsden*, Te Ahukaramū Charles Royal, ed. (Ōtaki: Estate of Rev. Māori Marsden, 2003).

92. Te Ahukaramū Charles Royal, "Books," *Dr. Te Ahukaramū Charles Royal*, n.d., http://www.charles-royal.nz/writings/ (accessed July 12, 2018).

93. Marsden, "God, Man and Universe," p. 136.

94. *Ibid.*

95. *Ibid.*

96. *Ibid.*, 137.

97. *Ibid.*, p. 117.

98. *Ibid.*

99. *Ibid.*, pp. 130–132.

100. *Ibid.*, pp. 132–133.

101. Anglican Church in Aotearoa, New Zealand and Polynesia/Te Hahi Mihinare ki Aotearoa ki Niu Tireni, ki Nga Moutere o Te Moana Nui a Kiwa, *Anglican Church in Aotearoa, New Zealand and Polynesia/Te Hahi Mihinare ki Aotearoa ki Niu Tireni, ki Nga Moutere o Te Moana Nui a Kiwa*, n.d., http://www.anglican.org.nz/ (accessed July 13, 2018).

102. *Ibid.*, "About."

103. *Ibid.*

104. *Ibid.*, "About"/"History," See "A Revised Constitution."

105. *Ibid.*, "About."

106. *Ibid.*, "About"/"History," See "A Revised Constitution."

107. *Ibid.*, "About."

108. *Ibid.*, "About"/"History," See "The General Synod /Te Hinota Whanui."

109. Tauroa, *Te Marae*, p. 29.

110. Tillich, "Religion as a Dimension in Man's Spiritual Life," pp. 3–9.

111. Tillich, "Aspects of a Religious Analysis of Culture," pp. 40–51.

112. *Ibid.*, pp. 41–42.

113. *Ibid.*, p. 42.

114. *Ibid.*

115. James Luther Adams, "Introduction," in *What Is Religion?*, by Paul Tillich, James Luther Adams, ed. (New York: Harper Torchbooks, 1969), pp. 22–24.

116. Tillich, "Aspects of a Religious Analysis of Culture," p. 42.

117. *Ibid.*

118. For an application of Whitehead's philosophy to religious pluralism see David Ray Griffin, ed., *Deep Religious Pluralism* (Louisville: Westminster John Knox Press, 2005).

119. For a brief discussion of transcendent and immanent levels of religious symbols see Tillich, "The Nature of Religious Language," pp. 61–65.

Chapter Eight

1. Clifford Geertz, "Person, Time, and Conduct in Bali," Chap. 14 in *The Interpretation of Cultures*, by Clifford Geertz, pp. 360–411 (New York: Basic Books, 1973), pp. 407–408.

2. Richard G. Fox, *Lions of the Punjab: Culture in the Making* (Berkeley: University of California Press, 1985), p. 190.

3. *Ibid.*, p. 191.

4. Geertz, "Thick Description," p. 5.

5. *Ibid.*, p. 29. Geertz describes "meaning" as "that elusive and ill-defined pseudoentity."

6. Geertz, "Religion as a Cultural System," pp. 90, 109.

7. Hanson, "The Making of the Maori," p. 890. Hanson cites Lamont Lindstrom, "Leftamap Kastom: The Political History of Tradition on Tanna, Vanuatu," *Mankind*, Vol. 13, pp. 316–329 (1982), p. 317.

8. Hanson, "The Making of the Maori," p. 890.

9. *Ibid.*

10. *Ibid.*

11. Roy Wagner, *The Invention of Culture*, Revised and Expanded ed. (Chicago: University of Chicago Press, 1975).

12. Jocelyn Linnekin, "Cultural Invention and the Dilemma of Authenticity."

13. Hanson, "Reply to Langdon, Levine, and Linnekin," p. 450.

14. Roy Wagner, *Symbols That Stand for Themselves* (Chicago: University of Chicago Press, 1986), p. x.

15. Mead, "Understanding Mātauranga Māori," p. 14.

16. Richard Handler and Jocelyn Linnekin raise this question in "Tradition, Genuine or Spurious," *Journal of American Folklore*, Vol. 97, No. 385, pp. 273–290 (July–September, 1984), p. 275, http://kodu.ut.ee/~cect/teoreetilised%20seminarid_2010/folkloristika_uurimisr%C3%BChma_seminar/Handler_Linnekin--Tradition-Genuine_or_Spurious--JAF_1984_vol_97_no_385.pdf (accessed August 1, 2018); also see Richard Handler and Jocelyn Linnekin, "Tradition, Genuine or Spurious," in *Folk Groups and Folklore Genres: A Reader*, Elliot Oring, ed., pp. 38–42 (Logan: Utah State University Press, 1989), p. 40.

17. *Ibid.*

18. Hanson, "The Making of the Maori," p. 890.

19. The similarity in Tillich's and Geertz's concept of meaning was first recognized by John H. Morgan. See Morgan, "Religion and Culture as Meaning Systems: A Dialogue Between Geertz and Tillich."

20. Tillich, "Religion as a Dimension in Man's Spiritual Life," p. 6.

21. Geertz, "Religion as a Cultural System," p. 100.

22. For a brief discussion of Māori education in traditional times see Ross Calman, "Māori Education: Mātauranga," *Te Ara: The Encyclopedia of New Zealand*, 20 June 2012, p. 1, https://teara.govt.nz/en/maori-education-matauranga (accessed August 2, 2018).

23. Among the online sources that explain Aotearoa/New Zealand's educational structure are: Nancy Swarbrick, "Primary and Secondary Education," *Te Ara: The Encyclopedia of New Zealand*, 20 June 2012, https://teara.govt.nz/en/primary-and-secondary-education (accessed August 2, 2018); Ministry of Education/Te Tāhuhu o te Mātauranga,

"Education in New Zealand," *Ministry of Education/Te Tāhuhu o te Mātauranga*, n.d., https://www.education.govt.nz/ministry-of-education/our-role-and-our-people/education-in-nz/ (accessed August 2, 2018); and Ministry of Business, Innovation, and Employment/Hīkina Whakatutuki, "The School System," *New Zealand Now*, 17 April 2018, https://www.newzealandnow.govt.nz/living-in-nz/education/school-system (accessed August 2, 2018).

24. The Government affirmed its commitment to the Māori language in the Māori Language Act 2016, No. 17.

25. For a brief discussion of the *kōhanga reo*, see Calman, "Māori Education: Mātauranga."

26. For a brief discussion of *kura kaupapa Māori* see *Ibid.*; also see Te Kura Kaupapa Māori o Hoani Waititi Marae, "About Us," *Te Kura Kaupapa Māori o Hoani Waititi Marae: Indigenous Māori Education Center*, n.d., http://hoaniwaititi.school.nz/about (accessed August 2, 2018), Our History sec.

27. Moorfield, "kaupapa Māori," in *Te Aka*.

28. For a brief discussion of *wānanga* see Calman, "Māori Education: Mātauranga"; also, see Kerryn Pollock, "Tertiary Education," *Te Ara: The Encyclopedia of New Zealand*, 20 June 2012, https://teara.govt.nz/en/tertiary-education (accessed August 2, 2018).

29. For a brief discussion of the first mission schools see Calman, "Māori Education: Mātauranga," p. 2.

30. "Education Act 1847, No. 10," *New Zealand Legal Information Institute*, http://www.nzlii.org/nz/legis/hist_act/ea184711v1847n10224/ea184711v1847n10224.html (accessed August 3, 2018).

31. Tānia M. Ka'ai provides a timeline of dates and events in "Te Mana o te Reo Me Ngā Tikanga: Power and Politics of the Language," Chap. 19 in *Ki te Whaiao: An Introduction to Māori Culture and Society*, Tānia M. Ka'ai, John C. Moorfield, Michael P.J. Reilly, and Sharon Mosley, ed., pp. 201–213 (Auckland: Pearson Education New Zealand, 2004), 202–204.

32. For a discussion of the *poutama* educational model see *Ibid.*, pp. 207–213.

33. For a brief discussion of the origin of knowledge in Māori mythology see Rāwiri Taonui, "Ranginui: The Sky," *Te Ara: The Encyclopedia of New Zealand*, 12 June 2006, p. 2, https://teara.govt.nz/en/ranginui-the-sky (accessed August 3, 2018).

34. See *Ibid.*, Taonui attributes this approach to the Reverend Māori Marsden.

35. Tānia M. Ka'ai associates Tāne's journey and his return with the baskets of knowledge with 12 levels of thought and achievement, and sketches the *poutama* holistic model. See "Te Mana o te Reo Me Ngā Tikanga."

36. *Ibid.*, p. 202.

37. *Ibid.*, p. 213.

38. The Ministry of Justice website furnishes information about its organization, mission, strategy, and goals. See Ministry of Justice/Tāhū o te Ture, "About Us," *Ministry of Justice/Tāhū o te Ture*, 2018, https://www.justice.govt.nz/about/about-us/ (accessed August 4, 2018).

39. Ministry of Justice/Tāhū o te Ture, *He Hīnātore ki te Ao Māori: A Glimpse Into the Māori World (Māori Perspectives on Justice)* (Wellington: Ministry of Justice/Tāhū o te Ture, 2001), p. iii, http://www.justice.govt.nz/publications/publications-archived/2001/he-hinatore-ki-te-ao-maori-a-glimpse-into-the-maori-world (accessed August 4, 2018).

40. Moorfield, "tikanga," in *Te Aka*.

41. Moorfield, "tika," in *Te Aka*.

42. Ministry of Justice/Tāhū o te Ture, *He Hīnātore ki te Ao Māori*, p. 5.

43. For a discussion of common law see Albert Roland Kiralfy, Mary Ann Glendon, and Andrew D.E. Lewis, "Common Law," *Encyclopaedia Britannica*, 26 July 2018, https://www.britannica.com/topic/common-law (accessed August 4, 2018).

44. Ministry of Justice/Tāhū o te Ture, *He Hīnātore ki te Ao Māori*, p. v.

45. *Ibid.*, p. vii.

46. Moana Jackson, "Why Did Māori Never Have Prisons?," *YouTube*, [Video],16 November 2017, https://www.youtube.com/watch?v=2vtpA_PbDJU (accessed August 4, 2018).

47. Ministry of Justice/Tāhū o te Ture, *He Hīnātore ki te Ao Māori*, p. iv.

48. *Ibid.*

49. Tillich, "Religion as a Dimension in Man's Spiritual Life," pp. 6–8.

50. Ministry of Education/Te Tāhuhu o te Mātauranga, "The Arts: Learning Area Structure," *The New Zealand Curriculum Online*, 25 March 2014, http://nzcurriculum.tki.org.nz/The-New-Zealand-Curriculum/The-arts/Learning-area-structure (accessed August 6, 2018).

51. Tāmaki Paenga Hira/Auckland War Memorial Museum, "The History of Auckland Museum," *Tāmaki Paenga Hira/Auckland War Memorial Museum*, n.d., http://www.aucklandmuseum.com/your-museum/about/history-of-auckland-museum (accessed August 6, 2018).

52. Museum of New Zealand: Te Papa Tongarewa, "Our History/Te Whakapapa o te Papa," *Museum of New Zealand: Te Papa Tongarewa*, n.d., https://www.tepapa.govt.nz/about/what-we-do/our-history (accessed August 6, 2018).

53. For a discussion of the colonial and provincial governments see Malcolm McKinnon, "Colonial and Provincial Government," *Te Ara: The Encyclopedia of New Zealand*, 20 June 2012, https://teara.govt.nz/en/colonial-and-provincial-government (accessed August 6, 2018).

54. Calman, "Māori Education: Mātauranga," p. 2.

55. "Native Schools Act 1858, No. 65," *New Zealand Legal Information Institute*, http://www.nzlii.org/nz/legis/hist_act/nsa185821a22v1858n65306/ (accessed August 6, 2018).

56. "Native Schools Act 1867, No. 41," *New Zealand Legal Information Institute*, http://www.nzlii.org/nz/legis/hist_act/nsa186731v1867n41290/ (accessed August 6, 2018).

57. For a brief discussion of the native school system see Calman, "Māori Education: Mātauranga," p. 3.

58. "Education Act 1877, No. 21," *New Zealand Legal Information Institute*, http://www.nzlii.org/nz/legis/hist_act/ea187741v1877n21224/ (accessed August 6, 2018).

59. Calman, "Māori Education: Mātauranga," p. 3.

60. For a discussion of the colonial and provincial governments see Malcolm McKinnon, "Colonial and Provincial Government."

61. Nancy Swarbrick, "Country Schooling," *Te Ara: The Encyclopedia of New Zealand*, 24 November 2008, p. 1. https://teara.govt.nz/en/country-schooling (accessed August 7, 2018).

62. For a discussion of historical events that have affected art education in Aotearoa/New Zealand and what they may mean for the future of art education in the country see Jill Smith, "Art Education in New Zealand: Framing the Past/Locating the Present/Questioning the Future," *Australian Art Education*, Vol. 31, No. 2, pp. 100–117 (2008), http://publicationslist.org/data/j.smith/ref-6/Art%20Education%20in%20NZ.%20Framing%20the%20Past.pdf (accessed August 7, 2018).

63. For a biographical sketch of Arthur Gordon Tovey see Carol Henderson, "Tovey, Arthur Gordon," *Dictionary of New Zealand Biography (Te Ara: The Encyclopedia of New Zealand)*, 2000, https://teara.govt.nz/en/biographies/5t17/tovey-arthur-gordon (accessed August 7, 2018).

Postscript

1. Human Rights Commission/Te Kāhui Tika Tangata, "What Will New Zealand Be Like in 2040? Asks Report on Race Relations," *Human Rights Commission/Te Kāhui Tika Tangata*, 17 March 2005, no longer available online.

Bibliography

Adams, James Luther. "Introduction." *What Is Religion?*, by Paul Tillich, edited by James Luther Adams. New York: Harper Torchbooks, 1969.

Alchin, Linda. "Star Spangled Banner Lyrics." *Siteseen Limited.* 1 July 2017. http://www.american-historama.org/1801-1828-evolution/star-spangled-banner-lyrics.htm (accessed May 29, 2018).

"America's Founding Documents: The Bill of Rights: A Transcription." *The U.S. National Archives and Records Administration.* 26 June 2017. https://www.archives.gov/founding-docs/bill-of-rights-transcript (accessed May 28, 2018).

"America's Founding Documents: The Constitution of the United States." *The U.S. National Archives and Records Administration.* 13 September 2017. https://www.archives.gov/founding-docs/constitution (accessed May 28, 2018).

The Analytical Greek Lexicon. Sixth Printing. Grand Rapids: Zondervan Publishing House, 1970.

Anglican Church in Aotearoa, New Zealand, and Polynesia/Te Hahi Mihinare ki Aotearoa ki Niu Tireni, ki Nga Moutere o te Moana Nui a Kiwa. *Anglican Church in Aotearoa, New Zealand and Polynesia/Te Hahi Mihinare ki Aotearoa ki Niu Tireni, ki Nga Moutere o te Moana Nui a Kiwa.* n.d. http://www.anglican.org.nz/ (accessed July 13, 2018).

Ballara, Angela. "Hongi Hika." *Dictionary of New Zealand Biography (Te Ara: The Encyclopedia of New Zealand).* 1990. https://teara.govt.nz/en/biographies/1h32/hongi-hika (accessed May 11, 2018).

Bell, Zana. "Marsden's First Christmas." *New Zealand Geographic,* no. 077 (January-February 2006): https://www.nzgeo.com/stories/marsdens-first-christmas (accessed May 11, 2018).

Benton, Richard A. "David Simmons, MBE (1930–2015) Obituary." Edited by Melinda S. Allen. *The Journal of the Polynesian Society* (Polynesian Society [Inc.]) 125, no. 4 (December 2016): 339–340. http://www.jps.auckland.ac.nz/document/Volume_125_2016/Volume_125%2C_No._4/David_Simmons%2C_MBE_%281930-2015%29_Obituary%2C_by_Richard_A._Benton%2C_p_339-340?action=null (accessed July 9, 2018).

Berger, Peter L. *The Sacred Canopy: Elements of a Sociological Theory of Religion.* First. Garden City: Doubleday, 1967.

Best, Elsdon. "The Cult of Io: The Concept of a Supreme Deity as Evolved by the Ancestors of the Polynesians." *Man* 13 (1913): 98–103. https://www.jstor.org/stable/pdf/2787812 (accessed July 5, 2018).

Best, Elsdon. "Maori Eschatology: The Whare Potae (House of Mourning) and Its Lore; Being a Description of Many Customs, Beliefs, Superstitions, Rites, &c., Pertaining to Death and Burial Among the Maori People, as Also Some Account of Native Belief in a Spiritual World." Edited by A. Hamilton. *Transactions and Proceedings of the Royal Society of New Zealand 1868–1961: Volume 38, 1905* (John Mackay, Government Printing Office), 1906: Article XXV, 148–239. Available from the "National Library of New Zealand/Te Puna Mātauranga o Aotearoa": http://rsnz.natlib.govt.nz/volume/rsnz_38/rsnz_38_00_002700.html (accessed May 12, 2018).

Best, Elsdon. "Maori Religion: Notes on the Religious Ideas, Rites, and Invocations of the Maori People of New Zealand." *Report of the Twelfth Meeting of the Australasian Association for the Advancement of Science* (Anthony James Cumming, Government Printer), 1910: sec. F., 2., pp. 457–464. Available from the Smithsonian Institution Website: https://www.biodiversitylibrary.org/item/52764#page/1/mode/1up (accessed July 4, 2018).

Best, Elsdon. *The Maori: Volume I.* Wellington: Board of Maori Ethnological Research, 1924. Available from "The New Zealand Electronic Text Collection": http://nzetc.victoria.ac.nz/tm/scholarly/tei-Bes01Maor.html (accessed July 3, 2018).

Best, Elsdon. *Some Aspects of Maori Myth and*

Religion: Illustrating the Mentality of the Maori and His Mythopoetic Concepts. Wellington: W.A.G. Skinner, Government Printer, 1922. Available from the "Internet Archive": https://archive.org/details/someaspectsofmao01bestuoft (accessed 3 July 2018).

Binney, Judith. "Papahurihia, Penetana." *Dictionary of New Zealand Biography (Te Ara: The Encyclopedia of New Zealand)*. June 1990. https://teara.govt.nz/en/biographies/1p4/papahurihia-penetana (accessed May 11, 2018).

Binney, Judith. "Taonui, Aperahama." *Dictionary of New Zealand Biography (Te Ara: The Encyclopedia of New Zealand)*. 1993. https://teara.govt.nz/en/biographies/2t7/taonui-aperahama (accessed May 11, 2018).

Bologna, Caroline. "The History of the National Anthem in Sports: How 'The Star-Spangled Banner' Became a Part of American Sports Culture." *HuffPost*. 21 May 2018. https://www.huffingtonpost.com/entry/history-national-anthem-sports_us_5afc9bcfe4b06a3fb50d5056 (accessed May 29, 2018).

Byrnes, Giselle M. "Smith, Stephenson Percy." *Dictionary of New Zealand Biography (Te Ara: The Encyclopedia of New Zealand)*. 1993. https://teara.govt.nz/en/biographies/2s33/smith-stephenson-percy (accessed July 4, 2018).

Calman, Ross. "Māori Education: Mātauranga." *Te Ara: The Encyclopedia of New Zealand*. 20 June 2012. https://teara.govt.nz/en/maori-education-matauranga (accessed August 2, 2018).

Central Intelligence Agency. "Australia-Oceania: American Samoa." *The World Factbook*. 2018. https://www.cia.gov/library/publications/the-world-factbook/geos/aq.html (accessed May 10, 2018).

Central Intelligence Agency. "Australia-Oceania: Cook Islands." *The World Factbook*. 2018. https://www.cia.gov/library/publications/the-world-factbook/geos/cw.html (accessed May 10, 2018).

Central Intelligence Agency. "Australia-Oceania: French Polynesia." *The World Factbook*. 2018. https://www.cia.gov/library/publications/the-world-factbook/geos/fp.html (accessed May 10, 2018).

Central Intelligence Agency. "Australia-Oceania: Samoa." *The World Factbook*. 2018. https://www.cia.gov/library/publications/the-world-factbook/geos/ws.html (accessed May 10, 2018).

Central Intelligence Agency. "Australia-Oceania: Tonga." *The World Factbook*. 2018. https://www.cia.gov/library/publications/the-world-factbook/geos/tn.html (accessed May 10, 2018).

"Civil Union Act." *New Zealand Legal Information Institute*. 2004, No. 102. http://www.nzlii.org/nz/legis/hist_act/cua20042004n102166/ (accessed August 21, 2018).

Colenso, William. "On the Maori Races of New Zealand." *Transactions and Proceedings of the New Zealand Institute-Volume 1, 1868* (James Hughes), May 1869: 1–75 (Essays sec., essay 10 of 10; Page numbers repeat for each essay). Available from the National Library of New Zealand/Te Puna Mātauranga o Aotearoa: http://rsnz.natlib.govt.nz/volume/rsnz_01/rsnz_01_00_002170.html (accessed February 7, 2019).

The Commonwealth. "Member Countries." *The Commonwealth*. 2018. http://thecommonwealth.org/member-countries (accessed May 10, 2018).

Coogan, Michael D., ed. *The New Oxford Annotated Bible with the Apocrypha*. New Revised Standard Version. New York: Oxford University Press, 2010.

Cook, Karen S., Coye Cheshire, and Alexandra Gerbasi. "Power, Dependence, and Social Exchange." Chap. Nine in *Contemporary Social Psychological Theories*, edited by Peter J. Burke, 194–216. Stanford: Stanford University Press, 2006.

Cox, James L. *The Invention of God in Indigenous Societies*. Durham: Acumen Publishing Limited, 2014.

Craig, Elsdon. W.G. *Man of the Mist: A Biography of Elsdon Best*. Wellington: A.H. & A.W. Reed, 1964.

Culpitt, Ian. "Bicultural Fragments: A Pākehā Perspective." *Social Policy Journal of New Zealand*, no. 2 (July 1994): http://www.msd.govt.nz/about-msd-and-our-work/publications-resources/journals-and-magazines/social-policy-journal/spj02/02-bicultural-fragments.html (accessed April 22, 2018).

Davis, C.O. *The Life and Times of Patuone, the Celebrated Ngapuhi Chief*. Christchurch: Capper Press, 1974, original work published in Auckland in 1876 by J.H. Field. Available from "The New Zealand Electronic Text Collection": http://nzetc.victoria.ac.nz/tm/scholarly/tei-DavLife.html (accessed July 4, 2018).

"Education Act." *New Zealand Legal Information Institute*. 1847, No. 10. http://www.nzlii.org/nz/legis/hist_act/ea1847l1v1847n10224/ea1847l1v1847n10224.html (accessed August 3, 2018).

"Education Act." *New Zealand Legal Information Institute*. 1877, No. 21. http://www.nzlii.org/nz/legis/hist_act/ea1877l4v1877n21224/ (accessed August 6, 2018).

Ehrman, Bart D. *Jesus: Apocalyptic Prophet of the New Millennium*. New York: Oxford University Press, 1999.

Electoral Commission/Te Kaitiaki Take Kōwhiri. *Elections*. n.d. http://www.elections.org.nz/ (accessed April 7, 2018).

Emerson, Richard M. "Power-Dependence Relations." *American Sociological Review* 27, no. 1 (February 1962): 31–41. https://www.jstor.org/stable/2089716 (accessed February 16, 2019).

Emerson, Richard M. "Social Exchange Theory." *Annual Review of Sociology* 2 (1976): 335–362. http://www.jstor.org/stable/2946096 (accessed April 23, 2018).

Erickson, Paul A., and Liam D. Murphy. *A History of Anthropological Theory.* Fourth. North York: University of Toronto Press, 2013.

Falloon, Malcolm. "The Night That Transformed a Mission and Established a Church." *NZCMS.* 3 December 2014. http://www.nzcms.org.nz/our-story-the-night-that-transformed-a-mission-and-established-a-church (accessed May 11, 2018).

Firth, Raymond. *Economics of the New Zealand Maori.* Second. Wellington: Government Printer, 1959.

Firth, Raymond. *Essays on Social Organisation and Values: School of Economics Monographs on Social Anthropology.* London: Athlone Press, 1964.

Fisher, Robin. "Williams, Henry." *Dictionary of New Zealand Biography (Te Ara: The Encyclopedia of New Zealand).* 1990. https://teara.govt.nz/en/biographies/1w22/williams-henry (accessed May 11, 2018).

"Forest Act." *New Zealand Legal Information Institute.* 1949, No. 19. http://www.nzlii.org/nz/legis/hist_act/fa19491949n19143/ (accessed August 20, 2018).

"Forest Act." *New Zealand Legislation.* 1949, No. 19. http://www.legislation.govt.nz/act/public/1949/0019/latest/whole.html#DLM255632 (accessed February 6, 2019).

"Forest Amendment Act." *New Zealand Legal Information Institute.* 1993, No. 7. http://www.nzlii.org/nz/legis/hist_act/faa19931993n7223/ (accessed February 6, 2019).

Foster, Bernard John. "Kororareka." *An Encyclopedia of New Zealand 1966.* 1966. https://teara.govt.nz/en/1966/kororareka (accessed May 11, 2018).

Fox, Richard G. *Lions of the Punjab: Culture in the Making.* Berkeley: University of California Press, 1985.

Geertz, Clifford. "Art as a Cultural System." *MLN* (The Johns Hopkins University Press) 91, no. 6 (December 1976): 1473–1499.

Geertz, Clifford. "Art as a Cultural System." Chap. 5 in *Local Knowledge: Further Essays in Interpretive Anthropology,* by Clifford Geertz, 94–120. New York: Basic Books, 1983.

Geertz, Clifford. "Common Sense as a Cultural System." *The Antioch Review* 33, no. 1 (Spring 1975): 5–26.

Geertz, Clifford. "Common Sense as a Cultural System." Chap. 4 in *Local Knowledge: Further*

Essays in Interpretive Anthropology, by Clifford Geertz, 73–93. New York: Basic Books, 1983.

Geertz, Clifford. "Ethos, World View, and the Analysis of Sacred Symbols." Chap. 5 in *The Interpretation of Cultures,* by Clifford Geertz, 126–141. New York: Basic Books, 1973.

Geertz, Clifford. "Ideology as a Cultural System." Chap. 8 in *The Interpretation of Cultures,* by Clifford Geertz, 193–233. New York: Basic Books, 1973.

Geertz, Clifford. "Ideology as a Cultural System." *Ideology and Discontent,* edited by David E. Apter, 47–76. New York: The Free Press of Glencoe, a Division of the Macmillan Company, 1964.

Geertz, Clifford. "Introduction." *Local Knowledge: Further Essays in Interpretive Anthropology,* by Clifford Geertz, 3–16. New York: Basic Books, 1983.

Geertz, Clifford. "Person, Time, and Conduct in Bali." Chap. 14 in *The Interpretation of Cultures,* by Clifford Geertz, 360–411. New York: Basic Books, 1973.

Geertz, Clifford. "Religion as a Cultural System." Chap. 4 in *The Interpretation of Cultures,* by Clifford Geertz, 87–125. New York: Basic Books, 1973.

Geertz, Clifford. "Thick Description: Toward an Interpretive Theory of Culture." Chap. 1 in *The Interpretation of Cultures,* by Clifford Geertz, 3–30. New York: Basic Books, 1973.

Gibbons, P.J. "Stowell, Henry Matthew." *Dictionary of New Zealand Biography (Te Ara: The Encyclopedia of New Zealand).* 1996. https://teara.govt.nz/en/biographies/3s38/stowell-henry-matthew (accessed July 4, 2018).

Greenwood, William. "The Upraised Hand or the Spiritual Significance of the Rise of the Ringatū Faith." *The Journal of the Polynesian Society* (The Polynesian Society [Incorporated]) 51, no. 1 (March 1942): 1–80. http://www.jps.auckland.ac.nz/document.php?wid=2250&action=null (accessed May 10, 2018).

Griffin, David Ray, Ed. *Deep Religious Pluralism.* Louisville: Westminster John Knox Press, 2005.

Handler, Richard. "Cultural Property and Culture Theory." *Journal of Social Archaeology* 3, no. 3 (October 2003): 353–365. http://web.williams.edu/AnthSoc/IJCP/Handler2003.pdf (accessed February 7, 2019).

Handler, Richard, and Jocelyn Linnekin. "Tradition, Genuine or Spurious." *Folk Groups and Folklore Genres: A Reader,* edited by Elliot Oring, 38–42. Logan: Utah State University Press, 1989.

Handler, Richard, and Jocelyn Linnekin. "Tradition, Genuine or Spurious." *Journal of American Folklore* 97, no. 385 (July–September 1984): 273–290. http://kodu.ut.ee/~cect/teoreetilised%20seminarid_2010/folkloristika_uurimisr%C3

%BChma_seminar/Handler_Linnekin—Tradi tion-Genuine_or_Spurious—JAF_1984_vol_ 97_no_385.pdf (accessed August 1, 2018).

Hanson, Allan. "The Making of the Maori: Culture Invention and Its Logic." *American Anthropologist* 91, no. 4 (December 1989): 890–902. https:// www.jstor.org/stable/681587 (accessed June 26, 2018).

Hanson, Allan. "Reply to Langdon, Levine, and Linnekin." *American Anthropologist* 93, no. 2 (June 1991): 449–450. http://www.jstor.org/ stable/681308 (accessed June 27, 2018).

Harper, Douglas. *Online Etymology Dictionary.* n.d. https://www.etymonline.com/ (accessed June 26, 2018).

Hearn, Terry. "English." *Te Ara: The Encyclopedia of New Zealand.* 25 March 2015. https://teara. govt.nz/en/english (accessed June 11, 2018).

Heidler, Jeanne T., and David S. Heidler. "Manifest Destiny." *Encyclopaedia Britannica.* n.d. https:// www.britannica.com/event/Manifest-Destiny (accessed May 29, 2018).

Henderson, Carol. "Tovey, Arthur Gordon." *Dictionary of New Zealand Biography (Te Ara: The Encyclopedia of New Zealand).* 2000. https:// teara.govt.nz/en/biographies/5t17/tovey- arthur-gordon (accessed August 7, 2018).

Higgins, Rawinia, and John C. Moorfield. "Tangihanga: Death Customs." Chap. 8 in *Ki te Whaiao: An Introduction to Māori Culture and Society,* edited by Tānia M. Ka'ai, John C. Moorfield, Michael P.J. Reilly and Sharon Mosley, 85–90. Auckland: Pearson Education New Zealand Limited, 2004.

Hīroa, Te Rangi (Sir Peter Buck). *The Coming of the Maori.* Second. Wellington: Whitcombe and Tombs, 1950. Available from "The New Zealand Electronic Text Collection": http://nzetc. victoria.ac.nz/tm/scholarly/tei-BucTheC.html (accessed July 3, 2018).

Human Rights Commission/Te Kāhui Tika Tangata. "History of the New Zealand Sign Language Act." *Ministry of Social Development/Te Manatū Whakahiato Ora.* n.d. https://www. hrc.co.nz/your-rights/people-disabilities/ your-rights/new-zealand-sign-language-act/ (accessed April 7, 2018).

Human Rights Commission/Te Kāhui Tika Tangata. "What Will New Zealand Be Like in 2040? Asks Report on Race Relations." *Human Rights Commission/Te Kāhui Tika Tangata.* 17 March 2005. No longer available online.

Internal Affairs/Te Tari Taiwhenua. "Local Government in New Zealand: Local Councils." *Internal Affairs/Te Tari Taiwhenua.* n.d. http:// www.localcouncils.govt.nz/lgip.nsf/wpg_url/ about-local-government-index (accessed April 7, 2018).

Irwin, Geoff. "Pacific Migrations." *Te Ara: The Encyclopedia of New Zealand.* 8 February 2017. https://teara.govt.nz/en/pacific-migrations (accessed May 9, 2018).

Irwin, Geoffrey. *The Prehistoric Exploration and Colonization of the Pacific.* Cambridge: Cambridge University Press, 1994.

Jackson, Moana. "Why Did Māori Never Have Prisons?" *YouTube.* [Video], 16 November 2017. https://www.youtube.com/watch?v=2vtpA_ PbDJU (accessed August 4, 2018).

Johnson, Martenzie. "Let's Take the National Anthem Literally, and the Songwriter at His Word: A Deeper Look at the Song, the Man Who Wrote It—and the History Attached." *The Undefeated.* 30 August 2016. https://theunde feated.com/features/lets-take-the-national- anthem-literally-and-the-songwriter-at-his- word/ (accessed May 29, 2018).

Ka'ai, Tānia M. "Te Mana o te Reo me ngā Tikanga: Power and Politics of the Language." Chap. 19 in *Ki te Whaiao: An Introduction to Māori Culture and Society,* edited by Tānia M. Ka'ai, John C. Moorfield, Michael P.J. Reilly and Sharon Mosley, 201–213. Auckland: Pearson Education New Zealand Limited, 2004.

Ka'ai, Tānia M., John C. Moorfield, Michael P.J. Reilly, and Sharon Mosley, Ed. *Ki te Whaiao: An Introduction to Māori Culture and Society.* Auckland: Pearson Education New Zealand Limited, 2004.

Ka'ai, Tānia M., and Rawinia Higgins. "Te Ao Māori: Māori World-View." Chap. 2 in *Ki te Whaiao: An Introduction to Māori Culture and Society,* edited by Tānia M. Ka'ai, John C. Moorfield, Michael P.J. Reilly and Sharon Mosley, 13–25. Auckland: Pearson Education New Zealand Limited, 2004.

Keane, Basil. "He Whakaputanga: Declaration of Independence." *Te Ara: The Encyclopedia of New Zealand.* 20 June 2012. https://teara. govt.nz/en/he-whakaputanga-declaration-of- independence (accessed June 23, 2018).

Kiralfy, Albert Roland, Mary Ann Glendon, and Andrew D.E. Lewis. "Common Law." *Encyclopaedia Britannica.* 26 July 2018. https://www. britannica.com/topic/common-law (accessed August 4, 2018).

Land Information New Zealand (LINZ)/Toitū te Whenua. "Maritime Boundary Downloads [Map]." *Land Information New Zealand (LINZ)/ Toitū Te Whenua.* 2 February 2018. http:// www.linz.govt.nz/sea/nautical-information/ maritime-boundaries/maritime-boundary- downloads (accessed February 5, 2019).

Lawler, Edward J. "An Affect Theory of Social Exchange." *American Journal of Sociology* 107, no. 2 (September 2001): 321–352. http://www. uvm.edu/~pdodds/files/papers/others/2001/ lawler2001b.pdf (accessed April 20, 2018).

Lindstrom, Lamont. "Leftamap Kastom: The Political History of Tradition on Tanna, Vanuatu." *Mankind* 13 (1982): 316–329.

Lineham, Peter J. "Missions and Missionaries." *Te Ara: The Encyclopedia of New Zealand.* 13 March 2017. https://teara.govt.nz/en/missions-and-missionaries (accessed May 11, 2018).

Linnekin, Jocelyn. "Cultural Invention and the Dilemma of Authenticity." *American Anthropologist* 93, no. 2 (June 1991): 446–449. https://www.jstor.org/stable/681307 (accessed August 1, 2018).

Mackay, David. "Colenso, William." *Dictionary of New Zealand Biography (Te Ara—the Encyclopedia of New Zealand).* 1990. https://teara.govt.nz/en/biographies/1c23/colenso-william (accessed July 7, 2018).

Macky, Ian. *PAT [Portable Atlas].* 28 November 2018. (public domain maps). https://ian.macky.net/pat/ (accessed February 19, 2019).

"Maori Affairs Act." *New Zealand Legal Information Institute.* 1953, No. 94. http://www.nzlii.org/nz/legis/hist_act/maa19531953n94152/ (accessed August 20, 2018).

"Maori Affairs Amendment Act." *New Zealand Legal Information Institute.* 1967, No. 124. http://www.nzlii.org/nz/legis/hist_act/maaa19671967n124232/ (accessed August 20, 2018).

"Māori Language Act." *New Zealand Legal Information Institute.* 1987, No. 176. http://www.nzlii.org/nz/legis/hist_act/mla19871987n176159/ (accessed August 20, 2018).

"Māori Language Act." *New Zealand Legislation.* 2016, No. 17. http://www.legislation.govt.nz/act/public/2016/0017/latest/whole.html#DLM6174509 (accessed February 4, 2019).

Māori Language Commission/Te Taura Whiri i te Reo Māori. *Annual Report for the Year Ended 30 June 2012.* Commentary, Wellington: Māori Language Commission, 2012. http://www.tetaurawhiri.govt.nz/assets/Uploads/Corporate-docs/Annual-reports/Annual-Report-2012-English.pdf (accessed April 7, 2018).

"Marriage (Definition of Marriage) Amendment Act." *New Zealand Legal Information Institute.* 2013, No. 20. http://www.nzlii.org/nz/legis/consol_act/momaa2013343/ (accessed August 21, 2018).

Marsden, Māori. "God, Man and Universe: A Maori View." *Te Ao Hurihuri: Aspects of Maoritanga,* edited by Michael King, 117–137. Auckland: Reed Publishing (NZ), 1992.

Marsden, Māori. *The Woven Universe: Selected Writings of Rev. Māori Marsden.* Edited by Te Ahukaramū Charles Royal. Ōtaki: Estate of the Rev. Māori Marsden, 2003.

Mason, Herbert M. "National Anthem Celebrates 78 Years, Thanks to VFW." *VFW: Veterans of Foreign Wars.* 3 March 2009. https://www.vfw.org/media-and-events/latest-releases/archives/2009/3/national-anthem-celebrates-78-years---thanks-to-vfw (accessed May 28, 2018).

McKinnon, Malcolm. "Colonial and Provincial Government." *Te Ara: The Encyclopedia of New Zealand.* 20 June 2012. https://teara.govt.nz/en/colonial-and-provincial-government (accessed August 6, 2018).

Mead, Sir Hirini Moko. "Understanding Mātauranga Māori." *Conversations on Mātauranga Māori,* edited by Haemata, Professor Taiarahia Black, Daryn Bean, Waireka Collings and Whitney Nuku, 9–14. N.P.: New Zealand Qualifications Authority/Mana Tohu Mātauranga o Aotearoa, 2012. http://www.nzqa.govt.nz/assets/Maori/ConversationsMMv6AW-web.pdf (accessed August 1, 2018).

Metge, Joan. "Returning the Gift-Utu in Intergroup Relations: In Memory of Sir Raymond Firth." Edited by Judith Huntsman. *The Journal of the Polynesian Society* (Polynesian Society [Inc.]) 111, no. 4 (December 2002): 311–338. http://www.jps.auckland.ac.nz/document.php?wid=5182&action=null (accessed April 21, 2018).

Milroy, Wharehuia. "Tamarau Waiari." *Dictionary of New Zealand Biography (Te Ara: The Encyclopedia of New Zealand).* 1993. https://teara.govt.nz/en/biographies/2t6/tamarau-waiari (accessed June 9, 2018).

Ministry for Culture and Heritage/Manatū Taonga. "The Census." *An Encyclopedia of New Zealand 1966.* Edited by A.H. McLintock. 1966. https://teara.govt.nz/en/1966/population/page-2 (accessed April 26, 2018).

Ministry for Culture and Heritage/Manatū Taonga. "A Frontier of Chaos?: Kororāreka." *New Zealand History/Nga Korero a Ipurangi o Aotearoa (Ministry for Culture and Heritage/Manatū Taonga).* 13 January 2016. http://www.nzhistory.net.nz/culture/missionaries/kororareka (accessed May 11, 2018).

Ministry for Culture and Heritage/Manatū Taonga. "A Frontier of Chaos?: Overview." *New Zealand History/Nga Korero a Ipurangi o Aotearoa (Ministry for Culture and Heritage/Manatū Taonga).* 13 January 2016. https://nzhistory.govt.nz/culture/maori-european-contact-before-1840/overview (accessed May 28, 2018).

Ministry for Culture and Heritage/Manatū Taonga. "A Frontier of Chaos?: The Boyd Incident." *New Zealand History/Nga Korero a Ipurangi o Aotearoa (Ministry for Culture and Heritage/Manatū Taonga).* 11 March 2014. http://www.nzhistory.net.nz/culture/maori-european-contact-before-1840/the-boyd-incident (accessed August 9, 2018).

Ministry for Culture and Heritage/Manatū

Taonga. "Missionaries: Wesleyans and Catholics." *New Zealand History/Nga Korero a Ipurangi o Aotearoa (Ministry for Culture and Heritage/Manatū Taonga).* 6 June 2017. https://nzhistory.govt.nz/culture/missionaries/new-arrivals (accessed May 11, 2018).

Ministry for Culture and Heritage/Manatū Taonga. *New Zealand History/Nga Korero a Ipurangi o Aotearoa.* n.d. https://nzhistory.govt.nz/ (accessed February 18, 2019).

Ministry for Culture and Heritage/Manatū Taonga. "Overview of NZ in the Nineteenth Century: *New Zealand History/Nga Korero a Ipurangi o Aotearoa (Ministry for Culture and Heritage/Manatū Taonga).* 4 August 2014. https://nzhistory.govt.nz/classroom/ncea3/19th-century-history-overview (accessed April 26, 2018).

Ministry for Culture and Heritage/Manatū Taonga. "Population, Population Trends, and the Census." *An Encyclopedia of New Zealand 1966.* Edited by A.H. McLintock. 1966. https://teara.govt.nz/en/1966/population (accessed April 26, 2018).

Ministry for Culture and Heritage/Manatū Taonga. "The Seal of the Ringatū Church." *New Zealand History/Nga Korero a Ipurangi o Aotearoa (Ministry for Culture and Heritage/Manatū Taonga).* 20 December 2012. https://nzhistory.govt.nz/media/photo/seal-ringatu-church (accessed May 8, 2018).

Ministry for Culture and Heritage/Manatū Taonga. *Te Ara: The Encyclopedia of New Zealand.* n.d. https://teara.govt.nz/en (accessed May 12, 2018).

Ministry for Culture and Heritage/Manatū Taonga. "Te Wiki o te Reo Māori–Māori Language Week: History of the Māori Language." *New Zealand History/Nga Korero a Ipurangi o Aotearoa (Ministry for Culture and Heritage).* 10 October 2017. https://nzhistory.govt.nz/culture/maori-language-week/history-of-the-maori-language (accessed May 9, 2018).

Ministry of Business, Innovation, and Employment/Hīkina Whakatutuki. "The School System." *New Zealand Now.* 17 April 2018. https://www.newzealandnow.govt.nz/living-in-nz/education/school-system (accessed August 2, 2018).

Ministry of Education/Te Tāhuhu o te Mātauranga. "The Arts: Learning Area Structure." *The New Zealand Curriculum Online.* 25 March 2014. http://nzcurriculum.tki.org.nz/The-New-Zealand-Curriculum/The-arts/Learning-area-structure (accessed August 6, 2018).

Ministry of Education/Te Tāhuhu o te Mātauranga. "Education in New Zealand." *Ministry of Education/Te Tāhuhu o te Mātauranga.* n.d. https://www.education.govt.nz/ministry-of-education/our-role-and-our-people/education-in-nz/ (accessed August 2, 2018).

Ministry of Education/Te Tāhuhu o te Mātauranga. "The New Zealand Curriculum/Official Languages." *The New Zealand Curriculum Online.* 8 December 2017. http://nzcurriculum.tki.org.nz/The-New-Zealand-Curriculum (accessed February 16, 2019).

Ministry of Justice/Tāhū o te Ture. "About Us." *Ministry of Justice/Tāhū o te Ture.* 2018. https://www.justice.govt.nz/about/about-us/ (accessed August 4, 2018).

Ministry of Justice/Tāhū o te Ture. *He Hīnātore ki te Ao Māori: A Glimpse Into the Māori World (Māori Perspectives on Justice).* Wellington: Ministry of Justice/Tāhū o te Ture, 2001. http://www.justice.govt.nz/publications/publications-archived/2001/he-hinatore-ki-te-ao-maori-a-glimpse-into-the-maori-world (accessed August 4, 2018).

Molm, Linda D., Jessica L. Collett, and David R. Schaefer. "Building Solidarity Through Generalized Exchange: A Theory of Reciprocity." *American Journal of Sociology* 113, no. 1 (July 2007): 205–242. http://www3.nd.edu/~jcollet1/pubs/2007-113.pdf (accessed April 20, 2018).

Moorfield, John C. *Te Aka: Māori-English English-Māori Dictionary.* n.d. http://maoridictionary.co.nz/ (accessed February 22, 2019).

Morgan, John H. *"In the Beginning...": The Paleolithic Origins of Religious Consciousness.* South Bend: Cloverdale Books, 2007.

Morgan, John H. "Religion and Culture as Meaning Systems: A Dialogue Between Geertz and Tillich." Chap. Two in *Being Human: Perspectives on Meaning and Interpretation (Essays in Religion, Culture and Personality),* by John H. Morgan, 17–33. South Bend: Cloverdale Books, 2006.

Morgan, John H. "Religion and Culture as Meaning Systems: A Dialogue Between Geertz and Tillich." *The Journal of Religion* 57, no. 4 (October 1977): 363–375.

Morgan, John H. "Theology and Symbol: An Anthropological Approach." Chap. Five in *Being Human: Perspectives on Meaning and Interpretation (Essays in Religion, Culture and Personality),* by John H. Morgan, 93–105. South Bend: Cloverdale Books, 2006.

Morris, Paul. "Diverse Religions." *Te Ara: The Encyclopedia of New Zealand.* 13 February 2017. https://teara.govt.nz/en/diverse-religions (accessed May 11, 2018).

Museum of New Zealand: Te Papa Tongarewa. "Our History/Te Whakapapa o te Papa." *Museum of New Zealand: Te Papa Tongarewa.* n.d. https://www.tepapa.govt.nz/about/what-we-do/our-history (accessed August 6, 2018).

National Police Headquarters. *New Zealand Crime Statistics 2014: A Summary of Recorded and Resolved Offence Statistics.* Tables, N.P.: National

Police Headquarters, 2015. http://www.police. govt.nz/sites/default/files/publications/crime-stats-national-20141231.pdf (accessed April 6, 2018).

"Native Schools Act." *New Zealand Legal Information Institute.* 1858, No. 65. http://www.nzlii.org/nz/legis/hist_act/nsa185821a22v1858n65306/ (accessed August 6, 2018).

"Native Schools Act." *New Zealand Legal Information Institute.* 1867, No. 41. http://www.nzlii.org/nz/legis/hist_act/nsa18673lv1867n41290/ (accessed August 6, 2018).

"New Zealand Bill of Rights Act." *Parliamentary Counsel Office/Te Tari Tohutohu Pāremata.* 1990, No. 109. http://www.legislation.govt.nz/act/public/1990/0109/latest/whole.html?search=y_act_2016_1990_ac%40ainf%40anif_an%40bn%40rn_25_a&p=1#DLM224792 (accessed February 4, 2019).

New Zealand Diversity Action Programme. *Languages in Aotearoa New Zealand/Te Waka Reo: Statement on Language Policy.* N.P.: New Zealand Human Rights Commission, 2008. https://www.hrc.co.nz/files/3414/2388/3771/25-Aug-2008_11-45-14_Language_Policy_Aug_08.pdf (accessed April 7, 2018).

New Zealand Parliament/Pāremata Aotearoa. n.d. http://www.parliament.nz/en/ (accessed May 12, 2018).

"New Zealand Sign Language Act." *New Zealand Legal Information Institute.* 2006, No. 18. http://www.nzlii.org/nz/legis/hist_act/nzsla 20062006n18248/ (accessed August 21, 2018).

Newman, Keith. "Rātana Church: Te Haahi Rātana." *Te Ara: The Encyclopedia of New Zealand.* 14 March 2017. http://www.teara.govt.nz/en/ratana-church-te-haahi-ratana (accessed May 8, 2018).

Ngata, A.T. "The Io Cult-Early Migration-Puzzle of the Canoes." *The Journal of the Polynesian Society* (The Polynesian Society [Inc.]) 59, no. 4 (December 1950): 335–346, Transcript. http://www.jps.auckland.ac.nz/document/Volume_59_1950/Volume_59%2C_No._4/The_Io_Cult_-_early_migration_-_puzzle_of_the_canoes%2C_by_A._T._Ngata%2C_p_335-346?action=null (accessed July 12, 2018).

Orange, Claudia. "Treaty of Waitangi." *Te Ara: The Encyclopedia of New Zealand.* 20 June 2012. https://teara.govt.nz/en/treaty-of-waitangi (accessed May 26, 2018).

Orbell, Margaret. *The Illustrated Encyclopedia of Māori Myth and Legend.* Christchurch: Canterbury University Press, 1995.

Owens, J.M.R. "Taylor, Richard." *Dictionary of New Zealand Biography (Te Ara: The Encyclopedia of New Zealand).* 1990. https://teara.govt.nz/en/biographies/1t22/taylor-richard (accessed July 7, 2018).

Paraone, Tiwai. "A Maori Cosmogony." *The Journal of the Polynesian Society* (Thomas Avery) 16, no. 3 (September 1907): 109–119. http://www.jps.auckland.ac.nz/document.php?wid=695&action=null (accessed July 4, 2018).

Parsons, M.J. "Jury, Hoani Te Whatahoro." *Dictionary of New Zealand Biography (Te Ara: The Encyclopedia of New Zealand).* 1990. https://teara.govt.nz/en/biographies/1j6/jury-hoani-te-whatahoro (accessed July 5, 2018).

Pawley, Andrew. "Obituary: Bruce Grandison Biggs 1921–2000." Edited by Judith Huntsman. *The Journal of the Polynesian Society* (Polynesian Society (Inc.)) 109, no. 4 (December 2000): 341–346. http://www.jps.auckland.ac.nz/document//Volume_109_2000/Volume_109%2C_No._4/%5BFront_matter%5D_p_337-346/p1 (accessed July 9, 2018).

Photos for Work. n.d. https://www.photosforwork.com/ (accessed February 19, 2019).

Pollock, Kerryn. "King Country Region-Arts, Culture and Heritage." *Te Ara: The Encyclopedia of New Zealand.* 30 March 2015. https://teara.govt.nz/en/photograph/34923/te-tokanganui-a-noho-wharenui (accessed May 10, 2018).

Pollock, Kerryn. "Tertiary Education." *Te Ara: The Encyclopedia of New Zealand.* 20 June 2012. https://teara.govt.nz/en/tertiary-education (accessed August 2, 2018).

The Polynesian Society. "About the Polynesian Society." *The Polynesian Society.* n.d. http://www.thepolynesiansociety.org/about.html (accessed July 4, 2018).

The Polynesian Society. "A Short History of the Polynesian Society (Abridged from M.P.K. Sorrenson's *Manifest Duty: The Polynesian Society Over 100 Years* with an Update to 2011)." *The Polynesian Society.* n.d. http://www.thepolynesiansociety.org/history.html (accessed July 4, 2018).

The Polynesian Society. "Volume III: Memoirs of the Polynesian Society: 'The Lore of the Whare Wānanga.'" *The Journal of the Polynesian Society* (Thomas Avery) 21, no. 4 (December 1912): 181, http://www.jps.auckland.ac.nz/document/Volume_21_1912/Volume_21%2C_No._4/Volume_III._Memoirs_of_the_Polynesian_Society._The_lore_of_the_whare_wananga%2C_p_181?action=null (accessed July 5, 2018).

Pool, Ian, and Tahu Kukutai. "Taupori Māori-Māori Population Change: Māori Urbanization." *Te Ara: The Encyclopedia of New Zealand.* 5 May 2011. https://teara.govt.nz/en/graph/31326/maori-urbanisation (accessed May 9, 2018).

Reed, A.W. *Maori Myths & Legendary Tales.* 1999. Auckland: New Holland Publishers (NZ), 1999.

Reilly, Michael P.J. "White, John." *Dictionary of*

New Zealand Biography (Te Ara: The Encyclopedia of New Zealand). 1990. http://www.teara.govt.nz/en/biographies/1w18/white-john (accessed July 3, 2018).

Reilly, Michael P.J. "Te Tīmatanga Mai o Ngā Atua: Creation Narratives." Chap. 1 in *Ki te Whaiao: An Introduction to Māori Culture and Society,* edited by Tānia M. Ka'ai, John C. Moorfield, Michael P.J. Reilly and Sharon Mosley, 1–12. Auckland: Pearson Education New Zealand Limited, 2004.

Reserve Bank of New Zealand/Te Pūtea Matua. "Monetary Policy: Inflation." *Reserve Bank of New Zealand/Te Pūtea Matua.* 2018. https://www.rbnz.govt.nz/monetary-policy/inflation (accessed April 4, 2018).

"The Ringatū Seal." *The Journal of the Polynesian Society* (The Polynesian Society [Inc.]) 51, no. 1 (March 1942): 81. http://www.jps.auckland.ac.nz/document//Volume_51_1942/Volume_51%2C_No._1/The_Ringatu_seal%2C_p_80/p1 (accessed May 8, 2018).

Rosenfeld, Jean E. *The Island Broken in Two Halves: Land and Renewal Movements Among the Maori of New Zealand.* University Park: The Pennsylvania State University Press, 1999.

Royal, Te Ahukaramū Charles. "Books." *Dr. Te Ahukaramū Charles Royal.* n.d. http://www.charles-royal.nz/writings (accessed July 12, 2018).

Royal, Te Ahukaramū Charles. "Māori Creation Traditions." *Te Ara: The Encyclopedia of New Zealand.* 8 February 2005. https://teara.govt.nz/en/maori-creation-traditions (accessed July 12, 2018).

Royal, Te Ahukaramū Charles. *Mātauranga Māori and Museum Practice: A Discussion,* edited by David Green. National Services Te Paerangi, Museum of New Zealand Te Papa Tongarewa, Wellington: National Services Te Paerangi, Museum of New Zealand Te Papa Tongarewa, 2007. https://static1.squarespace.com/static/5369700de4b045a4e0c24bbc/t/578e13812994cafd4eaabde3/1468928943167/Matauranga+Maori+and+Museum+Practice+-+a+discussion.pdf (accessed February 16, 2019).

Ryle, Gilbert. "Thinking and Reflecting." Chap. 36 in *Collected Papers, Volume 2: Collected Essays 1929–1968,* by Gilbert Ryle, 479–493. New York: Routledge, 2009.

Ryle, Gilbert. "The Thinking of Thoughts: What Is 'le Penseur' Doing?" Chap. 37 in *Collected Papers, Volume 2: Collected Essays 1929–1968,* by Gilbert Ryle, 494–510. New York: Routledge, 2009.

Shirres, Michael P. "Tapu." Edited by Geoffrey Irwin. *The Journal of the Polynesian Society* (The Polynesian Society [Inc.]) 91, no. 1 (March 1982): 29–52. http://www.jps.auckland.ac.nz/ document.php?wid=3806&action=null (accessed April 24, 2018).

Shortland, Edward. *Maori Religion and Mythology.* Auckland: Upton and Co., 1882. Available from "The New Zealand Electronic Text Collection": http://nzetc.victoria.ac.nz/tm/scholarly/tei-ShorMaor.html (accessed June 23, 2018).

Simmons, D.R. "A New Zealand Myth: Kupe, Toi and the Fleet." *The New Zealand Journal of History* (Department of History at the University of Auckland) 3, no. 1 (April 1969): 14–31. http://www.nzjh.auckland.ac.nz/document.php?wid=1620&action=null (accessed July 4, 2018).

Simmons, David, and Bruce Biggs. "The Sources of 'The Lore of the Whare-Wānanga.'" Edited by Mervyn McLean. *The Journal of the Polynesian Society* (The Polynesian Society [Inc.]) 79, no. 1 (March 1970): 22–42. http://www.jps.auckland.ac.nz/document.php?wid=4356&action=null (accessed July 9, 2018).

Simpson, Jane. "Io as Supreme Being: Intellectual Colonization of the Māori?" *History of Religions* 37, no. 1 (August 1997): 50–85. http://www.jstor.org/stable/3176563 (accessed July 3, 2018).

Sissons, Jeffrey. "Best, Elsdon." *Dictionary of New Zealand Biography (Te Ara: The Encyclopedia of New Zealand).* 1993. https://teara.govt.nz/en/biographies/2b20/best-elsdon (accessed July 4, 2018).

Smith, Jill. "Art Education in New Zealand: Framing the Past/Locating the Present/Questioning the Future." *Australian Art Education* 31, no. 2 (2008): 100–117. http://publicationslist.org/data/j.smith/ref-6/Art%20Education%20in%20NZ.%20Framing%20the%20Past.pdf (accessed August 7, 2018).

Smith, Jonathan Z. "The Unknown God: Myth in History." Chap. 5 in *Imagining Religion: from Babylon to Jonestown,* by Jonathan Z. Smith, 66–89. Chicago: University of Chicago Press, 1982.

Smith, S. Percy. "Introduction." *The Lore of the Whare-Wānanga or Teachings of the Maori College on Religion, Cosmogony, and History,* by H.T. Whatahoro, translated by S. Percy Smith, 1–18. Lexington: Forgotten Books, 2008; original work published in New Plymouth in 1913 by Thomas Avery as *The Lore of the Whare-Wānanga: Part I.-Te Kauwae-Runga, or 'Things Celestial.'*

Smith, S. Percy. "The Lore of the Whare-Wānanga: Introduction." *The Journal of the Polynesian Society* (Thomas Avery) 22, no. 85 (March 1913): 1–2. http://www.jps.auckland.ac.nz/document/Volume_22_1913/Volume_22%2C_No._85/The_lore_of_the_whare_wananga._Introduction%2C_p_1-2?action=null (accessed July 5, 2018).

The Star-Spangled Banner Project: National

Museum of American History, Behring Center, in Cooperation with Public Inquiry Services, Smithsonian Institution. "Star-Spangled Banner and the War of 1812." *Smithsonian.* n.d. https://www.si.edu/spotlight/flag-day/banner-facts (accessed May 28, 2018).

"State-Owned Enterprises Act." *New Zealand Legal Information Institute.* 1986, No. 124. http://www.nzlii.org/nz/legis/hist_act/sea19861986n124301/ (accessed August 20, 2018).

Statistics New Zealand/Tatauranga Aotearoa. *New Zealand in Profile 2011: An Overview of New Zealand's People, Economy, and Environment.* N.P.: Statistics New Zealand/Tatauranga Aotearoa, 2011. http://archive.stats.govt.nz/browse_for_stats/snapshots-of-nz/nz-in-profile-2011.aspx (accessed May 12, 2018).

Stats NZ/Tatauranga Aotearoa. *Age-Specific Fertility Rates by Ethnicity.* Tables, N.P.: Stats NZ, 2013. http://archive.stats.govt.nz/browse_for_stats/population/births/births-tables.aspx (accessed April 5, 2018).

Stats NZ/Tatauranga Aotearoa. *Births and Deaths: Year Ended December 2014.* Commentary, N.P.: Stats NZ, 2015. http://archive.stats.govt.nz/browse_for_stats/population/births/BirthsAndDeaths_HOTPYeDec14/Commentary.aspx (accessed April 5, 2018).

Stats NZ/Tatauranga Aotearoa. *Births and Deaths: Year Ended December 2017.* Tables, NP: Stats NZ, 2018. https://www.stats.govt.nz/information-releases/births-and-deaths-year-ended-december-2017 (accessed April 5, 2018).

Stats NZ/Tatauranga Aotearoa. *Demographic Trends 2010.* Tables and Narrative, Wellington: Stats NZ, 2011. http://archive.stats.govt.nz/~/media/Statistics/browse-categories/population/estimates-projections/demographic-trends/2010/Demographic%20Trends%202010.pdf (accessed February 8, 2019).

Stats NZ/Tatauranga Aotearoa. *Estimated Total Population by Sex, Year Ended 31 December 1926–2017 and 30 June 1937–2017.* Tables, NP: Stats NZ, 2018. http://archive.stats.govt.nz/browse_for_stats/population/estimates_and_projections/historical-population-tables.aspx (accessed April 5, 2018).

Stats NZ/Tatauranga Aotearoa. *Key Graph Data.* Tables, NP: Stats NZ, 2018. https://www.rbnz.govt.nz/statistics/key-graphs/ (accessed April 4, 2018).

Stats NZ/Tatauranga Aotearoa. *Marriages, Civil Unions, and Divorces: Year Ended December 2014.* Tables, N.P.: Stats NZ, 2015. http://archive.stats.govt.nz/browse_for_stats/people_and_communities/marriages-civil-unions-and-divorces/MarriagesCivilUnionsandDivorces_HOTPYeDec14.aspx (accessed April 6, 2018).

Stats NZ/Tatauranga Aotearoa. *Marriages, Civil Unions, and Divorces: Year Ended December 2015.* Tables, NP: Stats NZ, 2016. http://archive.stats.govt.nz/browse_for_stats/people_and_communities/marriages-civil-unions-and-divorces/MarriagesCivilUnionsandDivorces_HOTPYeDec15.aspx (accessed April 6, 2018).

Stats NZ/Tatauranga Aotearoa. *Marriages, Civil Unions, and Divorces: Year Ended December 2016.* Tables, NP: Stats NZ, 2017. http://archive.stats.govt.nz/browse_for_stats/people_and_communities/marriages-civil-unions-and-divorces/MarriagesCivilUnionsandDivorces_HOTPYeDec16.aspx (accessed April 6, 2018).

Stats NZ/Tatauranga Aotearoa. *New Zealand Abridged Period Life Table: 2015–17 (Provisional).* Commentary, NP: Stats NZ, 2018. https://www.stats.govt.nz/information-releases/new-zealand-abridged-period-life-table-201517-provisional (accessed April 6, 2018).

Stats NZ/Tatauranga Aotearoa. *Overseas Merchandise Trade: February 2018.* Tables, NP: Stats NZ, 2018. https://www.stats.govt.nz/assets/Uploads/Overseas-merchandise-trade/Overseas-merchandise-trade-February-2018/Download-data/overseas-merchandise-trade-february-2018-tables.xlsx (accessed April 4, 2018).

Stats NZ/Tatauranga Aotearoa. *Population Aging in New Zealand.* Tables and Commentary, NP: Stats NZ, 2000. http://archive.stats.govt.nz/browse_for_stats/people_and_communities/older_people/pop-ageing-in-nz.aspx (accessed May 8, 2018).

Stats NZ/Tatauranga Aotearoa. *Population Clock.* Current date. http://archive.stats.govt.nz/tools_and_services/population_clock.aspx (accessed May 8, 2018).

Stats NZ/Tatauranga Aotearoa. "Statistical Standard for Religious Affiliation." *Religious Affiliation.* n.d. http://archive.stats.govt.nz/methods/classifications-and-standards/classification-related-stats-standards/religious-affiliation.aspx (accessed April 6, 2018).

Stats NZ/Tatauranga Aotearoa. *2013 Census QuickStats About Culture and Identity.* Tables, N.P.: Stats NZ, 2014. http://archive.stats.govt.nz/Census/2013-census/profile-and-summary-reports/quickstats-culture-identity.aspx (accessed April 5, 2018).

Stats NZ/Tatauranga Aotearoa. *2013 Census QuickStats About National Highlights.* Tables, N.P.: Stats NZ, 2013. http://archive.stats.govt.nz/Census/2013-census/profile-and-summary-reports/quickstats-about-national-highlights.aspx (accessed April 5, 2018).

Stats NZ/Tatauranga Aotearoa. *Urban Area Population Projections, by Age and Sex, 2013(base)-2043 Update.* Table, NP: Stats NZ, 2017. https://www.stats.govt.nz/information-releases/

urban-area-unit-population-projections-2013 base2043-update-nz-stat-tables (accessed May 11, 2018).

Stefanu, Vic-World Travels and Adventures. "Cook Islands, Exploring a Historic, Religious, and Sacred Site (Marae Kainuku in Rarotonga)." *YouTube.* 18 October 2015. https://www.youtube.com/watch?v=iNvAd0acUCQ (accessed May 10, 2018).

Stefanu, Vic-World Travels and Adventures. "Tahiti, Exploring the Ancient Sacred Religious Sites (Marae), Pacific Ocean." *YouTube.* 16 December 2015. https://www.youtube.com/watch?v=wxvV1qxjm0w (accessed May 10, 2018).

Stenhouse, John, and Lachy Paterson. "Ngā Poropiti Me Ngā Hāhi: Prophets and the Churches." Chap. 16 in *Ki te Whaiao: An Introduction to Māori Culture and Society,* edited by Tānia M. Ka'ai, John C. Moorfield, Michael P.J. Reilly and Sharon Mosley, 171–180. Auckland: Pearson Education New Zealand Limited, 2004.

Swarbrick, Nancy. "Country Schooling." *Te Ara: The Encyclopedia of New Zealand.* 24 November 2008. https://teara.govt.nz/en/country-schooling (accessed August 7, 2018).

Swarbrick, Nancy. "Primary and Secondary Education." *Te Ara: The Encyclopedia of New Zealand.* 20 June 2012. https://teara.govt.nz/en/primary-and-secondary-education (accessed August 2, 2018).

Sweetman, Rory. "Catholic Church." *Te Ara: The Encyclopedia of New Zealand.* 3 February 2017. https://teara.govt.nz/en/catholic-church (accessed May 11, 2018).

Tāmaki Paenga Hira/Auckland War Memorial Museum. "The History of Auckland Museum." *Tāmaki Paenga Hira/Auckland War Memorial Museum.* n.d. http://www.aucklandmuseum.com/your-museum/about/history-of-auckland-museum (accessed August 6, 2018).

Taonui, Rāwiri. "Ranginui: The Sky." *Te Ara: The Encyclopedia of New Zealand.* 12 June 2006. https://teara.govt.nz/en/ranginui-the-sky (accessed August 3, 2018).

Taonui, Rāwiri. "Whakapapa-Genealogy." *Te Ara: The Encyclopedia of New Zealand.* 1 July 2015. https://teara.govt.nz/en/whakapapa-genealogy (accessed June 9, 2018).

Tauroa, Hiwi, and Pat. *Te Marae: A Guide to Customs & Protocol.* Auckland: Reed Publishing (NZ), 2007.

Taylor, the Rev. Richard. *Te Ika a Maui or New Zealand and Its Inhabitants.* London: Wertheim & MacIntosh, 1855. Available from "The New Zealand Electronic Text Collection": http://nzetc.victoria.ac.nz/tm/scholarly/tei-TayTeik.html (accessed July 7 2018).

Te Haupapa-o-Tane. "Io: The Supreme God and Other Gods of the Maori." *The Journal of the Polynesian Society* (Thomas Avery) 29, no. 115 (September 1920): 139–143. http://www.jps.auckland.ac.nz/document.php?wid=1683&action=null (accessed July 3, 2018).

Te Kura Kaupapa Māori o Hoani Waititi Marae: Indigenous Māori Education Center. "About Us." *Te Kura Kaupapa Māori o Hoani Waititi Marae: Indigenous Māori Education Center.* n.d. http://hoaniwaititi.school.nz/about (accessed August 2, 2018).

Te Rūnanga o Ngāi Tahu. "The Settlement." *Te Rūnanga o Ngāi Tahu.* n.d. http://ngaitahu.iwi.nz/ngai-tahu/the-settlement/ (accessed May 26, 2018).

"Te Ture Whenua Maori Act/Maori Land Act." *New Zealand Legal Information Institute.* 1993, No. 4. http://nzlii.org/nz/legis/hist_act/ttwmmla19931993n4326/ (accessed August 21, 2018).

Tillich, Paul. "Aspects of a Religious Analysis of Culture." Chap. IV in *Theology of Culture,* by Paul Tillich, edited by Robert C. Kimball, 40–51. New York: Oxford University Press, 1964.

Tillich, Paul. "The Nature of Religious Language." Chap. V in *Theology of Culture,* by Paul Tillich, edited by Robert C. Kimball, 53–67. New York: Oxford University Press, 1964.

Tillich, Paul. "Religion as a Dimension in Man's Spiritual Life." Chap. I in *Theology of Culture,* by Paul Tillich, edited by Robert C. Kimball, 3–9. New York: Oxford University Press, 1964.

Tillich, Paul. *Systematic Theology: Three Volumes in One.* Chicago: University of Chicago Press, 1967.

Toelken, Barre. *The Dynamics of Folklore.* Revised and Expanded. Logan: Utah State University Press, 1996.

"Treaty of Waitangi Act." *New Zealand Legal Information Institute.* 1975, No. 114. http://www.nzlii.org/nz/legis/hist_act/towa19751975n114226/ (accessed August 20, 2018).

"Treaty of Waitangi Act." *New Zealand Legislation.* 1975, No. 114. http://www.legislation.govt.nz/act/public/1975/0114/latest/whole.html?search=ts_act_treaty+of+waitangi+act_noresel&p=1#DLM435368 (accessed August 20, 2018).

"Treaty of Waitangi Amendment Act." *New Zealand Legal Information Institute.* 1985, No. 148. http://www.nzlii.org/nz/legis/hist_act/towaa19851985n148306/ (accessed August 20, 2018).

Tregear, Edward. *The Maori Race.* Whanganui: A.D. Willis, 1904. Available from "The New Zealand Electronic Text Collection": http://nzetc.victoria.ac.nz/tm/scholarly/tei-TreRace.html (accessed July 4, 2018).

Tūrei, Mohi. "He Aha Tatou I Kiia Ai He Maori." *National Library of New Zealand/Te Puna Mātauranga o Aotearoa: Papers Past. Te Pip-*

iwharauroa (Newspaper). 1 January 1911. https://paperspast.natlib.govt.nz/periodicals/pipiwharauroa/1911/01/01/4 (accessed June 11, 2018).

United Nations Educational, Scientific and Cultural Organization. "Taputapuātea." *United Nations Educational, Scientific and Cultural Organization.* 2017. http://whc.unesco.org/en/list/1529/ (accessed May 10, 2018).

University of Otago/Te Whare Wānanga o Ōtākou. "The Marae and Its Place." *University of Otago/Te Whare Wānanga o Ōtākou.* n.d. https://www.otago.ac.nz/profiles/themaraeanditsplace.html (accessed May 9, 2018).

Van Meijl, Toon. "Changing Property Regimes in Māori Society: A Critical Assessment of the Settlement Process in New Zealand." Edited by Judith Huntsman. *The Journal of the Polynesian Society* (Polynesian Society [Inc.]) 121, no. 2 (June 2012): 181–208. http://www.jps.auckland.ac.nz/document/Volume_121_2012/Volume_121%2C_No._2/Changing_Property_Regimes_in_Maori_Society%3A_A_Critical_Assessment_of_the_Settlement_Process_in_New_Zealand%2C_by_Toon_Van_Meijl%2C_p_181-208 (accessed June 25, 2018).

Van Meijl, Toon. "Historicising Maoritanga: Colonial Ethnography and the Reification of Maori Traditions." Edited by Ray Harlow. *The Journal of the Polynesian Society* (Polynesian Society [Inc.]) 105, no. 3 (September 1996): 311–346. http://www.jps.auckland.ac.nz/document.php?wid=4939&action=null (accessed June 22, 2018).

Wagner, Roy. *The Invention of Culture.* Revised and Expanded. Chicago: The University of Chicago Press, 1975.

Wagner, Roy. *Symbols That Stand for Themselves.* Chicago: The University of Chicago Press, 1986.

Walker, Ranginui J. "Marae: A Place to Stand." *Te Ao Hurihuri: Aspects of Maoritanga,* edited by Michael King, 15–27. Auckland: Reed Publishing (NZ), 1992.

Walrond, Carl. "Cook Islanders." *Te Ara: The Encyclopedia of New Zealand.* 25 March 2015. https://teara.govt.nz/en/cook-islanders (accessed May 10, 2018).

Ward, Keith. *More Than Matter? Is There More to Life Than Molecules?* Grand Rapids: William B. Eerdmans Publishing Co., 2011.

We Are. LGNZ. "Community Boards." *We Are. LGNZ.* 31 October 2018. http://www.lgnz.co.nz/nzs-local-government/community-boards/ (accessed February 6, 2019).

Whatahoro, H.T. *The Lore of the Whare-Wānanga or Teachings of the Maori College on Religion, Cosmogony, and History.* Translated by S. Percy Smith. Lexington: Forgotten Books, 2008; original work published in New Plymouth in 1913 by Thomas Avery as *The Lore of the Whare-Wānanga: Part I.-Te Kauwae-Runga, or 'Things Celestial.'*

White, John. *The Ancient History of the Maori, His Mythology and Traditions (Volume II of VII): Horo-Uta or Take-Tumu Migration.* Wellington: Whitcombe and Tombs, 1950; original work published in Wellington in 1887 by Government Printer. Available from "The New Zealand Text Collection": http://nzetc.victoria.ac.nz/tm/scholarly/tei-Whi02Anci.html (accessed July 3, 2018).

White, Te Taru. "A Maori Point of View." *YouTube.* 13 March 2007. https://www.youtube.com/watch?v=WkoR8qBSUtY&feature=youtu.be (accessed March 15, 2019).

Williams, Herbert W. *A Dictionary of the Maori Language.* Sixth. Wellington: Government Printer, 1957, original work by William Williams published in 1844. Available from "The New Zealand Electronic Text Collection": http://nzetc.victoria.ac.nz/tm/scholarly/tei-WillDict.html (accessed February 7, 2019).

Wilmshurst, Janet M., Atholl J. Anderson, Thomas F.G. Higham, and Trevor H. Worthy. "Dating the Late Prehistoric Dispersal of Polynesians to New Zealand Using the Commensal Pacific Rat." Edited by Patrick V. Kirch. *Proceedings of the National Academy of Sciences of the United States of America (PNAS)* 105, no. 22 (June 2008): 7676–7680.

Zafirovski, Milan. "Social Exchange Theory Under Scrutiny: A Positive Critique of Its Economic-Behaviorist Formulations." *Electronic Journal of Sociology.* 2005. http://citeseerx.ist.psu.edu/viewdoc/download?doi=10.1.1.454.7467&rep=rep1&type=pdf (accessed April 20, 2018).

Index

www.ingramcontent.com/pod-product-compliance
Lightning Source LLC
Chambersburg PA
CBHW081738270326
41932CB00020B/3311